PANIC IN PARADISE

PANIC IN PARADISE
Florida's Banking Crash of 1926

Raymond B. Vickers

THE UNIVERSITY OF ALABAMA PRESS
TUSCALOOSA AND LONDON

designed by Paula C. Dennis

∞

The paper on which this book is printed meets the minimum
requirements of American National Standard for Information
Science-Permanence of Paper for Printed Library Materials,
ANSI Z39.48-1984.

Library of Congress Cataloging-in-Publication Data

Vickers, Raymond B., 1949–
    Panic in paradise : Florida's banking crash of 1926 / Raymond B.
Vickers.
        p.   cm.
    Includes bibliographical references (p.   ) and index.
    ISBN 0-8173-0723-0 (alk. paper)
    1. Bank failures—Florida and Georgia—History.   2. Banks and
banking—Florida and Georgia—Corrupt practices—History.   I. Title.
HG2611.F6V53   1994
332.1′09759′09042—dc20   93-35974

Library of Congress Cataloguing-in-Publication Data available

For
Mary Taylor Vickers

"Governments are instituted among men, deriving their just powers from the consent of the governed."

—Declaration of Independence

"A popular government, without popular information, or the means of acquiring it, is but a prologue to a farce or a tragedy; or, perhaps both. Knowledge will forever govern ignorance: And a people who mean to be their own governors must arm themselves with the power which knowledge gives."

—James Madison

"Sunlight is said to be the best of disinfectants; electric light the most efficient policeman."

—Louis D. Brandeis

"Secrecy means impropriety."

—Woodrow Wilson

CONTENTS

PREFACE

Writing a history of banking is difficult because regulators and bankers have barricaded themselves behind a wall of secrecy. As long as a bank or a savings and loan survives, the regulatory records of the institution—which have been prepared by government employees at taxpayers' expense—remain confidential. Since the Great Depression and despite federal deposit insurance, regulators and bankers have argued that secrecy was necessary to prevent bank runs. They have persuaded Congress that the public would panic if the government disclosed the true condition of the nation's financial institutions.

This policy of official secrecy continues after the failure of a financial institution. The public is prohibited from seeing the federal government's regulatory and liquidation records of a defunct bank or savings and loan for another fifty years. The federal records of an institution that failed in 1990 will be sealed until the year 2040.[1]

Bank secrecy at the state level is even more restrictive. In forty-four states, the banking departments have either destroyed their regulatory and liquidation records or permanently prohibited public access. After his 1926 indictment for gross negligence, Comptroller Ernest Amos sealed his regulatory records and established Florida's secret regulatory system.

In 1974, while under federal grand jury investigation "for peddling bank charters," Comptroller Fred O. Dickinson preserved the tradition of bank secrecy in Florida. In an effort to plug newspaper leaks, he defeated a bill that would have opened some of his regulatory records. Dickinson, who was later indicted for extortion but convicted for income tax evasion, lobbied through that same legislature a law making it a third-degree felony to release any regulatory records of existing banks.[2]

Florida's bank regulatory records remained sealed until this study. In February 1988 Edward F. Keuchel and I began a time-consuming campaign to gain access to the regulatory and liquidation records of state banks that failed during the 1920s. Comptroller Gerald A. Lewis, who had defeated Dickinson by promising to "open the comptroller's office to public scrutiny," blocked the release of the antique records for a year and a half. Extending Dickinson's secrecy law to failed banks, Lewis refused to release any banking records, and his office warned that disclosure of the more than sixty-year-old banking records was a crime.[3]

After a year of research and arguments, a lawyer for the Florida State Archives agreed that, based on the state's public records law, the records should be opened. But the comptroller's office rejected that legal opinion, adamantly arguing that release of the historical records would establish a "dangerous precedent." State officials were then notified that a lawsuit would soon be filed. The Florida Historical Society also adopted a resolution that urged the opening of the records "within guidelines established by the National Archives (50 years after closing)."[4]

The power of publicity finally carried the day. On May 23, 1989, the *Wall Street Journal* published my article "Sleazy Banking in the '20s and Today," which called on Congress to enact a sunshine law to abolish bank secrecy and criticized the state of Florida for permanently sealing its banking records. In response, the *St. Petersburg Times* published an article, "Law Keeps Public in Dark about Banks' Well-Being," about this study and Florida's antiquated bank secrecy law. A week later, Comptroller Lewis, facing litigation and adverse publicity, unilaterally reversed his interpretation of the law to allow the opening of the state's secret vault.[5]

The Florida State Archives then proposed and the legislature passed a law to ensure that the historical banking records remain open. The law provided that records in the possession of the state archives become public documents after fifty years. Following on the heels of this public debate, the legislature attempted to make Florida the leading disclosure state. The Financial Institutions Regulatory Reform Act of 1992 provided that those portions of the state's bank and savings and loan "examination, operation, or condition reports" dealing with the finances of "directors, officers or controlling stockholders" would become public one year after the appointment of a receiver. But Lewis, after surviving an impeachment effort and shielding his deplorable regulatory record from public scrutiny, implemented the new law in such a way as to nullify its effect.[6]

In thirty-three states, bank regulatory records remained sealed until they were destroyed. State archivists who have fought to preserve this "wealth of economic history" have been no match for the powerful banking lobby. Within the last few years the states of Washington and Alabama suffered "a terrific loss" when they destroyed their banking records from the 1920s and 1930s. Sidney McAlpin, the state archivist of Washington for three decades, had "never seen such a successful lobbying effort to deny public access." After a careful review of the examination reports and other regulatory records, he discovered that "the only impact of disclosure would be to embarrass a lot of bank officials regarding their loan policies and bank management." Failing to persuade state regulators to release the records after "50 or a 100 years," McAlpin concluded that they are "scared of the industry they are regulating."[7]

After the Alabama banking records were destroyed, a state archivist explained: "We considered the possibility of an eventual change in the law creating a time limit on the [bank secrecy] restriction, but felt that this was a rather remote possibility given the lobbying strength of the banking industry in Alabama and on the federal level."[8] The following states have also destroyed their bank regulatory records from the 1920s and 1930s: California, New York, Texas, Pennsylvania, Illinois, Ohio, Michigan, Minnesota, Indiana, Massachusetts, Connecticut, New Jersey, New Hampshire, Maryland, West Virginia, Kentucky, Tennessee, South Carolina, Georgia, Mississippi, Louisiana, Nebraska, Iowa, Missouri,

Kansas, Nevada, North Dakota, South Dakota, Montana, Utah, and Hawaii.[9]

Eleven states have retained bank regulatory records that are now more than sixty years old but refuse to release them because of bank secrecy laws or the narrow interpretation of those laws. When North Carolina commissioner of banks William T. Graham denied access to his state's banking records, he acknowledged that the bank secrecy law is "ridiculous." In response to my request to review Delaware's historical banking records, the attorney general's office issued a legal opinion declaring that "the penalty for disclosure of such information is a fine and imprisonment of not more than two years." The opinion narrowly interpreted Delaware's bank secrecy law, ignoring its "public duty" exemption. Access was denied to the examination reports of the Newport Trust Company, which failed in 1930, on the basis of a secrecy statute that was not in existence in 1930.[10]

Wisconsin follows a novel procedure. Before gaining access to confidential examination reports, a historian must sign an agreement that prohibits disclosure of "individually identifiable information from these records (e.g. names, addresses) either directly or through deductive disclosure (e.g. recognizable physical descriptions)." The eight other states that have retained banking records but have permanently sealed them are Maine, Vermont, Rhode Island, Virginia, Arkansas, Colorado, Arizona, and Wyoming.[11]

Only Florida, New Mexico, Idaho, Oregon, Oklahoma, and Alaska permit the study of records of their failed banks from the 1920s. This study established that an accurate economic history of the United States cannot be written without using bank regulatory records. Until they are stopped, state regulators will continue to destroy the evidence.[12]

ACKNOWLEDGMENTS

No book of this scope can be completed without the help of many people. I am especially indebted to Edward F. Keuchel and William Warren Rogers of Florida State University for their guidance, extensive readings, and commitment to this project. I was also fortunate to have been a student of the late Vincent P. Carosso of New York University, who was the nation's foremost banking historian. His critical readings and considerable advice greatly improved the book.

Malcolm MacDonald, whose appreciation of Florida has enriched the state, deserves special recognition. The meticulous comments of Trudie Calvert turned the manuscript into a book. I am also indebted to Richard B. Gray, James P. Jones, and Earl R. Beck for their careful readings and many suggestions. Alan Neigher was always available for sound legal advice, and James Ring Adams shared his keen insights into the politics of banking.

The secrets of the banking industry were unlocked with the assistance of Keuchel, Rogers, Adams, Melanie Kirkpatrick of the *Wall Street Journal,* James Greiff of the *St. Petersburg Times,* Bill Friedlander, Craig Kiser, Jim Berberich, Ben Poitevent, and the Florida Historical Society. In addition, Leland Hawes of the *Tampa*

Tribune and Phillip Longman of *Florida Trend* enhanced my understanding of the state's colorful political history.

Jesse Stiller, the historian for the comptroller of the currency, was generous with his time. I also benefited from the aid of many archivists, especially William Sherman, John Butler, and Gayle Peters of the National Archives, Nan Dennison of the Historical Society of Palm Beach County, Peggy McCall of the Boca Raton Historical Society, Cheryl Schnirring of the Illinois State Historical Library, and Sidney McAlpin of the state of Washington. And I thank Paul Saavedra, who compiled the failed bank records of New Mexico.

A special thanks goes to Cherry Strickland, who manages my law office, Mary Lou Miller for providing valuable research, and Neil Betten and Debbie Perry for assisting me along the way. I must acknowledge the support of Amadeo Lopez-Castro, Hans and Erik Hvide, Jean Fitzgerald, Gene Douglas, John Christo, Joe Muldoon, Ted Steinmeyer, John Folsom, Ed Duggar, Sam Griffis, Louie Wainwright, Marie Robinson, Debra Munro, Martha Barrett, Walt Kinsey, Bridget Burke, Bill and Susan Dawkins, Lynn and Jeff Fenster, Burt Horwitz, Lex Hood, and Bob Rackleff. I also want to thank Howell and Tom Boney and remember their late brother George, who was my mentor when he was the chief justice of the Alaska supreme court.

The support and good humor of my remarkable family made this effort endurable. I am grateful to Si Slocumb, Greg Winkler, Edite Vickers, Barbara Jac and John Carter, Annie Houston, and the Maggie dog. My brother Bill, a professor of anthropology, established the precedent and set the pace. And the constant encouragement of my mother, to whom this is dedicated, and my sister Sally, who recently received her doctorate in history, ensured the completion of this book.

PANIC IN PARADISE

INTRODUCTION

This is the first work to analyze state and national regulatory records to determine why bank failures in the 1920s reached epidemic proportions. It is a book about the breakdown of the United States bank regulatory system. As America struggles to pay for the speculative mania of the 1980s, it is essential to view the banking system from a historical perspective. Bank secrecy laws prohibit an objective analysis of recent bank and thrift failures. Without primary source materials, an accurate interpretation of the current savings and loan debacle is impossible. Accordingly, this study goes beyond merely describing the banking crisis of the 1920s. It searches for an answer to the central financial question of our time: How can banking disasters be prevented in the future?

Irresponsibility, corruption, and regulatory complicity are not new to the American banking system. Today's thrift calamity ominously parallels the banking crisis of the 1920s. In both periods of wildcat speculation, state and federal regulators had the statutory authority to protect the public from unscrupulous bankers.[1] In fact, in 1932 a federal appeals court complained that the comptroller of the currency's power was "too sweeping and imperialistic." Nevertheless, that same court upheld those powers: "Unquestionably Congress contemplated the upheaval and cataclysm to which the financial structure is subject, the importance of its stability, and the necessity which exists for action unhampered by technicality in emergency."

Regulators had the power to remove or prosecute "dishonest, incompetent or reckless" bankers and the mandate to seize insolvent banks. Nevertheless, in most instances compliant regulators refused to assert their "sweeping and imperialistic" powers. This regulatory void allowed rogues to operate freely within the banking system.[2]

During the 1920s and the 1980s, America had the most elaborate bank regulatory system in the world. Although regulators examined banks and thrifts in every state, this country had the highest number of failures. Despite six decades of ever-increasing regulatory authority and bureaucracies, the sheer magnitude of the current savings and loan problem has proved that the regulatory system cannot police thousands of financial institutions. In both periods the soundness of the banking system has depended exclusively on regulators operating behind closed doors. The only fundamental change to the regulatory system has been that taxpayers, not depositors, now have to pay for bank and thrift failures.

BANKING IN THE SUNSHINE

The argument made in this book is that the bank regulatory system needs a drastic overhaul with disclosure, not secrecy, as its basis. Applying the words of James Madison to current events: the secret regulatory system is a "farce" whose failure caused the savings and loan "tragedy." Now the American people "must arm themselves with the power which knowledge gives" by demanding that Congress enact a banking-in-the-sunshine law.[3]

Does the public have a right to know how its money is invested? Because of federal deposit insurance and taxpayer bailouts, banks and thrifts are public institutions whose true conditions should be on the public record. Taxpayers have a right to know if a borrower defaults on a loan at a federally insured institution. If a bank chooses to sue a delinquent borrower, the bad loan becomes public knowledge. Bankruptcy proceedings also are public, so it seems reasonable to require disclosure of delinquent borrowers before they file for federal protection. Public release of the examination reports of existing banks as soon as they are finalized must be a basic provision of the new law. Delinquent borrowers would then be treated the same as delinquent homeowners: listed in the local newspaper when they miss the deadline to pay property taxes. Disclosure of self-dealings and bad loans would have a chilling effect on bankers who misuse their public trust for private profit and borrowers who take advantage of public institutions.[4]

Another conclusion of this study is that bankers are public officials who should be exposed to the same scrutiny as other public officials. Broad classifications of state and federal officials must file financial disclosure statements. But bankers, who use the public's federally insured money for private profit, are not required to disclose their finances. Bankers exercise more influence over the public interest than most other officials. And their power is disproportionate to the amount of money they have at risk. Banks and thrifts are unique entities because stockholders own less than 10 percent of their assets and depositors own more than 90 percent, which are insured by taxpayers. As trustees of the public's money and to prevent conflicts of interest, bankers should be required to make full disclosure of their finances.[5]

Throughout American history, industries vital to the nation's economy have been compelled to disclose their finances. Charles Francis Adams and Louis D. Brandeis, whom historian Thomas McCraw called "prophets of regulation," were responsible for opening the books of the railroad and investment banking industries. Adams, grandson and great-grandson of two American presidents, was the author of the Massachusetts sunshine law of 1869, which made railroad companies of the Gilded Age disclose their finances.

After the Panic of 1907, Brandeis, later a U.S. Supreme Court justice, made the call for an end to bank secrecy in *Other People's Money and How the Bankers Use It*. His 1914 book became a national sensation by sharply criticizing the influence of the "money trust" on the nation's economy. It publicized the majority findings of the Pujo subcommittee's investigation of insider abuses in the banking and securities industries.

Brandeis declared that "sunlight" was the "best of disinfectants; electric light the most efficient policeman." He believed disclosure would cure the bankers of the business disease of greed. Congress debated Brandeis's ideas of disclosure for twenty years before taking action. After the Bank Holiday of 1933, Congress opened the investment banking industry to public scrutiny with the passage of the securities acts.

Commercial bankers escaped disclosure during the New Deal by convincing Congress that revealing the true conditions of the nation's banks would cause violent bank runs. The history of federal deposit insurance has eliminated that argument. The current banking and thrift crisis has proved that depositors do not panic when their deposits are insured. Though the press has published the names of insolvent banks and savings and loans, Depression-style runs have not occurred.

Any regulatory system would fail, Brandeis argued, if it denied public access to financial information and relied solely on the government. He called for "real disclosure" by revealing banking activities to the public. The publicity would create an informed consent similar to the labeling requirements of the Pure Food Law. But the power of bankers in Washington and in state capitals has kept their activities in a shroud of secrecy. The cost of that secrecy has been staggering.[6]

Official secrecy permitted the current thrift debacle to grow beyond control while regulators deceived the public. M. Danny Wall, chairman of the Federal Home Loan Bank Board, maintained throughout the presidential election year of 1988 that a taxpayer bailout was unnecessary. He claimed in March 1988 that the problem could be solved with $17 billion. By May, Wall's calculation had risen to $22.7 billion. In July, Wall increased that figure to $30.9 billion, and in October he put the cost between $45 and $50 billion. After the election in November 1988, the same month that Wall told industry executives to "hold your heads high," estimates rose to $75 billion. Conservative estimates now calculate that the cost of the savings and loan bailout, including interest on government bonds, will exceed $500 billion.[7]

The 1920s was also a period of instability for the nation's banking system. More than fifty-five hundred banks closed during the nine roaring years before the crash of 1929. If the 1920s, like the 1980s, was a period of prosperity, why did so many banks fail? In such a healthy economy, did the bankers cause their banks to fail?

In the 1920s, state and federal regulators were quick to absolve bankers of any blame for the failures. Florida's elected comptroller and banking commissioner, Ernest Amos, praised the bankers in his state, declaring that they were "splendid businessmen." U.S. Comptroller of the Currency John W. Pole, a professional regulator who had been the chief of national bank examiners, proclaimed that the system had "broken down through [economic] causes beyond the control of the individual banker."[8]

The breakdown was particularly acute in Florida and Georgia, where uninsured depositors lost an estimated $30 million in 1926 alone. After violent runs by depositors, 150 banks failed in the two states. Eighty-three banks in Georgia and 32 banks in Florida were members of the Manley-Anthony banking chain. Following the financial havoc, James R. Smith, a principal of the banking system who was also the president of the Atlanta Real Estate Board, committed suicide.[9]

Florida was a bellwether state for the American economy in the 1920s. Its real estate boom, according to John Kenneth Galbraith, was a "classic speculative bubble" and a prelude to the stock market crash. The 1926 banking crash devastated Florida's economy and drove its recession into a depression. Bank assets in Florida fell more than $300 million in 1926. Between 1926 and 1929, they declined 60 percent, from $943 million to $375 million.[10]

Heretofore, the banking calamity has been blamed on the collapse of the Florida land boom. It was believed that a precipitate drop in real estate values created a regional recession that caused the unprecedented number of bank failures. Previous studies have not analyzed the cause of each bank failure, and thus bankers and their regulators have not been regarded as the primary problem.[11]

Using government documents, which stayed secret for sixty-three years, I have determined why so many banks failed in Florida during the 1920s. The sad story told by these records is that insiders looted the banks they pledged to protect. They tried to get rich by wildly speculating with depositors' money, and when their schemes failed so did their banks. Despite official disclaimers and historical accounts, more than 90 percent of the banks that failed in Florida during the 1920s involved abuse or fraud by insiders.[12]

The study of banking practices during the 1920s has particular relevance to the modern banking and thrift crisis. The same pattern of self-dealing and corruption existed in both periods. In 1988, the U.S. General Accounting Office (GAO) reviewed examination reports and other regulatory records of twenty-six failed thrifts and found that they did not fail because of "economic downturns in certain regions." Without releasing the specifics, the GAO concluded that "fraud or insider abuse existed at each and every one of the failed thrifts." The GAO also discovered that federal regulators knew about the abuses: "Despite the fact that examiners reported numerous and extensive violations of laws, regulations, and related unsafe practices, thrift regulators were unable to halt the practices."[13]

Responding to the impotency of the regulatory system, Representative Henry B. Gonzalez, chairman of the House Committee on Banking, Finance and Urban Affairs, declared: "The savings and loan scandals grew in the dark basements of official government secrecy." During the 1920s and 1980s, bank fraud and insider abuse flourished because secrecy allowed unscrupulous bankers and politicians to corrupt the regulatory system.[14]

BRIBES DISGUISED AS LOANS

In the United States, banking has always subsidized politics. Since the early days of the republic, bankers have used the public's money to capture public officials. They have corrupted the financial system by making "policy loans" to politicians and regulators. These so-called loans, even if they became gifts after being written off the books of the banks, have not been regarded as bribes because government secrecy has hidden the deals from the public. The American tradition of insider banking has endured because the public has been unaware of the extent of the corruption.

Aaron Burr established the precedent in 1799, when he and his political friends formed the Bank of the Manhattan Company, which later became the Chase Manhattan Bank. Burr, a member of the New York Assembly at the time, was in need of easy money because of his extravagant life-style and political aspirations. Burr used his public position to form the bank by passing its charter through the New York Assembly. He then became an organizing director of the new bank, receiving huge loans after it opened. Three years later, a report of the Bank of the Manhattan Company showed that it had made loans of $98,036 to Burr, who was then the vice-president of the United States.[15]

Insider abuse and influence peddling led Andrew Jackson, in 1832, to declare war on the Second Bank of the United States and its president, Nicholas Biddle. As head of the privately controlled central bank, Biddle was the nation's most powerful banker. Quietly operating in regal grandeur, Biddle made loans to Daniel Webster and Henry Clay to ensure that Congress passed the Second Bank's recharter bill. Biddle also appointed Webster as a director of the bank's Boston branch and hired the legendary senator as its attorney. Biddle's payments to Webster went far beyond his services as an attorney. When the Second Bank was fighting for its life, Webster wrote to Biddle: "I believe my retainer has not been renewed or *refreshed* as usual. If it be wished that my relation to the Bank should be continued, it may be well to send me the usual retainer."[16]

Jackson abolished the Second Bank of the United States with "the most important presidential veto in American history." With no central bank, however, a system of wildcat state banks developed throughout the country. After several financial panics and in the middle of the Civil War, Congress created the national banking system in 1863. But Jackson's enduring legacy was the entrenchment of state banking, which led to the creation of a dual banking system with thousands of state and national banks. This uniquely American system welded politics and banking together, making effective regulation impossible.[17]

BANK FAILURES IN THE WEST

During the 1920s insider abuse and fraud were not limited to the South. Between 1921 and 1925, 92 percent of the bank failures in the United States were west of the Mississippi River. The agricultural regions of the West had experienced a land boom during World War I which collapsed after hostilities ended in Europe. The banking records of New Mexico and Idaho, two of the six states that allow public access, reveal the extent of reckless speculation in farming and ranching operations.[18]

While Europe was fighting a war instead of producing commodities, the prices of agricultural products in the United States rose to spectacular levels. Beef cattle, lamb, wool, and wheat prices soared. After the signing of the Treaty of Versailles and the resumption of European production, the prices of American farm products dropped 54 percent between the spring of 1920 and the summer of 1921. Farmers and ranchers, who had expanded their holdings with debt to take advantage of the wartime boom, watched their land sold at public auctions.[19]

The decline in the value of commodities, however, was not the cause of the outbreak of bank failures in New Mexico. In the vast majority of cases, insider abuse and regulatory complicity—not "losses due to unforeseen agricultural disasters such as floods, drought or boll weevil"—led to the bank failures. During the first half of the decade fifty-seven banks failed in the state. For example, the McKinley County Bank of Gallup failed on August 20, 1923. It had been looted by the directors, who had made illegal loans of $242,942, which was 243 percent of its capital.[20]

The largest delinquent "loan" at the Farmers State Bank of Maxwell, New Mexico, was an unsecured note of the state's top banking regulator, State Bank Examiner James B. Read. Read chartered the bank on January 29, 1922. The day after the bank opened, in violation of state law, Read borrowed $11,716 from the fledgling bank. Because there was only $25,000 of stockholders' equity, the "excess" loan represented 47 percent of the bank's capital. Read made no payments on the 180-day loan, and when the bank failed two and a half years later it was still outstanding.[21]

Read was proud of his relationship with the state's bankers. In 1921, he told Governor Merrit C. Mechem that "relations" with the industry had been "most cordial and as never before the banks have availed themselves of the facilities offered by this office." But Read also believed he was overworked and underpaid. He complained to the governor that "the present salary of the State Bank Examiner is inadequate and should be increased." By chartering the Farmers State Bank and then procuring the loan, Read more than doubled his income.[22]

Bank failures also plagued Idaho when agricultural prices and land values fell drastically. Idaho farmers had sold potatoes for $1.51 a bushel in 1919. By 1922 the price had collapsed to 31 cents a bushel. During the 1920s, forty-three state banks and twenty-five national banks failed in the state. Most of the failures occurred in the first half of the decade. In 1922, after nearly a quarter of the state's banks had been lost, State Bank Commissioner J. G. Fralick had nothing but praise for the bankers of Idaho. Because of their "high standard of business ability and integrity," Fralick said he had been as "lenient" in his "requirements as circumstances would permit."[23]

Only a few of the banks failed because of the state's weak economy. In most of the cases the banks failed because of insider abuse, not depressed farm prices. The State Bank of Idaho Falls, whose officers and directors were in a hurry to make their fortunes, was representative of the pattern of self-dealing and irresponsibility that occurred in the boardrooms.[24]

The president of the bank, V. K. Tuggle, did not limit his activities to the banking business. He owned the Thousand Springs Land and Irrigation Company, which the bank examiner described as a "defunct corporation." Nevertheless, it borrowed $11,500 from the bank. Tuggle loaned himself $22,861, and he personally guaranteed $12,500 of other loans. He also sold the bank a worthless $4,000 note, which had been past due for two years. And Tuggle's father borrowed $5,000 from his son's bank. Considering most of the loans as a complete loss, the bank examiner reported that they violated the legal limit on loans to one borrower.[25]

Every member of the board of directors had loans from the bank, which failed on November 23, 1921. The vice-president, cashier, assistant cashier, and teller were also borrowers, and most of their loans were worthless. They used the bank to fund their speculative ventures. L. A. Hartert, one of the directors, received financing for his local Ford dealership, real estate office, and undeveloped land. In violation of state law, his obligations totaled $48,140. He was also partners with J. W. Hays, a major stockholder of the bank, in the Market Lake Reservoir Company. Hays, a farmer, was involved in eleven loans at the bank amounting to $41,652.[26]

The State Bank of Idaho Falls collapsed after insiders had taken more than $220,000 from its treasury, 220 percent of its capital. Instead of appointing a disinterested liquidator to protect the depositors, Bank Commissioner Fralick named C. I. Canfield, an officer and stockholder of the bank. He was also a recipient of two loans from the bank which were classified as "slow."[27]

THE FLORIDA CRASH OF 1926

By the middle of the decade, when receivers were busy liquidating banks in western states, a land boom erupted in Florida. Excitement again centered on land, but this time its use was for development, not farming and ranching. This book focuses on the banking crash which accompanied that mania. Angry crowds packed the streets of Florida and Georgia more than three years before panic struck Wall Street. The frenzy of speculation and flurry of bank failures parallel the savings and loan fiasco of the 1980s.

Florida's state and national bank failures during the 1920s can now be studied because both levels of regulatory records are finally open to the public. Though the state of Georgia destroyed its bank examination and liquidation records from the 1920s, Florida's records explain why scores of Georgia banks failed. Extensive transactions were conducted between the Florida and Georgia members of the Manley-Anthony banking system, so analysis of this vast body of inextricably entwined information provided the reasons for those failures.

The methodology of this study was to review every aspect of the banking business and its regulatory system to determine why so many banks failed. The book is divided into three parts, each covering a fundamental weakness of the American banking system. The first part investigates the influence and impact that promoter-bankers had on the system. The second part shows how bank secrecy allowed government officials to deceive the public. It compares what regulators told the press and public at the time with what the regulatory records prove they knew—but concealed. The last part of the book assesses the system's impact on the bankers, regulators, and depositors in the aftermath of the banking collapse. It also reveals how lawyers with ties to regulators and politicians turned the calamity into a bonanza.

The first chapter examines the role that speculation played in the bank failures. It begins in the spring of 1925, when the boom was in full bloom, and centers on Addison Mizner's dream development of Boca Raton. Mizner, whose extravagant imagination outstripped his budget and the market, was typical of the high-flying developers in the 1920s and 1980s. He began funding his Boca Raton development by attracting the rich and famous of society. But after a nasty split with his partner, Senator T. Coleman du Pont of Delaware, Mizner used depositors' money to keep his operations afloat.

The rise of James R. Anthony and Wesley D. Manley, the two most powerful bankers during the boom, is discussed in the second chapter. Anthony and Manley became dominant forces in

Florida and Georgia by using their financial clout to capture bank regulators. Bank secrecy fostered their cozy relationships with regulators and enabled their banking empire to grow to nearly two hundred banks in Florida, Georgia, New York, and New Jersey.

Chapter 3 describes how Mizner and his partners acquired and looted the Palm Beach National Bank. Mizner used the bank to finance his fantasy. Instead of restraining the wild speculation, regulators joined in the plunder. After the Mizner Development Corporation was sued for fraud, depositors of the Mizner bank panicked. The bank's collapse triggered the panic in paradise as word spread to affiliated banks in the Manley-Anthony banking system. The panic crossed state lines when W. D. Manley was sued for bank fraud in Atlanta.

As the title of Chapter 4 indicates, state and federal regulators tried to stop the panic by deceit, but it spun out of control. The system of secrecy ran the losses up to tens of millions of dollars, devastating depositors who waited for as long as a decade to receive less than half of their savings. Abuses by insiders took years to develop into a crisis while bank examiners reported the self-dealings to senior regulators. No action was taken to stop the looting, and no effort was made to inform the public of the misuse of the funds. The regulators refused to exert their awesome powers to remove Manley, Anthony, and their cohorts as officers and directors of the banks. Even after the Mizner and Manley lawsuits disclosed the fraud, regulators deliberately misled the public. This chapter shows the consequences of official secrecy and provides a compelling reason for abolishing it.

The complicity of state regulators is revealed in Chapters 5 and 6. Unknowing depositors left their savings in troubled state-chartered banks while state officials protected their political friends. T. R. Bennett, Georgia's superintendent of banks, an appointed official, was as deceitful as Florida comptroller Ernest Amos, an elected regulator. Each blamed the "hysterical" public and the other state for the catastrophe. There was one significant difference between the two regulators. Bennett was forced to resign three months after the fiasco. But Amos held fast to his high office for six years and six months, which enabled him to politicize the liquidation process.

These two chapters compare Florida's elected banking commissioner to Georgia's appointed regulator. In 1919, Georgia tried to remove politics from regulation by establishing a banking department headed by an appointed professional. Florida's reputation for lax enforcement persists today because the state legislature has refused to change the worst regulatory system in the country: an elected banking commissioner operating in secret. Florida has the only bank regulatory system in the nation headed by an elected official. The other forty-nine states and the federal government appoint their bank regulators. Chapter 6, however, shows that changing Florida's system will not solve the problem. Even with an appointed banking commissioner, the disaster in Georgia occurred because the regulator was captured by dishonest bankers.

After the regulators failed to regulate, prosecutors moved to punish W. D. Manley, the most visible culprit. Chapters 7 and 8 describe how J. R. Anthony and other bankers who had been Manley's partners influenced prosecutors to limit their exposure. The judicial system failed to dispense justice because able defense lawyers sat on both sides of the courtroom. They built barriers to confuse the issues in the complicated cases, and the Anthony brothers made loans to Comptroller Amos, which ensured his loyalty. Prosecutors were reluctant to file charges against prominent bankers when Amos and other regulators, who held possession of the secret files, obstructed the legal process. Depositors paid for the cover-up while Anthony and his colleagues lived the good life. One of his associates, Clarence M. Gay, went on to become comptroller of Florida.

Political interference with the defunct state and national banks continued throughout their liquidations. As discussed in Chapters 9 and 10, Comptroller of the Currency Joseph W. McIntosh repeatedly hired Senator Lawrence Y. Sherman to represent bank receiverships in Florida. Instead of preserving the remaining assets, Sherman, operating in secret, devoted himself to collecting exorbitant fees and protecting the interests of Vice-President Charles G. Dawes, his confidant of thirty years. Sherman's private interests compromised his public position, forcing depositors to wait in line for years. Comptroller McIntosh encouraged the abuse by personally approving the excessive fees charged by the former United States senator.

Chapter 11 chronicles the fight of Florida's elected comptroller, Ernest Amos, to retain political power and to stay in office. The state's history of bank regulation during the 1920s parallels the controversial reign of Gerald Lewis, the comptroller during the 1980s. Amos and Lewis continued to win elections even after they were disgraced by scandal. Both professional politicians won those campaigns with the heavy financial support of the industry they were regulating. Their cozy relationships with bankers who looted some of the state's leading financial institutions resulted in impeachment resolutions being filed against them. To survive the impeachment efforts, they masqueraded as reformers while quietly defeating every effort of the legislature to change the system.[28]

The inescapable conclusion of this book is that bankers and regulators, bound by a code of secrecy, have created an invisible regulatory system within the government. It is a system of covert regulators with imperialistic powers but without public accountability. Now that every American taxpayer is bailing out this clandestine government, it is time to eliminate the code of secrecy that separates the public from the truth. When Jefferson wrote the phrase "consent of the governed" in the Declaration of Independence, he meant informed consent. The following pages will prove that secrecy protects government officials and their friends, not the public.

PART I
Promoter-Bankers

Castle Mizner, with its medieval drawbridge,
was to become Addison Mizner's $1 million
dream-house and the center of his Boca
Raton extravaganza.
(Courtesy, Historical
Society Palm
Beach County)

1

PROMOTERS IN
PARADISE

California's gold rush of 1849 and the Klondike gold rush of 1898 pale when compared to the Florida land rush of 1925. Florida's boom was the greatest speculative frenzy in history. The madness in the Sunshine State reflected the mood of the country during the Roaring Twenties.[1]

America rebelled against the so-called morality of the Great War and Prohibition. The efforts of the Anti-Saloon League made Scarface Al Capone a leading citizen of Chicago while law-abiding citizens broke the law, drinking bootleg whiskey and bathtub gin. Making money was the national obsession as business became the new religion. Bruce Barton's *Man Nobody Knows* was the most popular nonfiction book in 1925. Barton called Jesus of Nazareth "the founder of modern business." "He picked up twelve men from the bottom ranks of business and forged them into an organization that conquered the world."[2]

President Calvin Coolidge, who agreed that business was a religion, was the nation's foremost promoter. He declared that "the man who builds a factory builds a temple . . . the man who works there worships there." Coolidge preached to the nation that "the chief business of the American people is business." Because unemployment was low and production was high, Coolidge prosperity seemed real to most Americans, who thought it would last forever. Between 1920 and 1929 annual automobile production more than doubled, and by 1929 26.7 million cars were traveling on thousands of miles of new roads. As people moved to the suburbs, housing construction boomed and the sale of electricity tripled during the decade. Appliances bought on installment credit furnished the new houses, and radios became the home entertainment center. More than 10 million radios were sold during the 1920s.[3]

President Coolidge hailed an era of permanent prosperity when he spoke to Congress for the last time in December 1928: "No Congress of the United States ever assembled, on surveying the state of the Union, has met with a more pleasing prospect than that which appears at the present time. In the domestic field there is tranquility and contentment . . . and the highest record of years of prosperity. In the foreign field there is peace, the goodwill which comes from mutual understanding." Coolidge overlooked the nation's farmers, who suffered through a postwar depression throughout the decade. And he ignored the thousands of depositors of failed banks.[4]

The leading businessman of the day was Henry Ford, whose methods of mass production created the "car culture." He gave the middle class a new life-style and a feeling of limitless opportunity. By 1927, the Ford Motor Company had sold 15 million cars at a cost as low as $290.[5]

Behind the wheel of a Model T, the average American felt prosperous and free. The car liberated the farmer from the farm and the factory worker from the city. It turned the country into a "nation of nomads." Searching for adventure and bonanza, hordes of modern pioneers drove to the "last frontier." They found a speculative boom of historic proportions. "All of America's gold rushes," wrote Mark Sullivan, "all her oil booms, and all her free-land stampedes dwindled by comparison . . . with the torrent of migration pouring into Florida during the early fall of 1925."[6]

Florida's climate, new roads, and low taxes had appeal, but the chance of easy money fueled the hysteria. Real estate promoters littered the state with "the joyful and confident devastation of development." Anything could happen as subdivisions rose from "snake-infested" mangrove swamps. Not since the days of the carpetbaggers had so many opportunists and swindlers migrated south.[7]

THE PROMOTERS

Tales of quick profits caught the attention of the nation. Even William Jennings Bryan, the former secretary of state and three-time Democratic nominee for president, made more than $500,000 by speculating in his adopted state. Bryan became a believer in Florida. When he was not crusading for anti-evolution laws, Bryan lectured about the virtues of "God's sunshine."[8]

At the end of his career, Bryan used his considerable credibility to peddle Florida real estate. George Edgar Merrick, the developer of Coral Gables, paid Bryan as much as $100,000 a year, with half in real estate, to promote his project. The "Great Commoner" tried to conceal the fortune made from speculating in Florida. A few months before his death, Bryan reported his net worth at less than $500,000. After his death in July 1925, his will disclosed a net worth of $860,000. A friend explained the discrepancy as his real estate profits.[9]

Bryan died at the height of the boom. He spent his last days telling prospects that Miami was "the only city in the world where you can tell a lie at breakfast that will come true by evening." Bryan's fervor was not lost on his benefactor. Merrick, who would be remembered for his "aesthetic vision," was a captive of his own publicity. He continued to expand and improve his "Miami Riviera" until the magnitude of the project doomed it. When in 1925 the development encompassed more than ten thousand acres and six miles of Biscayne Bay frontage, Merrick announced that he planned to add $100 million of improvements over the next decade. His grand plans included the Miami Biltmore Hotel and Club, a $10 million complex.[10]

Merrick received major financial backing from W. D. Manley and J. R. Anthony, who controlled the preeminent banking chain in Florida and Georgia. Telfair Knight, who was vice-president and general manager of Merrick's Coral Gables Corporation, was the link between the two organizations. He was also president of

Preaching under the palm trees about "God's sunshine," William Jennings Bryan made a fortune as a land speculator in Coral Gables. (Courtesy, Florida State Archives)

the Bank of Coral Gables, a member of the Manley-Anthony system. And as an accommodation to Anthony, he served as vice-president and director of the Anthony Investment Company.[11]

Access to liberal financing enabled Merrick to expand Coral Gables into insolvency. The records of defunct banks reveal the high cost of Merrick's unrestrained optimism. The Coral Gables Corporation received loans from the following members of the Manley-Anthony system: Bank of Coral Gables, Palm Beach Bank and Trust Company, Commercial Bank and Trust Company of West Palm Beach, Bank of Dania, Bank of St. Cloud, Citizens Bank of Eustis, First State Bank of Clermont, Bank of Oviedo, Bank of Mt. Dora, Exchange Bank of Sycamore, Georgia, Peoples Exchange Bank of Tennille, Georgia, and Lodi Trust Company of Lodi, New Jersey.[12]

Manley and Anthony also provided financing for Addison Mizner and his Boca Raton development. Historian George Tindall described Mizner as "one of the great charlatan-geniuses of the Twenties." Mizner designed a grandiose plan to transform obscure Boca Raton into the world's premier resort. Its centerpiece would be Castle Mizner, his proposed $1 million house, to be built on an island in the middle of Lake Boca Raton. The flamboyant architect planned a grand entrance for his "medieval castle," complete with a functioning drawbridge.[13]

With a straight face, Mizner announced that his residence would be "a Spanish fortress of the twelfth century captured from its owner by a stronger enemy, who, after taking it, adds on one wing and another, and then loses it in turn to another who builds to suit his taste." A brochure of the Mizner Development Corporation declared: "Addison Mizner has planned his home to endure through the ages and house for the enjoyment of posterity, the art and architectural treasures which he has brought from the old world. No finer contribution to the architectural splendor of Boca Raton could be made by its founder."[14]

The ego and imagination of Mizner epitomized the promoters in paradise. He advertised Boca Raton as "undoubtedly the most tremendous land development project ever launched in the state of Florida." Mizner's company purchased two miles of oceanfront and sixteen thousand undeveloped acres, an immense project even by boom standards.[15]

In April 1925, Mizner announced that the development would

feature a $6 million oceanfront hotel named "'Castillo del Rey' (Castle of the King)." It would be "the most beautiful hotel in the world," with 1,000 rooms and 250 apartments. The "social capital of the south" would include polo fields to "assure an aristocracy of sport," three world-class golf courses, tennis courts, private beaches, an airport, and a marina to house the yachts that would be cruising through the "lazy lagoons" and lakes of Boca Raton's twenty miles of waterways. A cabaret run by Irving Berlin, the famous composer, and a casino, even though casino gambling was illegal in Florida, would provide nighttime entertainment.[16]

A new generation of conquistadors would know when they reached the enchanted land. They would leave behind the "congested and tormented" Dixie Highway to enter the "palm-arcaded and flower-bordered" El Camino Real. Mizner planned "a truly royal highway 160 to 220 feet wide . . . inspired by Rio de Janeiro's famous Botafogo." The King's Highway would become "the world's most beautiful boulevard." To capture the romance of the Old World, "a bridge-arched Venetian Canal" would run through the center of the road, and imported Italian gondolas would ferry prospects and guests throughout the development.[17]

Mizner tried to emulate Henry Flagler, who, catering to the rich and famous, built the Royal Poinciana and Breakers in Palm Beach in the 1890s. Flagler's hotels stayed full because he controlled the transportation system on the east coast of Florida. He built the grand hotels after buying the Florida East Coast Railway and expanding it to West Palm Beach. With captive customers, Flagler minimized risk by building superb resorts in strategic locations.[18]

A different kind of "snowbird" migrated to Florida in the 1920s. Instead of traveling in private railroad cars, middle-class boomers headed south in their Fords. Mizner's isolated development had to compete with established subdivisions in Miami and Miami Beach, so he aimed his marketing at high society: "Get the big snobs and the little snobs will follow."[19]

Unlike Flagler, Mizner depended on other people's money. He raised most of the equity for his project by seducing the elite of society with his fantasy. Paris Singer, heir to the sewing machine fortune, had been Mizner's closest friend and booster for years. Singer gave Mizner his start in Palm Beach. He hired Mizner in 1918 to design a hospital for convalescent soldiers, which was converted to the exclusive Everglades Club. The Everglades Club introduced Mizner's Spanish architectural style to the cream of society. Its success generated a clientele for Mizner which made him one of the nation's leading architects. With Singer's backing, in 1925 Mizner persuaded Senator T. Coleman du Pont of Delaware to become chairman of the newly formed Mizner Development Corporation, and his lawyer, Congressman George S. Graham of Philadelphia, to join the board of directors.

Harold S. Vanderbilt, William K. Vanderbilt II, the Duchess of Sutherland, and Elizabeth Arden eagerly bought stock in Mizner's company. Clarence H. Geist, who had been a partner of United States vice-president Charles G. Dawes and who acquired the Mizner properties in 1927, was also one of Mizner's original stockholders. Henry C. Phipps, of the Pittsburgh steel family, and Jesse L. Livermore, the Wall Street speculator, also supported Mizner's dream. Another luminary investing in the future of Boca Raton was Irving Berlin, who was good friends with Addison's brother Wilson.[20]

Mizner leveraged his project by selling stock to local bankers and then arranging large loans from their banks. After the boom cooled and lot sales slowed, the promoter-bankers made their depositors unwitting participants in Mizner's reckless venture. Mizner put William A. White, who later became president of the Palm Beach National Bank, on the board of Mizner Development Corporation. Mizner also sold stock to D. Lester Williams and Howard P. Smith, officers and controlling stockholders of the same bank.[21]

Williams, whose name appeared in Mizner's advertisements, and Smith were important because they also controlled a state bank, the Palm Beach Bank and Trust Company, which had a different set of regulators. Its president, Benjamin R. Clayton, was another stockholder in the Boca Raton venture. Both banks were affiliated with the Commercial Bank and Trust Company of West Palm Beach, whose president, Thomas M. Cook, and vice-president, Adrian E. Pearson, were stockholders of Mizner's company. The three Palm Beach County banks were affiliated with the Manley-Anthony banking system. W. D. Manley and J. R. Anthony also had a personal financial interest in the Mizner Development Corporation.[22]

Addison Mizner gladly took money, but not advice, from his high-powered partners. He relied primarily on his brother Wilson, whom he appointed as the company's secretary and treasurer. When lot sales were generating millions of dollars, Addison entrusted the company's checkbook to Wilson, a "slick con man" and professional gambler with a criminal record. In complete control of the project, Addison and Wilson did not take long to squander the deal of their lifetime.[23]

THE BIG CON

Exposed to privilege and influence at an early age, the Mizner brothers knew they could make easy money by associating with high society. They came from a family of fortune hunters. Their father, Lansing, who was a member of the Society of California Pioneers, had sought his fortune in California during the gold rush of 1849. He became an influential lawyer, land developer, and politician in the San Francisco area. After serving as president of the California Senate, Lansing Mizner worked for Benjamin Harrison in the presidential campaign of 1888. President Harrison appointed him as the envoy extraordinary and minister plenipotentiary to Central America, the highest-ranking diplomatic position in Guatemala, El Salvador, Honduras, Nicaragua, and Costa Rica. Addison's fascination with Spanish architecture began when his family lived in Guatemala City and was enhanced when he studied at the University of Salamanca in Spain.[24]

Savoring champagne and caviar, the Mizner brothers associated with the high rollers of society for four decades. Addison, whose weight seemed to increase in proportion to his fame until it exceeded three hundred pounds, enjoyed being a creative eccentric, while Wilson acted the part of playwright and wit. They began their careers by resorting to confidence games and keeping on the move. During the Klondike gold rush of 1898, they endured the hardships of Alaska and the Yukon Territory in their quest for fame and fortune. They made the arduous journey to Dawson City after receiving an urgent message from their brother Edgar that gold had been found near the confluence of the Yukon and Klondike rivers.[25]

Wilson "sparkled with larceny" under the northern lights. He never intended to accumulate gold by panning the ice-cold creek beds and digging, with pick and shovel, through the frozen gravel for minute specks of gold dust. His plan for "gold and glory" was to become rich by using his wits to separate the gold from the prospectors.

At the time, Wilson, who was the best-dressed man in the territory, stood six feet four and weighed 220 pounds. He "dazzled" the rowdy miners and charmed the dance hall girls. While he played cards, he would survey the Monte Carlo Dance Hall and declare that "flesh beats scenery." His girlfriend was "Nellie the Pig" Lamore, a tough but attractive dance hall girl. In a campaign to win her affections, he risked arrest by the North West Mounted Police by robbing—masked and at gunpoint—a restaurant in an effort to supply Nellie with chocolates, which were more valuable than gold.[26]

In search of a fresh supply of suckers, Wilson joined the next wave of stampeders to Nome, Alaska, where gold had been discovered on the black beaches of the Bering Sea. In the treeless, barren town that stood on frozen tundra, Wilson became known as the "Prince of Nome." His quick wit and indoor talents flourished under Alaska's corrupt system of bush justice. He established the McQuestion, a casino with a saloon and dance hall. As one of the city's "founding fathers" he was appointed as a deputy sheriff. Wilson later quipped that his primary duty was "to warn Eskimos that they'd have to smell better." After four years of smoothly fleecing miners, Wilson left the land of the midnight sun to run a banana plantation in Honduras. He lasted only a few months in the jungles of Central America and returned to San Francisco to resume his career as a professional gambler.[27]

Addison had left Dawson City in 1899. He continued to acquire entertaining anecdotes for his memoirs by traveling to Hawaii, Samoa, Australia, Manila, Siam, India, and Shanghai. While in Hawaii he coauthored a small book of quotations, *Cynic's Calendar,* and in Australia he fought a prizefight with "the Pride of Australia." Searching for a way to make his fortune and using his father's contacts, he then tried to establish a coffee business in Guatemala. After failing as an entrepreneur, he moved to New York and finally found his niche as a society architect.[28]

Once Addison had established himself, Wilson joined him in Manhattan. Trading on Addison's talent and Wilson's tales of Arctic adventures, the brothers made inroads with the upper crust of the eastern seaboard. In 1906, Wilson, aged twenty-nine, made headlines when he married Myra Adelaide Yerkes, forty-eight, whom Addison thought was one of the richest widows in the country. Mrs. Yerkes was the recent widow of Charles T. Yerkes, who at one time controlled Chicago's railway system. She was also the owner of a $4 million mansion on Fifth Avenue decorated with oil paintings by Rembrandt, Van Dyke, and other European masters. Wilson was a member of the leisure class for only a few months. The publicity generated numerous letters from California and Alaska warning the new Mrs. Mizner about her husband's past criminal activities. After her lawyers finished with Wilson, he agreed to dissolve the marriage and started looking for a new confidence game.[29]

Wilson then made his living by gambling on luxury ocean liners between New York and London. He called himself a "deep-sea fisherman," luring suckers to play poker, craps, and other games of chance. When the Cunard and other liners cracked down on sting operations, he became the manager of Stanley Ketchel, "the Michigan Assassin," who was the greatest middleweight prizefighter of his time until he was murdered. Wilson then sold his adventures to Broadway.[30]

Collaborating with other playwrights, Wilson helped write several successful plays. *Deep Purple,* a play about the badger game of extortion, made Wilson a celebrity. He became known as the "Shakespeare of the Underworld." Irving Berlin composed a song, "Black Sheep Has Come Back to the Fold," about Wilson's success. But after his second Broadway hit, *The Greyhound,* about a cardsharp on transatlantic ocean liners, his short-lived success faded. His productivity as a playwright was affected by a hatred of writing and an addiction to drugs. He much preferred smoking opium with his friends. After his days on Broadway ended, he began running an illegal gambling house on Long Island. In 1919, the year of the great Red Scare and increased law enforcement activity, Wilson was convicted for gambling and received a suspended sentence. Trying to reverse his streak of bad luck, he went to Hollywood, where the nascent film industry was making millionaires out of many who had far fewer experiences to peddle. After working on a few movie scripts, Wilson rushed to Florida to join his brother at the great barbecue. His training prepared him for a central role in the boom and bust that made Florida "the con man's capital."[31]

During World War I, Addison Mizner moved to Palm Beach,

following the wintering aristocrats of New York. By 1925 his lavish architectural style had won him an impressive clientele. Alva Johnston, in *The Legendary Mizners,* described Mizner's work as the "Bastard-Spanish-Moorish-Romanesque-Gothic-Renaissance-Bull-Market-Damn-the-Expense Style." Mizner said his goal was "to make a building look traditional and as though it had fought its way from a small unimportant structure to a great rambling house that took centuries of different needs and ups and downs of wealth to accomplish. I sometimes start a house with a Romanesque corner, pretend that it has fallen into disrepair and been added to in the Gothic spirit, when suddenly the great wealth of the New World has poured in and the owner has added a very rich Renaissance addition."[32]

Addison's clients gave him the credibility to set up what Wilson called a "platinum sucker trap" in Boca Raton. Though little work had been completed on the "Golden City of the Gold Coast" during the first six months of the project, the *Palm Beach Post* declared that Mizner had really "put it over!"[33] The newspaper could speak with authority because its publisher, Donald Herbert Conkling, was involved in the deal.

AN UNHOLY ALLIANCE

Besides owning an influential newspaper, Conkling was a real estate promoter and banker who played a key role in the Mizners' confidence game. He was an organizing stockholder of the Mizner Development Corporation and owned fifteen hundred shares of the company. Conkling's *Palm Beach Post* proudly listed him as one of the "noted personages" joining Mizner's syndicate. His newspaper fueled the real estate frenzy with its promotional articles about the Mizner Development Corporation and other boom projects. The articles may have helped temporarily to inflate the value of Conkling's real estate holdings, but they were a disaster for the depositors of Palm Beach County.[34]

As a banker, Conkling knew how to play the insider's game. He bought stock in local banks and then borrowed many times more from those banks. He owned stock in the same banks that were financing Mizner: the Palm Beach National Bank, Commercial Bank and Trust Company, and First American Bank and Trust Company of West Palm Beach. After the banks failed, Conkling defaulted on his obligations. For example, he bought 1 percent of the stock of the Commercial Bank and Trust Company, became a vice-president, and then borrowed more than 10 percent of its capital. After the bank failed, he defaulted on his stock assessment.[35]

Conkling was also a stockholder and director of the First American Bank and Trust Company of West Palm Beach, which failed for the first time in March 1927. Two months later, news of its reorganization made front-page headlines in the *Palm Beach Post*. His newspaper devoted almost an entire page to the "gala event" on the day of its reopening. But the bank kept its doors open only until June 1928, when it failed again. By then Conkling's Post Holding Company, which was affiliated with the *Palm Beach Post,* had borrowed thirty-eight times his investment from the bank.[36]

Conkling's banks also generously loaned money to Mizner, and the publisher's involvement ensured favorable publicity for the developer. By hyping the boom, the *Palm Beach Post* advanced Conkling's economic interest. His newspaper derived most of its revenues from the Mizner Development Corporation and other real estate companies that ran full-page advertisements. Buyers then bought lots at inflated prices, providing Conkling and the other promoters with the cash to repay their bank loans. The pyramid scheme worked as long as new buyers believed in paradise.[37]

Addison Mizner reached the pinnacle of promoters in large part because of Conkling's newspaper. The *Palm Beach Post* depicted him as a "genius" who had a "keen, far-sighted" vision of the future. Effusively, the paper proclaimed that he had done "what no other man had been able to do in the world's history, and may never do again." He was "backed by the greatest of development companies" and was turning his magnificent dream into a reality. Boca Raton would become a "city old in romance, restful in atmosphere, poised in buildings, orderly in plan and in every feature beautiful . . . a cornerstone to American architectural prestige and a monument to American money."[38]

Advertisements in the *Palm Beach Post* trumpeted the same message. Carried away with his imagination, Mizner decreed that the Spanish conquistadors "had COURAGE . . . IMAGINATION . . . the spirit of ADVENTURE. But they lacked FORESIGHT. And so Spain lost what might have been the greatest empire the world has ever seen." Spain wasted the chance to develop "a new race of Spaniards" in the New World and be "DICTATOR among nations." In contrast, Mizner and his partners would "win empires of profit in Florida" because they were inspired prophets.[39]

The advertisements served the dual purpose of selling lots in the development and stock in the company. The Mizner Development Corporation invited the public "to Share in the Profits of an Enormous Land Development." The company sold a $500,000 public stock offering in one week. Anyone could participate by sending a check "direct to Addison Mizner" in Palm Beach.[40]

In September, when Mizner finally hired a general contractor for "actual work," the *Palm Beach Post* made the event a front-page story. Working in concert with the free publicity, advertisements kept lot sales moving by describing Mizner and his partners as the "magicians of art and commerce." For hundreds of years Florida had lain "barren, peopled only by a few breech-clouted savages." Now the wasteland was visited by "the men of genius and enterprise at whose magic touch Florida awakened to fulfill her destiny." These great men were a natural resource, as vital as Florida's sunshine. They had "the powers of brain, muscle and money . . . the vision that inspires and the energy that builds armies . . . the magic touch that pulls cities from the earth and draws people from all parts of the world to fill them."[41]

THE NIGHTMARE

When the cost of construction created a cash shortage, Mizner crossed the line. The Mizner Development Corporation surpassed its other promotional gimmicks by guaranteeing that the extravagant improvements would be built: "Attach this advertisement to your contract for deed. It becomes a part thereof." Lot buyers were also promised that they would "make quick and large profits." The advertisements pledged that the project could not possibly fail because the developers backing it owned "considerably over one-third of the entire wealth of the United States." Mizner's advertising strategy exposed Senator du Pont and the other wealthy directors to tremendous personal liability.[42]

Recognizing his exposure and sensing an end to the boom, du Pont tried to salvage his investment and distance himself from Mizner. Because many of the state's promoters were selling swampland, Florida was receiving negative publicity throughout the country. Concerned about the loss of deposits, bankers in Ohio had financed an anti-Florida advertising campaign to warn northern residents about "get-rich-quick" schemes. In October, du Pont organized a rally of "heavy" investors in New York City to generate positive press. Florida governor John W. Martin participated in the public relations disaster, complaining that unscrupulous promoters had victimized Florida. Ironically, Senator du Pont, whose Palm Beach partners were making some of the most outlandish advertising claims, blamed the state for not prosecuting confidence men. He said the state should "bag about four of them and give them the limit." Then other illegal operators would stop the false advertising. [43]

The *New York Times* interpreted the unusual conference as evidence that the bubble had burst. It proved that the leaders of Florida now understood the "dangers that lie in a boom, or rather in the after-effects of one when it has gone the lengths." The *Times* surmised that the prominent men were "worried" about the day when "'investors'" could not find new buyers for their speculations. [44]

After the futile attempt to change Florida's image, Senator du Pont tried to reorganize the Mizner Development Corporation by demanding the resignations of Wilson Mizner and Harry Reichenbach, the public relations man who was issuing the false advertisements. Du Pont produced evidence of Wilson's 1919 gambling conviction as proof that the company needed a new treasurer. When his demands were ignored, du Pont resigned as chairman of the board. He accused the Mizners of mismanaging the company, adding that Boca Raton had "wonderful possibilities" if properly managed. Du Pont's resignation sent shock waves through Florida. Addison Mizner blamed du Pont's departure on internal politics. He said the dispute was merely a struggle for control of the company and that du Pont had failed in his attempt to stack the board of directors with his cronies. According to Mizner, his group's efforts—not du Pont's—had produced sales of $30 million in just six months. His arrogant response prompted four more outside directors to resign within a week. They denied losing a takeover fight and castigated Mizner for falsely using their names in advertisements. With much fanfare, the business leaders denounced the "exaggerated" promotional campaign. The negative publicity crippled the company and raised serious doubts about a boom based solely on consumer confidence.[45]

Mizner's dream had become a nightmare. No guests would be royally entertained at Castle Mizner or the Castillo del Rey, the original thousand-room, $6 million oceanfront hotel, because they were never built. The Cloister Inn, a charming but small hotel with only one hundred rooms, was constructed on the Intracoastal Waterway. The company's administration buildings and twenty-nine small houses "of little architectural merit" in the Old Floresta district of Boca Raton were also completed. El Camino Real, with its twenty lanes of traffic, was finished for only half a mile, and its Venetian canal resembled a muddy ditch instead of a grand European waterway.[46]

Although 3,750 lot buyers executed sales contracts of nearly $21,900,000, the Mizner Development Corporation was insolvent. After squandering millions of dollars, Mizner was confronted with a liquidity crisis. As the volume of lot sales dropped dramatically, he relied on the Manley-Anthony banking system for financing. Its officers and directors held personal stakes in the Mizner Development Corporation, and the chain banks financed the development until depositors forced them to lock their doors.[47]

After provoking a banking crash of historic proportions, Mizner enticed Vice-President Charles Dawes and his brothers to become his partners. The Dawes brothers, through the Central Equities Corporation, kept the company floating for less than a year. In the process they secured $10.5 million of the unpaid purchase contracts for themselves. Mizner and the Dawes brothers then left the obligations and debts of the Mizner Development Corporation for the bankruptcy court.[48]

2

CAPTURING THE REGULATORS

To finance paradise, bankers became promoters and promoters became bankers. Operating under a spell of greed, these bankers corrupted Florida's economic and regulatory systems. The state went through a period of lawlessness, both sophisticated and crude, which finally ended with the Great Depression. Bank robbery by bandits was easier for the public to understand than bank fraud committed by officers of financial institutions. Depositors remained calm when the infamous Ashley gang robbed banks at gunpoint in south Florida. Using the Everglades as a hiding place, the gang was less of a threat to society than its counterparts in stiffly starched white shirts.[1]

Besides controlling the economy of boom-time Florida, bankers dominated its government at both the state and local levels. The governor of Florida from 1921 to 1925 was Cary A. Hardee, who was simultaneously the president of the First National Bank of Live Oak. Hardee understood the relationship between banking and politics. In 1909, he was selected as president of the Florida Bankers Association, and in 1915 he was chosen by his colleagues to be Speaker of the House before becoming a member of the

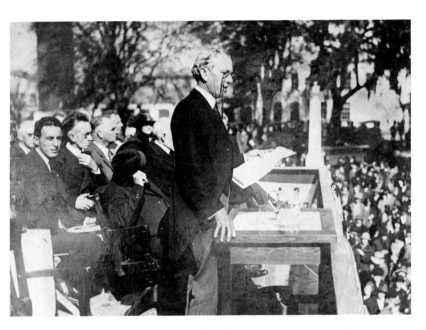

Cary A. Hardee, governor of Florida and president of the First National
Bank of Live Oak, was one of the leading promoters of the
Sunshine State prior to the boom.
(Courtesy, Florida State Archives)

legislature. He served two terms as Speaker and then was elected
governor in 1920.[2]

Speaking to enthusiastic members of his "banking fraternity" in
1922, Governor Hardee declared that they did not need "to apolo-
gize for being bankers." Hardee urged his friends to exert more
"influence" in politics and government. He praised Miami's
"banker government" and proclaimed that "the government of this
country is not run by the Bolsheviks or by demagogues entirely.
. . . Constructive forces can always control, if they will. You can
have your influence along that line if you will only exert it, and the
constructive forces ought to control this country. They ought to
control the politics of this country, which incidentally of course,
means the government of the country."[3]

The promoter George Merrick, who was a Coral Gables city
commissioner, agreed with the governor and attributed Miami's
phenomenal success to its banker government. In 1920, the

"bankers ticket," composed of five bank presidents, was swept into office. Merrick told the *New York Times* that Miami was "the most cosmopolitan and American of American cities," a progressive city, "where capitalism and industry work ideally together." In other words, a promoter could borrow money from a banker and rezone his property at the same time. This linkage between bankers, promoters, and politics led to a reckless expansion of the economy which inflated real estate values to irrational levels.[4]

Between 1921 and 1925, all five members of the Miami city commission were bankers. Members of the bankers commission were James H. Gilman, president of the Bank of Bay Biscayne; James E. Lummus, president of the Southern Bank and Trust Company; James I. Wilson, president of the Dade County Security Company; Charles D. Leffler, president of the Miami Bank and Trust Company; and Edward C. Romfh, president of the First National Bank of Miami, who was mayor of Miami from 1923 to 1927. Fueling the boom, the bankers commission issued bonds of $27 million for streets, bridges, and sewers. By 1932, the taxpayers of Miami and Dade County carried $60 million of local debt, almost three times the $21,348,000 debt of Jacksonville and Duval County, an area with a comparable population. Miami and Dade County, with a poor credit rating, struggled to pay for its bonded indebtedness throughout the 1930s. Years later, former mayor Romfh took credit for the huge expansion program, though he admitted it was "so big it toppled over in the crash."[5]

Its taxing authority enabled Miami to survive the mismanagement of the banker commissioners. But four of their five banks collapsed after the boom cooled off. The Bank of Bay Biscayne, Southern Bank and Trust Company, Dade County Security Company, and Miami Bank and Trust Company failed because of insider abuse and bad loans to real estate promoters. By 1930 Merrick's Coral Gables Corporation was insolvent and he was running a fishing camp in the Florida Keys that his wife, Eunice, had inherited from her father.[6]

THE BANK CHARTERING SYSTEM

Andrew Jackson's veto of the Second Bank of the United States led to the proliferation of state and national banks, each with its own charter and political mandate. Under the American system of *de novo* banking, new banks are formed by local groups receiving a charter from a state or federal regulator. During the 1920s a promoter needed political connections, not banking experience, to become a banker.

During Florida's land boom, promoters eagerly sought bank charters, which regulators willingly provided. The newly sanctioned bankers then used depositors' money to fund their own projects. And with their new source of money, they bought regulatory protection by making loans to banking officials. The corruption of the regulatory system created a bewildering array of bank openings and closings. Between 1921 and 1929, Florida comptroller Ernest Amos approved 127 bank charter applications, and 122 state banks closed. During the same period, the U.S. comptroller of the currency chartered 36 national banks in Florida, and 16 national banks failed.[7]

The liberal granting of state bank charters declined markedly after 1926. In September of that year, a Palm Beach County grand jury indicted Comptroller Amos for gross malpractice. Jurors blamed Amos for the failure of the Palm Beach Bank and Trust Company and the Commercial Bank and Trust Company of West Palm Beach. The grand jury also indicted officers of the two banks for making secret insider loans to their own companies, including the Mizner Development Corporation. Mizner's company and the banks were affiliated through common ownership and interlocking directors. Officers of the banks, who failed to disclose their ownership interest in Mizner's company, loaned more than 100 percent of the capital of both banks to Mizner and his partners. When the Boca Raton development failed, so did the banks.[8]

Amos and his staff were intimately aware that Mizner's project endangered the state banks, but they refused to stop the speculation. Instead, Amos and two of his bank examiners procured unsecured loans from the same bankers who were wildly speculating with Mizner. Amos defaulted on his note, and a "loan" to E. M. Porter, the state's chief bank examiner, was repaid by Howard P. Smith, vice-president of the state-chartered Palm Beach Bank and Trust Company and former president of the Palm Beach National Bank. Smith was also a major stockholder of the Mizner Development Corporation. Another stockholder of Mizner's company, Thomas M. Cook, president of the Commercial Bank and Trust

Company, made a loan to T. C. Hawkins, the state examiner in charge of that bank.[9]

Smith and Cook were partners in their banking activities with J. R. Anthony, the founder of the Palm Beach Bank and Trust Company. Anthony and W. D. Manley controlled the Commercial Bank and Trust Company by owning 52 percent of its stock. Anthony was the most powerful banker in Florida until July 1926, when his banking empire crashed. Understanding "the power of money," Anthony knew how easy it was to capture bank regulators. He and his brother A. P. Anthony preyed on Amos's "weakness" and greed. They supported him politically and financially.[10]

The state comptroller's regulatory records of the Peoples Bank of Jacksonville, sealed for sixty years, confirm Amos's intimate relationship with the Anthonys. When the Peoples Bank failed in 1929 with Augustus P. Anthony as its president, Amos owed the state bank $12,632 in six unsecured loans. The final examiner's report also revealed that the partnership of Anthony, Amos, and Bowers had endorsed a $4,347 loan.[11]

THE CRACKER REGULATOR

Ernest Amos had no banking training or experience to qualify him for the position of state banking commissioner. He rose to prominence in state government through the political process. His political career began when he became the law clerk for Senator Charles J. Perrenot of Milton, who served as president of the Florida Senate during the 1897 session. Amos was elected to the Florida House of Representatives in 1900 but served only one term. He then held the office of state auditor from 1904 to 1917, which prepared him for the comptroller's constitutional function as the chief fiscal officer of the state. In 1916, Amos was elected comptroller of Florida and a member of the state's cabinet.[12]

Amos projected the image of a cracker politician who was born and raised in Milton, the county seat of Santa Rosa County. But his family had been prominent in the panhandle of Florida for generations. Amos's father, Joseph W. Amos, who proudly served as a sergeant in the Confederate army, worked for his son, alongside his daughter-in-law, Mrs. Ernest Amos, in the comptroller's office. Amos's office was no exception to the state cabinet's tradition of nepotism.[13]

Florida Comptroller Ernest Amos granted bank charters to promoter-bankers and then accepted unsecured loans from them. (From a campaign brochure, Courtesy, P. K. Yonge Library of Florida History, University of Florida)

After conducting a statewide campaign and serving in the cabinet for four years, Amos gained name recognition throughout Florida. He was reelected with little opposition in 1920 and 1924. His real advantage was the ability to raise campaign funds from the state banking industry, which he regulated with unbridled discretion. His regulatory power could be used as a fund-raising club any time he needed money. Bankers could play the game or face the economic consequences.

Another important political advantage for Amos was his statewide organization. Most communities had a state bank, and each one could serve as a local political headquarters for the comptroller. Each bank had influential community leaders serving on its board of directors. Customers who obtained loans from the bank were a good source of campaign funds and political support. Investors forming new state banks were also reliable contributors. Bank charter applicants were eager to contribute to the official who would be approving their applications.[14]

Failed banks were valuable political assets for the comptroller as well. The power to appoint receivers and attorneys provided him with a patronage system. Amos hired local politicians and state legislators to ensure their support in his future campaigns and legislative sessions. He used his patronage to thwart efforts by angry depositors to oust him at the polls and to reform the system. Because his friends were in charge of defunct state banks and in the halls of the legislature, Amos survived the banking crash of 1926.[15]

His role as a cabinet member was also a significant political benefit. The Florida cabinet system, which remains strong today, divided the executive authority among the governor and six cabinet members. Cabinet members were more powerful than the governor because they could serve unlimited terms. Prohibited from a second consecutive term by the constitution of 1885, a governor only had four years to make an impact and usually failed in attempts to change the system. By the 1920s, only William D. Bloxham, who had been elected in 1880 and 1896, had served as governor for two terms. Machinators in Florida knew that the power of state government rested in the hands of the six elected cabinet members and not with the governor. Florida's cabinet system developed its stronghold after Reconstruction. State Democratic party leaders realized that the Republican party might someday be able to elect the governor but not all six cabinet seats. By dividing the executive power, they guaranteed that their political exclusion would be neither total nor ruinous.

Amos developed ties with individual cabinet members and their friends. Common friends often supported the various cabinet members. An owner of a citrus grove regulated by Commissioner of Agriculture Nathan Mayo would also own stock in a bank regulated by Comptroller Amos. A close relationship existed between the comptroller's office and the treasurer's office. Treasurers J. C. Luning and later William V. Knott, who were responsible for depositing the state's funds in banks, traveled in the same banking circles as Amos. At cabinet meetings a majority vote was required for action to be taken so it made political sense for members to work in harmony. Four votes were required, even if the governor voted against a proposal. Governors who came to Tallahassee with plans to reform state government soon discovered that they did not have the votes in the cabinet to implement their programs. If the governor exercised his legislative veto power to try to shape state policy, he found that any four cabinet members could veto his proposals.[16]

By 1926, Amos had enjoyed the benefits of sitting on the state's board of directors for nine years. Into his third term as the chief bank regulator, he was accustomed to the trappings of his office, which included the ability to borrow on an unsecured basis from state banks. Because no banking commissioner had been defeated for reelection in Florida's history, he could feel secure in his position as long as he stayed close to the industry he regulated. Throughout the 1920s, Amos maintained his bond with the banking industry and its most powerful member, J. R. Anthony.[17]

ANTHONY BECOMES A BANKER

James Rembert Anthony, Jr., rose to preeminence in Florida's banking community by the skillful use of money and politics. He was not trained as a banker. Yet his relationship with Comptrollers William V. Knott and Ernest Amos enabled him to develop a Florida banking system of sixty-one banks with deposits of more than $120 million. Known as the "King of Chain Banks," Anthony was so influential that his banks could ignore the state's banking laws with impunity. Because Knott and Amos approved dozens of charters for Anthony, the likelihood of a banking catastrophe increased with the opening of each new bank.[18]

The Anthonys were one of Florida's pioneer families who migrated to Titusville from Georgia in the early 1890s. J. R. and his two brothers, Augustus P. and Henry J., pooled their insufficient resources and obtained a loan from the Indian River State Bank of Titusville, where Henry worked as a clerk, to purchase a jewelry and newspaper store in Titusville, which they named Anthony Brothers. After Flagler expanded his railroad to West Palm Beach in 1895, the brothers borrowed more money from their banker and opened stores in West Palm Beach and Palm Beach. Through negotiations and persistence, they were able to win an important concession from Flagler that enabled them to make a fortune. They secured an exclusive lease on the grounds of Flagler's Royal Poinciana Hotel in Palm Beach and specialized in fashionable men's clothes that appealed to its wealthy patrons wintering in Florida. After developing a successful business and speculating in real estate, the brothers decided to expand their influence by becoming bankers.[19]

With limited capital but unlimited ambitions, the Anthony brothers developed plans for opening the First National Bank of Miami, which would be the first national bank in the city. Miami was a frontier community with only one state bank, the Bank of Bay Biscayne, and competing against it would be a formidable challenge. The Bank of Bay Biscayne had opened as a state bank in 1896, shortly after Flagler's railroad began operations to Miami. The bank was formed under the direction of Flagler, who suggested its name and supplied it with deposits of his Florida East Coast Railway Company.

The Anthonys confidently moved forward with their bold plan because they had inside knowledge about their future competitor. William M. Brown, the former cashier of the Indian River State Bank of Titusville, had financed the Anthony Brothers stores for years. When Brown became president of the Bank of Bay Biscayne, his former clerk, Henry Anthony, moved to Miami to work for the bank as a bookkeeper. The Anthonys also promised to hire Edward Coleman Romfh, the assistant cashier of the Bank of Bay Biscayne, as the cashier of the new bank for $75 a month.[20]

The Anthonys facilitated the project by forming an alliance with the Romfh brothers. As a base of operations, the Anthonys opened a clothing store in downtown Miami with Eugene B. Romfh as its manager. He was also named secretary of Anthony Brothers. Edward Romfh, the city's future mayor, arrived in Miami with twenty cents in his pocket in 1898 and was hired by William Brown as a $50-a-month assistant cashier. His lack of money did not interfere with his passion for becoming a banker but may have affected his business ethics. He helped convince the Anthonys of the unique opportunity in Miami by leaking confidential information about his employer's bad loans and unsound condition. The Bank of Bay Biscayne would be the only competition, and if it failed the First National Bank would dominate the development of Miami. If the Bank of Bay Biscayne survived its worthless loans and the rumors from its former employee, the new bank would have access to its customers.[21]

Before the Anthonys could start opening new accounts, they had to navigate through the highly politicized bank chartering process. Henry Anthony, the chairman of the Dade County Democratic Campaign Committee, and his brothers appreciated the political clout of the Bank of Bay Biscayne and its customers. They could assume that Florida comptroller A. C. Croom, who had been appointed in 1901 by Governor William S. Jennings and who would be running in a statewide election in 1904, would deny any new state bank charters in Miami. Applying for a national bank charter was also risky because of Flagler's involvement with the competition. Flagler had friends in Washington capable of persuading Comptroller of the Currency William B. Ridgely to deny the bank application. To ensure approval of their application, the Anthonys became partners with some of the most powerful political and business leaders in the country.[22]

J. R. Anthony's contacts secured the charter and guaranteed the success of the venture. He had witnessed the linkage between politics and business during the 1890s, when he was affiliated with William Gibbs McAdoo, then a Wall Street lawyer, who would become chairman of the Federal Reserve Board, secretary of the treasury, and a Democratic United States senator from California. Anthony observed at close hand that money did not distinguish between political parties and was not concerned with political ideology. His education in high finance began in 1893, when he went to work for a Paterson, New Jersey, streetcar company owned by Garret A. Hobart, a corporation lawyer and future Republican vice-president of the United States. McAdoo's brother Malcolm was the manager of the streetcar company, and Anthony was his able assistant. After Vice-President Hobart sold his company in 1900 for a huge profit, Malcolm McAdoo became the general manager for the Pittsburgh, McKeesport and Connellsville Railway Company, whose president was Congressman William H. Graham. McAdoo then hired Anthony to work in Pittsburgh as the general superintendent for expansion of the railroad. Besides being a powerful member of Congress and a wealthy industrialist, Graham was president of the Mercantile Trust Company, a large Pittsburgh bank. Recognizing that influence was more important than financial strength and ability in the organization of a bank, Anthony offered the congressman a high-yield, no-risk deal. He guaranteed Graham an 8 percent dividend if he would purchase stock in the First National Bank. Graham then became a stockholder and director of the fledgling bank. The Miami bank also established a correspondent relationship with Graham's Pittsburgh bank.[23]

Congressman Graham's participation ensured regulatory approval and oversubscription of the bank's stock. His involvement also meant that Flagler would not oppose the bank charter application. His influence with Flagler derived from his support of federal appropriations for the deepening of Biscayne Bay, which created a harbor for the port of Miami. With the backing or neutral position of Flagler's Florida East Coast Railway Company, the most powerful organization in the state, the Anthonys could gain the upper hand over the Bank of Bay Biscayne.[24]

After Edward Romfh resigned from Bank of Bay Biscayne, the bank's president, William Brown, tried to block the First National Bank by filing a charter application with the comptroller of the currency for the Fort Dallas National Bank of Miami. Romfh, a small man with a malicious side to his character, wanted to retaliate against his former employer by having a receiver appointed for the Bank of Bay Biscayne. But the Anthonys considered Brown a friendly competitor, not an enemy to be destroyed, so they responded to Brown's maneuver with a subtle approach.[25]

Playing power politics and taking nothing for granted, the Anthonys moved to erode Brown's influence with the Florida East Coast Railway by tying their bank closer to Flagler. They sold part of the bank and offered a directorship to C. C. Chillingworth, a Miami lawyer who represented the railroad and was an adviser to Joseph R. Parrott, Flagler's general manager and confidant. Miami mayor James E. Lummus, a local merchant aligned with Flagler, also bought stock and was invited to join the board of directors. Now the First National Bank could compete for the deposits of the Florida East Coast Railway.[26]

Faced with two formidable groups applying for charters in the same town, Comptroller Ridgely took the safe route and approved both applications. By manipulating the political process and the sale of stock, the Anthonys controlled the First National Bank with their Pittsburgh connections, which included Graham's partner, M. K. Salsbury, president of the Midland Coal Company of Pittsburgh, who was also a director of the bank.[27]

The Anthonys were now doing business on a grand scale. They wanted to be associated with the nation's elite business leaders, and working with men like Graham and McAdoo assured them of reaching that goal. William McAdoo was interested in the success of the First National Bank because he had recently received a charter from Ridgley for the Equitable National Bank in New York City. McAdoo's bank, which was a depository for New York City, was interested in becoming a correspondent of Anthony's Miami bank.[28]

To garner deposits, the Anthonys attracted a prominent group of local directors. They named Edmund Munger Brelsford as president of the new bank. Brelsford, a pioneer of south Florida, migrated to Lake Worth in 1881. He opened a general store in 1884, and three years later President Grover Cleveland appointed him the postmaster of Palm Beach. Brelsford had previous banking experience as an organizing director of the Dade County State Bank at West Palm Beach. The Anthonys also invited William M. Burdine, founder of the department store chain, to become an organizing director of their bank.[29]

Besides increasing their prestige and borrowing capacity, a primary motivation of the Anthonys for forming the bank was to locate it on the "Anthony Block," which they hoped would include a department store, real estate office, newspaper, and other businesses. The bank significantly increased the value of their land in downtown Miami. The insider deal increased their net worth before opening day.[30]

After the First National Bank opened, the competition between Romfh and Brown for customers became fierce. Weary of Romfh's ruthless methods and eager to make a profit for Congressman Graham and his partners, the Anthonys decided to sell their bank stock to a group headed by Romfh in 1905. Holding majority control of the bank and the power in Washington, Anthony's group could name the price for its stock. J. R. Anthony gave Romfh an ultimatum. He had thirty days either to buy the Anthony group's stock at their price or to resign as cashier of the bank. Romfh saved his job by raising the money to buy the controlling shares.[31]

The animosity between Romfh and Brown lasted until the Panic of 1907. Rumors flew that the Fort Dallas National Bank was insolvent, and on July 5, 1907, a frantic run of depositors forced Brown's bank to close. The comptroller of the currency appointed a receiver for the bank that same day. Three days later, Brown was fired as president of the Bank of Bay Biscayne, which had survived the panic. Romfh later told the *Miami Daily News* that the First National Bank had weathered the run because he "had reason to believe that the Fort Dallas National Bank was unsound" so he prepared for the panic by asking other bankers in the state to bail out his bank. Working with the comptroller of the currency's office and ignoring the law, Romfh survived the Panic of 1907 by refusing to pay any depositor more than $25 a day until the runs stopped. The close call scared Romfh, but the doors of his bank stayed open and his nemesis had been destroyed.[32]

Romfh did not have to compete with another national bank for the next fourteen years. Between 1907 and 1921, the comptroller of the currency did not approve any bank charters for Miami. After United States senator Duncan U. Fletcher of Florida intervened with Comptroller Daniel R. Crissinger, the Anthonys received the next charter in 1921 for the Miami National Bank. Yet Romfh's main competition remained the state-chartered Bank of Bay Biscayne until 1930, when it failed after a bank run.[33]

THE FINANCIAL COLOSSUS

With control of his bank firmly established and his competition limited, Romfh decided to enter politics. He was elected to the Miami city commission in 1912 and served until 1917. He returned to city government on the "bankers ticket" of 1920 and was mayor of Miami during the boom period. The prestige and influence of being the mayor of the winter playground helped Romfh advance his banking business. If the comptroller of the currency wanted to go sport fishing, Romfh's yacht, the *Marinette,* was available. When Comptroller Joseph W. McIntosh and Vice-President Charles Dawes came to Miami in March 1927, McIntosh stayed at Romfh's house. During that trip, Romfh's *Marinette* was part of a "flotilla of yachts" that sailed with Vice-President Dawes and his entourage out of Miami. Comptroller McIntosh relied on Romfh for advice regarding the appointment of receivers and the approval of bank charters. Romfh's access to the comptroller's office was of concern to McIntosh's professional staff because the banker-mayor used his personal relationship with McIntosh to lobby against the approval of new national banks in the Miami area. At the height of the boom, in 1925, only two national banks were operating in the Miami area: the First National Bank of Miami and Romfh's Miami Beach First National Bank. In 1926, Romfh received his third national bank charter when McIntosh approved the Coral Gables First National Bank. McIntosh's relationship with Romfh continued after he resigned as comptroller. McIntosh became a member of the board of directors of Romfh's First National Bank of Miami.[34]

Community bankers' aversion to competition was adopted as the official policy of the Coolidge administration. In June 1926, Comptroller McIntosh and his predecessor, Henry Dawes, called for the nation's independent bankers to support the banking bill of Congressman L. T. McFadden, which prohibited nationwide branch banking. As a salute to the Democratic tradition of Andrew Jackson, the Republican administration opposed the Canadian system of interstate branch banking. McFadden's legislation enhanced the value of Romfh's banks and the Dawes family bank, the Central Trust Company of Chicago. This hostility to competition mandated into the American banking system increased the wealth and influence of independent bankers such as Romfh, Dawes, and Anthony.[35]

Romfh rose from a clerk to the "financial colossus" of Miami by using cutthroat tactics against his competitors and conservative lending practices with his customers. The First National Bank of Miami survived the Panic of 1907, the land boom, and the Great Depression to become the largest bank in Florida. Romfh's battles with his competitors seemed to be forgotten in 1935, when he told the Florida Bankers Association: "We pioneers in Southeast Florida faced hard times—sometimes accompanied by yellow fever and malaria. We suffered from floods, fruit flies, freezes and hurricanes, but . . . we lived through it all and plugged to make this part of Florida what it is today."[36]

THE PALM BEACH BANK AND TRUST COMPANY

After the profitable First National Bank deal, J. R. and A. P. Anthony realized they could make more money speculating in bank stock than running clothing stores. While south Florida was recovering from the Panic of 1907, they reentered the banking industry in a major way by forming the Bank of Palm Beach, a state bank in West Palm Beach.

The Anthonys applied the same political methods to secure the state bank charter that they had used in the application for a national bank charter. They recruited John T. Dismukes, president of the First National Bank of St. Augustine, who had been four times the president of the Florida Bankers Association, to join in the Palm Beach venture. Dismukes's father, Senator Elisha P. Dismukes of Quincy, was the author of the Florida Banking Code of 1889 and president of the Quincy State Bank, which was the first bank chartered under the new law. With John Dismukes as an organizer, the bank charter application was assured of approval. On September 4, 1909, Florida comptroller A. C. Croom issued the certificate of authority for the Bank of Palm Beach.[37]

A. P. Anthony was the initial president and J. R. Anthony the vice-president, and both sat on the board of directors. Their brother Roscoe became the assistant cashier. In 1916, when A. P. and J. R. Anthony moved to Jacksonville, they put E. M. Brelsford out front as the president. Brelsford's son-in-law, David Forrest Dunkle, a lawyer who became mayor of West Palm Beach, was a real estate promoter and major borrower of the bank. Dunkle was also president of the Palm Beach Guaranty Company, a high-flying finance company in which Anthony had once owned an interest. After the bank failed in 1926, he defaulted on his loans. In 1928, Dunkle was convicted of embezzlement and sentenced to five years in the state prison. Represented by Ezra Ballard Donnell, he appealed the verdict to the Florida Supreme Court, which reversed it in 1929. Federal prosecutors then indicted Dunkle and two bankers for conspiracy to defraud the government of $106,604 in income taxes. A Miami jury acquitted him after a complicated conspiracy trial, which was plagued by statute-of-limitations problems.[38]

In 1919 the bank received trust powers and changed its name to Palm Beach Bank and Trust Company. J. R. Anthony acquired complete control of the bank in 1922 and succeeded Brelsford as its president. The Anthony family built a "splendid" new structure named the Seward Building and leased it to the bank. The new building, called "the finest of any banking institution south of Jacksonville," increased the bank's quarters by more than seven times. The Palm Beach Bank and Trust Company leased from the

Anthonys enough space to accommodate the bank for "the next two or three generations." Property values in downtown West Palm Beach leaped when Anthony announced his plans for the new bank building. Yet like most insider deals, the transaction was of great benefit for the Anthonys but not for the bank.[39]

His wealth was increasing rapidly, and J. R. Anthony formed the Anthony Investment Company to shelter his valuable assets. He transferred some of his prime real estate into the entity. He also exchanged stock in his investment company for stock he owned in the Peoples Bank of Jacksonville, Peninsular Casualty Company of Jacksonville, Bankers Investment Company, and Anthony Brothers, Incorporated. He used the investment company to speculate in bank stock and to engage in insider deals with the Palm Beach Bank and Trust Company and other banks he controlled.[40]

In 1924, Anthony's decision to concentrate his energies in the banking industry seemed like a brilliant move. Anthony Brothers, Incorporated, the family clothing business, was insolvent because of aggressive expansion plans and the construction of an extravagant building in West Palm Beach. But the Palm Beach Bank and Trust Company appeared to be prosperous. J. R. Anthony now controlled nine of the thirteen Palm Beach County banks, and he was the most influential banker in Florida.[41]

THE WITHAM BANKING SYSTEM

Anthony's meteoric rise in the banking industry resulted from his partnership with Wesley D. Manley. By 1914, Anthony had political strength at both state and national levels. But he lacked the capital to expand his operations. He solved that problem by helping W. S. Witham of Atlanta maintain control of the Bank of Delray. Witham was impressed by Anthony and introduced him to Manley, who was the current head of the Witham chain banking system, which had sixteen member banks in Florida. They formed a partnership that combined Manley's financial resources with Anthony's political muscle.

Witham, who was raised in LaGrange, Georgia, during the Civil War, moved to New York City in 1867 as an ambitious teenager. After developing his business skills and some capital, in 1888 he returned to his native state and started building the banking system by forming new banks in small communities throughout Georgia.

With the Farmers and Traders Bank of Atlanta as the lead bank, he operated the system like a modern bank holding company but with local boards of directors.[42]

In 1900, Witham hired W. D. Manley of Augusta as his personal secretary. Witham then named Manley, who had no banking experience but was a loyal employee, as cashier of the Farmers and Traders Bank. Witham ran into legal trouble in 1903 when the Barnesville Savings Bank and the Bank of Warrenton failed. He overcame these problems, however, and continued to expand his banking chain.[43]

Witham introduced Manley to creative financing in 1905 when he organized the Bankers Financing Company of Atlanta, which purportedly had $100,000 of capital. He raised the capital stock by personally borrowing $100,000 from his Farmers and Traders Bank and the Maddox-Rucker Banking Company. He used the money to buy a thousand shares of the Bankers Financing Company. When the company opened for business and held its first board meeting, the directors approved the payment of $100,000 to Witham for his contracts to act as financial agent for sixty-one banks in Georgia. Witham, who then paid off his unsecured loans, owned a finance company that appeared to be well capitalized. But its capital was nothing more than "goodwill" that was later charged off the books.[44]

"Because his credit was gone," Witham named his wealthiest board member, Asa G. Candler, president of the Coca-Cola Company, as president of the Bankers Financing Company. Board meetings of the Bankers Financing Company were held at the corporate offices of the Coca-Cola Company in Atlanta. As a board member, Candler approved the $100,000 payment to Witham. He also served as a trustee of the Depositors Guarantee Fund, which Witham and Manley used to entice banks into their system, from November 26, 1903, to July 6, 1914. Candler was elected mayor of Atlanta in 1916, and by then he had resigned his positions with the Bankers Financing Company and most other entities. In an effort to raise capital from the public, in 1911 Witham and Manley organized the Bankers Trust Company, announcing that it would have a solid capital base of $400,000. The Bankers Trust Company then acquired the Bankers Financing Company by paying Witham $250 a share for his one thousand shares. Because the purchase price was paid with shares of the Bankers Trust Company, Witham ended up with 62.5 percent of the company. The public bought the remaining $150,000 of stock, which was the only cash raised. On paper the Bankers Trust Company had $400,000 of capital and appeared to be one of the strongest financial companies in the South.[45]

The Witham system now consisted of 108 banks, located primarily in Georgia. After the corporate reorganization, Witham spent most of his time and money in Miami speculating in real estate. In a highly leveraged transaction, Manley purchased a major block of stock in the Bankers Trust Company and became its president. During the next fifteen years the Bankers Trust Company, which operated as a central clearinghouse for member banks, expanded its services until it was the financial agent of nearly 200 banks in Georgia, Florida, New York, and New Jersey.[46]

Manley was also named president of the Farmers and Traders Bank. His close friend James R. Smith, a powerful real estate developer in Atlanta, became vice-president of the bank. They immediately began an ambitious expansion program. The Georgia part of the system culminated in the formation of the Georgia State Bank in 1922. Georgia superintendent of banks T. R. Bennett quickly approved the charter application for the bank, whose capitalization during the first year of operation was purportedly $500,000, five times the minimum capital requirement. The Georgia State Bank and the Bankers Trust Company had interlocking directors. Manley was president of both, and Lorne R. Adams, the secretary-treasurer of the Country Bankers Association, of Georgia, was vice-president of the financial institutions. The center of operations for the banking empire remained Atlanta, where Manley and his partners ran the Bankers Trust Company, Farmers and Traders Bank, and Georgia State Bank. At the time of the banking crash, state and federal regulators tried to calm depositors by stating that Manley's banks were small country banks that operated as independent units. But before its collapse in July 1926, the Georgia State Bank was one of the state's largest banks, with its branching network of twenty offices throughout the state.[47]

After his leveraged buyout of the Witham system, Manley was seen by the elite of Atlanta as a dynamic banker whose success illustrated the greatness of the free enterprise system. He had begun his banking career at the turn of the century as a $50-a-month apprentice. By the early 1920s his family lived like royalty in an Atlanta mansion surrounded by sixty-two acres. Unlike Addison

Mizner, Manley built his dream castle. In 1923, a reporter described her visit to his estate: "As I turned off Pace's Ferry Road and rolled slowly up the long driveway toward the Italian Villa, [I felt] the pleasant thrill always experienced when one's eyes see and recognize perfection."[48]

Manley's butler opened the door for dinner guests, while his driver waited to chauffeur the rich and powerful around town in his Cadillac limousine. When the Manleys and their four children went on shopping excursions to New York or Europe their maid accompanied them, and while in town they motored around in flashy cars. During the reckless months leading to the crash, Manley bought a new limousine, a 1926 Rolls-Royce, and a large Marmon sedan. He also bought his teenage daughter a Marmon sports car.[49]

Caught up in the fantasy, Valeria Rankin Manley was a compulsive spendthrift. In 1926, when her husband's banks were suffering a cash crisis, she went on a spending spree. Sharing a joint account with her husband and unconcerned about its balance, she wrote checks "whenever she wanted to." She especially enjoyed shopping at Atlanta's Chamberlin-Johnson-DuBose Company, which had been operating since 1866. Chamberlin's, with its impressive five-story building, was one of the most exclusive department stores in the South. During the first half of 1926, she purchased on credit at Chamberlin's 101 pairs of hose, 32 pairs of gloves, 23 dresses, 12 pairs of shoes, 10 handbags, 5 girdles, and a kimono. She also bought shirts, blouses, and costly jewelry, along with chairs, rugs, and other items to decorate her home. After Mrs. Manley defaulted on the charges, Chamberlin's filed suit and received a judgment against her. Apparently Mrs. Manley was not the only customer with a poor payment history. The Atlanta landmark was forced out of business in 1931.[50]

Mrs. Manley also borrowed heavily from friendly banks in her husband's banking empire. One of her last loans from a Florida bank seemed to reassure her. After closing the loan, one month before the crash, she made three more expensive shopping trips to Chamberlin's during the next week. Her purchases at the Chamberlin store from January to July 1926 represented 10 percent of the capital of Farmers and Traders Bank. Her obsessive spending habits, like her husband's wild speculations in Florida and the stock market, were symptomatic of the troubled banking system.[51]

THE MANLEY-ANTHONY PARTNERSHIP

In 1914, Manley's lack of political clout in Florida was causing problems with the state comptroller's office. Comptroller William V. Knott, who was planning to run for governor in 1916, was the impediment because his core political supporters, the bankers under his jurisdiction, were opposed to deposits flowing to Georgia. J. R. Anthony's connections in Tallahassee made him the ideal partner for Manley. Anthony met privately with Knott and received his blessings to form the Bankers Financing Company of Jacksonville, which was jointly owned by Anthony and the Bankers Trust Company of Atlanta. Anthony then moved to Jacksonville, the state's banking center, to become vice-president of the company—Manley was its president. Anthony also used his connections in Washington to advance the partnership. His former mentor, William McAdoo, was now the secretary of the treasury, in whose department the comptroller of the currency resided. For a dozen intoxicating years Manley and Anthony formed new banks, managed them for a period of time, then sold out to local people reaping huge profits.[52]

While building his empire in Florida, Anthony carefully preserved his relationships in Tallahassee. When former comptroller Knott struggled with his personal finances, Anthony helped him with loans. Knott's term as state comptroller ended in 1917, but he remained active in Democratic politics and became state treasurer in 1928. He lost the governor's race to Sidney J. Catts, the Prohibition party's anti-Catholic candidate, in 1916. After the campaign, Knott was named superintendent of the Florida State Hospital in Chattahoochee. In 1927, Governor Martin appointed Knott as state auditor and the next year named him as state treasurer and insurance commissioner.[53]

Throughout his long public career Knott recklessly speculated in real estate. Many of his deals went sour, and he tried to solve his financial problems by using his political influence. After leaving the comptroller's office, Knott converted his relationship with Anthony into generous loans from the Bankers Financing Company. As the state's banking commissioner, Knott, always the compliant regulator, had been instrumental in the success of the Manley-Anthony banking system. Now he expected Anthony to return the favor.[54]

As Florida's comptroller from 1912 to 1917, William V. Knott *(left)* helped J. R. Anthony *(right)* develop a statewide banking system and then received loans from his company. (Knott photo, Courtesy, Florida State Archives and Anthony photo from J. E. Dovell's *History of Banking in Florida*)

In 1921, after Knott had been in default on his loans for more than six months, Anthony's company agreed to accept a small payment and renew the loans for another ninety days. But Knott ignored the problem for a year. He then wrote a *"PERSONAL"* letter to F. O. Spain, an officer of the Bankers Financing Company, to call in a political chit: "I am not presuming on that fact but it is a fact nevertheless that my attitude has always been exceedingly friendly towards the Company that you are with and there was a time when such friendship was worth something to [Manley and Anthony]. I am not asking that they lose any money by me but this is not an ordinary situation and I trust that I will not be forced into an embarrassing situation by any precipitate action that would not be of any good to anyone but hurtful to me. I feel that you will appreciate my situation. A little delay at this time will not cause your people to suffer any loss."[55]

In a longer letter dated the same day, Knott emphasized to Spain that he hoped his request for a deferral of the loan payments would not be interpreted as "trying to take advantage of personal friendship." Anthony responded to Knott by return mail. He assured the influential Democrat, who was still the superintendent of the Florida State Hospital, that the Bankers Financing Company would not initiate legal action against him. Anthony's company continued to renew Knott's indebtedness, and the matter dragged on for years.[56]

The Anthony brothers were also the private bankers of Ernest Amos, Knott's successor as comptroller and banking commissioner. If Amos wanted to speculate in a land deal or was short of cash he had access to unsecured loans. In addition, when A. P. Anthony was chairman of the state bank section for the Florida Bankers Association, his committee lobbied the legislature to give the comptroller and his staff a substantial increase in salary.[57]

The Anthonys strived to meet the needs of Amos's staff. Assistant Comptroller Robert Anderson Gray, who later served in the state cabinet as secretary of state for more than thirty years, was not immune to influence peddling. In 1921, A. P. Anthony, president of the state-chartered Peoples Bank of Jacksonville, wrote to Gray inviting him to come to Jacksonville to discuss a business deal. The banker told his regulator that the proposal would be quite profitable for him. Anthony also offered to pay Gray's expenses if they did not reach an agreement.[58]

By acquiring troubled state banks, J. R. Anthony solved several sensitive problems for Comptroller Amos between 1917 and 1925. And in 1919, when the dual banking system came under attack by the Federal Reserve System, Anthony helped Amos organize a state bankers association. Amos reciprocated by granting Anthony dozens of bank charters, more than all other groups in Florida combined. The comptroller also appointed A. P. Anthony as the receiver of the United States Trust Company of Jacksonville. Amos remained a loyal friend and patron of the Anthonys long after the Manley-Anthony banking system crashed in 1926. That relationship proved invaluable to J. R. Anthony. It shielded him from criminal investigation because state attorneys were reluctant to prosecute a complicated banking case without the assistance of the comptroller.[59]

Anthony enhanced his position in Tallahassee through strong ties to the Democratic party of Florida and the Florida legislature. He was the partner of James B. Hodges of Lake City, a former legislator who was chairman of the state Democratic Executive Committee, in the State Exchange Bank of Lake City which failed in July 1926. During the chaotic period following the crash, Hodges remained a staunch defender of Amos, arguing against the publication of the comptroller's regulatory records. At the time Hodges was negotiating with Anthony to buy his stock in the State Exchange Bank as part of a reorganization plan. Amos then approved the plan, which did not require Hodges, Anthony, and the other stockholders to pay for the bank's capital deficiency. Hodges became president of the bank after its reopening in October 1926.[60]

In the legislature, the comptroller could rely on the steady hand of Anthony's partner, Jesse J. Parrish of Titusville, who was Speaker Pro Tempore during the boom year of 1925 and president of the Senate in 1929. Parrish was a director and stockholder of the Brevard County Bank and Trust Company of Cocoa, and J. R. Anthony was its president. The bank collapsed under the weight of insider loans in 1929. Senator Parrish defaulted on his unsecured loan at the Brevard County Bank. With full membership privileges, he also used his bank stock to arrange financing with the Bank of Little River, a Miami member of the Manley–Anthony system which failed in July 1926 because of insider abuse.[61]

The chain system grew by attracting member banks with its services. The Bankers Trust Company of Atlanta operated as a financial agent for member banks, which placed demand deposits at 6 percent interest and made loans to other member banks and their customers. It also provided fidelity insurance to members and supervised them with a staff of examiners, who regularly audited the banks and then reported the findings to their boards of directors.[62]

Its most attractive service was to provide members with private deposit insurance, two decades before federal deposit insurance. Deposit insurance was an effective advertising gimmick for the system's members. Banks that joined the "scientific" insurance fund would immediately begin an aggressive advertising campaign that stressed the "SAFETY" of the Depositors Guarantee Fund. The message was that the deposit insurance and the banking system were "strong enough to pay off every depositor." Truth in advertising was not a concern: "This Bank is connected with the Manley System which means that every dollar of your deposit is insured against loss from whatsoever cause. You can't lose when you are a depositor here."[63]

Anthony's career and the boom peaked at the same time. By 1925, the Bankers Financing Company of Jacksonville and Manley's Bankers Trust Company were the financial agents of sixty-one banks in Florida. Anthony and Manley exercised dictatorial power over their banking system. By controlling so many community banks, Anthony dominated the Florida Bankers Association (FBA), in which his influence enabled him to hand-pick the presidents. Anthony joined forces with Forrest Lake, a state representative and president of the Seminole County Bank, Dr. Louis A. Bize, president of the Citizens Bank of Tampa, and Dr. J. H. Therrell, president of the Commercial Bank of Ocala. Lake, Bize, and Therrell were promoter-bankers who were elected as president of the FBA with Anthony's help. Lake was convicted for bank fraud after his bank failed in 1927, and Bize's bank failed in 1929 because of massive insider abuse.[64]

In 1922, at the same convention that elected Bize, Anthony and his associates decided that Florida needed to prove its conservatism to the nation by passing a state constitutional amendment to prohibit income and inheritance taxes. Following the lead of Secretary of the Treasury Andrew Mellon, they believed that the anti-tax message would ignite an unparalleled economic boom. Florida's economy was healthy and it had experienced significant expansion, but it was not in a frenzy. They did not need to convince the governor of the soundness of the policy.[65]

The administration of Governor Cary Hardee, the "banker-governor," was a striking departure from Florida's constitution of 1838, which had banned bank officers and directors from holding public office. That constitution recognized the unique public role of bankers in American society. It read: "No president, director, cashier, or other officer, of any banking company in this state shall be eligible to the office of governor, senator or representative to the general assembly of this state, so long as he shall be such president, director, cashier, or other officer, nor until the lapse of twelve months, from the time, at which he shall have ceased to be such president, director, cashier, or other officer."[66]

Riding high, Anthony shared Governor Hardee's hopes of a banker-dominated government. In 1924 it was Anthony's turn to be elected president of the Florida Bankers Association. Forrest

Lake nominated the "popular Jacksonville financier," who was elected by acclamation. The next year Anthony presided over the FBA's convention in West Palm Beach, and in the president's annual address he revealed the involvement of the bankers in the passage of the landmark changes to Florida's constitution.[67]

Anthony spoke to "the best as well as the biggest" FBA convention in history, which was attended by more than four hundred conferees, about the "outstanding accomplishment" of the association in passing the state's income and estate tax amendments. He described how the FBA had "inaugurated" the effort in 1922, successfully lobbied the legislature to pass the proposals in 1923, and spearheaded the election campaign of 1924. Anthony acknowledged that the association had concealed its involvement in the movement:

> It had no appearance of, and we studiously avoided anything that would make it appear to be a "banker's movement." Every effort was made to keep the activities of the association in the background. But these activities were none the less real, earnest and effective. I think it can safely be said—and without boasting—that the general policy followed in the handling of this important matter was planned and directed by your association's officers and members. The resolution was the work of your association . . . the policy of an intensive publicity campaign commencing shortly after the primary election, and continuing up to the day of the voting, was again the policy of your association. . . . The result is known. The details of how it was accomplished and the men and organizations most active in it probably will not be made public. But it is with great pleasure that you are advised of your association's most active and prominent part in this matter which already is beginning to bring far-reaching results to the state of Florida. I think the lesson to be learned from the activity of the association in connection with this matter from its inception to its conclusion, is the great power and public influence of a body of men like this properly led and directed.[68]

Anthony's speech confirmed that the bankers had thrown caution to the wind. The provisions, which Anthony said "justified the existence of the association," remain in Florida's constitution: the prohibition of both a state income tax and a state inheritance tax. The "far-reaching results" of those provisions still have a somber effect on the Florida legislature when it attempts to balance the budget of the fourth largest state in the nation. Those well-advertised constitutional provisions fueled the speculative frenzy of the last eighteen months of the boom.[69]

The bankers had a hidden agenda in their desire to prohibit a state income tax. Because their banks were domestic corporations in Florida, the constitutional amendment prohibited a tax on their corporate profits. According to a resolution passed by the FBA at the 1925 convention, the adoption of the amendment made it "more advantageous to form corporations under the laws of Florida than under the laws of any other state." Though the corporate tax break was a well-kept secret, the bankers praised the wisdom of the people of Florida for their action "to invite capital into the state and to protect it after it is invested here." They declared: "The great glory of this state is not so much its unequalled soil, its wonderful resources, its great possibilities and its matchless climate, but its splendid conservatism."[70]

By prohibiting state personal income and corporate profits taxes, the FBA institutionalized "conservatism" in the tradition of Andrew Mellon, who was slashing federal taxes in the upper brackets while speculating with his excess income. Just a few years after the Russian Revolution of 1917, Anthony, like most of his colleagues, believed that maximizing profit by paying less taxes was the way to stop the spread of bolshevism. Anthony told the FBA: "The unprecedented prosperity of the state and the country is coupled with high wages and high costs everywhere. A readjustment in the near future is inevitable. . . . Unless this big subject is handled with the greatest care the growth of radicalism in this country will be much more rapid than in the past and in time constitute a serious menace."[71]

While Anthony was running the Florida Bankers Association, Manley was running the Georgia Country Bankers Association. Lofty speeches about protecting capitalism disguised their "invisible hands" that were recklessly speculating with depositors' money. Simple greed, not enlightened self-interest, was their driving force. Fearing a "re-adjustment," Anthony and Manley tried to pocket a lifetime of profit in a few years. Their high-stakes deals and Manley's lavish life-style sent warning signals to regulators. Yet these were ignored, as were the critical examiners' reports, by top officials. The appearance of wealth impressed the regulators and influenced them to do nothing.[72]

At the 1925 convention and despite Anthony's platitudes, the bankers who were part of his system were privately expressing "serious complaints and criticisms" about their reckless way of doing business. In particular, the financing of subsidiary companies was "causing considerable comment" among affiliated bankers. They recognized that the risks of being a member bank were enormous. But with the boom still going strong, the profits seemed to outweigh the risks.[73]

3

THE MIZNER
BANK

The fever at Boca Raton broke after the resignation of Senator du Pont. Without a fresh supply of buyers, the pyramid scheme was doomed to fail. Scrambling to maintain control of the Mizner Development Corporation, Addison Mizner participated in a bank fraud conspiracy that financed his extravaganza with depositors' money. His partners acquired control of the Palm Beach National Bank, an affiliate of the Manley-Anthony banking system, and operated it as a criminal enterprise. Mizner looted the bank by using worthless promissory notes to procure loans.[1]

Regulatory records of the Palm Beach National Bank reveal the inside story of the bank regulatory system. They provide an eyewitness account of political corruption reaching to the highest levels of the American government. Comptroller of the Currency Joseph McIntosh reported to Congress that the Palm Beach National Bank failed because of "unforeseen" economic conditions and not because of "incompetent management" or "dishonesty." But the secret records of the comptroller of the currency prove that the bank failed because of fraud and insider abuse.[2]

Howard P. Smith and D. Lester Williams, who were partners of Addison Mizner and J. R. Anthony, organized the Palm Beach National Bank. Smith was president of the bank, Williams the vice-president and chairman of the board. Comptroller of the Currency Henry M. Dawes approved the bank's charter in November 1924. Henry Dawes was the brother of Charles Dawes, formerly the comptroller of the currency under President William McKinley, who had been elected vice-president of the United States that same month.[3]

J. R. Anthony taught Smith and Williams the art of promoter banking. As Anthony's partners in the Palm Beach Bank and Trust Company, they learned how insiders could load a bank with their loans and then sell out to another promoter who had the same plans. In January 1925, Anthony sold a major block of stock in the Palm Beach Bank and Trust Company to Smith and Williams. Although he continued to own 13.33 percent of the bank's stock, his family left behind loans amounting to 45 percent of its capital. Following his lead, Smith and Williams formed the Palm Beach National Bank, borrowed directly 44 percent of its capital, and sold out to another promoter who did the same thing.[4]

During the organizational period, Smith and Williams sold stock to influential businessmen to capitalize the bank at $50,000. They also appointed several public officials to the board of directors. West Palm Beach mayor Henry Stephen Harvey, Palm Beach County tax assessor James M. Owens, Jr., and Judge R. P. Robbins bought stock and joined the board. E. B. Donnell, a lawyer and former circuit court judge who represented Addison Mizner and J. R. Anthony, also bought stock in the bank. Less than two years later, Donnell represented Smith and Williams when they were indicted for bank fraud.[5]

After the Palm Beach National Bank opened, Howard Smith used it to influence the regulation of his state bank, the Palm Beach Bank and Trust Company. Smith arranged for the national bank to make "policy loans" to the state's top regulators. At a time when a new Ford could be purchased for $290, the Palm Beach National Bank loaned $1,750 to Comptroller Ernest Amos. After both banks failed, Amos defaulted on his loan.[6]

During a routine examination in February 1926, Victor H.

Northcutt of the comptroller of the currency's office discovered that the Palm Beach National Bank had loaned $2,000 to E. M. Porter, the state's chief bank examiner, who was in charge of the Palm Beach Bank and Trust Company. Northcutt immediately called for the collection of the Porter loan, which was more than 50 percent of his yearly state salary. Criticizing the loan in his report, Northcutt wrote: "E. M. Porter, State Bank Examiner. No statement or security. Put in bank by Mr. Smith. *Need to collect.*" Northcutt failed to elaborate on the propriety of the loan, although he knew that Smith was vice-president of the Palm Beach Bank and Trust Company, which was under the direct supervision of Porter.[7]

When Northcutt returned to the Palm Beach National Bank on June 15, 1926, he found that Porter had defaulted on his "loan." Four days after the examiner left the bank and in an attempt to avoid criticism, Smith paid off Porter's loan. Nevertheless, Northcutt classified the loan, listing it in the "slow and doubtful paper" category of his confidential report: "$2,000, E. M. Porter, Tallahassee, Fla. State Bank Examiner. Paid 6/19/26 by H. P. Smith former President of the Bank."[8]

Smith made the loans after Comptroller Amos had placed the Palm Beach Bank and Trust Company on the state's troubled bank list. Smith's state bank had been criticized for "excessive" insider abuses and other "irregularities." Though the survival of the national bank depended on the affiliated state bank, federal regulators did nothing to stop the brazen influence peddling. A federal investigation could have resulted in bribery charges against Porter and Smith. Instead, Porter did not even lose his position.[9]

Public disclosure of bank examination reports also would have exposed impropriety at the affiliated Commercial Bank and Trust Company of West Palm Beach. In furtherance of the multibank scheme, the Manley-Anthony bank made an unsecured $500 loan to T. C. Hawkins. Hawkins was the state bank examiner responsible for the Commercial Bank and Trust Company.[10]

INSIDER ABUSE

With corruption permeating the secret regulatory system, Smith and Williams abused their fiduciary positions at the Palm Beach National Bank with reckless abandon. Before the ribbon-cutting ceremony, they leased the bank's quarters from William A. White, a real estate promoter and director of the Mizner Development Corporation. The sweetheart lease ran for twenty years and required the payment of a full year's rent in advance. After the bank opened, they purchased the building and began collecting the rent payments. Later they sold their bank stock and the building back to White, who continued to loot the bank until it collapsed.[11]

Smith and Williams initially owned 25 percent of the Palm Beach National Bank. But they and their partners borrowed at least 182 percent of the bank's capital. Smith and Williams also used about 200 percent of the national bank's capital to purchase loans from their Palm Beach Bank and Trust Company. Regulators knew exactly what was happening. The comptroller of the currency's office examined the bank four times in a one-year period, much more frequently than is done today. Yet federal officials merely watched the insider deals and reported the abuse to each other.[12]

Why did the federal regulatory system fail? The problem was not a lack of competent regulators. Northcutt, the examiner in charge, was a veteran auditor with thirteen years of experience, seven of those as a bank examiner. He had served as a state bank examiner in Alabama and as a national bank examiner in Texas and Florida. But he planned to become a banker and refused to endanger his career. Although he reported the chicanery to his superiors, he was unwilling to recommend strong enforcement action. His forbearance was rewarded in 1928 when he entered the revolving door between the comptroller of the currency's office and the banking industry. He accepted the position as vice-president of the First National Bank of Tampa, where he remained for fifty years, becoming its president and chairman. Northcutt was president of the Florida Bankers Association in 1944 and chairman of the congressional committee of the American Bankers Association.[13]

In June 1925, the conspicuous wealth of Palm Beach fascinated the thirty-three-year-old examiner. He described the opulence in his report: "Palm Beach . . . is one of the winter playgrounds of the Florida East Coast. Wealthy people from various sections of the country come here to spend winter months in palatial private homes and hotels." The growth in deposits of the Palm Beach National Bank impressed Northcutt, who measured its performance by the rapid increase in liabilities. He seemed unconcerned that its highest overhead item, the cost of funds, outstripped management's ability to attract good loans. Even without the insider abuse, management faced a serious challenge because the bank lacked sufficient business to offset interest expense on its deposits with interest income from its loans.[14]

Critical problems surfaced during the initial examination. Northcutt expressed concern about the quality of the bank's assets, which consisted primarily of real estate loans. Many of the boomtime developers were delinquent on their obligations. He alerted his supervisors to the shaky loan portfolio: "For a new bank just getting started there is entirely too much past due paper."[15]

The national bank was affiliated with the Palm Beach Bank and Trust Company through interlocking officers and directors. Three of the directors of the national bank sat on the board of the state bank. Northcutt reported that Smith and Williams were also vice-presidents of the affiliated state bank. Recognizing the conflict of interest, he warned that the national bank had purchased "excessive" loans from the state bank. In a suspicious move, those loans were "reduced within the lawful limit" only two days before Northcutt arrived at the Palm Beach National Bank. Yet he excused the violations of federal banking regulations as merely "ignorance of the law."[16]

Three months later, Northcutt returned to Palm Beach and learned that his previous criticisms had been ignored. No board meeting had been held in months so the outside directors had not seen the June examination report. Finding the books and records in disarray, he uncovered evidence of embezzlement. Despite the "irregular cash items," he declined to recommend a criminal investigation, but he cited the bank for failing to record an overdraft of Assistant Cashier C. C. Gilbert, Jr. The examiner could not even determine who controlled the bank because the "stock ledger and stock book [were] not properly kept." Alarmingly, the bank also failed to require financial statements from borrowers on "large unsecured lines" of credit.[17]

In spite of these unsafe and unsound banking practices, Northcutt reported that the bank was "getting along very nicely." Its high earnings misled him. The bank appeared healthy because its borrowers had made their interest payments during the summer of 1925. As the loans matured, they were renewed throughout the autumn and winter. When the real estate recession hit the state in the spring of 1926, the bank's lack of liquidity forced it to call in its mature loans. The illusion of profitability disappeared when borrowers defaulted on principal payments. Huge losses followed.[18]

In February 1926, when Northcutt examined the Palm Beach National Bank for the third time in eight months, he learned that Mizner's group had begun its raid on the bank. He also found that the bank was inundated with deposits, which had increased by 248 percent since September 1925. The phenomenal growth in deposits was not an isolated case. Bank deposits in Florida soared to spectacular levels during the winter of 1925–26. The first quarter call reports of state banks for 1926 showed that deposits totaled $440,708,004 as compared to $294,373,906 a year earlier. Deposits increased by more than $146.3 million or 50 percent in one year. If the banks had maintained adequate liquidity, they could have overcome the recession. Instead, nearly fifty state banks were on the verge of collapse because promoter-bankers had loaned millions of dollars to themselves.[19]

The flood of deposits at the Palm Beach National Bank occurred after the public became suspicious of Addison Mizner and other boom promoters. Local residents exercised restraint by depositing their money in the bank rather than speculating in real estate. But Mizner and his partners followed the money into the bank's vault. By February they had borrowed nearly twice the capital of the Palm Beach National Bank.[20]

Northcutt warned his supervisors of the danger. He criticized the Mizner loans "as representing unwarranted extensions of credit to the same or affiliated interests." His report focused on the Mizner loans: "Mizner Development Corporation are carrying on large development at Boca Raton. The loans to Addison Mizner, Antiqua Shops, Inc. and Mizner Industries, Inc. and secured by notes of parent company are claimed to represent bonafide purchases. Parent organization claimed to have large assets and to be in strong hands. Total accommodation viewed as concentration and *material curtailment urged.*"[21]

Northcutt chided Smith and Williams, who were undisclosed stockholders of the Mizner Development Corporation, for excess loans and violations of federal banking law. He advised his supervisors that the national bank was now dependent on their state bank for survival. Two more directors of the Palm Beach Bank and Trust Company had been added to the board of the Palm Beach

National Bank, increasing the interlocking directors to five. Smith, Williams, and Mizner could now borrow from either bank and sell those loans to the other without answering embarrassing questions from outside directors.

The examination exposed many other unsafe and unsound banking practices. The report portrayed a grossly mismanaged bank: "Inadequate credit data. . . . Past due paper . . . in need of constant close attention. . . . One illegal real estate loan. . . . Irregular cash items. . . . General detail of the bank in poor shape. Bank statements had not been reconciled for several months; both savings and individual ledgers were out of balance. . . . The Cashier and Assistant Cashier are apparently very indifferent and negligent." Nevertheless, Northcutt did not recommend an increase in the loan loss reserve, and he agreed to the distribution of dividends. He concluded that, because of its high profits, the bank had "enjoyed a very good year."[22]

Summarizing his findings, the examiner revealed the most alarming development. Smith and Williams were in the process of selling control of the bank to William White, the Mizner director, who would now be its president. Though he had no banking experience, White impressed Northcutt. White bragged that he had "made some very successful deals in real estate," which increased his net worth to more than a million dollars. Without investigating further, Northcutt reported that White was "a man of fine intellect and business qualifications." Yet the examination report disclosed that White had already borrowed 60 percent of the bank's capital and that his obligations to the bank were second only to those of Addison Mizner.[23]

The insider abuse described in the examination reports and the examiner's feeble conclusions are contradictory. Northcutt, a seasoned examiner who had worked for both state and federal banking departments, recognized the risk involved in recommending tough action against well-connected bankers. So he played it safe by recording the problems but stating the politically acceptable conclusions.

CHANGE OF CONTROL

After the examiner left town and his confidential report was filed away, Mizner's inner circle acquired more than 50 percent of the Palm Beach National Bank, making it an affiliate of the Mizner Development Corporation. In addition to White, the following collaborators joined the bank's board of directors: Congressman Graham, a legal adviser to Addison Mizner and director of Mizner Development Corporation; H. Halpine Smith, business manager of Mizner Industries; Ward A. Wickwire, an original stockholder and director of Mizner Development Corporation; and Willey Lyon Kingsley, a Mizner client and banker from Rome, New York, who became chairman of the bank's board. Majority control of the bank's stock was ensured when two influential newspaper executives participated in the bank deal. Donald H. Conkling, publisher of the *Palm Beach Post* and a major stockholder in the Mizner Development Corporation, bought bank stock along with Christopher J. Dunphy, assistant to the president of the *Washington Post,* who became a vice-president of the bank and then defaulted on his loans.[24]

Addison Mizner and his partners, controlling the board of directors, increased their loans to more than 200 percent of the bank's capital. According to Receiver John B. Cunningham, Mizner used "worthless" promissory notes of the Mizner Development Corporation as collateral for his loans. His interests, including Mizner Industries, Antiqua Shops, and Clay Products Company, were the largest borrowers with loans of $38,600, which represented 77 percent of the bank's capital.[25]

With the Palm Beach National Bank as an affiliate of the Mizner Development Corporation, Addison Mizner tried to bail out his failing development by manipulating his newly acquired colleagues in the banking fraternity. Using bogus collateral, Mizner procured large loans from friendly bankers, who in turn received loans from the Palm Beach National Bank. After its insolvency, the Mizner Development Corporation borrowed $57,982 from the Palm Beach Bank and Trust Company and $47,500 from the Commercial Bank and Trust Company; both were affiliates of the Palm Beach National Bank. He also arranged loans of $101,689 from the First American Bank and Trust Company of West Palm Beach, a member of the Manley-Anthony banking system, $99,636 from the Farmers Bank and Trust Company of West Palm Beach, and $99,500 from the Chelsea Exchange Bank. The Palm Beach Bank and Trust Company, First American Bank and Trust Company, and Chelsea Exchange Bank lost all the principal of their Mizner Development Corporation loans.[26]

Addison Mizner and his brother Wilson also procured large personal loans from the Palm Beach National Bank and its affiliated banks. Other Mizner insiders also took their share of the spoils. They included his nephew Horace B. Chase, who worked for Mizner Industries; Harry L. Reichenbach, his public relations agent; C. R. Crandall, auditor for Mizner Industries; and Anderson T. Herd, vice-president and general manager of Mizner Development Corporation.[27]

Operating the Palm Beach National Bank as a subsidiary, officials of the Mizner Development Corporation could make bank loans to lot buyers at the real estate office. On behalf of Mizner's company, Anderson Herd made a $6,000 unsecured, interest-free loan to former United States senator Joseph W. Bailey of Texas. After originating the loan, the Mizner Development Corporation sold it to the bank with Herd as the guarantor.[28]

After Senator Bailey defaulted on the loan, Herd hid from the receiver. Cunningham told Comptroller McIntosh: "Every endeavor to locate the address and present whereabouts of Anderson T. Herd has not been successful. He has a woman in Palm Beach call for his mail and she then re-addresses same to wherever he may be. No forwarding address or any information of any sort or character can be obtained from her. Great secrecy seems to be the order of procedure with her and she absolutely refuses to give any information directly or indirectly regarding Anderson T. Herd. There are many, many summons awaiting personal service on Herd."[29]

Mizner's director, William White, was president of the bank until it failed. Shortly after his appointment, Cunningham uncovered that White had obtained a fraudulent loan from the bank by having his secretary sign a $6,000 note. The deposit ticket and withdrawal records showed that White had received the money, and his secretary confessed that he "never received one penny" of the loan. With evidence of other fraudulent loans, Cunningham recommended to Comptroller McIntosh that the Justice Department immediately investigate the Palm Beach National Bank. In response, the comptroller's office filed a routine criminal referral with the attorney general, who in turn referred the matter to the U.S. attorney in Tampa.[30]

Appalled by the criminal activities at the bank, Cunningham also urged the swift prosecution of Assistant Cashier Gilbert, who was a relative of Howard Smith's. The receiver had gathered solid evidence showing that Gilbert had stolen a large amount of cash from customers. In July 1926, the comptroller of the currency's office filed a criminal referral regarding "willful irregularities in the accounts" of Gilbert. The transactions consisted "of frequent shortages in his tellers cash, added to extreme carelessness in his records, coupled with extravagant methods in which he lived." Before leaving town, he defaulted on his loans and was drinking heavily and engaging in fistfights.[31]

Receiving no response from the U.S. attorney's office, in August Cunningham renewed his efforts to prosecute White and Gilbert. He repeated to his superiors in Washington that Gilbert had "systematically embezzled the funds of the bank" and that he was a "fugitive from justice, every effort to locate him has been nil." He recommended that a "special request be made on the Department of Justice to locate and apprehend" Gilbert. Indicting him for embezzlement "would have a decided moral effect with the community and command respect and observance of the National Bank Act." In September, the frustrated receiver complained to John W. Pole, the chief of national bank examiners, that Comptroller McIntosh was not treating his repeated reports of bank fraud as a priority matter. Cunningham wrote Pole: "The general public in this community cannot understand why action has not been taken." He said that an accountant from the Justice Department could complete the investigation in "three or four days inasmuch I have all the facts and evidence available." In spite of Cunningham's efforts, no charges were filed against White or Gilbert.[32]

A close look at the major participants explains the reluctance of the Justice Department to investigate the Palm Beach National Bank. A public trial of White would have disclosed the relationship between the bank and the Mizner Development Corporation at a time when Vice-President Charles Dawes and his brothers controlled the company. It also would have exposed the involvement of Senator Bailey and Congressman Graham, who Northcutt described as a "Washington D.C. Judge."[33]

THE POLITICS OF BANKING

Because the Palm Beach National Bank was regulated by the federal government, the Mizner group had turned to their partner in Washington, Congressman George S. Graham, for assistance with Comptroller of the Currency Joseph McIntosh. Graham remained on the board of the Mizner Development Corporation after his client, Senator du Pont, resigned. His influence with federal bank regulators was crucial to the survival of Mizner's company. Graham asserted his clout and gained concessions from the regulators for the Palm Beach National Bank. The powerful congressman then bought stock in the bank and joined its board of directors.[34]

Representative Graham was a power broker in Washington for two decades. He served in the U.S. House of Representatives from 1913 to 1931, becoming dean of the House and chairman of the Judiciary Committee, with jurisdiction over the Department of Justice. Despite a forceful personality, he was known for his "quiet but effective work." Operating out of the limelight for most of his political career, he developed two lucrative law firms. The millionaire lawyer simultaneously headed the firms of Graham and Gilfillan in Philadelphia and Graham, McMahon, Buell and Knox in New York City. Besides the du Pont family interests, Graham and his law firms represented many large corporations. In addition to the Mizner Development Corporation, he sat on the boards of numerous public companies.[35]

In January 1926, William White asked his colleague in Congress to intervene with the regulators so that the Palm Beach National Bank could sell more stock to the public. Graham immediately put pressure on Comptroller McIntosh for a quick approval. He considered it a special favor for McIntosh to help his friend. McIntosh, a political appointee linked to Vice-President Dawes, responded promptly to the request from the chairman of the House Judiciary Committee.[36]

Comptroller McIntosh and his staff expedited White's request so thoroughly that they approved the application three weeks before it was filed. The comptroller of the currency's office received the application on April 1, 1926, but its approval was dated March 11, 1926. The confidential memorandum approving the new stock issue stated that the bank was in excellent condition and that it had no "doubtful" or "undesirable" loans. The comptroller's office estimated that the bank would suffer no losses on its loan portfolio. In fact, insider loans had already rendered the bank insolvent.[37]

Congressman Graham personally benefited by gaining regulatory approval for the bank to sell its worthless stock to the public.

Soon after pulling the strings, he took a seat on the board of directors of the Palm Beach National Bank, which had become part of the life support system for the Mizner Development Corporation. Graham was now a stockholder and director of both the bank and the land development company.[38]

Congressman Graham was not the only powerful politician to receive special treatment from McIntosh. Senator Joe Bailey used his connections to take advantage of the Palm Beach National Bank. Bailey, who was known as the "Lion of Texas," served in the U.S. House of Representatives for a decade and in the U.S. Senate for a dozen years. In 1897, he was elected as the Democratic nominee for Speaker of the House. He was a rugged man, whose bombastic personality was legendary. His toughness and unorthodox style commanded respect in a city that gave power to those who demanded it.[39]

After his resignation from the Senate in 1913, Bailey became a lawyer-lobbyist in Washington. He later opened a law practice in Dallas with his son Joseph, Jr., who served one term in the U.S. House of Representatives. The Bailey law firm was so confident of its position in the financial community that it listed as its references "any bank or trust company in Dallas."[40]

Speculative land deals had always enticed Senator Bailey. His efforts to accumulate a fortune, however, often conflicted with his public position. His reputation suffered from the wheeling and dealing, and a scandal eventually forced him to quit the Senate. He was caught accepting an unsecured, interest-free "loan" from an oil company executive. After leaving the Senate, Bailey continued to demand and to receive the privileges of high office.[41]

Northcutt criticized Bailey's interest-free loan at the Palm Beach National Bank and urged immediate repayment. The examiner's efforts resulted in a $5,000 reduction, but Bailey flatly refused to pay the remaining $1,000. McIntosh resisted collection efforts that would have embarrassed the legendary senator so the controversy dragged on for several years.[42]

Congressman Graham's intervention with the regulators and Senator Bailey's loan were typical of the pattern of influence and abuse that existed during the 1920s and 1980s. In times of intense speculation, the system finally reaches a breaking point when the public perceives that it is threatened by the greed of its leaders. That point was reached in the summer of 1926.

PANIC STRIKES

By the time of the gala opening of Addison Mizner's Cloister Inn on February 6, 1926, the public had become wary of his charade. Nevertheless, he entertained five hundred socialites with an extraordinary gastronomic experience, properly presented on New York's finest china. Uninvited depositors had no way of knowing that they were paying for the dinner. Neither did the manufacturer of the china, who had rushed 906 dozen plates, teacups, and other items to Boca Raton.[43]

Less than a week after the dinner party, Northcutt examined the Palm Beach National Bank, which was already hopelessly insolvent. He immediately reported its unsound condition and the Mizner loans to McIntosh. But instead of McIntosh seizing the bank, the Federal Reserve Bank of Atlanta loaned it $43,550. The federal government was now subsidizing Mizner's extravagance. The federal bailout and regulatory secrecy kept the bank open until June 29, 1926. Meanwhile, the insider abuse and outright fraud continued.[44]

Federal regulators had front-row seats to the Mizner fiasco and other bizarre land deals at the Palm Beach National Bank. Northcutt repeatedly warned that the survival of the bank depended on the solvency of the Mizner Development Corporation. Although McIntosh had full knowledge of the bank's precarious condition and its entanglement with Mizner, he failed to take enforcement action. Northcutt and his superiors also knew that the Palm Beach National Bank was affiliated with the state-chartered Palm Beach Bank and Trust Company through common ownership and interlocking directors. Since the first examination, Northcutt had been alerting his superiors of the reckless interbank deals and the dependency of the national bank on the state bank. The national bank had used 200 percent of its capital to buy bad loans from the state bank. In four consecutive examinations, Northcutt reported its rapidly deteriorating condition to federal bureaucrats, who shuffled the reports, held meetings, and worried about newspaper leaks. Regulators in Palm Beach, Atlanta, and Washington took no action until angry depositors forced the bank to close.[45]

Regulators kept a tight lid on the impending disaster, so depositors unknowingly continued to fund Mizner's project. Regulatory secrecy and favorable publicity deceived depositors. Mizner made

Addison Mizner *(left)* and Wilson Mizner *(right)* at the gala opening of the
Cloister Inn *(below)* on February 6, 1926.
(Courtesy, Historical Society Palm Beach County)

big news in March by announcing that Otto H. Kahn had invested "a considerable sum totaling six figures" in the Mizner Development Corporation. Kahn, the head of Kuhn, Loeb and Company and one of the most respected bankers in the world, also bought property at Boca Raton. Kahn said the investment demonstrated his "faith in the state." He was confident that "the Mizner imagination and genius will eventuate into as splendid an accomplishment as our continent knows."[46]

When a lawsuit was filed accusing Mizner of fraud, the pyramid scheme ended. On June 21, Guy C. Reed, a New York stockholder of Mizner Development Corporation, charged in open court that the company was insolvent and had engaged in fraudulent advertising. Reed demanded that a federal court appoint a receiver for the company. The case was dismissed, but news of the controversy started a quiet run among wealthy depositors of the Commercial Bank and Trust Company of West Palm Beach, whose president, Thomas Cook, was one of Mizner's banker partners. By the end of the week, the bank was closed permanently.[47]

Early Monday morning, June 28, a state bank examiner posted a curt notice on the front door of the Commercial Bank and Trust Company announcing that it would not be opening for business. Word of the closing triggered "fierce" runs at affiliated banks. "Coffee cooled in china cups" as depositors rushed to their banks. By noon, a "tornado" of humanity swirling around the Palm Beach Bank and Trust Company forced its tellers to lock their cages. By nightfall, a motorcade of guards—armed with rifles—escorted a cash-laden armored car through the crowded downtown. The show of strength was supposed to calm the "hysterical" depositors. One "formerly friendly banker" reportedly told a depositor who made a withdrawal "to go to hell and never set foot inside the bank again." Despite insults and cajolery, depositors continued to demand the return of their money. The Palm Beach National Bank closed the next day, and panic spread through the Manley-Anthony banking chain in south Florida.[48]

Two weeks later a lawsuit accused W. D. Manley of operating a massive bank fraud conspiracy. Depositors stampeded in Georgia, and the suit had a sensational impact in both states. In a matter of days eighty-three Georgia state banks, 20 percent of the state banking system, failed. The disastrous news from Georgia caused a second wave of bank failures in Florida. Regulators had attempted to prevent the panic by concealing the magnitude of the problem. Instead of curbing the crisis, official deception caused the banking debacle to grow beyond control. The collapse of the chain banking system shattered Georgia's economy and drove Florida's recession into a depression. Thousands of depositors, who had believed officials, lost most of their life savings. By the end of 1926, 150 banks had locked their doors in the two states. More than $30 million was missing.[49]

PART II

Regulatory Complicity

Panic in Florida. Depositors run to claim their
savings after banks in West Palm Beach lock
their doors.
(Courtesy, Historical Society
Palm Beach County)

4

OFFICIAL
DECEIT

The lawsuit against W. D. Manley accused him of defrauding member banks of the chain system. It also charged that the Bankers Trust Company of Atlanta was insolvent. After an Atlanta judge appointed a receiver for Manley's company, panic swept through Georgia and Florida, forcing 117 banks to close in ten days.[1]

The dramatic first week of the crash concluded with the suicide of Manley's partner, James R. Smith. On the night of July 16, 1926, Smith, aged fifty-eight, desperately reviewed his financial affairs for the last time. Sitting alone behind the locked door of his bedroom, the respected civic leader ended his life with one final pull on the trigger of his shotgun. Frantically forcing the door open with a hatchet, the butler and Smith's daughter found him lying on the bed next to his desk, where he had been studying canceled checks drawn on a closed bank.[2]

The suicide shocked Atlanta. Smith was a pillar of the establishment, having climbed from an office boy to a wealthy banker. Raised on a small rural farm, he enjoyed saying that the only education he received was at "the handles of the plow." As president of the Atlanta Real Estate Board, he was a developer with considerable political pull. He had been the campaign manager for Joseph M. Brown, son of Civil War governor Joseph E. Brown, who was elected governor in 1908 and 1912. He had also managed the congressional campaigns of Hoke Smith, a two-term governor who represented Georgia in the U.S. Senate from 1911 to 1921, and William S. Howard, who was elected to represent Atlanta in the U.S. House of Representatives in 1910. And Smith had been a key supporter of Asa G. Candler, who had been his partner at the Bankers Financing Company, in his successful race for mayor of Atlanta in 1916.[3]

Smith and Manley made their fortunes together in banking and real estate. They controlled the chain banking system in Georgia through ownership of the Bankers Trust Company of Atlanta. They also owned J. R. Smith and Company and jointly developed Morningside Park, an exclusive Atlanta subdivision. Manley was the beneficiary of a $5,000 life insurance policy on Smith's life.[4]

Smith's "desperate act" baffled the *Atlanta Constitution.* He was facing "unfortunate financial entanglements," but he had the love of his family, "the trust of friends, and the strong arm of public confidence always about him." Bank regulators in Georgia guarded his secrets by destroying their confidential records. The dark side of his character was buried in Florida's confidential banking records for sixty-three years.[5]

The Florida records reveal that Smith and Manley had looted banks throughout the state. Their insider loans, backed by worthless paper, led to the collapse of their chain banking system. On Smith's last day, sixteen more banks in their empire crashed. A few hours before his suicide, the Fulton County grand jury had begun a criminal investigation into their financial manipulations.[6]

The mystery surrounding the suicide enveloped the Florida and Georgia bank failures. Even after the Mizner and Manley lawsuits disclosed the fraud, regulators continued to deceive the public. As panic spread, state regulators blamed the public for the debacle. Florida comptroller Amos warned depositors about loose talk, declaring that "the public [has] no need to become panicky for the trouble . . . has spent itself and the sky is already clearing." T. R. Bennett, Georgia superintendent of banks, proclaimed: "The trouble . . . is not with the banks, it is with the people . . . agitators and hysterical people are doing incalculable harm."[7]

The creed of state regulators that required them to protect the banking industry instead of the public raised the question, Why not abolish the provincial state banking systems? The nation's extensive system of state banks is the legacy of Andrew Jackson and his war against the Second Bank of the United States. Since the Civil War, America has had a duplicative banking system with state and national banks. But a review of federal banking records shattered the argument for a single system of national banks. Federal officials deceived the public in the same deliberate manner as state regulators.[8]

FEDERAL DECEPTION

Politics and money corrupted the federal system as well as the state systems. Smith rose in financial circles by his fund-raising skills so he and Manley had friends in high places at the state and federal levels of government. One of those friends, M. B. Wellborn, was governor of the Federal Reserve Bank of Atlanta.[9]

By 1922, Wellborn knew that Manley's banking system was engaging in unsafe and unsound practices and had suffered heavy losses from bad loans. Yet when the professional staff of the Georgia Department of Banking became alarmed, Wellborn intervened to defend Manley and J. R. Anthony. As the federal government's top banker in Atlanta, he told state regulators that Manley and Anthony were "splendid business men" and their banking system was "most excellently managed." He said Manley had done Georgia a great service during difficult economic times because his "splendid" Florida banks had provided liquidity for their Georgia counterparts. Wellborn acknowledged that he was "well acquainted" with Manley: "I have always found him sound and reliable in his views, and I have a high regard for him as a business man."[10]

In spring 1926, Wellborn, who was still head of the Federal Reserve Bank of Atlanta, was aware of the precarious condition of the Manley-Anthony banking system and its affiliates. The affiliated Palm Beach National Bank was insolvent and on the brink of failure. Nevertheless, the Federal Reserve Bank of Atlanta attempted to bail out the bank with a loan that represented 87 percent of its capital. The irresponsible loan was consistent with Wellborn's protective attitude toward the Manley-Anthony system.[11]

When the panic struck, Wellborn tried to stop the bank runs by praising Georgia's economy. He announced that the bank failures would have "no material effect on the general prosperity of the state." Thus if the public left money in the banks, everything would return to normal. He also praised Florida and its banks: "Many banks in Florida are in a more liquid and stronger position than many banks in our financial centers and big cities. The progress of Florida will not be retarded at all by the collapse of the real estate boom."[12]

After the Bankers Trust Company failed, Comptroller McIntosh and Daniel R. Crissinger, chairman of the Federal Reserve Board, rushed to defend the bankers in the federal system. Crissinger, one of Warren Harding's cronies who Herbert Hoover later said was "utterly devoid of . . . banking sense," told the public that national banks were in "good shape." McIntosh and Crissinger said that "sound conditions soon would be restored." They concealed the failure of the Palm Beach National Bank by declaring that "there was no trouble involving national banks or member banks of the Reserve system in either Florida or Georgia."[13]

Comptroller McIntosh had detailed knowledge of the bank fraud at the Palm Beach National Bank. Receiver John Cunningham had repeatedly urged him to have the bankers prosecuted for embezzlement and criminal fraud. McIntosh said he read the receiver's letters "with great interest," but he refused to prod the Justice Department into action. The comptroller's official explanation to Congress was that the bank failed because of a "local financial depression from unforeseen agricultural or industrial disaster." Privately, he told his staff that he appointed a receiver for the bank because excessive insider loans and other "foolishness" proved "bad management."[14]

While McIntosh misled Congress, Cunningham told depositors that all "information relative to the affairs of the bank" was strictly confidential. He also advised the receiver of the affiliated Palm Beach Bank and Trust Company to refuse similar requests from depositors of that bank. The examination and liquidation reports of the Palm Beach National Bank, which disclosed the insider abuse and fraud, were sealed for fifty years.[15]

McIntosh and the comptroller of the currency's office had known for years that Manley's chain banking operation was a dangerous threat to the nation's banking system. As early as 1923, federal examiners issued warnings that member banks had carried bad loans on their books for years "without any reduction." To negate the examiners and stop their "raids" on affiliates, Manley's partner, John D. Russell, went to Washington to convince the top echelon of the comptroller's office that examiners in the field were "misleading" their superiors. The professional staff of the comptroller's office had been "very critical" of excessive loans made to companies owned by Manley, Smith, Anthony, and their partners. Examiners "severely criticized" Manley's reckless banking practices and called his accounting procedures a "joke." They denounced the practice at affiliated national banks in New York and New Jersey of placing unsecured deposits with the Bankers Trust Company of Atlanta. Reporting on his meeting in Washington, Russell told Manley: "The Federal Reserve Bank in New York are our enemies and are at the bottom of this whole thing. I gathered during my interview that they tried to call all of our business last January, but the [comptroller of the currency's office] would not let them but stood by us very strongly, in fact, Mr. McIntosh said this."[16]

Russell considered his meeting a success because he "had a good chance to tell them that their examiners had been knocking us constantly and criticizing every action of our banks." His "explanation seemed to satisfy Mr. McIntosh very thoroughly." He bragged that he "shut [John W. Pole] up very effectively on the use of such words as disastrous and catastrophe." Pole was the chief of national bank examiners, who, according to Russell, backed off "his objections in the presence of his superiors." The comptroller's office was now "friendly towards" them and Russell had "every assurance of this fact." He concluded his report by saying: "We will soon have the [comptroller's office] entirely in line again." Tragically, his prediction came true, and the comptroller of the currency's office did nothing to prevent the calamity or even to limit the losses.[17]

NATIONAL BANKS IN PALM BEACH COUNTY

After the crash, depositors took federal banking authorities at their word and hurried to deposit their money in the national banks of Palm Beach County. When depositors lost confidence in state banks, one beneficiary was the newly chartered National Bank of West Palm Beach, which was not affiliated with the Manley-Anthony chain system. Its advertisements boasted that it was the only bank in the city "under U.S. Government Supervision." The bank's grand opening was on May 14, 1926, and its deposits increased by more than 400 percent during the month of June. During the crisis month of July its deposits increased by 72 percent. The upward trend continued as depositors searched for a safe harbor during the autumn of 1926. Between July and November deposits increased another 152 percent.[18]

Senior staff members of the comptroller of the currency's office were impressed with the growth in deposits. Deputy Comptroller E. W. Stearns complimented the bank for "doing so well." On August 5, officers of the bank told local newspapers that the rapid growth of deposits indicated that the economy of West Palm Beach was "normal for this season of the year and compared favorably with conditions in other sections of the state." They said the bank's success in garnering deposits demonstrated that management had gained the respect of the community. What it really showed was the public's lack of confidence in state banks and the advantage of being "the only national bank and the only member of the Federal Reserve System in West Palm Beach."[19]

A few miles south, the First National Bank of Lake Worth also enjoyed the confidence of its depositors throughout the summer and autumn of 1926. The independent bank opened in 1920 and was dominated by its cashier, A. D. Clark, who was also the mayor of Lake Worth. His forceful personality, according to Examiner Northcutt, made it a "one man bank." Northcutt regarded the board of directors as a "bunch of figureheads."[20]

Mayor Clark projected the image of a "highly religious man," who was conservative in his actions. He was noted for leading "a crusade to clean up the town of every sort of evil." Despite his reputation, Northcutt had good reason to be "dubious as to his honesty." In 1923, the examiner had informed the comptroller of the currency that Clark, J. W. Means, president of the bank, and John L. Bosley, clerk of the city of Lake Worth, had been arrested for embezzling $2,000 from the city. The comptroller's senior staff asked, "Are these people running a bank or a political machine?"[21]

Clark overcame his legal problems and continued to intertwine his public position as mayor with his private position as bank cashier. By the summer of 1925, the city of Lake Worth had deposited $412,038 in the First National Bank of Lake Worth. Palm Beach County and the South Lake Worth Inlet District had deposited another $46,593 in the bank. Clark's bank also held public deposits of the state treasurer and the city of Saferno of $9,000 and $5,458, respectively. It had public deposits of $473,089, more than 30 percent of its total deposits.[22]

Mayor Clark used the bank and the city of Lake Worth to promote his third career as a real estate promoter. He borrowed heavily from the bank as an individual and as a partner in the El Nuevo Hotel Company, which was trying to develop Lake Worth's first premier hotel. By June 1925, Clark's interests had borrowed $47,323 or 47 percent of the bank's capital.[23]

The consequences of Clark's "political machine" were realized when the bank was forced to close after a second wave of turbulent bank runs struck Palm Beach County in March 1927. The *New York Times,* in a front-page article, described efforts to halt the near riot of depositors. An armored car with $2 million in cash raced from Miami as great crowds of "frantic" depositors gathered in the streets. Despite efforts to restore public confidence, worthless insider loans at the First National Bank of Lake Worth prevented it from reopening. Individual depositors finally discovered the extent of their losses when the receivership ended six and a half years later. More than half of their savings had been squandered by Clark and his partners.[24]

Insider abuse and "laxity" by the directors created an environment that condoned "malicious and willful violations of the National Bank Act." Receiver Cunningham reported to McIntosh that Walter S. Porter, an officer of the bank, "broke down and confessed to several acts of embezzlement" and fraud. Porter was arrested and released after posting a $5,000 bond. But he "jumped" bail, changed his name, and fled to Seattle. He was apprehended after traveling back across the country to New Orleans. Porter then pled guilty to embezzlement charges and was sentenced to one year in the Atlanta federal penitentiary.[25]

A stock manipulation scheme was uncovered by the receiver early in the liquidation process. Cunningham found that the stock ledgers of the bank had been falsified. One of the directors sold his stock, which had been financed by the bank, back to the First National Bank at a profit. Board members then purchased the same shares from the bank at two-thirds the price paid to the director, creating a loss for the bank.[26]

McIntosh and his senior staff had full knowledge of the insider abuse, embezzlement, and fraud at the bank. But they were more concerned about the publicity surrounding Porter's arrest than about telling the truth to Congress. Advancing his legacy of deception, McIntosh officially reported that the bank failed because of a "local financial depression from unforeseen agricultural or industrial disaster."[27]

When the First National Bank of Lake Worth dissolved, deposits at the National Bank of West Palm Beach increased by 145 percent. Regulatory secrecy concealed the wheeling and dealing at the West Palm Beach bank and fostered its growth. Beginning with its first examination, the comptroller of the currency's office knew that this was a promoter bank on a fast track.[28]

Two high-flying real estate promoters controlled the bank. Its president was Fred A. Franck, and his partner, G. W. Bingham, was vice-president. The bank's other vice-president was regarded by regulators as "nothing more than a dummy." Franck and Bingham also controlled a state bank, the Northwood Bank and Trust Company, where they switched positions with Bingham as president and Franck as vice-president. The problem was that neither one of them was a "real banker." They were interested only in funneling funds from both banks into the Pinewood Development Company and other companies they owned.[29]

Comptroller McIntosh had intimate knowledge of the insider abuse at the National Bank of West Palm Beach. In April 1927, after the affiliated Northwood Bank and Trust Company failed, McIntosh told the board of directors that he was "astounded" when he personally reviewed the examiner's report. He declared that the bank's "door seems to be wide open to excess loans, illegal real estate and overdrafts." He admonished the directors for using the institution as their own private bank and borrowing "money at will regardless of its condition." McIntosh was upset because he had personally met with Franck and Bingham in West Palm Beach, and they had promised to "clean up" the bank. He warned that irresponsible behavior would not be tolerated and threatened to revoke the bank's charter if the unlawful conduct continued.[30]

Franck and Bingham ignored the idle threat and resumed their pillage of the bank. Instead of taking decisive regulatory action, McIntosh passively watched the looting. He refused to act even after he was informed that Bingham, the "dominating officer" of the National Bank of West Palm Beach, was involved in a conspiracy to defraud the state-chartered Central Farmers Trust Company of West Palm Beach. In a "strictly confidential" letter, Cunningham, the receiver of the First National Bank of Lake Worth, recommended that McIntosh take immediate action against Bingham to "save the reputation of the National Bank and the Federal Reserve System."[31]

Bingham admitted that he had submitted a "fraudulent financial statement" to the Central Farmers Trust Company as an inducement for a $50,000 loan. In the loan transaction, Bingham was acting in his capacity as vice-president of the Pinewood Development Company. The financial statement omitted a $150,000 loan that his company owed to the First American Bank and Trust Company of West Palm Beach.[32]

Bingham's loans of $19,602 at the defunct First National Bank of Lake Worth complicated matters and made the situation acute. He had defaulted on the loans, and Cunningham was afraid that a lawsuit against the vice-president of the National Bank of West Palm Beach would cause a run on that bank. Although the financial manipulations were well known to McIntosh, he failed to take action against Bingham or his bank.[33]

McIntosh and his staff knew that Franck and Bingham had committed "illegal acts," which had a devastating impact on the National Bank of West Palm Beach. Yet "fearing the disastrous effects, which would occur, if called upon to publish statement showing capital impaired," the comptroller's office "agreed" with Franck and Bingham to the issuance of a fraudulent call report. After the deception failed and the bank collapsed, Franck told the press that the bank had "closed voluntarily and is in a solvent condition." McIntosh continued to mislead the public by refusing to disclose that the bank failed because of dishonesty.[34]

Federal prosecutors waited until 1930 to indict Franck and Bingham for conspiracy to defraud the Internal Revenue Service of $106,604 in taxes. Prosecutors accused them of wrecking the Pinewood Development Company between 1926 and 1928 in anticipation of filing for bankruptcy. Allegedly evading federal income taxes, Franck and Bingham diverted the assets of the real estate company for their own purposes, including the bailout of their state bank. They won an acquittal after a lengthy trial, which was complicated by a three-year statute of limitations and a stale prosecution.[35]

T. R. Bennett, Georgia's superintendent of banks, also shielded depositors in his state from the truth. While the panic spread, he maintained that the banks under his jurisdiction were in "cleaner and sounder condition than at any time since 1920." Bennett announced: "The atmosphere is clearing . . . there is nothing wrong with Georgia or her financial institutions. The present flurry is due entirely to causes outside the state and does not indicate any weakness on the part of Georgia banks." He blamed the failures on a "wave of hysteria" and condemned those who were spreading "wild rumors."[36]

Throughout his tenure, Bennett allowed Manley's banks to manipulate their books by carrying loans at "fictitious values." Commodity prices fell during the postwar deflation period, and the Georgia economy slid into a recession. After funding Manley's reckless ventures during the wartime boom, his banks faced financial ruin. Manley and Lorne R. Adams, vice-president of the Bankers Trust Company, had purchased control of the Parker Motor Company in 1918. Selling the Marmon, Chandler, and Cleveland cars, they rapidly expanded into the largest automobile dealership in Atlanta with branches in Jacksonville, Macon, and Birmingham. By 1920 their company was hopelessly insolvent. The grand headquarters for the business, the Parker Building, was encumbered by mortgages of $831,600. The company also had a $100,000 line of credit at both the Citizens and Southern Bank and the Fourth National Bank of Atlanta. And it owed $50,000 to the Fourth National Bank of Macon. As the recession deepened, the dealership was caught with an inventory of $350,000 to $400,000 of cars parked in fancy showrooms and on lots in three states.[37]

To avoid personal bankruptcy, which would have triggered a run on his banking chain, Manley formed the Amortization Corporation to acquire the Parker Motor Company and assume its liabilities. The Bankers Trust Company used the deposits of member banks to fund loans for the Amortization Corporation, which replaced the loans of the Parker Motor Company. Pyramiding the debt, Manley later formed the United Realty Corporation to assume the obligations of the Amortization Corporation. The Bankers Trust Company then sold participating loan certificates of the United Realty Company to member banks in Florida and Georgia. By allowing Manley to play this shell game, Bennett delayed his bankruptcy for more than five years and enabled him to expand his banking system.[38]

When his examiners reported the worthless loans, Bennett allowed Manley's banks to continue operating by counting as assets unpaid assessments of their stockholders. These promissory notes from the stockholders clearly violated the state banking code, which required that assessments be paid in cash. Like the Federal Home Loan Bank Board's policy of capital notes during the 1980s, Bennett invented stockholder notes to bolster the capital of Manley's banks in published call reports. Bennett condoned this fraud on the public by saying that "if every jot and tittle of the law had been enforced, more than four hundred banks in this state would have failed in 1920 and 1921." His forbearance may have been approved by the Georgia bankers, but the Fulton County grand jury determined that his failure to close insolvent banks in the early 1920s caused the panic of 1926. The banking problem was ignored until it exploded.[39]

Bennett fostered the growth of Manley's banking system. He never criticized the reckless banking practices and later explained that his "hands [had been] tied" by the banker's influence in the Georgia legislature. Manley's support or opposition dictated the fate of banking bills in the state. His influence may have intimidated Bennett, but he also respected and used it. Manley's lieutenants vigorously lobbied the legislature to pass the banking act of 1919. After Bennett became the first appointed superintendent of banks, he stayed in "constant touch" with Lorne Adams, Manley's partner. Adams assisted Bennett in the "inauguration of the department and the application of the new banking law." He remained "very close" to his friend and regulator until his federal indictment for bank fraud.[40]

Bennett refused to accept any responsibility for the banking disaster. He also absolved Georgia's bankers. To a large extent this was because he was a banker. A major flaw in the Georgia banking code required the superintendent of banks to have "at least five years active experience in the banking business." The mandate ensured that the top bank regulator would be a member of the banking industry, which he was supposed to regulate. Not surprisingly, the author of the banking code was Orville A. Park, general counsel of the Georgia Bankers Association.[41]

Georgia's bankers came to Bennett's side during the crisis. He cherished his friends in the "banking fraternity," who were "a source of great comfort and help." The regulator was indebted to the bankers because they had "supported the Department, financially and otherwise." In fact, the operating budget of the Department of Banking was funded entirely by the banking industry. Now he needed their political support to remain in office.[42]

In turn, Bennett called for deregulation of the banking industry. He asked the legislature to create a banking commission comprised of three "outstanding" bankers and the superintendent of banks. All candidates for the commission would be selected by the banking industry. The governor would appoint the members of the commission from a list provided by the state's bankers, and the commission would have "direct supervision and control over the Department of Banking." Bennett said that such a regulatory system would "remove the department from politics."[43]

Georgia made an attempt to remove bank regulation from politics in 1919. The expansion and collapse of the Manley banking system proved that the effort failed. Nevertheless, the state's regulatory system, with the banking commissioner appointed by the governor, had moved in the right direction. The banking commissioner was one step removed from the fund-raising process. But no regulatory system that operates in secret can insulate public officials from influence.

In Bennett's case, the system faltered because he was a captive of the industry. He spent his time having pleasant dinners with bankers and making promotional speeches for the Georgia Bankers Association. Manley's private secretary said it best when she testified that the crash would not have occurred if Bennett and his staff had been "vigorous" regulators. Instead, Bennett commended Manley "for his watchful care of the banks of Georgia."[44]

Florida had—and still has—an elected banking commissioner. State bankers have enjoyed the streamlined system of influence peddling for more than a hundred years. In the 1920s, as in the 1980s, bankers contributed directly to their regulator, bypassing the governor and legislators. Comptroller Amos reciprocated by ignoring their insider abuses and rushing to their defense when the panic started.

FLORIDA'S ELECTED REGULATOR

Amos, a seasoned politician, moved quickly to put the proper spin on the bad news. He chastised Georgia and federal banking officials for making "untrue" statements about Florida's real estate market. The misrepresentations were "calculated" to damage "perfectly safe" Florida banks. He insisted that Florida's economy and its banks were "sound, absolutely." Scolding the "panicky" public for losing faith in the banks, the backwoods politician preached to his constituency: "Let us sit steady in the boat and the whole situation will rapidly right itself here in Florida. The cause of the trouble does not lie within our borders. . . . A little public confidence now is the thing most needed to put an end to this unfortunate situation."[45]

The *Tampa Morning Tribune* united with Amos in the misinformation campaign. After twenty-seven Florida banks failed in less than a week, the newspaper ran the following front-page headline: "Amos Announces Banks in Florida in Good Shape." The owners of the paper had a good reason to slant coverage of the crisis: they owned the Citizens Bank and Trust Company, the largest bank in Tampa. Dr. Louis A. Bize, president of Tampa Tribune, Inc., was also president of the state bank. Bize, a former president of the Florida Bankers Association, was a partner of Manley and Anthony in the Florida Title Insurance Company of Miami.[46]

Bize's *Tribune* blamed the public for the crisis: "When the tattler, the gossiper, the idler, the doubter and the skeptic are silenced from further prattle, there will be less runs and fewer failures." Believing Amos and their local newspaper, depositors of the Citizens Bank and Trust Company remained calm in 1926. Bize sold the paper in 1927 to S. E. Thomason and John Stewart Bryan, but he continued to control the bank.[47]

During the banking crisis of 1929, the new owners of the *Tribune* refused to sugarcoat the news and the Citizens Bank and Trust Company failed after a bank run. Because Amos allowed the insolvent bank to remain open, Bize and his associates had the opportunity to abuse the Tampa landmark for another three years. Bank secrecy laws left depositors in the dark so they had to wait ten years to get back less than 25 percent of their money.[48]

In 1926, bankers throughout Florida joined hands with Amos and Bize in the public relations sham. They denied that the state's banks were loaded with bad real estate loans, and they insisted that the boom was still going strong. Dr. J. H. Therrell, president of the Florida Bankers Association, who was J. R. Anthony's partner at the Commercial Bank and Trust Company of Ocala, declared: "Florida banks are in excellent condition. . . . Fundamentally,

Florida is financially in better position than ever in her history. The banks are in a strong liquid position."[49]

Disproving his own case, Therrell argued that the state's prohibition of branch banking and its lack of deposit insurance strengthened the system. He said, "Every bank in Florida is under government supervision, but not government control, or the communistic so-called 'guarantees of deposits' by the supervising government." Therrell theorized that 30 percent of the bank failures were caused by "drastic legislation," 20 percent by "overinflation," and 50 percent by "idle gossip."[50]

The concerted effort continued when the Jacksonville Clearing House Association issued a press release for the benefit of north Florida's bankers: "Close investigation has shown that the Florida condition has never been healthier than at the present time . . . the bankers of Florida have the greatest confidence in the future of the State and fail to show the slightest uneasiness on account of a condition which is due to causes originating outside of Florida."[51]

James H. Gilman, president of the Bank of Bay Biscayne and one of Miami's banker-commissioners, fought to calm his depositors. He "hit back" by accusing the banks of Georgia of causing the problems in Florida. At the helm of a "hopelessly insolvent" bank, Gilman bluffed his way through the crisis. During the next four years, worthless insider loans increased his bank's negative net worth by $8 million. Despite the red ink, Amos allowed the powerful banker to remain in business. The regulator closed only his eyes when Gilman issued fraudulent statements. So depositors were led to believe that the Bank of Bay Biscayne was in "a flourishing and prosperous condition." Finally, in 1930, Miami's largest bank collapsed with disastrous consequences for its ten thousand depositors. Enraged by the regulatory collusion, depositors had Amos arrested for official malfeasance.[52]

After the panic of 1926 subsided, Amos admitted that he had known of the impending crisis. He said the fiasco was "a plain case of misplaced confidence." He defended the bankers associated with Manley, saying they were "justified" in trusting him because his banking network had operated successfully for years. Amos acknowledged receiving complaints from bankers that Manley had defaulted on his obligations. Alarmed by the size of Florida bank deposits placed with Georgia banks and loans made to Manley's affiliated companies, Amos said he tried to avert the crisis by meeting with Manley and Anthony on May 14, 1926. Manley satisfied his concerns by promising to make "substantial payments" to Florida banks.[53]

Amos's public explanation contradicted his private letters and bank examiners' reports. His official statements also conflicted with sworn testimony given during Manley's legal proceedings. In April 1925, word of a disaster circulated at the Florida Bankers Association convention in West Palm Beach. Affiliated bankers feared the Manley-Anthony system was near the brink because of insider loans. And by December 1925, Manley's Farmers and Traders Bank of Atlanta had stopped making payments to Florida banks. Amos then requested that state banks report to him the exact amount of deposits and loans made with the chain system. By the time of his meeting with Manley and Anthony, Amos had known about the crisis for months.[54]

Amos, Assistant Comptroller R. A. Gray, and Chief Examiner E. M. Porter huddled privately at Anthony's office with the two principals and Lorne Adams and John Russell of the Bankers Trust Company for most of May 14. The regulators went to Jacksonville to negotiate a plan to salvage the Manley-Anthony banking system. Amos began the meeting by presenting "a tabulated statement of all the loans, participating certificates, call money, and other obligations that had been placed in the Florida banks by the Bankers Trust Company of Atlanta and the Bankers Financing Company of Jacksonville." Florida member banks had loaned Manley and related corporations in Georgia $6.2 million. The state banks had also deposited $4.2 million in Manley's Georgia banks. Millions more loaned to affiliated entities in Florida would cause the member banks to collapse if Manley's Georgia system failed.[55]

Manley refused to show Amos a financial statement for the Bankers Trust Company. Instead, he produced an Ernst and Ernst audit of the Bankers Financing Company which documented that the company's assets had been diverted to seven companies owned by Manley and Anthony. Caught between two sets of partners and a regulator, Manley piously declared that if his partnership with Anthony "had diverted any assets that should properly belong to the Bankers Financing Company of Jacksonville then the partnership would have to put them back." In a private deal, Manley and Anthony had secretly transferred an estimated $1 million out of the Bankers Financing Company. Consequently, the Atlanta company lost between $40,000 and $75,000 a year in income from the operations in Florida.[56]

Instead of investigating or reporting the evidence of misappropriation to state and federal prosecutors, Amos conspired with Manley and Anthony to cover up the looming catastrophe. To save his investment and limit his liability, Anthony had a plan to divide $5 million of assets that he and Manley personally owned in Florida. Amos approved the plan although it reduced Anthony's exposure for the $10.4 million of worthless paper held by the Florida banks. He also agreed to stall collection efforts and to force all demands for the payment of loans and deposits through Anthony's Jacksonville office. The regulator ran interference for the bankers, obstructing efforts of Florida banks to collect from Manley's Georgia banks.[57]

The ability of Manley and Anthony to exert pressure on Amos and his staff was an indispensable element in the plan to stonewall the Florida creditors. A. P. Anthony's Peoples Bank of Jacksonville made six unsecured loans to the regulator. In addition, Amos's unsecured loan at the Palm Beach National Bank came due on July 1, 1926, and Porter's "loan" at the Palm Beach National Bank was repaid on June 19 of that year by J. R. Anthony's partner, Howard Smith.[58]

Amos was captured. When Thomas Cook, president of the Commercial Bank and Trust Company of West Palm Beach, complained about Manley's refusal to make loan payments or return demand deposits, he received a lecture from Amos. Manley and Anthony owned 52 percent of the Commercial Bank, but they borrowed more than 100 percent of its capital. The bank had deposited another 50 percent of its nonexistent capital with Manley's Georgia banking affiliates. Cook was desperate because Manley's defaults meant the bank was insolvent.[59]

Responding to Cook's appeal, Amos wrote to the "disloyal" partner of Manley and Anthony on June 1, 1926. "The time has come in banking circles for the exercise of the utmost brotherly feeling and assistance for another in the game." Amos said it was "a time for moderation." It was inappropriate for bankers to be "cold blooded" when collecting stale debts. The regulator preached to the banker about the need for compassion toward his colleague, who was in "an unfortunate situation." Amos said it was wrong for Cook to press his claims against Manley; Cook should work out the problem with Anthony. The comptroller's intervention stopped the critical collection process, assuring the collapse of the Commercial Bank and Trust Company.[60]

Less than a week after his meeting with Manley and Anthony to discuss the imminent crisis, Amos released a quarterly call report indicating that Florida's banks were in an "unusually healthy condition." According to the report, state bank assets had increased more than $164 million between April 1925 and April 1926. The comptroller allowed the bankers to deceive the public by counting millions of dollars of worthless loans as valuable assets. Amos made no mention of his secret report, which revealed the dependency of sixty-one Florida banks on the insolvent Manley banking system.[61]

Amos was intimately aware that the banks under his jurisdiction were not healthy. He also knew that Manley's insider abuse was only part of the problem. A confidential letter written by Amos to the directors of the Palm Beach Bank and Trust Company showed the extent of his knowledge. Six months before the panic, Amos had conclusive evidence of "habitual" insider abuse and "irregularities" by the local directors of the bank. Rather than demand their resignations, he merely wrote them a letter that outlined their "reckless practices."[62]

Amos's letter proved he had firsthand knowledge that the directors had violated the "rigid" legal limit by making "excessive" loans to themselves; customers were allowed to overdraw their accounts "at ruthless random without any regard whatsoever for banking principles," and the overdrafts totaled $138,000; the bank operated without a loan committee, and only two board meetings were held in 1925; 75 percent of the loans were concentrated in real estate; and cash items were in a "deplorable condition." A few weeks after writing the letter, Amos procured the unsecured loan from the Palm Beach National Bank, of which Howard Smith was the president. Amos then failed to take any enforcement action against the Palm Beach Bank and Trust Company, of which Smith was the vice-president.[63]

While regulators guarded their confidential records, depositors were led to believe the "encouraging indications" of the comptroller's call report and the advertisements of banks. For example, the Palm Beach Bank and Trust Company ran Mother's Day advertisements in May 1926. In the advertisements, the mother was a depositor who was looking forward to "reaping the reward" of her "years of careful investment" at the bank. Because her home was "secured by wisely managed finances," the "white-haired grandmother" would be the "uncrowned queen" in the "years of quiet rest toward the end." The collusion between the regulator and the bankers robbed the grandmother of 96 percent of her life savings on deposit at the Palm Beach Bank and Trust Company.[64]

Official deceit delayed—but could not prevent—the banking panic. Regulatory protection of Manley and Anthony caused ruinous losses for depositors when civil suits in Florida and Georgia blew the lid off the scandal. Depositors panicked when they finally learned the magnitude of the fraud.

Comptroller Amos blamed the crisis on Georgia banks, and Superintendent Bennett blamed it on Florida banks, while federal regulators pointed at state banks in both states. All agreed that the cause of the panic was outside their respective jurisdictions. The simple truth about Manley's insider abuse would have stopped the growth of his banking chain because depositors would have used other banks. Bank secrecy, which nourished his cozy relationships with regulators, allowed him to build an empire and live like a king with other people's money.[65]

State and federal regulators deceived the public. If depositors had known what the regulators knew, when they knew it, the panic would not have occurred. After more than a hundred bank failures, it became obvious that regulators had protected unscrupulous bankers instead of depositors. Desperate depositors in West Palm Beach and Atlanta became militant and demanded action.

5

THE INDICTMENT OF
FLORIDA'S COMPTROLLER

After the collapse of the Manley-Anthony banking system, depositors demanded that the Palm Beach County grand jury investigate the bank failures. Local authorities were "besieged" by elderly depositors whose life savings were ensnared in the "bank disgrace." They blamed the disaster on the political influence of J. R. Anthony and Amos's "hush-hush policy and secretive attitude."[1]

In a "fiery" speech, a lawyer for the Depositors League of Palm Beach County asked an irate crowd: "Who is your comptroller?" Answering his own question, he declared: "J. R. Anthony." Leaders of the movement were convinced that Amos was the puppet of the powerful banker. They believed Anthony dictated the naming of the receivers and attorneys for his defunct banks.[2]

Amos reinforced the belief that he was too cozy with Anthony by refusing to disclose any information about the closed banks. Drawing a "cloak of secrecy" around the disaster, Amos waited more than two months before filing the final examination report of the Palm Beach Bank and Trust Company in open court, which was the first step in the appointment of a receiver. In lieu of liquidating the bank, he proposed a plan of reorganization that would have required the depositors to "underwrite the losses" by giving up a large percentage of their deposits. With a "righteous howl," depositors demanded that Amos produce "definite information" about their "frozen" deposits. He responded that disclosure was dangerous, and he warned depositors to stop agitating. Disclaiming responsibility for the bank failures, he told the press: "The position of bank supervisor is one largely of 'locking the door after the horse is stolen.'" His callous attitude backfired. After being ignored, depositors organized a grass-roots movement dedicated to the indictment and removal of Amos.[3]

To protect themselves from further abuse, depositors of the Palm Beach Bank and Trust Company and the Commercial Bank and Trust Company united to form the Depositors League of Palm Beach County. All members pledged 2 percent of their deposits for a legal defense fund, and many made cash contributions to open an office and hire accountants and attorneys. They planned to take legal action against Amos, Anthony, and other bankers to ensure a maximum return of their money. During an organizational meeting, more than five hundred angry depositors rallied to protest Amos's "lax enforcement" of banking regulations. They unanimously passed a resolution demanding that the grand jury investigate the bankers who stole their money and the regulator who protected them. Believing it was impossible "for a bank to fail without criminal action on the inside," depositors formed a special committee to conduct their own investigation and to "aid and cooperate with the grand jury." Dr. Thomas E. Butler, chairman of the Depositors League, declared: "No honest man should have anything to fear from an investigation."[4]

While depositors vowed to "eliminate Comptroller Amos, Manley, Anthony, and chain banks," State Attorney L. R. Baker and the Palm Beach County grand jury launched an investigation. Using the grand jury's subpoena power, Baker gained access to the comptroller's correspondence and other regulatory records. The records revealed that the bankers had blatantly violated the banking code for years with Amos's acquiescence. They also disclosed that the prosecutor and six of the eighteen grand jurors had deposits frozen in the Palm Beach Bank and Trust Company. Two of those jurors, including W. C. Crittenden, the foreman, had outstanding loans at the bank.[5]

In September 1926, the grand jury indicted Amos, Howard

Smith, Lester Williams, Thomas Cook, and four other officers of the Palm Beach Bank and Trust Company and the Commercial Bank and Trust Company. Amos was charged with malpractice in office for his failure to remove the bankers though he "well knew" that they had made illegal loans to themselves and their entities, including the Mizner Development Corporation. Jurors urged the legislature to impeach and remove Amos from office. For years he had "wholly and shamefully failed in his duty to safeguard the interests of depositors by proper examination and proper control of irresponsible banks and bankers." The grand jury determined that he should have seized the banks because their loans were "so doubtful, extended, unliquid, and otherwise of depreciated value." Knowing the banks were insolvent, he allowed Smith, Williams, and Cook to operate them in an "unsafe and unsound" manner and to make loans to themselves "in excess of the extreme limit permitted by law." Amos took no action when the bankers borrowed more than 40 percent of the capital and surplus of the banks. Jurors charged that his failure to remove the bankers established an "evil example of all others in like cases offending, and against the peace and dignity of the State of Florida."[6]

Amos declared that he had "committed no wrong and had no fears as to the final outcome of a fair and impartial trial or other proceedings." He was arrested in Tallahassee by Leon County sheriff Frank Stoutamire, who assigned a deputy to "guard" the cabinet member at the capitol. Palm Beach circuit judge Curtis E. Chillingworth set his bond at $5,000. Remaining in office but realizing his freedom was in jeopardy, Amos used his powerful position to assemble a potent defense team. In light of the ugly mood in south Florida, a conviction by a local jury and a sentence by a West Palm Beach judge could result in three years at the state prison.[7]

CONFLICT OF INTEREST

While Amos was under siege in Tallahassee, the Depositors League focused on removing the receiver and law firm for the Palm Beach Bank and Trust Company. Depositors demanded that Amos dismiss his hand-picked receiver, Orel J. Myers, and the law firm of Blackwell and Donnell because of their glaring conflict of interest. They sought impartial liquidators who were not debtors and who had "no connection, either directly or indirectly with the suspended institution."[8]

Depositors feared that Amos and his cronies would misuse the funds of the receivership and wipe out what was left of their savings. Orel Myers, a local lawyer with political clout, had delinquent loans at the bank amounting to 13 percent of its capital. The members of Blackwell and Donnell not only owed substantial sums to the bank, but they represented its major borrowers. C. D. Blackwell also had been a director and stockholder of the bank, and he was liable for assessments on his stock. His partner, E. B. Donnell, had defaulted on loans amounting to 39 percent of the bank's capital. Blackwell and Donnell represented J. R. Anthony, the Mizner Development Corporation, and the Pinewood Development Company, which meant that they would be sitting on both sides of the negotiating table.[9]

The banking scandal split Palm Beach County down the middle, the business community, the debtors, on one side, and the creditors, who were the depositors, on the other. Donnell represented a disproportionate number of the debtors. Before the controversy the former judge had a good reputation and was well liked. His ascent began when he was the legal adviser to Sidney J. Catts, the gubernatorial candidate who defeated Comptroller Knott in 1916. After the campaign Governor Catts appointed him to the bench, where he stayed for a few years and made extensive contacts in the business community. He then resigned to develop a thriving law practice.

Donnell handled both corporate and criminal cases, frequently involving the same individuals. After the banking crash, his mainstay was the bankrupt Mizner Development Corporation and the defunct Palm Beach Bank and Trust Company. He stayed active in politics for the next three decades, serving several terms as mayor of West Palm Beach. He succeeded J. B. Hodges as chairman of the state Democratic Executive Committee. His law partner, Blackwell, who also continued to use the title of judge after leaving the bench, represented many well-heeled businessmen who were debtors of the Palm Beach Bank and Trust Company.[10]

With Blackwell and Donnell as the lawyers, depositors feared that, like the typical Amos-supervised receivership, the liquidation process would last a decade, so they pushed to wrap it up expeditiously and limit expenses. They hoped to get their money back within two years. Their anxiety was well-founded, according to Receiver Cunningham of the Palm Beach National Bank. Cunningham told the comptroller of the currency's office that "the liquidation of the Palm Beach Bank and Trust Co. will be a long, drawn-out affair and no doubt will cover a period of at least six or seven years."[11]

Amos could not risk the appointment of impartial liquidators, so he ignored the pleas of the depositors. Myers remained the receiver until his resignation in 1929, and he continued to use the services of Blackwell and Donnell. Besides its high legal fees that depleted the bank's dwindling assets, the law firm settled the debts of its clients against the interests of the bank. By compromising his own obligations at the bank, Donnell personally benefited at the expense of the depositors.[12]

AN INDEPENDENT NEWSPAPER

Joe L. Earman, an organizer of the Depositors League and the publisher of the *Palm Beach Independent,* was a catalyst for the investigation. His small weekly newspaper became the vociferous defender of the eight thousand depositors of the two failed banks. To ensure that they were treated fairly by Amos and his political appointees, he decided to put a "spotlight" on the liquidation process. Earman, a former owner of the *Palm Beach Post,* also recognized that the controversy would increase the circulation of his paper.[13]

Earman could lead the charge for the depositors because he was not indebted to the defunct banks. After hearing rumors of the imminent failure of the Palm Beach Bank and Trust Company, he paid a $5,000 loan at the bank four days before it collapsed. He also withdrew his deposits at the bank because he was not "foolish enough" to leave large sums in an insolvent bank.[14]

Prior to the bank failures Earman and Amos had been friends. Both had been involved in state Democratic politics for many years. Before he reviewed the regulatory records, Earman considered the comptroller a competent cabinet member. His perception began to change after attempts to reopen the Palm Beach Bank and Trust Company failed. Saying he did not intend to cause "embarrassment," Earman wrote Amos stressing the desperate situation in West Palm Beach. He assured Amos that he respected him and regarded his "mistakes" as "of the mind and not the heart." He urged Amos to release "full information" about the closed banks to restore public confidence.[15]

In his probing letter, Earman asked illuminating questions. He wanted to know if "it is right for a cloak of secrecy to be drawn around the two suspended financial institutions wherein it is alleged that seven million dollars are 'frozen up?'" Is the comptroller's office "a public office with the records of said office subject to scrutiny by the public?" Earman emphasized that the public had a right to know how its money had been invested. He pointed to the high level of taxpayers' deposits in the banks from the city, county, and state. Earman ended by "respectfully" requesting the release of "information about the people's money in Palm Beach County."[16]

Amos refused to answer any questions and provided no information. Furthermore, he issued a stern warning against publicity: "In those communities where closed banks have been reopened there has been no agitation to speak of but all have rolled up their sleeves and worked whole-heartedly to bring it to pass. Therefore, as I view it, no good purpose can be served by thrashing the matter out in the newspapers."[17]

After Earman received a copy of the final examiner's report of the Palm Beach Bank and Trust Company, he discovered why Amos was so opposed to disclosure. The crude self-dealings revealed in the report infuriated the idealistic editor. He was now convinced that disclosure of the insider abuse was the only way to prevent it from continuing during the liquidation process. He faced "pronounced opposition" from influential businessmen to the publication of the examiner's report, which was on file with the clerk of the circuit court. Orel Myers, the receiver, organized a lobbying effort to prevent the publication of the public document. The board of directors of the Palm Beach County Merchants Association unanimously passed a resolution that urged Earman "to withhold publication of any list which would show the depositors and debtors in detail of the Palm Beach Bank and Trust Company." The Merchants Association said that "any publicity of this nature would be detrimental to the welfare of the city."[18]

The president of the Merchants Association was E. D. Anthony, whose interests had borrowed 30 percent of the bank's capital. He was also the brother of J. R. Anthony. The vice-president of the association was City Commissioner Vincent Oaksmith, another major borrower of the bank. The names of six of the twelve officers and directors of the association appeared in the examiner's report as debtors of the bank. Publishing the report would offend the largest advertisers in the *Palm Beach Independent,* including the Anthony Brothers department store.[19]

Defiantly, the *Independent* published the examiner's report of the Palm Beach Bank and Trust Company and Amos's correspondence regarding the insider abuse at the two banks. Earman declared that the "AUTOCRATIC POWER VESTED IN THE STATE COMPTROLLER" could not silence his paper. Disclosure of the regulatory records enraged the depositors, who got a rare look at the secret relationship between a regulator and a bank. It was a shocking view.[20]

Earman was a participant in and reporter of the struggle. As the spokesman of the grass-roots movement, he said he was moved to militancy by "the tears of helpless women." He became the self-proclaimed champion of the fifty-five hundred depositors of the Palm Beach Bank and Trust Company who owed nothing to the bank. His loyalty to those "who furnished the money" made him the sworn enemy of Amos, Myers, and the law firm of Blackwell and Donnell.[21]

Earman, a political veteran, was no stranger to controversy. He was an insider of the Democratic party and had held influential positions at the local and state levels. He understood the role that money played in Florida politics. During the hard-fought 1916 governor's race, Earman made several personal loans to Sidney Catts. In the final two weeks of the campaign, he arranged a loan for Catts from the Barnett National Bank of Jacksonville. He then bought clothes for the governor and his family so they could be properly attired for the inauguration. Earman continued to subsidize the Baptist preacher throughout his administration by loaning him more than $15,000.[22]

Governor Catts rewarded his benefactor and appointed him chairman of the Board of Control for the university system and president of the State Board of Health. Earman, whom historian Wayne Flynt described as an "urban idealist," supported higher education, reapportionment, and a deposit insurance fund for state banks. Bank failures during the election year of 1916 helped defeat Comptroller Knott and made banking an important issue during the Catts administration. Although the Florida Bankers Association prevailed in the legislature and defeated measures to restrict insider loans and insure deposits, Earman recognized the need to reform the banking system. His knowledge of banking and his ownership of the *Palm Beach Independent* made him the natural leader of the Depositors League.[23]

Earman's caustic pen gave balance to the biased reporting of D. H. Conkling's *Palm Beach Post*. Conkling, the publisher and banker, was in partnership with Addison Mizner and other promoters. His incestuous relationships with the local banks and promoters prevented the *Post* from investigating the bank failures. Earman, who had no loans from the failed banks, was free to investigate and to publish the Palm Beach Bank and Trust Company's examination report. The *Independent* dedicated almost an entire issue to the report and created a storm of controversy. Out of the conflict several fresh ideas emerged.

APPOINTED BANKING COMMISSIONER AND DISCLOSURE

After reviewing the examination reports of the failed state banks, the Palm Beach County grand jury concluded that the impeachment and removal of Amos would solve only a personnel problem. To insulate the regulation and liquidation of banks from politics, jurors urged the legislature to strip the comptroller of the power to regulate banks. They endorsed the creation of an independent department of banking, headed by a professional banking commissioner. "Much of the evil inherent" in the banking system would be eliminated by the establishment of a "separate" department "wholly removed from the authority of the comptroller."[24]

Jurors recognized the awesome power that the comptroller held over bankers and the state's economy. Amos could use his life-or-death regulatory powers to stay in office. He could take retaliatory action against those who refused to give contributions, appearing as an effective regulator, or he could ignore the violations of those who supported his campaigns. Because the banking industry was tainted by so many corrupt bankers, jurors appealed for reform of the system before the next election. Defeating Amos would be almost impossible while the industry was "directly under the heel of the state comptroller." The delay in appointing a receiver for the Palm Beach Bank and Trust Company and then the appointment of Myers showed jurors how an insolvent bank could be manipulated for political benefit. The authority to appoint receivers and their attorneys provided the comptroller with a potent system of patronage. Depositors paid for the shenanigans with their savings. Jurors hoped that such blatant politics could be eliminated if the comptroller was removed from banking. Amos had been the state's banking commissioner for nine years, and because cabinet members could serve unlimited terms, his tenure in office seemed to be for life. Thus jurors proposed that the governor, whose power was limited by the 1885 constitution, would appoint the banking commissioner.[25]

The grand jury's recommendations were well received by the Depositors League. Its leading attorney, Halsted L. Ritter, who later became a federal judge in Miami, told the press that "a separate and exclusive banking department is one of the great needs of the state of Florida." Before moving to West Palm Beach at the age of sixty, Ritter had practiced law in Denver for twenty-eight years, serving as president of the Denver Bar Association and as a member of the Colorado railroad commission. After researching the laws of other states, Ritter knew that by 1926 the majority of states had specialized banking departments, headed by appointed commissioners. He believed public confidence could be restored if Florida's regulatory system was brought into the twentieth century. Ritter argued diplomatically that no comptroller could regulate banks effectively and perform his other important functions. He stressed that Amos was "the busiest and most burdened official at Tallahassee." Regulating banks was "just one of the multitudinous duties of the comptroller." Under the state constitution, the comptroller was the chief fiscal officer of the state, approving all expenditures. And his seat in the cabinet required him to oversee most of the departments in the state government. Ritter concluded that Florida needed a full-time banking commissioner who possessed "technical knowledge, experience, sound judgment and political neutrality."[26]

Ritter also advocated that the legislature open banking to public scrutiny. Abolishing bank secrecy would restore depositors' confidence. His call for disclosure came one year after the legislature repealed the state's 1913 sunshine law. That Progressive Era disclosure law, which was enacted after bank runs threatened the state's banking system during the Panic of 1907, compelled state banks to publish their examination reports in local newspapers. But it was never implemented by Knott and Amos.[27]

Amos ignored the new banking-in-the-sunshine proposal. After his indictment, he decided that his survival in office required a system of secrecy. For a short period after the crash, the final examiner's report of a closed state bank was available for public inspection. But after the furor created by the publication of the Palm Beach Bank and Trust Company's report, Amos unilaterally changed the procedure. He refused to release the examination report of the Commercial Bank and Trust Company because to do so was "inadvisable." He also delayed the appointment of a receiver at J. R. Anthony's bank for five months. Following Anthony's recommendation, Amos then appointed his partner, W. H. Tunnicliffe, as receiver.[28]

Understanding that "knowledge will forever govern ignorance," Amos permanently sealed the records of all state banks in Florida, an order that remained in effect until June 1989. He even refused to give the Depositors League the addresses of the depositors of the Palm Beach Bank and Trust Company. The Depositors League sued the receiver for the addresses, and Judge Chillingworth ordered Myers to release them. Amos defied the court order by refusing to authorize their release. For the rest of his administration, Amos denied access to liquidation reports because they were "quasi-confidential."[29]

In an attempt to save his seat in the cabinet, however, he recommended that the 1927 legislature create a separate banking department independent of the comptroller's office. Amos adopted Ritter's argument when he told Governor Martin: "A banking commissioner, with nothing else to do but look after state banks, building and loan associations, and small loan companies . . . should be in a better position to take care of the work than one who has many other exacting duties equally important to perform and consequently would be able to hold failures down to a minimum."[30]

Amos's position was good politics, but not good government. After the panic of 1926, Florida's way of choosing its banking commissioner seemed archaic even to conservative commentators. The *Madison Enterprise Record* supported "the removal of the banking department from the comptroller's office" in an effort to restore confidence and "insure safe banking." With an indictment

pending against him, Amos would have committed political suicide if he had publicly opposed the move for a separate banking
department.[31]

Always a nimble politician, he knew one of his powerful friends
in the legislature could kill the bill in a committee. During the
1920s, the Florida legislature met every other year for sixty days. It
was easy for a cabinet member, who exercised power on a daily
basis, to sabotage legislation. Yet if the banking crisis continued
and an indignant public forced the legislature to remove banking
from the comptroller's office, Amos would retain his constitutional post as a cabinet member and the state's chief fiscal officer.
He could afford to relinquish his statutory position as banking
commissioner, but the disgrace of losing the most prestigious part
of his office would probably defeat him at the next election, especially since his campaign coffers would be empty.[32]

Opening the 1927 legislative session, Governor Martin urged
the creation of a separate banking department headed by an appointed professional. Representative Franklin O. King of Orlando,
chairman of the House Banking Committee, prodded his colleagues to pass the governor's bill as "a certain remedy for present
ills in the Florida banking situation, and that it would provide
ample supervision and inspection of banks." Legislators listened to
their local bankers, who were satisfied with the status quo, and
refused to reform the system. A watered-down version passed the
House by a vote of fifty-eight to twenty-nine. It would have established a state banking commission, a five-member board with the
chairman serving as banking commissioner. The governor was the
appointing authority, but at least three of the members had to "be
either president, vice president, cashier, director or other executive
officer" of a state bank "or shall have had at least five years previous experience in such capacity." A majority of the commission
members could continue as bankers after their appointments. Despite this accommodation, the bill was killed in the Senate, at least
fifteen members of which had close ties to banks.[33]

Passing meaningful banking legislation was impossible while
the Florida Bankers Association opposed reform. Speaking for the
bankers, A. P. Anthony said they opposed changing the regulatory
structure because "under our present arrangement the state banks
are being well supervised and are receiving the finest kind of cooperation from the department." Working quietly with Amos, the

bankers also buried a bill to establish a state deposit insurance fund, which was modeled after Nebraska's successful system. Dr. J. H. Therrell, J. R. Anthony's partner who was head of the FBA, lobbied against any government guarantee of deposits because it was a "communistic" idea that would lead to central control of banking.[34]

PUBLIC DEPOSITS AND PRIVATE LOANS

The grand jury also investigated the preferential treatment received by city officials of West Palm Beach from banks they used as public depositories. Jurors realized the potential for private profit by officials responsible for public funds. Many of the banks that survived the banking crash did so because of public deposits. And many of those that failed delayed their closing by the misuse of public deposits. J. R. Anthony and other astute bankers knew it was easier to control a few politicians than thousands of depositors.[35]

Jurors named H. J. Daugherty, city clerk and treasurer of West Palm Beach, as a co-conspirator in the scandal. Daugherty had deposited, without proper security, $1,021,872 of city funds in the Palm Beach Bank and Trust Company. He also deposited $700,000 of taxpayer funds in the Commercial Bank and Trust Company, which was its largest account. Meanwhile, the city's checking account was overdrawn by $295,000 at the Palm Beach Bank and Trust Company. While he was managing city funds in what jurors called "a very slipshod and unbusinesslike manner," his personal checking account was "habitually overdrawn" at the Palm Beach Bank and Trust Company. On the day the bank failed he had bad checks outstanding of $6,775 in his personal account. He also had personal loans of $43,500 at the Palm Beach Bank and Trust Company, an enormous sum of money for a city employee to borrow. He was a borrower at the Commercial Bank and Trust Company as well.[36]

After the grand jury issued its report, Daugherty was fired by a unanimous vote at a special meeting of the West Palm Beach Commission. To protect its books and records, the commission ordered his office door nailed shut and assigned a policeman to guard the premises. His partner in real estate deals, City Manager C. A. Bingham, was dismissed by the city commission too. Bingham owed the Palm Beach Bank and Trust Company $31,000 when it closed, and he had a $3,000 loan at the Commercial Bank and Trust Company. Daugherty and Bingham were indicted for conspiracy to defraud the city of $200,000. Daugherty was also indicted for accepting compensation from the Palm Beach Bank and Trust Company in exchange for depositing city funds in the bank. Judge A. G. Hartridge, whose depositor status and delinquent loan at the Palm Beach Bank and Trust Company led to his disqualification in a related criminal trial, summarily dismissed the conspiracy charges against Daugherty.[37]

City Commissioner Vincent Oaksmith enjoyed the generosity of the Manley-Anthony system. He escaped criticism although he owed $17,200 to the Palm Beach Bank and Trust Company and had a loan at the Commercial Bank and Trust Company. Oaksmith was an audacious politician. He was a member of the Depositors League, and he tried to reorganize and reopen the Palm Beach Bank and Trust Company. He was also vice-president of the Palm Beach County Merchants Association, which opposed the publication of the bank's examination report.[38]

After both banks failed, Oaksmith moved his personal business to the First American Bank and Trust Company, which closed in March 1927. When the First American Bank reopened two months later, in his role as commissioner, Oaksmith introduced a resolution designating it as a city depository. The city then deposited $82,582 in the bank, and the commissioner borrowed $19,293 from it. The city suffered a significant loss when the bank closed permanently a year later.[39]

Moreover, Oaksmith defaulted on his personal loans at the First American Bank. In addition, he and his business partner, E. D. Anthony—J. R.'s brother—defaulted on their joint obligations at the bank. Because of bank secrecy, his irresponsible financial affairs did not affect his political career. He was a city commissioner for fourteen years and served as mayor of West Palm Beach three times.[40]

While the industrious grand jury was investigating the handling of municipal deposits, Governor Martin began probing "irregularities" of a "grave character" in the management of state funds. The governor suspected that taxpayers would sustain substantial losses because so many failed banks held state deposits. Martin insisted that Amos explain why millions of dollars under his control were deposited in interest-free, undersecured accounts. In particular, the governor accused the comptroller of mismanagement for leaving state deposits in a dormant account at the Barnett National Bank of Jacksonville for nine years. The comptroller's office had not received interest from the Barnett National Bank since 1917, and Amos had failed to make an accounting of the state funds throughout the administrations of Sidney Catts and Cary Hardee. Three days before Martin's press conference, Amos suddenly deposited $20,215 with the state treasurer. The sum presumably represented interest for nine years. The investigation revealed that Amos had deposited as much as $2.5 million in revolving accounts at various banks. He allowed the banks to use state funds for months before he deposited them with the state treasurer. Martin demanded to know if the state had received any interest on the accounts and if they were properly secured. He was trying to learn whether Amos had circumvented the law by depositing funds directly with preferred banks instead of with the state treasurer. The governor ordered a full accounting of the collateral Amos was holding to secure the funds.[41]

After traveling to Jacksonville to meet with his bankers, Amos responded that he had handled more than $40 million of public funds without losing a penny. Declaring that he had never "received a dollar's personal benefit" from the bankers, he ignored the question of interest lost on state deposits. He admitted, however, that the revolving account at the Barnett National Bank was unsecured. He said state law did not require security for those funds, except for the $5,000 bond he carried as a cabinet member.[42]

Amos had a special relationship with the Barnett National Bank because J. R. Anthony served on its board of directors. Barnett was the correspondent for many of the banks affiliated with the Manley-Anthony system, including the Palm Beach National Bank, Palm Beach Bank and Trust Company, and Commercial Bank and Trust Company. Amos's delinquent and unsecured loans at the Palm Beach National Bank and the Peoples Bank of Jacksonville confirmed that he had received far more than a dollar from his cozy relationship with Anthony.[43]

Taking issue with his Democratic colleague, Martin sent Amos another embarrassing interrogatory. The governor, formerly a Jacksonville lawyer, requested a breakdown of the comptroller's transactions with Florida banks. Specifically, he asked for the name of each bank acting as a public depository for the comptroller; a detailed statement of the public funds in each bank; the amount of interest, if any, paid on the deposits; and the collateral pledged as security for those funds. Martin then told Amos that his $5,000 bond would not "indemnify the state in case of a loss of state funds or even the interest on same, especially when you have from one to two and a half million dollars on hand which you refrain from depositing with the treasurer from thirty to sixty days or more."[44]

Amos and Martin had widely divergent philosophies regarding public deposits. With Florida's banks failing in record numbers, Martin was concerned about the loss of unsecured state funds. On the contrary, Amos argued that the taxpayers of Florida should bail out troubled banks: "It would help to leave state funds in the banks as long as practical and that necessary withdrawals thereof should be so distributed as to have the least possible effect."[45]

After front-page headlines in the state's major newspapers, the governor's investigation faded from public view. Joe Earman queried why Martin had fallen on Amos "like a ton brick and then like a winded race horse slowed down half way around the track." Because troubled banks held $500,000 of state funds, Martin feared his investigation would cause another panic. Earman then asked Amos the status of the unsecured deposits. The comptroller cautioned "against an unwarranted attack upon the good name and credit of a state bank." Amos warned Earman that he had "no right by innuendo and inference to attack a solvent institution" and that he could expect a lawsuit by the "injured bank" if he published its name. The threat of bank runs allowed Amos to seal the banking records, denying access to the governor, legislature, press, and depositors.[46]

THE CABINET AND THE COURT

To salvage his political career, Amos moved quickly to dispose of the indictment against him. He had to remove the cloud of suspicion hanging over his office before the legislators returned to Tallahassee in April 1927. Otherwise, the legislature would probably strip banking from the comptroller's office and consider impeachment charges against him. So he hired Speaker of the House Fred H. Davis of Tallahassee as his lawyer and began to fight back.

Davis, who later became the state's attorney general and then a supreme court justice, maneuvered to have the supreme court of Florida dismiss the case. Having the popular Speaker as his lawyer enhanced Amos's chances before the six statewide-elected justices.[47]

Davis hastily petitioned the supreme court for a writ of habeas corpus to release Amos from an "illegal detention." Four days later, the Tallahassee-based court asserted jurisdiction and removed the case from the circuit court of Palm Beach County. Amos was released without posting a bond, and his lawyer was granted the opportunity to argue technical procedural issues. The supreme court, now in control of the fate of the high-ranking cabinet member, could dismiss the charges or order him to face a jury in West Palm Beach.[48]

Davis advanced several novel immunity theories, including the view that impeachment was "the sole primary remedy and punishment" for the comptroller as a "superior" constitutional officer. A criminal indictment, according to Davis, had to follow an impeachment by the House of Representatives and the trial in the Senate. Moreover, he said, the comptroller was immune from prosecution for malpractice in office because the banking code granted him "highly discretionary powers" in the regulation of state banks. Amos had "wide discretion and far reaching power" and could not be prosecuted "for failure to exercise such discretion and judgment or improper or erroneous exercise of such discretion and judgment." Davis asked the court to reverse two of its previous decisions and rule that the doctrine of *ejusdem generis* required the strict construction of the malpractice statute to exclude the comptroller and other cabinet members from prosecution.[49]

Attorney General J. B. Johnson and Palm Beach County state attorney Baker filed a brief challenging the motion to discharge. Relying on established authority, they attacked the "fallacious premise" that the supreme court had jurisdiction to hear a case properly before the criminal court of Palm Beach County. They argued that no precedent cloaked the comptroller with prosecutorial immunity, and the state constitution mandated that cabinet members "shall nevertheless be liable to indictment, trial and punishment according to law." In addition, the banking code compelled the regulator to seize any state bank which he had "reason to conclude" was operating in an "unsound or unsafe condition." The code also required that officers of banks who violated the law "shall be subject to summary removal from office by the comptroller." They stressed that "shall" does not mean "may." Thus Amos's failure to seize the banks and remove their officers was "criminal neglect" of his "mandatory duty" and constituted malpractice in office. Finally, the brief reminded the court that the construction of the malpractice statute had been settled in *Smith* v. *State* and *Kirkland* v. *State,* two Florida Supreme Court cases.[50]

A badly divided court delayed the decision until January 1927 and then dismissed the charges against Amos on procedural grounds. He was freed by the vote of four of the six justices. Chief Justice William H. Ellis, whose political career began on the Quincy Town Council and Gadsden County Commission and who had been Amos's predecessor as state auditor, wrote the majority opinion. Ellis, who also was the state's attorney general before serving twenty-three years on the supreme court, tarnished his reputation when he retired from the court and soon represented a client before his colleagues. After other lawyers criticized the former justice, the supreme court adopted a rule prohibiting such a practice.[51]

Justices Armstead Brown, a good Democrat, who had been "consistently loyal to his party," and William Glenn Terrell, who served in the House and Senate before Governor Hardee appointed him to the high court, joined in Ellis's opinion. Justice James Bryan Whitfield, "an ardent Democrat" and a former member of the cabinet as both treasurer and attorney general, wrote a concurring opinion. Amos needed all four votes to avoid a trial on the merits.[52]

The majority had to create new law to immunize Amos for his regulatory misconduct. Chief Justice Ellis tried to justify the departure from precedent with some ingenious reasoning. He accepted Davis's interpretation of the malpractice statute. He used the *ejusdem generis* rule and reached for the logic of Chief Justice John Marshall to distinguish the Amos case from *Kirkland* v. *State,* which the same court had decided in 1923. In *Kirkland,* which involved a county commissioner, not a cabinet member, the supreme court held: "It is within the power of the legislature to dispense with the necessity for a criminal intent and to punish particular acts without regard to the mental attitude of the doer. And [the malpractice statute] denounces two offenses; one wilful extortion in the charging of fees or commissions by an officer of the state, and the other 'any malpractice in office not otherwise especially provided for' to which the word 'wilfully' does not apply and in which it is not an element." Nevertheless, the court dismissed the Amos indictment because it did not allege that he "charged, received or collected any money or other thing of value in consideration of his alleged failure to act" or that he "wilfully or corruptly neglected or failed" to close the banks or to remove their officers.[53]

Justice Whitfield argued in his concurring opinion that the court was not in conflict with *Kirkland*. In one sweeping statement he laid the predicate for ignoring any previous case: "In applying cases which have been decided, what may have been said in an opinion should be confined to and limited by the facts of the case under consideration when the expressions relied upon were made, and should not be extended to cases where the facts are essentially different." He then rejected *Kirkland* by concluding that no criminal prosecution for official malpractice could proceed without showing that Amos "corruptly acted or failed to act."[54]

Justices Louie W. Strum and Rivers H. Buford wrote dissenting opinions. Strum was a jurist respected by Democrats and Republicans alike. Governor Martin had appointed him to the Florida Supreme Court in 1925, and he served until 1931. He was then selected by President Hoover as U.S. district judge for the Southern District of Florida and by President Harry Truman for the Fifth Circuit Court of Appeals in 1950. Dissenting in the Amos case, Strum wrote: "I am unable to reconcile the majority opinion herein with the former opinion of this Court in *Kirkland* v. *State*."[55]

Justice Buford, another former attorney general, was a "colorful" judge known for his "homespun philosophy." He also criticized the majority opinion for contradicting the *Kirkland* precedent. He declared that the comptroller "stands as the representative of the people between the unscrupulous, the careless, the inefficient or the unfortunate banker and the public which entrusts its deposits to such institutions." His reading of the banking code was that it compelled the comptroller to take action if he found a bank in an unsound or unsafe condition. Buford concluded that the supreme court should not have exercised its jurisdiction in the case.[56]

When Buford wrote his dissenting opinion the row between Amos and Joe Earman was well-known in political circles. He had served on the cabinet with Amos, but he had a special relationship with Earman. In 1925, Earman made a personal loan of $8,000 to Buford for the construction of his residence in Tallahassee. Earman asked J. B. Hodges, the chairman of the Democratic Executive Committee, to draft the papers, which included an assignment of the mortgage to the Ocean and Lake Realty Company, a West Palm Beach corporation.[57]

Bank secrecy laws hid the examination reports of the Palm Beach National Bank and the Peoples Bank of Jacksonville. The "loans" received by Amos from those banks were concealed from the Palm Beach County grand jury and the supreme court. Evidence that the bankers had bought influence with Amos would have shown "corrupt intent" and forced him to stand for trial.[58]

The reasoning of the majority opinion would have allowed prosecution of Amos under the malpractice statute if he had been charged with "misconduct in the disbursement of public funds," which amounted to "a breach of good faith." His misuse of public deposits at the Barnett National Bank of Jacksonville and other banks could have been grounds for a malpractice indictment. Amos was indicted two more times for malpractice in connection with bank failures. But the indictments did not charge him with corruption or misuse of public funds, and the supreme court dismissed both of them.[59]

The Amos case emasculated the malpractice law and made it almost impossible to remove negligent or incompetent public officials in Florida. The Amos doctrine controlled the definition of malpractice for the next fifty years. Its protection of cabinet members had a far-reaching effect on public administration in the state.[60]

6

THE RESIGNATION OF GEORGIA'S SUPERINTENDENT OF BANKS

While prosecutors in West Palm Beach investigated Florida comptroller Amos, Atlanta's solicitor general John A. Boykin initiated a criminal investigation into the regulatory failure of T. R. Bennett, Georgia's appointed superintendent of banks. With tens of thousands of depositors facing losses of as much as $30 million, the ambitious prosecutor also began probing Georgia's financial community.

At a press conference, which made the front page of the *New York Times,* Boykin declared that the Manley banking system had been looted. Feeling the pressure from Atlanta's business establishment, he said: "No local pride or influence of any kind brought to bear in the case will deter me from the most vigorous and exhaustive prosecution of the guilty parties." Making his point, the *Atlanta Constitution* ran a story on the investigation but omitted the "local pride" statement.[1]

Boykin immediately obtained a court order directing the Fulton County grand jury to investigate Manley's banking empire and the Georgia Department of Banking. After reviewing the state's confidential bank examination reports, the grand jury issued a scathing report condemning Bennett for "dereliction of duty." Jurors urged Governor Clifford Walker to dismiss his chief bank regulator for failing to protect the public from the criminal conduct of Manley and his associates.[2]

The grand jury determined that Georgia's banking code, if enforced, provided ample protection for depositors. Jurors concluded that the "underlying and precipitating" causes of the banking crash were not "chargeable to deficiencies in the law, or to the need for amendments thereto, but to unsound banking practices and to the failure of the department of banking to properly, promptly and rigidly enforce the state banking laws." The bank examination reports convinced jurors that the calamity could have been "averted" if Bennett had "properly acted" on the warnings from his staff about the rampant insider abuse.[3]

The bank examination reports astounded jurors. They saw that the banking chain was "loaded down" with $12.8 million of insider loans. The personal loans to Manley, his partners, and their affiliated companies were from member banks or from the Bankers Trust Company, which had recycled the demand deposits of member banks. The bank fraud conspiracy had created a severe liquidity crisis for member banks in Georgia and Florida. Jurors realized that the corruption went beyond Manley and his partners in Atlanta. Local officers and directors of member banks also flagrantly violated the law by financing their own pet projects.[4]

The confidential regulatory records proved that Bennett was intimately aware of the fraud and insider abuse. Jurors denounced him for failing to remove the bankers and for allowing the rogue banks to continue operating. They concluded that the regulator was "derelict in his duty in permitting these conditions to exist, which ultimately resulted in this great calamity injuring not only the depositors in these institutions but damaging the credit and good name of the state at large."[5]

BENNETT MISLEADS THE GRAND JURY

After the grand jury released its report, Bennett fought in vain to keep his position. Ironically, after years of shielding the Georgia banking industry from public scrutiny, Bennett attacked the grand jury for operating in secret. He sent a disingenuous letter to Governor Walker, criticizing the grand jury for not indicting him. An indictment would have given him an opportunity to clear his name in a public trial, he said. Hoping for vindication through the political process, Bennett asked Walker to conduct a "special investigation" of his performance.[6]

Because the state's bankers stood beside their embattled colleague, Bennett was well fortified for his fight. His reliance on the bankers was underscored when he hired Orville A. Park, the general counsel of the Georgia Bankers Association for more than twenty years, as his special counsel. Bennett appointed Park's law firm to represent the receiverships of more than eighty failed state banks. Park, a former judge and author of the state's banking code, also received fees from the defunct Bankers Trust Company.[7]

In a carefully orchestrated public relations campaign, Park declared that the grand jury was "misinformed" and "shellshocked." He accused the jurors of committing "a grave injustice" to "an honest, faithful and efficient public officer." While Bennett called for openness, his lawyer told the press to "quit talking about Georgia banks . . . quit trying to make a 'goat' out of the superintendent of banks." Park blamed the newspapers for causing "irreparable injury" to the state, and he advised everybody to just "forget it all and get down to business." His solution for the crisis was to "tell the world that Georgia is all right, that her financial institutions are sound, that her people for the most part are prosperous, that she has her face to the sun."[8]

Sounding like his elected counterpart in Florida, Bennett defended the integrity of Georgia's bankers. His candid response highlighted the problem. He asked the governor to give him the chance to exonerate himself "especially to the bankers whose servant in a popular sense I am." Bennett even defended the operations of Manley's Georgia State Bank, saying that the bank "exercised unusual care to have its loans within the letter of the law." Throughout the 1920s members of the banking chain regarded Manley's "gilt-edged" loans as the highest-quality paper.[9]

On one hand, Bennett admitted that, contrary to law, he had allowed Manley's insolvent banks to remain open for years. He failed to enforce the "technicalities" of the banking code because he believed his primary responsibility was to keep the banks open. His "liberal" policy negated the basic capital requirements of the banking code. During the postwar deflation of the early 1920s,

Bennett adopted the extralegal policy, which was "approved" by the state's bankers "individually and in conventions" and by Governor Walker and his predecessor, Governor Hugh M. Dorsey. By permitting the use of phony accounting practices, Bennett allowed Manley's system to operate with a negative net worth.[10]

On the other hand, Bennett blamed the legislature for refusing to provide sufficient staff to examine the more than four hundred state banks in Georgia. His complaint was contradicted by the banking code, which provided for the appointment of special examiners whose fees and expenses would be paid by the industry. Bennett admitted that his department had ignored the law by failing to examine Manley's banks on a regular basis. The problem was his lack of willpower, not a lack of manpower.[11]

Bennett relied on Manley's promise to guarantee the system with his net worth of "more than $4 million" and on unaudited financial statements prepared by bank officers. With those assurances, Bennett stood idle while Manley and his officers violated the banking code by receiving insider loans without approval from their boards of directors. He then accommodated the bankers by allowing retroactive loan approval.[12]

Groping in bureaucratic prose, Bennett denounced the legislature for refusing to grant the department additional regulatory power. He said his office lacked authority over the Bankers Trust Company because Manley's organization had killed every legislative attempt to regulate trust companies. Bennett "abandoned" the department's 1922 bill after "it met with no support" in the legislature. State bankers had told him that it was "impossible" to pass the bill because of the "peculiar conditions" that existed in Georgia. Bennett said he also proposed tough regulatory bills in 1924 and 1925, which were defeated by "strenuous opposition" from the Country Bankers Association, whose officers were members of Manley's system.[13]

Bennett did not mention that the most influential officer of the Country Bankers Association was his confidant Lorne Adams, who was also vice-president of the Bankers Trust Company. Even so, Bennett said he could have prevented the disaster if the legislature had granted his office the power to regulate trust companies. Despite his denials, Bennett had effective control over the Bankers Trust Company because he had complete regulatory power over the 134 state banking units that were affiliated with it. Indeed, the Farmers and Traders Bank, which acted as the conduit for the Bankers Trust Company, was a state bank.[14]

Between 1922 and 1924, Bennett had approved the establishment of Manley's Georgia State Bank and twenty of its branches. In an effort to consolidate control within his banking system, Manley received from Bennett the authority to form a system of branch banks in communities throughout Georgia. With full knowledge of the insolvent condition of his existing system, Bennett approved Manley's expansion plans. The grand jury rejected Bennett's theory that the superintendent of banks was simply a ceremonial post to promote the state's banking industry. Jurors believed that he could have prevented the disaster by enforcing the law.[15]

After reviewing regulatory records and listening to testimony, the grand jury found that the state's bank examiners understood the law and had repeatedly warned the superintendent about the excessive insider loans in Manley's system. Ignoring his examiners, Bennett allowed the perpetual renewal of the worthless loans, which in some cases had been on the books for fifteen years. When confronted by prosecutors, he disclaimed any specific knowledge of the examination reports. He said it was "impossible" for the superintendent to remember "the details of over 400 banks."[16]

Bennett's file of correspondence revealed that he had committed perjury. By April 1925 the Bankers Trust Company was insolvent and Bennett was urging its officers to "liquidate as many subsidiary companies as possible." In December he had a private meeting with Manley because he was "gravely concerned" about the "comatose condition" of many of the member banks. The system represented nearly a third of all the banks under his jurisdiction, and Bennett recognized that "any calamity" involving its members "would be an immeasurable disaster not only to Georgia and Florida but to the whole country." In January, Bennett asked Manley for the fourth time to submit detailed financial statements on his affiliated companies, which had borrowed millions of dollars from state banks in Georgia. Bennett told Manley that "prompt attention" was required to remove the insider loans from the banks and avoid the "necessity" of taking "radical action."[17]

Manley responded to the request in typical fashion by assuring

Bennett: "We have never had a failure among our banks in Georgia, and never will have, and I will use my own personal resources, to protect these institutions. . . . We are entitled to your confidence. . . . I am afraid you are overlooking the fact, that almost all of the notes you have inquired about, are secured by good collateral." Bennett waited more than a month to question Manley: "Up to this time no action appears to have been taken in any matters . . . we will be glad to cooperate with you in bringing these matters to a satisfactory conclusion." While the Florida frenzy was subsiding, Bennett told Adams that he felt "impelled to use the whole weight and power of his office if necessary."[18]

But Bennett "deferred action" and reached a supervisory agreement with Manley in early March "to handle the matter quietly and privately." Following Bennett's suggestion and as part of the agreement, Manley promoted Adams and John Russell, both of whom were special friends of the superintendent. Implementing the agreement, the Bankers Trust Company named Adams and Russell as vice-presidents "with authority equal to that of the president." That action, Russell later testified, meant that the operations of the company were "under the direction of the State Banking Department." Instead of removing Manley from the banks, Bennett "designated" Adams and Russell as his agents inside the trust company. After assuming their new positions on March 16, 1926, they reported to Manley that Bennett had given "the assurance of his heartiest cooperation."[19]

Bennett was gravely concerned about "the questioning and critical attitude toward the System and its officers in financial circles, both in the South and the East where he was faced with never ending questions on all occasions." He decided against taking enforcement action because it "would bring about a tremendous amount of talk and contain elements of danger and might prove destructive." Bennett reminded Adams that he had the authority to require "the elimination of any and all paper with which he was not satisfied and convinced are proper to be in banks."[20]

The supervisory agreement confirmed Bennett's power over the Bankers Trust Company, but the criminal convictions of his agents, Adams and Russell, certified his poor judgment. Beginning in the early 1920s and ending on July 13, 1926—the day of the crash—Manley's strategy was to "hold the Department off." Bennett's compliant attitude allowed the pyramid scheme to operate unrestrained for years. Though Bennett threatened "to use the whole weight and power of his office," he took no action and withheld evidence of fraud from prosecutors. His misconduct delayed the panic until creditors filed suit.[21]

GEORGIA'S MODERN BANKING CODE

In 1919, Georgia enacted a modern banking code designed to protect depositors by insulating bank regulation from politics. The heralded reform created a separate department of banking, headed by a professional superintendent of banks who was appointed by the governor. Before the new law, Georgia had an elected banking commissioner who was the state's treasurer.[22]

Georgia's bank regulatory system moved into the twentieth century because Treasurer W. J. Speer took the extraordinary political step of relinquishing power. Speer preserved his place in Georgia history by calling for a comprehensive revision: "The present laws are utterly inadequate to the proper protection of the large and annually increasing amounts of the people's money left with banks. These laws are in such a state of confusion and uncertainty, and are so unsatisfactory that their condition has been fittingly described by competent judges as being chaotic."[23]

Governor Hugh Dorsey, as chairman of the State Budget and Investigating Commission, joined with Treasurer Speer to pass the banking reform. A future governor, Attorney General Clifford Walker, a member of the Ku Klux Klan who was not known as reform-minded, was also a member of the powerful state board. In 1919, the commission informed the Georgia legislature: "The duties incumbent upon the State Treasurer take practically all of his time and leave none for the examination of banks required of him by law. . . . We recommend that provision be made for the establishment of a separate department for the examination of state banks; and a bill has been prepared for this purpose by the state bankers which has our endorsement and approval."[24]

As the appointing authority, Governor Dorsey naturally promoted the change to an appointed regulator. After losing the 1920 U.S. Senate race to Tom Watson, Dorsey became a banking lawyer. In 1926 the former governor was appointed as a receiver for the Bankers Trust Company.[25]

The banking bill could not have passed without the active support of the industry. Following the tradition of regulatory reform in the railroad industry, the bill was drafted by Orville Park, the general counsel of the Georgia Bankers Association, and lobbied through the 1919 legislative session. By changing to an appointed regulator, the "reform" had the appearance of professionalism. But by mandating that the superintendent be a member of the banking fraternity, the industry could control the professional and at the same time escape a public cry for state deposit insurance if a postwar banking disaster happened. Though the legislation granted the department of banking sweeping authority, bankers recognized that a captive regulator was a poor enforcer. Effortlessly, the consensus measure passed both chambers and was signed into law by Governor Dorsey, who appointed Bennett as the first superintendent of banks. Bennett was confirmed by the state Senate and took office on January 1, 1920.[26]

Bennett was from a banking family. His father, T. R. Bennett, Sr., was an organizer and director of the Bank of Camilla, and T. R. Bennett, Jr., was an officer and director of the bank. When appointed superintendent of banks, he was forty-eight years old. He would be the state's chief bank regulator for seven years.[27]

After the collapse of Manley's banking system, Bennett told Governor Walker: "Chain banking is fundamentally wrong, and that which is fundamentally wrong must fail." Yet throughout the 1920s Bennett favored the "Manley Chain of Banks" by approving the bank charter applications filed by that organization. For example, it was Bennett who approved the charter applications for the State Bank of Cochran in 1921, the Georgia State Bank in 1922, and the Richland State Bank in 1923. He also approved branch applications of the Georgia State Bank in twenty Georgia communities. The three banks and all twenty branches failed during the panic of 1926.[28]

Bennett eagerly approved the applications despite warnings from his bank examiners about the unsound chain banking system. He also allowed troubled member banks to continue operating after a dangerous impairment of capital. In January 1926 the Bank of Powder Springs filed an application to reduce its capital, which reflected serious loan losses. Instead of seizing the bank or requiring the stockholders to inject additional equity, Bennett authorized a 40 percent reduction of capital from $25,000 to $15,000. The Bank of Powder Springs failed on July 14, 1926.[29]

Under Georgia's modern code, Bennett had the authority to investigate the applicants for a bank charter and to deny applications if necessary. The superintendent of banks could request from the organizers any information which he "desired" to review. It was the "duty" of the organizers to supply the superintendent with the requested information. If depositors' money could not be "safely entrusted" to a group of organizers, Bennett was required to deny the application.[30]

The superintendent also had broad discretion in considering applications for branch banks. Because of its impaired capital, the Georgia State Bank failed to meet the test for branching. The capital requirements for a branch office were the same as those for a new bank. Bennett could deny any application if he deemed that "public convenience and advantage" would not be "promoted" by the establishment of the proposed branch office.[31]

Bennett later explained that the code did not grant the Department of Banking the power to appraise loans and that the department was not a credit agency. He flatly stated that the directors were solely responsible for determining the condition of state banks. Again he misrepresented the law. Georgia's code granted the superintendent and the department all-inclusive powers to regulate state banks. All state banks had to be examined at least twice every year. During each examination, the examiner had to determine the "true condition" of the bank, the lending and investment policies of management, the cashier's procedures for keeping the books, the conduct of the board of directors, "the safety and prudence of its management," and the managers' compliance with the department's regulations.[32]

The superintendent had wide latitude to conduct special examinations of any state bank to protect the public. In his sole discretion, Bennett could send in examiners if he believed "the management and condition of the bank [was] such as to render an examination of its affairs necessary or expedient." The code mandated that the superintendent investigate any bank that was operating in an unsafe manner.[33]

The legislature granted to the superintendent and his examiners the power to compel sworn testimony of "any person" in connection with the examination of a state bank. Bennett had the authority to take the depositions of Manley and any of the officers, directors, borrowers, and depositors of member banks in the chain banking system.[34]

If examiners discovered unsound loans and investments in a state bank, the superintendent could order the bank to divest those assets. If the president of the bank refused, Bennett had the authority to remove him from office for operating the bank in a "reckless" manner. The rarely used power to remove officers and directors may have been the most effective enforcement weapon in his arsenal.[35]

Bennett had the ultimate power to institute a proceeding for forfeiture of a bank charter. He could "take possession of all the assets and business" of any state bank that violated the department's regulations, operated in an "unsafe" manner, or had lost more than 10 percent of its capital. He had abundant authority to regulate the Manley system of banks in Georgia. If he had been concerned about the investments of Georgia banks in the Florida land boom, he could have halted that speculation long before the crash.[36]

FAVORITISM AND LIQUIDATIONS

Bennett offered no apology for his failure to enforce the banking code. Indeed, he blamed the ignorance of depositors for his troubles. He complained that "the average depositor who lost his money in institutions which were forced to suspend business does not understand how the Department operates." Uninformed depositors had "censured" the department when they should have denounced the legislature for establishing "preferences and priorities," which consumed the assets of the failed banks and left little for individual depositors.[37]

Jurors held a different view of the victims of the catastrophe. After hearing testimony from helpless depositors, they appreciated the human tragedy of the crash. Witnesses from "every walk of life" testified that the bank failures had caused "the crippling of business, loss of widows' and orphans' funds, and life savings of now aged people." The grand jury determined that bankers and regulators, not the depositors, were responsible for the calamity.[38]

Depositors had a reason to be dismayed by the priorities of claims established by the Georgia banking code. Their injury was compounded by a law skillfully drafted by liquidation lawyers. It discriminated against depositors by forming special classes of creditors. Before depositors were paid on a proportional basis, the following expenses and liabilities had to be satisfied in full: the cost of liquidation, including the fees of receivers, attorneys, and agents; secured judgments and debts; assets held by the bank as trustee; and taxes due to the Internal Revenue Service, the state of Georgia, or any county, district, or municipality of the state.[39]

Park, the author of the banking code and chief defender of Bennett, was a primary beneficiary of the statutory class of creditors. Bennett appointed Park and his law firm as the liquidation lawyers for more than eighty defunct banks in Georgia. Their legal fees had to be paid in full before depositors could receive proportional payments.[40]

Circuit Judge D. A. R. Crum of Cordele, however, issued an order denying Park's fees because they were "excessive." Park and his associates had charged a $1,000 retainer for each of the eighty banks that they represented. In addition to the $80,000, Bennett petitioned the various circuit courts to approve Park's fees of 10 percent of collections and for other fees deemed necessary. Judge Crum protected the depositors of three defunct banks in his circuit by rejecting the excessive liquidation expenses.[41]

Park's fees and the Department of Banking became major issues in the hotly contested governor's race of 1926. Bennett was criticized for failing to regulate Manley's banks and for allowing "exorbitant" liquidation expenses. Even with the state's appointed regulator, politics was always only one step away.

THE GEORGIA GOVERNOR'S RACE

The scandal was fully debated during the gubernatorial campaign of 1926 because the Georgia legislature—unlike the Florida legislature—had granted to the chief executive the power to dismiss the superintendent of banks. When four of the state's best-known politicians qualified for the Democratic primary, the banking issue was assured of receiving the level of media exposure that it deserved.

The candidates were Dr. Lamartine Griffin Hardman, John N. Holder, chairman of the state highway commission, state representative J. O. Wood of Fulton, and George H. Carswell of Wilkinson. Hardman won the September primary with a slim lead over Holder. Hardman, running as the businessman's candidate, pledged to investigate the banking department and strengthen the state banking code.[42]

Hardman was a surgeon, gentleman farmer, and banker. He was president of the First National Bank of Commerce, Georgia. At age seventy, he enjoyed statewide name recognition after serving for many years in the Georgia General Assembly. As a state representative and state senator, he sponsored many laws, including the creation of the state highway board and the state board of health. Yet Hardman's popularity derived from his sponsorship of the Georgia prohibition law of 1908.[43]

John Holder of Jefferson was also an influential politician. Holder, formerly a member of the state legislature, had as his power base his chairmanship of the highway department. During the campaign, Hardman accused Holder of turning the highway department into a political machine.[44]

With seventy-five of the state's counties in the throes of a financial calamity, Holder made Bennett the central issue in the runoff election. In an unrelenting assault, he denounced the system of "parasites" which allowed the governor's cronies to extract exorbitant fees from insolvent banks. Launching the attack in counties suffering from bank liquidations, he charged that Bennett's receivers, attorneys, and auditors were "milking dry the depositors' moneys."[45]

Holder criticized Governor Walker, who was supporting Hardman, for ignoring the grand jury findings of Bennett's gross negligence. He declared that the banking crisis occurred because the weak regulator refused to enforce the law. He promised, if elected, to fire Bennett and "clear out" the banking department.[46]

To stop Holder's momentum, the Hardman campaign labeled him a hypocrite who represented the problem not the solution. Hardman assailed Holder for using the highway department as a "monstrous vehicle of graft and corruption." He allegedly deposited $21,000 of state funds in a non-interest-bearing account at an insolvent bank in Union County for the "sole purpose" of promoting his campaign. Holder carried Union County in the first primary, but the state lost money when the bank failed.[47]

Hardman, the banker, enjoyed the active support of the banking industry. Even so, he assured voters that he could best reform the banking system. Following Bennett's advice, he pledged to launch his own investigation of the banking department as soon as he was inaugurated. But he emphasized that his "business-like" administration would revive the state's crippled economy.[48]

Hardman's strategy worked. Hoping for good roads and full employment, voters elected him by a landslide. He defeated Holder in the runoff election by a two-to-one margin, carrying 110 counties. Holder carried only 51 counties. Hardman received 80,925 popular votes to Holder's 60,244. Hardman's winning of the Democratic primary meant that he would become governor in the one-party state.[49]

Bennett resigned soon after the election. He said his "health had been shattered" by the ordeal. Outgoing governor Walker distanced himself from his disgraced regulator. He explained that Governor Dorsey had originally appointed Bennett, and he had reappointed him because of the urging of the banking community. In fairness to Bennett, Walker said he had tried to stop Manley from engaging in the "wild speculative Florida situation."[50]

In his resignation letter, Bennett accused irresponsible politicians for his problems. The concerns of depositors had been "artificially multiplied by political strife." He said the politicians had damaged the banking industry, whereas his actions had always been in its best interests. His remedy for a regulatory system permeated with politics was to relinquish government supervision over the banking industry. After the inauguration of a new governor, the former regulator's ideas of deregulation failed to gain serious consideration.[51]

To the end, Bennett refused to criticize any banker. Even after the indictment and conviction of Manley and his partners, he refused to acknowledge the bank fraud conspiracy. He blamed the Florida recession, the people of Georgia, and the legislature for the disaster. In his final banking report he philosophized about business cycles and delivered a postmortem: "Deflation followed inflation just as night follows day."[52]

PART III

The Aftermath:
Indictments, Bankruptcies, and Lawyers

Using their influence to exploit the panic, U.S. Vice-President Charles G. Dawes and his brothers gained control of the assets of the Mizner Development Corporation, leaving its debts for the bankruptcy court. *Front:* Rufus and Charles. *Back:* Beman and Henry. (Courtesy of the Evanston Historical Society, Evanston, Illinois)

7

THE MAD
BANKER

After violent bank runs shocked Georgia's banking system, state and federal prosecutors quickly indicted W. D. Manley for orchestrating the elaborate bank fraud conspiracy. The prosecution of the South's most influential banker threatened to expose his secret dealings with the rich and powerful of the region. A few weeks earlier he had been treated with the reverence that great fortunes command. Now, with subpoenas being served on prominent bankers, the banking community rushed to blame its fallen colleague and to disclaim any responsibility for the disaster.[1]

Pointing well-manicured fingers at Manley, the bankers who had been members of his system swore that they knew nothing about the fraud and insider abuse. Prosecutors had solid evidence, however, that they were concealing their own involvement. Authorities knew that they had enjoyed the profits and ignored the problems of Manley's system for years. Yet prosecutors limited the scope of their inquiry and settled for merely taking action against the most visible culprit.

Manley's internal memorandums proved that his associates had decided the profits outweighed the risks. In January 1923, John

Russell, an officer of the Bankers Trust Company, reported to Manley after visiting with member bankers in the Northeast: "Very few of them want to cancel our contracts, because it has been profitable to them, and since I told them last October that we were voluntarily going to quit unless we could stop being harassed constantly, they seem to have been doing some figuring, and if we can hold the [comptroller of the currency's examiners] off them somewhat, we will probably have many years of connection with them yet, with a few exceptions."[2]

The bankers remained affiliated with Manley after the comptroller of the currency's examiners had "severely criticized practically everything" from the Bankers Trust Company. Member banks continued to make unsecured loans with Manley's company although previous loans had not been reduced in years. They withstood "lots of embarrassment" from bank examiners because Manley withheld the financial statement of the Bankers Trust Company. Instead, he sent participating banks "an unsigned condensed statement" of the Farmers and Traders Bank of Atlanta, which was "written on plain paper, not certified to by an authorized officer of the bank." Examiners considered the bogus financial statement "a joke." Despite being "warned" that they would be held "*personally* responsible," the bankers continued to send unsecured loans and deposits to Atlanta. They refused "to give up the profits," which represented as much as 50 percent of a member bank's earnings, so they stayed with the system until its collapse.[3]

Atlanta solicitor John Boykin ignored the complicity of the affiliated bankers. He accepted their offer and allowed their attorneys to assist in the prosecution of Manley. With their private attorneys sitting at the table with prosecutors, the bankers were shielded from prosecution. The integrity of Boykin's investigation came into question because his private law firm, Austin and Boykin, accepted the representation of banks that had been members of the Manley system.[4]

The worthless insider loans of Manley and his partners were estimated at $12,796,569. If prosecutors were correct and $30 million was missing, then affiliated bankers were responsible for more than $17.2 million of additional worthless loans. Prosecutors and regulators allowed many of these culpable bankers to reorganize and operate their banks for several more years until they failed again. One of Manley's associates, Clarence M. Gay, who had worked for the Bankers Trust Company and supervised the Orlando Bank and Trust Company, a member bank that collapsed because of insider abuse, became the comptroller of Florida.[5]

BANKRUPTCY PROCEEDINGS

Depositors ran to get their money after the Bank of Umatilla, Florida, filed an involuntary bankruptcy petition against the Bankers Trust Company, which accused Manley of fraud. During the bankruptcy proceedings, Manley, who suffered a "nervous collapse" after testifying, provided a rare glimpse into the financial world.[6]

After his banking system nearly collapsed in the early 1920s, Manley had taken steps to insulate his assets. His banks survived the postwar deflation through the use of creative accounting and the forbearance of Superintendent Bennett. Realizing that his system was insolvent, in 1921 Manley bought the Pace's Ferry estate and put the title in his wife's name. She later testified that she had purchased the property with her own money, but all of the payments came out of her husband's checking account. On June 7, 1926, Manley's secretary signed another check on that account making a $10,000 principal reduction on the estate.[7]

On the night of July 7, 1926, as Manley huddled with his wife, secretary, and lawyer at his "fashionable" Pace's Ferry mansion, he desperately tried to preserve part of his empire. There was no time to spare. During the past ten days affiliated banks in Palm Beach and Miami had collapsed, and in another week his Georgia banks would crash. Sitting at the desk in his study, he convened back-to-back meetings of the stockholders and board of directors of W. D. Manley and Company, Inc., at which the company was activated so that it could hold property. He was trying to remove his most valuable assets, which had a face value of $781,936, from the reach of his creditors.[8]

The previous day Manley had met with his lawyer, Herbert J. Haas, to organize the company and effectuate the transfers. Haas represented several of Manley's insolvent companies: the Farmers and Traders Bank, Morningside Park, Inc., Bankers Security Company, Avondale Company, and United Realty Corporation. He was also the lawyer for James R. Smith, Manley's partner, who would soon commit suicide. After receiving stocks, bonds, and notes, Haas drafted the necessary instruments for his client's signature. He then placed the securities in a safe deposit box at the Fourth National Bank of Atlanta and prepared minutes and resolutions for the hastily called meetings.[9]

During the special stockholders' meeting, the Manleys elected themselves and Lena Long, his longtime secretary, to the board of directors. The board then convened and appointed Manley as the president, Mrs. Manley as the vice-president and treasurer, and Long as the secretary of the company. Manley, alert but nervous, followed the legal procedures and confirmed the transfer of assets into the company. Although the securities and real estate were in his sole name, minutes of the meetings would reflect that Mrs. Manley had been the joint owner of the assets.[10]

Manley also tried to preserve his winnings in the stock market. For years he had speculated on Wall Street by trading his margin accounts at Livingston & Company and Swartwout & Appenzellar, two New York City brokerage firms. Immediately after the crash, Manley instructed Livingston & Company to sell shares of American Express, American Hide & Leather Company, and other listed companies, which had a market value of $180,101. He had also withdrawn $25,405 from Swartwout & Appenzellar during 1926. While prosecutors and creditors closed ranks, he sent Swartwout & Appenzellar the following telegram: "Send check for balance direct to Valeria R. Manley, Pace's Ferry Road, Atlanta, Georgia." Mrs. Manley would later claim that the trading account had been part of her inheritance.[11]

The "midnight" transfers did not go unnoticed. The receiver for the Bank of Dania, Florida, which had been controlled by Manley and Anthony, filed suit to freeze Manley's personal assets. The complaint charged that he had devised a scheme "for the purpose of hindering, delaying and defrauding his creditors." It accused him of hiding assets in W. D. Manley and Company, which was nothing more than a dummy corporation. The receiver was trying to recover nearly $500,000 of loans and deposits that had been sent to Atlanta. After holding an emergency hearing, Fulton County Superior Court judge Edgar E. Pomeroy issued a restraining order freezing Manley's personal assets. Then Federal District judge Samuel H. Sibley nullified the transfer of assets and deposited them with the court-appointed receivers.[12]

Manley's manipulations generated expensive litigation as lawyers in four states ground out billable hours. Representing banks in Florida, Georgia, New Jersey, and New York, they filed lawsuits to collect millions of dollars in delinquent loans and frozen deposits. They also sued to recover insurance benefits under the Depositors Guarantee Fund. Banks had joined the chain system to gain the competitive edge. The private deposit insurance fund had given its members an advertising theme: "This bank is a member. Its depositors cannot lose." The marketing pitch was used on signs, stationery, brochures, and in the newspaper. Membership in the system, once a great advantage, became a disastrous liability when its highly advertised insurance fund paid depositors nothing.[13]

Civil suits to recover ill-gotten gains were as ineffectual as criminal prosecutions. For example, the receiver of the Bank of Coconut Grove, Florida, which had been controlled by Anthony, sued the Farmers and Traders Bank to recover deposits of $127,000. The receiver accused Manley and the other officers of the Farmers and Traders Bank of converting deposits for their personal use. The litigation revealed that the Atlanta bank had stopped paying interest in December 1925. Nevertheless, Anthony's board of directors took no legal action before the bank failed on July 1, 1926.[14]

After nearly four years of complex litigation, a Fulton County jury awarded a $14,000 judgment to the Bank of Coconut Grove. Because the court treated its deposits as a trust liability, the Bank of Coconut Grove received preference and moved ahead of the individual depositors of the Farmers and Traders Bank. But the bank had to stand in line behind the Internal Revenue Service, the state of Georgia, Fulton County, and the receiver's expenses. When the litigation finally ended and the lawyers on both sides were paid, depositors at the Bank of Coconut Grove were in no better shape than their counterparts in Georgia.[15]

Receivers and lawyers of Manley's bankrupt estate spent three years tracking down his personal assets, but they collected only $299,712. Not all of the money was lost in speculative ventures or squandered on extravagant life-styles. Receivers paid themselves $10,637, the lawyers $63,441, and the Internal Revenue Service $92,020 for Manley's back taxes. The remaining creditors of the purported multimillionaire had to divide the paltry sum of $128,180. Through a compromise worked out with their receivers, the Manleys were allowed to keep the sixty-two-acre estate on Pace's Ferry Road and their Cadillac limousine. But Manley was forced to sell his Rolls-Royce.[16]

THE FIRST INSANITY PLEA

The Manley case became a "G-man adventure" story when J. Edgar Hoover took extralegal steps to jail the former banker. The spectacle began when Manley asserted the defense of insanity in his first state criminal case. Maneuvering to prevent a trial on the merits, his defense team filed a petition for a writ of lunacy. It claimed that he was mentally incompetent and unable to assist in his defense and requested that Mrs. Manley be appointed as his guardian. His lawyers told the court that the stress of a public trial would kill him.[17]

Recognizing that the sudden declaration of insanity would create a credibility problem, the "former financial genius" sought refuge at the Piedmont Sanitarium in Atlanta. His lawyers said his current mental illness resulted from a brain hemorrhage he had suffered four and a half years earlier. Supposedly, his condition had improved while the business ran smoothly, but the crash had a "disastrous effect" on his health. The defense created a dilemma by using the insanity plea. It delayed the prosecution but jeopardized the transfers to W. D. Manley and Company.[18]

Solicitor Boykin vigorously opposed the insanity petition and vowed to press for more indictments. His assistant was one of the three members on the lunacy commission, and Boykin was allowed to turn the guardianship hearing into a circus by inviting creditors to attend. The prosecutor created mass hysteria by announcing that the claims of depositors and other creditors would be worthless if the court adjudicated Manley as insane.[19]

Mrs. Manley was the leading witness at the insanity hearing. She testified that her husband had acted "queer" for fourteen years. Late at night and dressed in pajamas, he often walked through his exclusive neighborhood. When she went looking for him, he would hide in the bushes. After the demise of his banking empire, the bizarre behavior took a violent turn. She said he threatened to hire a hit man to murder W. S. Witham, his former partner. Sounding as eccentric as her husband, she told the commission that she was forced to sleep in the hall with the butler or chauffeur standing guard.[20]

Under cross-examination, she admitted her husband handled the finances for the family. She testified that he was a skillful speculator in real estate and in the stock market. Her testimony contradicted the assertion that he could not manage his own affairs or assist in his defense. Manley had been disturbed about the marriage of his youngest daughter. In the bankruptcy proceedings, his secretary had testified that he was thrown "off the track" when his daughter eloped. Apparently the family's embarrassment prevented this crucial testimony from being used during the lunacy proceedings.[21]

Manley's longtime partner, Paul J. Baker, testified for the government. He had been the treasurer of the Bankers Trust Company and had worked with Manley for twenty-five years. He was also a vice-president and director of the Farmers and Traders Bank. Throughout their long association, he never thought Manley was "mentally unsound." Manley was consumed by speculation in the stock market and Florida, yet he found time to review every letter that left the office. Baker's theory for his strange behavior was his fear of going to jail. On the eve of the crash, regulators had threatened to prosecute him if the banking chain collapsed because of his insider deals.[22]

Carl N. Davie, an attorney representing the state banking department, argued that 110,000 depositors in eighty-three Georgia communities were suffering because Manley had looted their banks. He asked the commission why Manley should be afforded the "luxuries" and "comfort" of a private sanitarium "while poor people, whose life savings had been swept away in the bank failures, did not have even the necessaries of life." Former governor Dorsey, a receiver and attorney for the defunct Bankers Trust Company, reinforced that Manley had lived "in the lap of luxury" after depositors had "poured in their money" to his banks. In an impassioned closing argument, he declared that the insanity plea was "pure bunk," a desperate attempt to escape liability. Dorsey concluded that if Manley was declared insane, depositors would suffer ruinous losses. In less than two hours of deliberation, the lunacy commission unanimously pronounced Manley sane. After the ploy failed, the full weight of the judicial system fell on him and his partners.[23]

The Fulton County grand jury immediately issued multiple indictments against Manley, Baker, whose cooperation failed to mitigate the charges, John Russell and Lorne Adams, the vice-presidents of the Bankers Trust Company who acted as Bennett's agents, and Joseph Sasser, the senior vice-president of the company. They were accused of misappropriating deposits from 120 member banks in Florida, Georgia, New Jersey, and New York. Jurors charged that they had defrauded depositors by enticing them to insolvent banks with false claims of deposit insurance. Manley was separately indicted for engaging in a multibank check-kiting scheme and stealing a $50,000 promissory note. Although tens of millions of dollars were missing, Manley was allowed to return to his mansion after posting a $100,000 bond.[24]

A SPECIAL PLEA

Manley hired an army of lawyers to battle the prosecutors and creditors. Setting a precedent for the savings and loan operators of the 1980s, Manley paid significant retainers to his lawyers just before declaring bankruptcy. He paid $6,000 to Herbert Haas, the lawyer for W. D. Manley and Company; $10,000 for the services of Arthur G. Powell and Marion Smith of Little, Powell, Smith and Goldstein; $3,000 to Smith, Hammond and Smith; and $1,000 to Paul S. Etheridge. He also retained Walter Colquitt and Ben J. Conyers of Colquitt and Conyers and J. A. Branch of Branch and Howard. The prominent Atlanta lawyers delayed their client's incarceration at each step of the process. After losing the petition of lunacy, they attacked the initial indictment on the grounds that the Georgia banking code violated the state's constitution. Judge G. H. Howard denied the motion, and Manley's lawyers immediately filed an appeal with the Georgia Supreme Court.[25]

Manley had the resources to belabor his due process rights and used the defense of insanity in each criminal case. His prepaid lawyers sidetracked the new indictments by entering a special plea of insanity for the still formidable banker. A special plea of insanity compelled the selection of a separate jury, in lieu of the three-member lunacy commission, to determine the competency of Manley to stand for trial.[26]

Finding an impartial judge and jury was difficult because so many Georgians were touched by the catastrophe. Before the insanity trial began, Judge Howard announced that he might disqualify himself because his relatives owned stock in the Bank of Cusseta, a member of the Manley system that failed during the panic. After conferring with lawyers from both bitter sides, Howard decided to conduct the trial despite his family's business relationship with Manley. The reluctance of Manley's lawyers to object was a strategic blunder.[27]

Selecting the twelve-member insanity jury was tedious and time-consuming. Eighty potential jurors were examined by the lawyers. To eliminate those biased toward Manley, thousands of names of depositors and stockholders of member banks were read in the courtroom. Prosecutors and defense lawyers questioned the potential jurors about their connections with the failed banks. The defense team also probed for any relationship with the 119 banks that had contributed to a fund established to aid the prosecution.[28]

After the jury was selected, Manley, only fifty-two years old, played the role of the deranged financier who had been driven over the edge by the collapse of his far-flung empire. The jury saw a "gray-haired, emaciated, bespectacled, cane tapping" man, who sat staring at the courtroom floor. Throughout the proceedings, his face twitched constantly, and "occasionally his body would jerk in a terrific convulsion that would almost throw him from the chair."[29]

Mrs. Manley looked like the stoical wife who cared deeply for her poor husband but who knew that he had lost his mind. Struggling to salvage her world, she gave a performance that rose to a new level of absurdity. She testified under oath that since 1913 her husband had suffered from "spells" that caused him to beat on their bedroom walls at night. During one of these "hallucinations," he screamed that their lawn was "covered with blood." Tormented by fears of prosecution and ruin, he had threatened to commit suicide by jumping into a neighborhood lake. Appealing to the churchgoing jurors, Mrs. Manley said she became convinced of his insanity when he renounced faith in God. He suddenly began to use profanity and told her there was no God. He said he had seen heaven and nothing was there except an "ash can." Everybody who went there ended up in the trash heap. He had gained his insights into life after death by talking to his dead mother.[30]

The defense also tried to persuade jurors with high-paid expert witnesses. The "star witness" was Dr. Smith Ely Jelliffe of New York, whose testimony had saved several murderers from the electric chair. The renowned psychiatrist testified that Manley had "arteriosclerosis dementia in an advanced form." He said the condition could not be feigned "any more than you can measles or pneumonia, any more than you could make the moon." The most ludicrous testimony was presented by Dr. Barnes E. Sale, an x-ray expert. He showed the jury photographs of Manley's brain and explained that the "grooves" in his skull had "enlarged considerably" since 1922. But on cross-examination Sale admitted that he was unqualified to evaluate how the condition might affect Manley's state of mind. Assistant Solicitor Reuben Arnold retorted that the insanity defense was "a rotten fake." He declared in his closing argument: "It is the fake of a man who has functioned in this community for 52 years, who conducted many business enterprises and who made a great deal of money, with no one knowing he was crazy except his wife. Fifty-two years of saneness and 30 days of insanity."[31]

Although some doubts may have remained, the jury found Manley sane after deliberating for less than two hours. Judge Howard then ordered Manley to stand trial on the first of eighteen pending charges, which dealt with the fraudulent insolvency of the Farmers and Traders Bank of Atlanta. After numerous delays he was finally scheduled to face a jury of his peers.[32]

THE STATE TRIAL OF MANLEY

The insanity jury was disbanded and the laborious process of impaneling a new jury commenced. Prosecutors and defense lawyers eliminated five prospective panels. The twelve jurors who were selected had little in common with the defendant. They represented the middle class, not the leisure class: a plumber, a machinist, a fertilizer salesman, a carpenter, a candy maker, a florist, a restaurant manager, an optician, a bookkeeper, two cashiers, and a businessman.[33]

The prosecution had to convince them, beyond a reasonable doubt, that Manley caused the insolvency of the Farmers and Traders Bank by operating it in a fraudulent manner. The state's first witness, R. E. Bentley, an auditor, told the jury that Manley had used the bank as "a clearing house for kiting purposes." After conducting an "exhaustive audit," he documented that worthless loans to insiders had rendered the bank insolvent since 1915. Most of the bad loans were unsecured credits to the bank's officers and directors or to their dummy companies.[34]

Bentley found that the deposits of the Farmers and Traders Bank and the other chain banks were backed by a bogus insurance fund. He testified that the Bankers Trust Company, the agent of the insurance fund and the holding company for many of the Georgia and Florida banks, had been insolvent for years. Throughout the 1920s it had been losing about $100,000 a year and now faced a decade of liquidation proceedings. Depositors had been lured into system banks by false advertising.[35]

Prosecutors then called to the stand R. E. Lewis, the cashier of the Farmers and Traders Bank. He described Manley's practice of overdrawing his personal accounts and the accounts of his private companies. He withdrew $90,000, nearly four times the bank's capital, a month before it failed. Manley, the bank's president, simply took the money without signing a note or leaving any collateral. Insider abuse had wiped out the bank's capital long before Lewis became its cashier in 1925. The bank carried an extraordinary level of "worthless" loans on its books. The loans had remained in the bank for as long as sixteen years. Georgia's bank regulators reviewed the same bad loans during each examination and never required that they be charged off the books. The condition of the bank deteriorated until 55 percent of its assets were worthless, more than twelve times its capital.[36]

Clifford Cagle, an auditor in the Justice Department, testified that the Farmers and Traders Bank had collapsed after making "last-minute" wire transfers to other banks owned by Manley and his partners. Demand deposits of $422,000 from member banks in Florida had been funneled to the bank by the Bankers Trust Company. All of those deposits, with the exception of $6,000, were moved out of the Atlanta bank before it closed on July 12, 1926. At the end, Manley's lead bank was nothing but a shell.[37]

Carl Davie, the attorney for the state banking department, was called as a witness and confirmed that worthless insider loans caused the collapse of the chain banking system. The refusal of Manley and his partners to pay personal loans and to return demand deposits provoked the legal action that triggered the panic.[38]

The most damaging testimony came from Paul Baker, the treasurer of the Bankers Trust Company and vice-president of the

Farmers and Traders Bank. Continuing to cooperate with prosecutors, Baker admitted that member banks were defrauded when their deposits were commingled at the Farmers and Traders Bank. He said that Manley "ordered" him to place the $422,000 from Florida banks in the checking account of the Bankers Trust Company. Baker swore that he had "objected" to the commingling: "I told him that it wasn't right, but he declared that he would make it right." While Baker was grilled during the cross-examination, Manley, with a dazed look on his face but understanding the impact of his partner's testimony, collapsed and was carried to the judge's chambers.[39]

After the state rested, defense lawyers embraced the risky strategy of calling no witnesses. They argued that the prosecutors had failed to prove beyond a reasonable doubt that Manley had defrauded depositors. The insider dealings followed generally accepted practice in the banking industry. With a large crowd packing the courtroom, Ben Conyers, the eloquent defense lawyer, told the jury that the accused would come clean and "surrender every stick and stone of his property to make up the deficit of these banks."[40]

Boykin did not accept the rhetorical offer. In his closing argument, he proclaimed that Manley had clearly committed fraud and that "Georgia's system of justice was on trial." The ambitious prosecutor insisted that the banker be jailed for "not even 10 seconds under 10 years."[41]

The strategy of the high-powered defense team backfired. After three hours of deliberations, the jury declared Manley guilty of bank fraud. Judge Howard, whose relatives lost their investment in the Bank of Cusseta, sentenced him to serve between nine and ten years at "hard labor" in the state penitentiary. His lawyers immediately filed a motion for a new trial, and he was released after posting a reduced bond of $25,000. After the denial of the new trial, an appeal was filed with the supreme court of Georgia, which upheld the conviction in 1928. Fighting to stay out of state prison, Manley then filed an appeal with the United States Supreme Court.[42]

Meanwhile, Boykin attempted to bring Manley to trial on the outstanding indictments, but his lawyers successfully argued that a new trial would kill him. Judge N. B. Moore ordered yet another medical examination of Manley, who was now residing at a private sanitarium in Milledgeville, Georgia. His medical experts and lawyers frustrated prosecutors and delayed the state trial indefinitely.[43]

THE FEDERAL TRIAL OF THE ATLANTA PARTNERS

While his lawyers kept the state at bay, a federal grand jury in Atlanta began investigating Manley and his partners for using the U.S. postal system to advance their bank fraud scheme. Affiliated bankers throughout Georgia[44] and Florida[45] received subpoenas commanding them to appear before the grand jury.[46]

In September 1926, the federal grand jury issued a twenty-count indictment against Manley, Sasser, Baker, Adams, and Russell for using the mails to defraud member banks in Florida, Georgia, and New Jersey. The indictment charged that they induced banks to join the Depositors Guarantee Fund, which they managed as the board of trustees. While advertising that depositors were protected by "disinterested trustees," Manley and his partners had allegedly bilked the insurance fund.[47]

Manley's defense team used the same procedural tactics in federal court that they had used in state court. They filed a plea of insanity and a motion for continuance, claiming that a rigorous federal trial would kill the defendant. After his lawyers convinced District Judge Sibley to grant a continuance, Manley enjoyed a three-year reprieve. His Atlanta partners, however, were forced to face a local jury in February 1927, when the emotions of the community still ran high.[48]

During the trial of the partners, prosecutors demonstrated that the self-dealing at the Bankers Trust Company was not limited to Manley. H. E. Rank, a government auditor, testified that the lesser-known officers had abused their relationship with member banks by procuring personal loans. On the day of the crash, Baker had outstanding loans of $64,713 with member banks, Adams had loans of $37,906, and Russell had loans of $32,800. They had used the Bankers Trust Company, which had borrowed $194,700 from member banks, to funnel money into their private ventures. The auditor described some of their stale loans, which had been renewed as many as twelve times without the reduction of any principal.[49]

Prosecutors presented internal memorandums that showed the defendants had acted in concert with Manley. For example, John

Russell, who was promoted to vice-president of the Bankers Trust Company at the urging of Superintendent Bennett, told Manley in 1923: "A careful study should be made at once, with a view of immediately changing as near as possible all the notes we have at each bank. This can largely be accomplished by switching from Florida and other places notes to the East which have never been there, and switching notes from the East to Florida and other places. . . . The switching process should show the notes now held in the East actually 'paid' and not swapped, and no note should be renewed at the same place more than twice."[50]

The trial revealed that the Bankers Trust Company had operated in a fraudulent manner for more than a decade. George O. King testified that in 1915, when he was twenty years old, he worked at the Bankers Trust Company as a $63-a-month secretary for Baker. Baker and J. R. Smith, whose suicide thwarted his indictment, asked King to sign notes of $55,000 as part of a series of phony real estate transactions. The notes were sold to member banks and used to pay off loans of the Georgia Realty Company, an insolvent entity owned by Manley, Baker, and Smith. King made no payments on the notes and did not receive title to the lots that supposedly created the obligations. The fictitious notes were renewed every six months for three years and then "paid" by the substitution of identical notes of the Georgia Farm Loan Company, an insolvent subsidiary of the Bankers Trust Company.[51]

When the Bankers Trust Company collapsed, member banks held $280,706 in worthless notes of the Georgia Realty Company, which at the time had a negative net worth of $131,256. Rank, the auditor, compared the loan files of the Bankers Trust Company and the financial statements of the Georgia Farm Loan Company and discovered that the latter was nearly as deep in debt as the Georgia Realty Company. He testified that the Georgia Farm Loan Company had been insolvent since the early 1920s and had issued false financial statements for at least five years to conceal its condition. By the summer of 1925 the Georgia Farm Loan Company had a negative net worth of $93,199. Even so, the defendants continued to peddle its worthless promissory notes to member banks, and on July 13, 1926, the Georgia Farm Loan Company owed $228,900 to the Manley system.[52]

To prove the mail fraud case, the prosecution called to the stand the officers of member banks. Their testimony produced images of a high-flying world of finance in which new notes were swapped for old ones as business was conducted by a handshake. Prosecutors questioned E. M. Webster, who became the cashier and vice-president of the Fidelity Bank of New Smyrna, Florida, after forming a partnership with J. R. Anthony. He was asked why his bank had frequently renewed a $5,000 loan to the Georgia Farm Loan Company, when the only collateral was a $5,000 note of the Georgia Realty Company. He said the officers and directors of the bank "made no investigation of the value of the paper or the security behind it when it was accepted, but that it was accepted upon the confidence they had in W. D. Manley and J. R. Anthony."[53]

It had been an exciting autumn day for New Smyrna in 1917 when the Fidelity Bank announced its affiliation with the Bankers Financing Company of Jacksonville. Anthony was on hand to declare: "The Bankers Financing Company acts as financial agent for the institution and their connection with the bank is equivalent to its taking in a $20,000,000 partner. It is associated with some 48 of the most successful and progressive banks in the state. . . . The local bank now gets the advantage of its backing, its statewide connections, its progressive methods and rigid examinations, and, above all, the factor of safety for depositors. Its deposits are insured. In 28 years no depositor has ever lost a dollar in one of these banks and there are some 170 institutions associated with the system in the states of Florida, Georgia, New York and New Jersey." Anthony assured the depositors of New Smyrna that their bank was "backed by unlimited funds for any legitimate banking needs." After the Manley-Anthony system collapsed and the Fidelity Bank failed, depositors discovered that it had sounded too good to be true.[54]

Instead of serving "legitimate banking needs," Manley and his partners used the brokerage facilities to procure loans for their desk-drawer corporations. For example, the Amortization Corporation, which had assumed the liabilities of the Parker Motor Company, Manley's insolvent automobile dealership, owed $880,235 to member banks. The Amortization Corporation's paper also was used to secure loans of $96,750 for the Bankers Security Company, $93,800 for the United Realty Corporation, $79,500 for the Bankers Financing Company, and $32,250 for the Georgia Farm Loan Company. The obligations of the Amortization Corporation included loan guarantees of $84,500 for personal loans of Manley and his partners.[55]

The rift between Manley's two sets of partners became public during the trial. Sasser testified that he had become "suspicious" as early as 1920 that Manley and Anthony were diverting assets to their private companies in Florida. Russell confirmed that "certain assets of the Bankers Financing Company, which had become very valuable, and which the Bankers Trust Company, on account of its ownership of stock should have participated in, had been sold to other companies for a song." The dispute came to a head after the Atlanta partners hired the accounting firm of Ernst and Ernst to determine if "assets had been diverted from the proper channels." The audit verified that Manley and Anthony had engaged in "the switching of assets from one company to another which did not appear on the books nor was it shown just what each respective party owned."[56]

A showdown occurred on May 14, 1926, at the pivotal meeting in Anthony's Jacksonville office. Using Comptroller Amos's presence and influence to gain the upper hand, Anthony negotiated with Manley a one-sided formula for dividing their interests. Under the deal, Manley would make a $1 million payment to the Bankers Trust Company as "restitution" for the diverted assets. Anthony was to surrender his stock in the Bankers Financing Company, which was valued at $125,000, and walk away with an estimated $2 million. As part of the settlement, the Bankers Financing Company and Bankers Trust Company would release their claims against the Manley-Anthony companies in Florida.[57]

The disgruntled Atlanta partners viewed the secret settlement with Anthony as a prescription for disaster. When they returned to Atlanta, Adams and Russell sent Manley a memorandum: "We are compelled to feel that we are paying a terrific price for the peaceful ending of the present strain and at best are settling very cheaply. We see nothing to be gained by any settlement now which does not in the end enable the whole situation to be worked out. If we are to be swamped it had just as well be from one cause or another. . . . Nothing was said about any part of it being kept a secret and off of the records of the Bankers Trust Company. A large part of our troubles in the past have come from secret understandings and from things not on the record, and in this case we can not see our way clear to consent to any settlement or the execution of any release until both the first and second $500,000 go fully into the record. And the first $500,000 is to be CASH or its *equivalent.*"[58]

When Manley received the memorandum he became "violently angry." Nevertheless, Adams and Russell insisted that the books of the Bankers Trust Company and the Bankers Financing Company accurately reflected their assets. Manley never paid the $1 million in restitution to the Bankers Trust Company, and later creditors sought to dismantle the Manley-Anthony partnership. Seven banks took legal action to liquidate their holdings in Florida, which consisted of real estate, orange groves, and mortgages on apartments. The bulk of the assets were held in companies owned jointly by Anthony, who cleverly resisted the collection efforts.[59]

The airing of the partnership dispute did not help the Atlanta partners with the jury. They were all convicted of mail fraud and sentenced to prison. With the exception of Sasser, each of them served time in the Atlanta penitentiary. Sasser's wife died during the trial, and he died while his appeal was pending.[60]

MANLEY'S FEDERAL TRIAL

In 1929, the U.S. Supreme Court reversed Manley's state conviction, declaring that he was prosecuted under an unconstitutional law. This development caused J. Edgar Hoover, head of the Federal Bureau of Investigation, to ignore legal formalities to achieve his brand of justice.[61]

Hoover planted a federal agent, Charles S. Vail, in the Milledgeville sanitarium where Manley was residing. Disguised as a mental patient, Vail was admitted to the private hospital after his "niece" and her husband, both federal agents, told Dr. H. Dawson Allen, the proprietor, that he had a bad case of melancholia. Once inside, he peeked into Manley's room, went through his trash, and kept a diary of his observations. During one encounter Manley told the undercover agent that "his life had been stranger than fiction." Vail recorded that Manley spent his time making toys and working as a carpenter. Trailing him around the grounds of the hospital, he observed that Manley took long walks and often went fishing.[62]

Relying on the agent's diary, U.S. Attorney Clint W. Hager argued that Manley was healthy enough to be tried on the federal charges. When Judge Sibley set a date for an insanity hearing,

Manley went on a five-day hunger strike. On the day of the hearing, with standing room only in the courtroom and a hostile crowd waiting outside, the heavily bearded Manley was wheeled before the special insanity jury on a hospital cot. Flanked by his wife, a nurse, and an attendant, he laid motionless on the cot with a hat pulled down over his eyes.[63]

Unimpressed with his antics and unaffected by the government's misconduct, Judge Sibley ruled for the prosecution and allowed the testimony of lay witnesses to carry as much weight as that of psychiatrists. Vail then made the bizarre allegation that Manley was plotting to escape the sanitarium by private airplane. According to the sensational testimony, his leather hunting clothes were really an aviator's outfit. The government charged that he was studying Spanish in anticipation of fleeing to Colombia. Manley's psychiatrist, Dr. Allen, contradicted the agent's incredible testimony and insisted that his patient was mentally ill. In a move calculated to intimidate the defense and impress the jury, Hager had Allen indicted for perjury. The strategy worked, and after a four-day hearing the jury found Manley sane.[64]

After the sanity verdict Manley's lawyers capitulated. They announced their client was unable to confer with them so they were unable to present a defense. Thus the jury heard only evidence favorable to the government's case. No evidence of regulatory complicity was mentioned. Without access to bank regulatory records, defense lawyers were unaware that regulators had acquiesced to the illegal banking practices for years.

The trial jury was selected in less than ten minutes, and the uneven contest began. The prosecution showed that the Bankers Trust Company had lost $358,511 between 1920 and 1924, which had "wiped out" its capital and surplus. Fictitious intercompany transactions and phony financial statements were the customary practices of the banking system. John L. Grice, an officer of the Bank of Buena Vista, Florida, which made numerous loans to Manley's insolvent companies, testified that "as subordinates we investigated nothing." Banker after banker, who had once enjoyed a profitable relationship with Manley, denied knowledge of the condition of his companies except the financial statements he mailed to them. Based on their sworn testimony, at best, the bankers should have been banned from the industry.[65]

The government presented damning evidence concerning the

misappropriation of more than $445,000 from the Depositors Guarantee Fund. In 1917, Manley instructed his partners to use the fund for their private purposes. The prosecutor slowly read Manley's letter to the jury: "This depositors' guarantee fund money in other banks doesn't help us so let's draw it all out. We might as well make use of it." During the next nine years, Manley and the other trustees of the fund loaned $205,000 to the Bankers Trust Company, $166,052 to the Bankers Financing Company of Jacksonville, and $75,000 to Manley's Georgia Realty Company.[66]

Prosecutors also introduced into evidence a pamphlet, *The Depositors Guarantee Fund of the Witham System,* which was used to entice banks to join the system and then used by the members to attract depositors. The pamphlet described the fund and the system as "based on a scientific insurance principle," designed to protect depositors by keeping member banks in a "wholesome and sweet" condition. "The deposit of a member bank with the Depositors Guarantee Fund is kept in actual cash on deposit with some of the largest and strongest banks in the United States, where it is instantly available under any and all circumstances, and it is not invested in securities or other property, even though such investment would yield a larger interest than the 2% which now accrues on it." Oscar Dooley, the receiver of the Depositors Guarantee Fund, testified that at the time of the crash only $2,000 remained in the fund.[67]

At 11:30 in the morning of October 24, 1929, the government rested its case against the "mad" banker of Atlanta. At the same time, the stock market "surrendered to blind, relentless fear." While the jury deliberated through the lunch hour, the nation's most powerful bankers held a summit conference to decide how to stop the panic. By 1:30 in the afternoon the jury had convicted Manley of mail fraud. Judge Sibley comforted the former banker, who was still lying on his cot: "Pride rather than greed or criminal intent usually causes the failure of these great financial institutions and this seems to have been the case in this instance." By then the senior partner of J. P. Morgan and Company, Thomas W. Lamont, had told the world: "There has been a little distress selling on the Stock Exchange." He assured the public that the adjustment was merely "due to a technical condition of the market."[68]

Judge Sibley sentenced Manley to seven years in prison and a fine of $10,000. He did not appeal the conviction. After serving five years in prison, he was released in 1934 for "extra good behavior." Solicitor Boykin then dropped the pending state charges, saying that Manley had spent more time behind bars "than convicted Georgia murderers." Boykin said he had been punished enough and that a new trial would kill him. His assessment of Manley's health was accurate. Less than a year after his release, he died in a sanitarium in Asheville, North Carolina.[69]

No other federal prosecutions resulted from the banking crash of 1926, and Boykin dismissed the state charges against Manley's Atlanta partners because their federal convictions related to the "same transactions and business." The indictments in Palm Beach County were the only other state charges filed against affiliated bankers. But no bankers were convicted on any state charges in Florida or Georgia. Criminal prosecution was an idle threat. With the rewards so great and the risk so small, it was no deterrent to insider abuse and fraud.

For years J. Edgar Hoover used the Manley case as a leading example of the "Hoover-FBI victory over crime." Because the records of the FBI, Department of Justice, and comptroller of the currency's office remained sealed, Hoover did not have to explain why all of the other bankers affiliated with Manley were treated as victims instead of co-conspirators.[70]

8

A SYSTEM OF PROTECTION

M anley's principal partner in Florida, J. R. Anthony, was never charged with a crime. During the years after the crash, when Manley's criminal prosecutions were active, Anthony blamed his Atlanta partner for everything that went wrong in Florida. He disclaimed any responsibility for the disaster or knowledge of the fraud. But could Manley have hoodwinked Anthony so completely?

Anthony was the high-profile partner in Florida, becoming known as the "King of Chain Banks." Manley seldom traveled beyond Jacksonville. Anthony and Manley operated their banks with dictatorial power, and the records of their defunct banks confirmed that they procured personal loans at will. The local boards of directors obediently approved their loans. In turn, they allowed the affiliated directors to borrow as much as they wanted. Consequently, the chain banks were loaded with insider loans sent from headquarters and produced locally.[1]

Anthony was intimately aware of the unsound condition of their banks and the unsafe operating procedures of the chain system. He appreciated the situation in Florida more fully than his partner in Atlanta because he was the one responsible for their operations in the state. Fearing that a "re-adjustment in the near future" was "inevitable," he had a driving ambition in 1924 and 1925 to cash in his winnings.[2]

Leaving behind his personal loans, before the crash Anthony sold blocks of stock in the Palm Beach Bank and Trust Company for $130,000; the First American Bank and Trust Company of West Palm Beach for $480,000; the Brevard County State Bank of Cocoa for $150,000; and the Bank of Okeechobee for $65,000. He sheltered his most valuable assets by transferring them to the Anthony Investment Company and then to the Anthony family trust at the Barnett National Bank of Jacksonville. He also secretly formed the lucrative partnership with Manley, diverting income and assets from the Bankers Financing Company of Jacksonville.[3]

In spite of his secret understanding with Manley, the only investigative body to examine Anthony's activities was the Palm Beach County grand jury that indicted Comptroller Amos. Because his operations were based in Jacksonville, jurors petitioned Governor Martin to impanel a special grand jury to investigate Anthony, the Bankers Financing Company of Jacksonville, and his affiliated companies. He escaped prosecution altogether when Martin, a lawyer from Jacksonville, failed to take action on the grand jury's request.[4]

While Georgia and federal officials prosecuted Manley, the Anthony brothers ensured that Amos remained their loyal friend. With A. P. Anthony at the helm, the Peoples Bank of Jacksonville continued to make unsecured loans to the comptroller until it collapsed in 1929. Avoiding problems during the liquidation, Amos appointed Joseph R. Dunn, a stockholder of the bank, as its receiver.[5]

Amos refused to investigate the diversion of assets from the Bankers Financing Company of Jacksonville into entities personally owned by Anthony and Manley. Those assets could have been used to pay depositors for insider loans and stockholder assessments at failed state banks. The "irregularities" were documented in the Ernst and Ernst audit report, which was presented to Amos at the May 14, 1926, meeting in Jacksonville. He simply ignored the evidence of fraud.[6]

ACQUITTALS IN PALM BEACH COUNTY

The Palm Beach County grand jury indicted six of Anthony's partners for insider dealings at the Commercial Bank and Trust

Company and the Palm Beach Bank and Trust Company. Indictments charged that they made illegal loans to their own companies, including the Mizner Development Corporation. Jurors accused Thomas M. Cook, president of the Commercial Bank, of procuring loans of $117,540 for his interests and Adrian E. Pearson, the bank's vice-president, of arranging personal loans of $144,060 "in excess of the extreme limit permitted by law."[7]

Anthony's partners at the Palm Beach Bank and Trust Company—Benjamin R. Clayton, D. Lester Williams, Howard P. Smith, and Ralph Payne—were also indicted for flagrant insider abuse. Clayton, president of the bank, was charged with lending more than $500,000, or 667 percent of the bank's capital, to the other officers. Williams, the largest stockholder and a vice-president, was accused of making loans to his interests of $177,577. Smith, another major stockholder and a vice-president, was indicted for borrowing $233,177. Payne, the third vice-president, was charged with making personal loans totaling $133,357.[8]

Anthony eluded the grand jury because of the complicity of Amos and the policy of bank secrecy in Tallahassee and Washington. Official secrecy prevented prosecutors from understanding the cozy relationship between the regulators and the banks affiliated with Anthony. The Amos loans at the Peoples Bank of Jacksonville and the Palm Beach National Bank went undetected along with the loans to his bank examiners. Howard Smith's payoff of the "loan" to Amos's chief bank examiner neutralized the regulation of the Palm Beach Bank and Trust Company. The same corrupt practice occurred at the Commercial Bank and Trust Company, Anthony's other West Palm Beach bank. That bank made an unsecured loan to its state bank examiner.[9]

Bank secrecy tainted the judicial system when Anthony's partners went on trial. It prevented the jury from hearing evidence of the multibank conspiracy and the official corruption. Represented by a battery of lawyers, Howard Smith was acquitted. A vigorous defender was former judge E. B. Donnell, the lawyer for the Palm Beach Bank and Trust Company before and after its collapse, who had defaulted on obligations of $18,812 at the bank. "Blurring the continuity of the chain of evidence," Donnell and the defense team objected to almost every document presented by prosecutors. Smith's lawyers argued that Amos, not their client, was responsible for the bank failure. When L. E. Heisler, a former director, testified, he "seemed to have lost his memory." Frustrated by his lack of candor, Judge A. G. Hartridge ridiculed the witness: "Can't you testify without thinking?"[10]

Williams, a major player with Smith and Anthony, used the same defense team and faced the same judge. His lawyers moved to disqualify Judge Hartridge for "bias and prejudice" because he had lost "large sums of money as a depositor" in the Palm Beach Bank and Trust Company. They did not mention Judge Hartridge's delinquent and unsecured loan at the bank, which was two and one-half times larger than his checking account. The motion caused a spectacle in the courtroom. After reading it, Hartridge abruptly left the bench and walked straight at Williams shouting: "You swore to a damn lie." But he disqualified himself and dismissed the jury. Williams was assigned a new judge and after a complicated trial was acquitted of all charges.[11]

Without knowing the extent of the insider abuse and influence peddling, prosecutors were unable to convict any of the bankers. The acquittals had been predicted by James B. Hodges, chairman of the Democratic Executive Committee, who was Anthony's partner in the State Exchange Bank of Lake City. In a confidential letter, in which he urged Joe Earman of the *Palm Beach Independent* not to publish Amos's regulatory records, Hodges recognized there was "not any doubt" that Smith, Williams, and the other directors of the Palm Beach Bank and Trust Company had blatantly violated the banking code. But the powerful Democrat said the "JOKER" in the Florida law was that it provided no penalty for excessive loans to directors.[12]

ANTHONY'S ASSOCIATE BECOMES COMPTROLLER

Outside of Palm Beach County, none of the Florida bankers affiliated with Manley and Anthony were investigated. Clarence Gay, who had worked for Manley in Atlanta and Anthony in Orlando and who was involved in the defunct Orlando Bank and Trust Company, was spared the scandal of an investigation. In 1946, Gay became comptroller of Florida when Governor Millard F. Caldwell appointed him to succeed J. M. Lee, who had died in office.[13]

Although Gay became comptroller on October 9, 1946, the state Democratic Executive Committee nominated Senator Edwin G.

After working for the Manley-Anthony banking system, Clarence M. Gay became comptroller and chief regulator of Florida's scandal-ridden banking industry. (Courtesy, Florida State Archives)

Fraser as its candidate for comptroller in the November election. Without Republican opposition, Fraser was elected. Gay then filed suit to invalidate the election on constitutional grounds. The supreme court of Florida disqualified Fraser because the state constitution prohibited members of the legislature from serving in an office after participating in the raising of its salary. Fraser had been in the Senate when the comptroller's salary was increased.[14]

In the 1948 campaign, Fraser challenged Gay, declaring that he had been "robbed" on a legal technicality. In the "knock-down-drag-out fight," Gay displayed his knowledge of the politics of banking. After his appointment, he had adopted "a conservative policy" in the awarding of bank charters. By denying a number of applications, he enhanced his fund-raising prospects from groups waiting to enter the banking industry. Because there was no appellate procedure, applicants contributed generously to the comptroller's campaign.[15]

Gay used the full powers of his office to advance his campaign. One of his key supporters, Selden F. Waldo, an attorney in Gainesville, advised him of the fund-raising efforts in central Florida. Waldo reported to the comptroller that his local campaign manager was contacting "the persons who are interested in the new Citizens Bank of Gainesville to see whether or not we can secure financial assistance from that group, in addition to its personal support." With the active support of bankers throughout Florida, Gay defeated Fraser by a landslide vote. He was reelected in 1952 without opposition.[16]

ANTHONY DEFAULTS

The depositors of the Palm Beach Bank and Trust Company were left to pay for the impropriety of the bankers. Depositors did not know the full extent of the insider abuse until the bank's receiver was discharged in 1938. When the bank closed in 1926, it had deposits of $4,056,323. After twelve years of liquidating its assets, depositors received only $152,091 or 4 percent of their deposits. They lost ninety-six cents on the dollar.[17]

Because the capital of the Palm Beach Bank and Trust Company had been wiped out, Anthony and the other stockholders were required by law to reimburse the treasury to the extent of their stock ownership. Anthony's deficiency assessment was $10,000 because the bank's capital was $75,000 and he owned 13.33 percent of its stock. Although he had sold a block of his stock to Smith and Williams in 1925 for $130,000, Anthony refused to pay his assessment. Disregarding his obligation, Anthony avoided litigation because the bank's receiver, Orel Myers, who was also a major borrower of the bank, did not file suit. Oblivious to its conflict of interest, the law firm of Blackwell, Donnell and Moore represented both Receiver Myers and Anthony. In addition, Smith and Williams retained the same firm and then defaulted on their stock assessments.[18]

Anthony, whose family had founded the bank, remained a major stockholder of the Palm Beach Bank and Trust Company until it closed. On that day his wife, Rosa Seward Anthony, his brother E. D. Anthony, and Anthony Brothers, Inc., an insolvent entity, had loans at the bank amounting to 45 percent of its capital. Anthony, Manley, and their partners continued to load the bank with worthless insider loans until it collapsed. The defunct bank had played a central role in their interstate loan-kiting scheme.[19]

Anthony also refused to pay his $26,000 stock assessment at the Commercial Bank and Trust Company, though one of his companies, the Anthony Investment Company, had been worth in excess of $1.5 million in May 1926. Anthony and Manley were equal partners at the Commercial Bank and Trust Company, with each owning 26 percent of its capital stock of $100,000. Holding majority control of the bank, they pillaged it with insider deals and then defaulted on their obligations to depositors. Anthony dodged an embarrassing lawsuit when Amos accepted his recommendation and appointed W. H. Tunnicliffe as the receiver for the bank. Tunnicliffe had been Anthony's partner in the Peoples Bank of Sanford and in other bank deals.[20]

The banking crash of 1926 began when the Commercial Bank and Trust Company failed on June 26. Its affiliated banks, the Palm Beach Bank and Trust Company and the Palm Beach National Bank, failed on June 28 and June 29. When the Commercial Bank and Trust Company folded, Anthony and his companies had loans and guaranties of more than 75 percent of its capital. Manley's interests had obligations at the bank of 112 percent of its capital. Anthony, Manley, and their associates and affiliates, including chain banks in Georgia, owed the Commercial Bank and Trust Company more than $500,000, an astounding 500 percent of its capital.[21]

Reassured by Comptroller Amos, prosecutors accepted Anthony's explanation that he was unaware of the wrongdoing and that Manley was solely responsible for the disaster in Florida. Anthony, who became president of the Bankers Financing Company of Jacksonville before the crash by switching the position of vice-president with Manley, maintained the loyal support of Amos, which shielded him from scrutiny. Though they remained partners until the end, Anthony blamed the crash on Manley's lavish life-style and wild speculations, suggesting that his partner must have been insane to have been so reckless with other people's money. Yet Anthony had managed Manley's affairs in Florida, and just days before the crash he acted as the undisclosed trustee for Manley in a real estate deal in Ocala. The clever businessmen worked well together. They evaded banking laws and maximized profits by accommodating each other. Besides their banking activities, they jointly owned the following companies: Florida Mutual Investment Company of Jacksonville, Bankers Investment Company of Jacksonville, Bankers Trading Corporation of Jacksonville, Bankers Guaranty Company of Miami, First National Company, Campbell Building Company, and Church Street Holding Company of Orlando. The value of their joint holdings in May 1925 was approximately $5 million.[22]

The profitable relationship became one-sided after Manley was forced into bankruptcy. Anthony skillfully maneuvered through the maze of bankruptcy by compromising his debts and purchasing valuable assets from the federal court. On July 23, 1927, he bought ninety-nine shares of the Florida Mutual Investment Company for $1,500—$15.15 a share—from the receiver of Manley's estate. The Florida Mutual Investment Company was a bank holding company, which was owned jointly by the Anthony Investment Company and Manley. It owned a major block of stock in the Peoples Bank of Jacksonville, whose president was A. P. Anthony. On a financial statement dated December 31, 1927, the Anthony Investment Company listed the stock of the Florida Mutual Investment Company with a value of $112.50 a share.[23]

Anthony also purchased from Manley's receiver 450 shares of the Bankers Trading Corporation for a total of $666.66 for "the purpose of expeditiously winding up the affairs" of the company. Appraisers hired by the bankruptcy court, however, had valued the shares at $4,500. And they were worth more to Anthony because he now owned 100 percent of the company.[24]

Several of their partners declared bankruptcy to escape from creditors. Thomas Cook and Donald Conkling were inextricably intertwined with the Manley-Anthony banking system in the Palm Beaches. As stockholders, directors, officers, and borrowers of the member banks, they plunged into the real estate frenzy with reckless abandon. Cook bounced back after using the bankruptcy court as a safe haven, but Conkling lost his irreplaceable asset, the *Palm Beach Post*.[25]

THE BANKRUPTCY OF A BANK PRESIDENT

Under the protection of the federal bankruptcy court, Thomas McBride Cook, president of the Commercial Bank and Trust Company, resumed an active career while depositors of the bank struggled through twelve years of liquidation proceedings. Cook rose from the rubble by leaving his creditors with $824,926 in worthless paper. After his acquittal of criminal charges in 1927, he became a municipal bond salesman in West Palm Beach.[26]

Amos had chartered the Commercial Bank and Trust Company in February 1924. Anthony and Manley had formed the bank as a companion to the Palm Beach Bank and Trust Company. Cook, who had worked for the Manley banking system in Georgia as the vice-president and cashier of the Bank of Abbeville, was the hand-picked president for the West Palm Beach project. Manley, Anthony, and Cook destroyed the bank with their speculative ventures in twenty-eight months.[27]

After deflecting his creditors for six years, Cook filed a voluntary bankruptcy petition in 1932. His schedule of debts revealed that he was not a conservative banker but instead a reckless gambler with access to unlimited credit. His only assets of any value were one share in Thomas M. Cook and Company and less than $500 of "household effects, wearing apparel and other personal effects." Those assets, including the stock in his lucrative municipal bond company, were exempted from his creditors because he listed their value at less than $1,000. He offered his creditors no assets to offset his pile of debt.[28]

Cook's assets consisted primarily of stock in failed banks, some real estate concerns, and an insurance company. He was a stockholder in the following defunct entities: Commercial Bank and Trust Company, Bank of Abbeville, Greater Palm Beach Development Company, Florida Insurance and Investment Company, and Palm Beach Realty and Investment Company, which owned stock in the Mizner Development Corporation. Most of his worthless stock had been pledged as collateral for loans at the Bank of Coconut Grove, Bank of Buena Vista of Miami, First Bank and Trust Company of Palm Beach, Bank of Little River of Miami, Ocean City Bank of Delray, and First American Bank and Trust Company of West Palm Beach. In addition, Cook owned notes of $11,916, which were listed as having "no value" and pledged to secure loans at the First American Bank and Trust Company.[29]

Cook's debts revealed the extent of his speculation and the consequences for the depositors of the failed banks. He had borrowed $742,875 on an unsecured basis from banks, mortgage companies, real estate companies, and property owners. Moreover, his bank stock had a negative value because he was liable for unpaid stockholder assessments. For example, he owed $7,200 on his assessments at the Commercial Bank and Trust Company.[30]

Besides the Commercial Bank and Trust Company, Cook had procured unsecured loans from all the banks listed above and from the following financial institutions: Hanover National Bank of

New York, Atlanta Trust Company, Bankers Trust Company of Atlanta, Bankers Financing Company of Jacksonville, Peoples Bank of Jacksonville, Palm Beach National Bank, First National Bank of Palm Beach, Palm Beach Bank and Trust Company, Farmers Bank and Trust Company of West Palm Beach, Northwood Bank and Trust Company of West Palm Beach, Commercial Bond and Mortgage Company of West Palm Beach, Bank of Boca Raton, Bank of Coral Gables, First National Bank of Lake Worth, First Bank and Trust Company of Lake Worth, Bank of Boynton, Delray Bank and Trust Company, Kelsey City State Bank, Miami Bank and Trust Company, City National Bank of Miami, Bank of Dania, Bank of Homestead, American Bank and Trust Company of Daytona Beach, New Smyrna Bank and Trust Company, Fidelity Bank of New Smyrna, Bank of Osceola County, Dorsey Banking Company of Abbeville, and Bank of Abbeville.[31]

Cook had purchased vast amounts of real estate from numerous individuals and entities, including the Mizner Development Corporation, Coral Gables Corporation, Spanish River Land Company, and Clarence Geist. He had also borrowed substantial amounts from his local partners—Donald Conkling, Howard Smith, and A. E. Pearson. Though he was unable to pay his electric and dry cleaning bills, Cook went shopping on credit at Anthony's department store before filing bankruptcy. He then resolved his financial problems by declaring himself bankrupt.[32]

While disposing of his debts in federal court, he was busy selling Florida's municipal bonds throughout the nation. Although he swore to the court that his stake in Thomas M. Cook and Company was worth only $100, it was rapidly becoming the state's leading municipal bond dealer. His company had sold over $30 million of municipal bonds by 1937.[33]

THE GAMBLER AND THE NEWSPAPER

Donald H. Conkling, the publisher, banker, and real estate promoter, was driven into bankruptcy after accumulating debts of $610,405. He was Anthony's partner at the Commercial Bank and Trust Company, of which he was a vice-president. He was also a stockholder of the Palm Beach National Bank and the First American Bank and Trust Company of West Palm Beach. As an organizer of the Mizner Development Corporation, he became a major stockholder by trading advertisements in the *Palm Beach Post* for stock in the real estate company. Conkling received nothing from his investment with Addison Mizner, and the Post Publishing Company had to write off $20,503 for Mizner's unpaid advertisements.[34]

Conkling converted his bank investments into substantial loans from the banks, but they contributed greatly to his downfall. After the First American Bank and Trust Company failed for the first time in March 1927, he became a director by joining a syndicate that financed its reorganization and reopening. In the process, he endorsed loans of $110,000. When the bank failed for the second time in June 1928, he was sued on the notes.[35]

The reason behind the promotional fervor of the *Palm Beach Post* was exposed when its publisher filed his bankruptcy papers. Before the demise of the First American Bank and Trust Company, Conkling borrowed $37,953, which was ostensibly for the Post Publishing Company. But he had a practice of diverting the funds of the newspaper into his real estate ventures. It caught up with him when the publishing company went deeper in debt by issuing bonds of $160,000, which he guaranteed. By the time of his bankruptcy in 1932, he owed $61,999 to the publishing company. That liability would remain unpaid because his assets consisted of worthless stock and deflated parcels of real estate, whose mortgages were more than the value of the land.[36]

The proceedings also disclosed that one of his largest creditors was Edward Riley Bradley, the proprietor of the notorious Bradley's Beach Club, a private casino in Palm Beach. Conkling had borrowed $121,082 from Bradley and had pledged his stock in the Post Publishing Company to secure the loan. Colonel Bradley was a professional gambler and owner of the Idle Hour Farm of Lexington, whose thoroughbred horses won the Kentucky Derby four times. Bradley, who enjoyed immunity from prosecution because he maintained a special relationship with local politicians and publishers, became the most influential businessman in Palm Beach. Although operating a casino was a serious crime under the laws of Florida, Bradley's Beach Club was a popular gambling establishment for forty-eight years. Rules of the house restricted its membership to out-of-state citizens, which did not make it any less illegal. Members included Joseph P. Kennedy, Philander C. Knox, William K. Vanderbilt II, Vanderbilt, Stuyvesant Fish, George W.

Perkins, Henry C. Phipps, the Duke of Manchester, John Studebaker, and John W. "Bet a Million" Gates.[37]

A scandal in 1915 could have forced the closing of the club, but Bradley's influence quashed the trouble. Pressured by the Law and Order League of Palm Beach County, Governor Park Trammell hired a private detective to investigate allegations of gambling at the club. During a police raid, Colonel Bradley and his brother John R. Bradley were arrested for operating an illegal casino. Facing a possible three-year term in prison, John Bradley said: "We made [this restaurant] famous on account of food, service and guests' treatment. We have never had anything which indicated any gambling implement. It is nothing but jealousy of our successful business—and politics. We have nothing to fear." While members of the club, including John F. Fitzgerald, the former mayor of Boston, quickly left town, Palm Beach mayor Elisha Newton Dimick raised the bail for the Bradleys. The indictment was dismissed when no witnesses could be found to testify against them.[38]

During the Prohibition period, Colonel Bradley was so flush with cash that he became a leading philanthropist and private banker. He made significant contributions to Saint Edward's Catholic Church and financed Conkling's *Palm Beach Post* and Sheriff Robert Baker's *Palm Beach Times*. John Bradley also fostered their position in the community by joining with members of the Kennedy family to become stockholders of the Farmers Bank and Trust Company of West Palm Beach. The bank collapsed in 1927, but the newspaper loans resulted in Colonel Bradley acquiring the *Palm Beach Post* and the *Palm Beach Times* in 1934.[39]

THE BANKRUPTCY OF ANTHONY'S, INC.

J. R. Anthony's wealth survived the banking crash and the depression that followed. But many of his private companies, including the Bankers Financing Company of Jacksonville, Bankers Investment Company, and Bankers Guaranty Company, went into bankruptcy court. After the failure of the Peoples Bank of Jacksonville, his brother A. P. Anthony voluntarily petitioned the court for bankruptcy protection.[40]

Anthony preserved his fortune by forming the Anthony Investment Company and deeding valuable assets to his wife and three children. Creating another layer between his creditors, he and his wife formed Rosa Seward Anthony, Inc., which owned control of the Anthony Investment Company. As a further precaution, the Anthonys transferred assets of the Anthony Investment Company to a family trust administered by the Barnett National Bank of Jacksonville, of which he had once been a director. Behind their layered fortress, J. R. Anthony's family was prepared to resist any attack from creditors.[41]

Anthony and his brothers conducted their business in a grandiose manner. Their original clothing business had operated as Anthony Brothers, Inc. J. R. Anthony was president from 1894 to 1918, and then E. D. Anthony became head of the company. With borrowed money, the brothers expanded their business to twelve stores by the early 1920s. Reckless expansion choked the concern with $320,000 of debt. By procuring loans from J. R. Anthony's banks, it was able to avoid bankruptcy court. But creditors forced it through a liquidation process in 1923. Ten of the stores were sold or liquidated, and the two stores in Palm Beach and West Palm Beach were transferred to a new company called Anthony's, Inc., with E. D. Anthony as the president.[42]

Leaving behind the delinquent bank loans of its predecessor, the new Anthony's operated until 1932 before creditors filed a bankruptcy petition against it. This was the second time in nine years that the family clothing business had been through a liquidation. The bankruptcy created a crisis for J. R. Anthony because his private entity, the Anthony Investment Company, was the owner and landlord of the flagship store of Anthony's, Inc., in West Palm Beach.[43]

The Anthony Investment Company had raised $90,000 to build the majestic department store by issuing 8 percent mortgage bonds to investors. The building was built on a lot already owned by the Anthony Investment Company, yet its final cost exceeded $135,000. By 1932, $70,000 remained on the bonds issued by J. R. Anthony's private company. Though he began transferring assets out of the Anthony Investment Company after the banking crash, it still had a net worth of $386,200. Nevertheless, for several years it had reneged on its bond payments and owed the bondholders more than $15,000. It also failed to pay property taxes on the building for 1929, 1930, and 1931. Tax certificates had been sold for the delinquent taxes, which exceeded $12,000. Faced with these menacing obligations, J. R. Anthony engaged in a series of maneuvers to transfer a majority of the remaining assets of the investment company to other members of his immediate family and their entities. He was now in a position to negotiate a favorable settlement with the bankruptcy court.[44]

Anthony had prepared for disaster by appointing the Palm Beach Bank and Trust Company as the trustee for the bonds. When the bank failed, its receiver, Orel Myers, became the trustee for the bondholders. Using the same law firm as Anthony, Myers allowed the Anthony Investment Company to ignore its obligations. After Myers finally resigned, the new trustee moved to foreclose because the Anthony Investment Company had "for long periods of time heretofore elapsed, neglected, failed and refused to comply with the terms and provisions" of the bondholders agreement. The trustee "ousted" the Anthony Investment Company from the building, but Anthony avoided a deficiency judgment. Because the bankruptcy referee limited the scope of the inquiry, his Machiavellian tactics went undetected.[45]

Anthony's, Inc., was insolvent long before 1932. When clothing sales suffered a downturn, it stopped paying rent to the Anthony Investment Company, which in turn defaulted on the mortgage bonds. For several years this precarious situation threatened to force Anthony's, Inc., into bankruptcy because it had guaranteed the bonds. Concealing its financial condition from creditors and trying to avoid yet another liquidation, Anthony's transferred its leasehold interest in the building to a newly formed, wholly owned subsidiary, the Anthony Holding Company, in June 1930. Though Anthony's, Inc., remained obligated for the bonded indebtedness, the $70,000 liability disappeared from its balance sheet after the transfer. Issuing false financial statements, the clothing business avoided bankruptcy for two more years by buying merchandise on credit and borrowing from local banks.[46]

By creating the Anthony Holding Company, the Anthony brothers converted a liability into an asset, a remarkable accounting feat. It came to light after H. U. Feibelman, an attorney representing creditors, vigorously cross-examined Luella E. McGuire, the bookkeeper of Anthony's, Inc., at a hearing in federal court on April 30, 1932. The following exchange took place as McGuire was trying to explain how $70,000 of debt was erased from the balance sheet of Anthony's, Inc., by the transfer to the Anthony Holding Company.

FEIBELMAN: Nowhere after [June 1930] does the indebtedness of $70,000 of bonds appear?
McGUIRE: Except as it appears as a contingent liability.
FEIBELMAN: Where does it appear as a contingent liability?
McGUIRE: Anthony Holding.
FEIBELMAN: Any balance sheet wherein that shows?
McGUIRE: Not on the balance sheet.
FEIBELMAN: Why doesn't it show on the balance sheet?
McGUIRE: It is on our balance sheet not in just that way. It is shown right here on the balance sheet as an asset.
FEIBELMAN: Please tell me, does the insertion of an asset in any way reflect a liability for a contingent debt?
McGUIRE: There is bound to be a contingent debt.
FEIBELMAN: How would anybody reading that statement know there is any liability because that asset is owned by the corporation, anyone unfamiliar?
McGUIRE: If they were sufficiently interested could they not go into the records? I am just wondering.
FEIBELMAN: So that the only place, according to your contention, that there is any allusion whatever to any liability on those bonds is in the representation of an asset known as the Anthony Holding Company $80,708.34?
McGUIRE: That is the only place it is mentioned, yes.
FEIBELMAN: Any other liabilities of this corporation that are not shown on that balance sheet?
McGUIRE: Not to my knowledge.[47]

The deceptive accounting entry changed Anthony's, Inc., from a tenant in the building to its owner. The financial statement of Anthony Holding Company listed the building as an asset, worth $100,474. But according to J. R. Anthony's sworn statement, Anthony's, Inc., "had no right, title or interest in said premises other than that of tenant." After deducting the bogus interest in the building, the Anthony Holding Company had a negative net worth of $36,302.[48]

Jacob Elishewitz and Sons of New York accused Anthony's, Inc., of committing fraud by buying 173 hats knowing that it was "hopelessly insolvent, and was without ability or means, present or future, to pay for the merchandise." Under the laws of bankruptcy, a fraud occurred when the buyer concealed its insolvency and had "no well founded expectations or hope of payment." Consequently, L. Earl Curry, the referee in bankruptcy, rescinded the last of three transactions because Anthony's, Inc., "knew or should have known" that it was insolvent.[49]

The bankruptcy also came as a surprise to the Florida Bank and Trust Company of West Palm Beach. Less than two weeks before its declaration of bankruptcy, Anthony's, Inc., obtained a $10,000 unsecured loan from the bank by using a stale financial statement. It omitted the $70,000 debt and failed to report "very severe" losses which had occurred in the late summer and autumn of 1931. This pattern of misrepresentation was repeated at the Palm Beach Bank and Trust Company and the First American Bank and Trust Company of West Palm Beach, from which Anthony Brothers, Inc., the predecessor entity, had substantial loans years after its insolvency.[50]

Representing Anthony's, Inc., the law firm of Blackwell, Donnell and Moore negotiated a friendly settlement with Joseph D. Farish, the creditors' lawyer. On the advice of counsel and over the objection of 72 creditors, the controversial plan was approved by a majority of the 189 unsecured creditors. Under the plan, unsecured creditors received "deferred payments" amounting to twenty-five cents on the dollar. Farish's law firm, Beall and Farish, had been indebted to the Anthony Investment Company for years. J. R. Anthony, who practiced the art of gentle persuasion by making loans to law firms, had cultivated Beall and Farish, and that relationship was now indispensable.[51]

Farish orchestrated the proceedings by working closely with the Anthonys. He met with them before filing the involuntary bankruptcy petition, and two days after the proceedings began, E. D. Anthony agreed to the appointment of a receiver. Farish then nominated Charles H. Warwick, Jr., to be the receiver. Soon after creditors approved the original plan, the Anthonys requested approval of an amended plan that allowed the sale of the assets of Anthony's, Inc., to a newly chartered company called Anthony and Sons, Inc. Following Farish's advice, the creditors agreed to the switch, and the Anthonys were back in business with first-class merchandise that was free of liens. E. D. Anthony continued as president of the enterprise, which operated from the same locations. Shedding creditors along the way, in less than a decade the family clothing business had passed through Anthony Brothers, Inc., to Anthony's, Inc., and then to Anthony and Sons, Inc.[52]

To facilitate the sale of assets, E. D. Anthony issued shares in Anthony and Sons, Inc., to George W. Slaton. Slaton was employed by I. G. Atwell, the vice-president of the Florida Bank and Trust Company. Atwell also was president of the Consolidated Florida Company, an unsecured creditor of Anthony's, Inc., which lost 75 percent of its claim against the company. The Florida Bank and Trust Company, whose law firm was Beall and Farish, loaned $15,000 to Anthony and Sons, Inc., to finance the purchase of assets. Finalizing the deal, Farish and his law partner, Egbert Beall, were members of the bank's board of directors, which approved the loan.[53]

The Anthonys had a history of defaulting on loans at banks affiliated with Atwell. Five years after its liquidation, Anthony Brothers, Inc., still owed $11,283 to the First American Bank and Trust, of which Atwell was a director and stockholder. Its successor company, Anthony's, Inc., and E. D. Anthony were also in default on loans at the bank. In addition, J. R. Anthony's Bankers Investment Company borrowed $9,073 from the bank in 1926 and then received bankruptcy protection. When the First American Bank and Trust Company failed in June 1928, all of the Anthony loans were in default.[54]

REGULATORY FORBEARANCE

Despite his legal problems, J. R. Anthony remained a proud man, living the remainder of his life in comfort and financial security. His substantial net worth assured his acceptance in political and financial circles. After the crash, he divided his time between meetings with lawyers and preserving his assets. Much of his efforts were directed at developing his insurance business. He entered the insurance industry in 1915, when he acquired an interest in the Peninsular Casualty Company of Jacksonville. For the next twenty-two years he was a major stockholder and secretary-treasurer of the Peninsular Casualty Company and its successor, the Peninsular Life Insurance Company.[55]

As was the case with the elected banking commissioner and the banking industry, Anthony knew that the value of his investment in the insurance industry was largely dependent on his relationship with the elected insurance commissioner. In 1928, Governor John Martin, a former mayor of Jacksonville, appointed William Knott as state treasurer and insurance commissioner. Despite the banking scandal, Knott maintained complete confidence in Anthony, who had made loans to him a few years earlier. Anthony had allowed Knott to ignore his obligations then, and now the position of power was reversed. Knott was the sole regulator of insurance companies operating in the state.[56]

When the Peninsular Life Insurance Company ran into trouble during the 1930s, Knott risked a major political scandal by ignoring the problems at Anthony's company. Knott's regulatory forbearance enabled Anthony not only to salvage his investment but to make one of the best deals of his career. In 1937, he sold his stock in the company for more than double its book value. Though in declining health, Anthony was ready to enjoy his fortune. But in 1940 he died at the age of seventy, leaving behind a large estate which he had accumulated during a controversial fifty-year career.[57]

9

FRIENDS OF
VICE-PRESIDENT DAWES

D epositors received a final insult when Comptroller of the Currency Joseph McIntosh allowed Charles Dawes, the vice-president of the United States, and his associates to deplete the assets of the defunct Palm Beach National Bank. McIntosh was far more interested in helping his political friends profit from the calamity than he had been in restraining bankers during the speculative frenzy.[1]

Immediately after the collapse of the bank, McIntosh retained former United States senator Lawrence Y. Sherman of Illinois as the lawyer for the failed bank. The hiring of Sherman and his newly formed Daytona Beach law firm was no coincidence. Sherman enjoyed the confidence of Vice-President Dawes, who had been his friend for thirty years. They had been business partners, and Dawes had used Sherman as his private attorney. Now the Dawes brothers were negotiating to acquire the Mizner Development Corporation, and Sherman would play a major role in closing the deal.[2]

McIntosh was part of the Dawes political and business organization. He had worked with Dawes and Sherman in Republican party politics for years. They were his mentors. He was the youngest of the three and came from the same hometown as Sherman, Macomb, Illinois. In 1923, after President Warren Harding appointed Henry Dawes as comptroller of the currency, McIntosh came to Washington as his deputy comptroller. Henry Dawes followed in the footsteps of his brother Charles, who had been McKinley's comptroller of the currency. In December 1924, after his brother had been elected vice-president, Henry resigned to become president of the Pure Oil Company, which was controlled by the Dawes brothers. President Calvin Coolidge then appointed McIntosh as the nation's chief bank regulator. During McIntosh's tenure, visitors to his office in the Treasury Building were reminded of his connection by the portrait of Charles Dawes that hung behind his desk. He remained part of the Dawes organization after he left the government. For fifteen years he sat on the board of directors of the Pure Oil Company.[3]

With Charles Dawes operating from the vice-president's chamber, the Dawes brothers were poised to turn Florida's banking crash into a bonanza. They had confidants in the key government positions necessary to gain control of the company that may have held Florida's most valuable real estate.

THE DAWES-MIZNER DEAL

The Mizner Development Corporation was temporarily rescued from bankruptcy at the expense of the depositors of the Palm Beach National Bank. The insolvent company was bailed out by the Central Equities Corporation of Chicago, owned by the Dawes brothers. Senator Sherman, who supposedly represented the depositors, facilitated the Dawes-Mizner deal for the benefit of Vice-President Dawes and his brothers.[4]

Shortly after the Palm Beach National Bank failed, the law firm of Blackwell and Donnell, on behalf of the Mizner Development Corporation, which was in the process of being acquired by the Dawes brothers, demanded that McIntosh release valuable securities held at the defunct bank. Receiver John Cunningham had refused Addison Mizner access to his company's safe deposit box. Because he and his companies owed the bank a "substantial amount," Deputy Comptroller E. W. Stearns wired Cunningham ordering him to keep possession of the "stocks, bonds, notes and other items convertible into cash." Stearns planned to use the securities to offset Mizner's worthless loans, and he instructed Cunningham to "immediately bring suit for attachment and ask for injunction and temporary restraining order prohibiting company from taking assets from its box."[5]

Sherman, who went to Chicago, the headquarters of Dawes Brothers, Inc., before reporting for duty at the Palm Beach National Bank, contradicted the deputy comptroller as soon as he arrived in Palm Beach. Sherman advised Cunningham to release the Mizner securities because he did not have a lien on them and he would lose in court. His legal advice was erroneous and violated the standard operating policy of the comptroller of the currency's office.[6]

While the Dawes reorganization was pending, officials of Boca Raton prodded Cunningham to release city tax warrants in Mizner's safe deposit box. His company owed real estate taxes to the city of Boca Raton, and the officials proposed trading the tax warrants for the delinquent taxes. The proposal highlighted Mizner's glaring conflict of interest at Boca Raton. He was both the city's primary land developer and the city land planner. His influence in Boca Raton and the Dawes takeover of his company put Cunningham, a career government employee, in an untenable position.[7]

Cunningham resisted the pressure by seeking approval from Washington to apply the warrants toward the retirement of the Mizner loans. He received tentative authorization, which would have forced Mizner to litigate for release of the warrants. But the receiver was instructed to be "governed by advice of local counsel." With counselor Sherman in an accommodating mood, Cunningham was in a weak negotiating position. So he released and swapped promissory notes of the Mizner Development Corporation with a face value of $25,000 for the Boca Raton warrants worth $12,000, which became collateral for the Mizner loans.[8]

When senior staff at the comptroller's office later discovered the "switch of collateral" during an audit, they asked the receiver for "a complete explanation." Cunningham said the collateral swap was a good transaction for the bank even though the city was "financially embarrassed" because the notes of the Mizner Development Corporation were "worthless." He neglected to mention that the Dawes brothers had refinanced the company.[9]

In October 1926, Comptroller McIntosh's office approved another collateral swap at the bank which helped the Dawes brothers take control of the Mizner Development Corporation. His office authorized the exchange of 512 shares of the Mizner Development Corporation, which the bank held as collateral for Mizner loans, for "stock trust certificates" in a voting trust agreement for the benefit of the Central Equities Corporation. Following Sherman's advice, Cunningham recommended the swap because the Mizner Development Corporation was "on the rocks" and the Central Equities Corporation, which he described as a company "organized and existing under the laws of the State of Delaware," had agreed to make substantial loans to it. Instead of using the opportunity to negotiate a favorable deal for the bank's depositors, Cunningham, who was in the middle between Sherman and McIntosh, closed his eyes and went along with the reorganization plan of Vice-President Dawes and his brothers.[10]

Cunningham, the professional liquidator, was no match for Senator Sherman and Comptroller McIntosh. Without the political interference, the receiver could have demanded full payment of the Mizner loans before releasing the Mizner Development Corporation stock. When the comptroller's office sanctioned the Dawes-Mizner deal, the depositors of the Palm Beach National Bank became the unwitting partners of the vice-president of the United States.[11]

CENTRAL EQUITIES CORPORATION

Central Equities Corporation was led by Rufus C. Dawes, who was also the president of Dawes Brothers, Incorporated. He served as an officer and director of companies in which the Dawes brothers had an ownership interest. For example, he was vice-president and director of the Seattle Lighting Company, in which Senator Sherman had owned stock. He held similar positions with gas and electric companies across the country and sat on the board of the Central Trust Company of Illinois, a Chicago-based bank controlled by the Dawes brothers. When Charles Dawes was appointed chairman of the reparations committee of experts in 1924, Rufus helped his brother develop the Dawes Plan, which eased Germany's payments of war reparations and stabilized the German currency. After the Dawes Plan resulted in France's withdrawal of troops from the Ruhr industrial district of Germany, Charles Dawes was a co-winner of the Nobel Peace Prize.[12]

In July 1926, Rufus Dawes reached an agreement with Addison Mizner to control and manage the Mizner Development Corporation. Central Equities Corporation publicly committed itself to loan as much as $1.5 million to Mizner's company in exchange for control of 51 percent of its stock. Mizner would remain as president of the company and have charge of architectural design for the Boca Raton development. The takeover would be effective within ninety days if Central Equities could reach "satisfactory agreements" with all interested parties, including Receiver Cunningham and Comptroller McIntosh.[13]

After the agreements were executed, the board of directors of Central Equities Corporation met in New York City to decide the fate of Boca Raton. The directors of Central Equities approved the transaction, and Conkling's *Palm Beach Post* proclaimed on October 19, 1926: "The dream which Addison Mizner originally had for Boca Raton seems assured of materialization. . . . It is the opinion of many realtors, that the importance of this transaction cannot be overestimated in its beneficial effects, not only to Boca Raton, but to the entire east coast of Florida, and it is generally regarded as conclusive evidence of the present soundness and future worth of America's Riviera, as was pointed out by Mizner officials."[14]

CREDITORS FORCE BANKRUPTCY

The Dawes bailout merely delayed the bankruptcy of the Mizner Development Corporation. During the early part of 1927 lawsuits were filed by disgruntled creditors in Palm Beach, Miami, and New York. In March, Jack Lindy, H. F. Underwood, and Sidney Adler sued the Mizner Development Corporation for $50,662, charging that the company was insolvent and had engaged in "false and fraudulent" sales tactics. They also accused the company of committing improper acts of bankruptcy by transferring its assets to several other creditors after becoming insolvent. Addison Mizner, fronting for the Dawes brothers, responded to the suit with typical irreverence by saying he had never heard of the petitioners and claiming that the company was in "very good condition." But in April, Harry M. and Ethel Chesebro commenced an action to foreclose on thirty-two acres, which included the Cloister Inn. They asserted that the company owed them $75,000 in principal and accrued interest.[15]

While litigating with creditors, Central Equities Corporation stripped the development company of its liquid assets and cash flow. By May 1927, Vice-President Dawes and his brothers had advanced $151,113, only 10 percent of their public commitment, to Mizner's company. Securing the advances, Central Equities, the controlling stockholder of the Mizner Development Corporation, seized the purchase contracts of lot buyers with an unpaid balance of $10,510,407. It also secured a priority position as a creditor by filing mortgages on 87.5 acres and 67 lots owned free and clear by the company. In addition, Central Equities placed liens on the furniture, equipment, and automobiles of the Mizner Development Corporation. The Dawes brothers had secured for themselves the unencumbered assets of the Mizner Development Corporation, leaving its debt and other liabilities to the unsecured creditors.[16]

The predatory practices of the Dawes brothers prompted the Riddle Engineering Company and two other creditors to file a bankruptcy petition against the Mizner Development Corporation on June 23, 1927. Karl Riddle's engineering firm, which was owed $30,764 for professional services, attacked the actions of the Dawes brothers as an unlawful depletion of assets designed "to hinder and delay" the creditors. A month later, the Mizner Development Corporation was adjudicated a bankrupt company.[17]

The bankruptcy trustees of the Mizner Development Corporation petitioned the federal court to set aside the transfers to Central Equities Corporation charging that they were based on "fraudulent" and "fictitious" claims. Central Equities had collected $41,446 from lot buyers on the purchase contracts from March to July 1927. The lawyers for the Dawes brothers, Evans and Mershon of Miami, denied the allegations of fraud and argued that the bankruptcy court lacked jurisdiction. They also asserted that the payments had been compensation for services rendered. Furthermore, they claimed that Central Equities must have been entitled to the $10.5 million of contracts because the Mizner Development Corporation failed to demand their return before the filing and adjudication of bankruptcy. This disingenuous argument ignored that Central Equities had complete control over the Mizner Development Corporation and had been its collection agent. Even so, the referee in bankruptcy, L. Earl Curry, ruled in favor of the vice-president's company because it had possession of the purchase contracts and mortgages before the involuntary bankruptcy petition was filed.[18]

The bankruptcy of the Mizner Development Corporation left 173 creditors with $4,192,000 in unsecured claims. They waited three more years to receive a dividend of .001 percent from the bankruptcy court. Riddle Engineering Company received $30.76 on its $30,764 bill. Mizner Development Corporation paid $57.98 to the Palm Beach Bank and Trust Company on unsecured loans of $57,982 and $101.68 to the First American Bank and Trust Company on unsecured loans of $101,689. The Chelsea Exchange Bank received only $95.50 on its unsecured loans of $95,500.[19]

The law firm of Congressman George S. Graham lost far less on its accounts receivable than the local law firm of the Mizner Development Corporation. At the time of the bankruptcy, Graham, McMahon, Buell and Knox of New York City had been paid for all of its legal services except for $1,500. So it received $1.50 as a creditor. The West Palm Beach firm of Blackwell, Donnell, and Moore was owed $67,650, and received $67.65. E. B. Donnell's firm continued to represent the company in bankruptcy, however, and recouped some of its losses by charging high fees to the trustees.[20]

The remaining creditors suffered heavy losses. For example, Warren and Wetmore of New York City, the architects of a proposed oceanfront Ritz-Carlton hotel, which was never built, received payment of $150 on their $150,000 commission. The Andrews Asphalt Paving Company received $93.36 of its $93,362 accounts receivable. And the Florida Power and Light Company, which supplied the electricity for the Cloister Inn, lost $3,080.[21]

In November 1927, Clarence Geist of Philadelphia, an original Mizner stockholder and a former partner of Vice-President Dawes and his brothers in midwestern gas and electric companies, purchased the real estate holdings of the Mizner Development Corporation for $76,350 and the assumption of $7 million of mortgage loans. The Dawes brothers, in the name of Rufus and Henry, then became stockholders of the Geist syndicate.[22]

MIZNER'S PRIVATE COMPANIES

Addison Mizner held worthless shares of the Mizner Development Corporation but still hoped to secure a profit from his ill-fated Boca Raton project. In the name of Mizner Industries, Inc., he filed a lien for labor and materials on the Cloister Inn, which was owned by the Mizner Development Corporation. By the summer of 1926, his business affairs had become a tangled web of intercompany transactions. Until his death on February 5, 1933, he kept a running balance of credits and debits between Mizner Industries, Inc., and Addison Mizner, Inc., his architectural business. Between June 30, 1926, and December 16, 1932, Addison Mizner, Inc., transferred $412,020 to Mizner Industries, Inc., which in turn transferred $355,305 to Addison Mizner, Inc. As a result of these transactions, Addison Mizner, Inc., had an outstanding balance of $56,715 with Mizner Industries. Despite Mizner's manipulations, both companies were forced into federal bankruptcy court.[23]

Mizner Industries, Inc., had been in the business of manufacturing floor and roof tiles, pottery, reproduction antique furniture, and decorative items made of iron, stone, and wood. Less than four months after Mizner's death, it was adjudicated bankrupt. After five years of proceedings, unsecured creditors received only $3,360 of $111,786 in debts. The Internal Revenue Service was a priority creditor because after 1928 Mizner Industries stopped paying federal taxes, which totaled $10,855 by 1933. The company also owed the tax collector of Palm Beach County, and it was delinquent for four years on its taxes to the city of West Palm Beach.[24]

Moreover, Mizner Industries defaulted on an unsecured loan at the West Palm Beach Atlantic National Bank, which had an outstanding balance of $3,795. After the bankruptcy of the Mizner Development Corporation, why would any bank make an unsecured loan to one of Addison Mizner's companies? Because Mizner Industries had issued a false financial statement showing a net worth of $152,239. Relying on that financial statement, the bank loaned Mizner Industries $6,100 on December 15, 1932. But appraisers hired by the trustee in bankruptcy reported that the company was worth only $11,300.[25]

The prized asset of Addison Mizner, Inc., was the five-story Via Mizner Building in Palm Beach. In February 1925, Mizner had personally borrowed $100,000 from the Atlantic National Bank of Jacksonville and other mortgage bondholders to construct the complex. The following September, while in the throes of the Boca Raton development and as a shield against his creditors, he transferred the building to Addison Mizner, Inc. The Via Mizner loan, which ballooned in February 1935, forced the company to reorganize its affairs through the bankruptcy court.[26]

The Via Mizner Building, located on Worth Avenue, one of the most exclusive shopping districts in the world, consisted of shops, offices, and apartments. It housed Mizner's architectural office and his private residence. Addison Mizner lived there in grand style without paying rent to his company. Surrounded by antiques and fine furnishings, he entertained like an Old World potentate. His butler served drinks to the guests as they listened to a group performing classical music, an artist explaining his work, or Mizner's anecdotes. After Mizner's death in 1933, Frank Gair Macomber, the curator of the Boston Museum of Fine Arts, appraised his personal silver, china, rugs, works of art, chandeliers, antiques, and other furnishings. Seven years after the Boca Raton fiasco, Mizner's personal belongings were valued at $191,432 in Depression-era dollars.[27]

10

SENATORIAL PRIVILEGE

When Comptroller of the Currency Joseph McIntosh misused the assets of the defunct Palm Beach National Bank to reward his political friends, he was following a well-established practice among regulatory authorities. So when the First National Bank of Lake Worth and the National Bank of West Palm Beach failed in 1927, he quickly appointed Senator Lawrence Sherman as their lawyer. Then, by personally approving Sherman's exorbitant legal bills, McIntosh ensured that his confidant was well paid on an expedited basis.[1]

Sherman, who abused his public position to advance his private interests, had been the beneficiary of this form of political largess before. Sherman and the Dawes brothers understood the patronage system that the comptroller of the currency controlled and the business opportunities associated with bank liquidations. Sherman was a recipient when both Charles and Henry Dawes had been the comptroller of the currency. He and the Dawes brothers became powerful allies after Charles Dawes entered national politics in 1896 as William McKinley's Illinois campaign manager. In 1897 President McKinley appointed Dawes, at the age of thirty-two, as his comptroller of the currency. While Dawes was the nation's chief bank regulator, Sherman was the Speaker of the Illinois House of Representatives.[2]

Preparing to run for the United States Senate from Illinois, Comptroller Dawes appointed Sherman as his special liquidation attorney. Though he had already hired local counsel, Dawes retained Sherman's small law firm to represent some of the nation's largest insolvent national banks in the states of Washington, Colorado, Montana, Oregon, and Maryland. Dawes guaranteed that his political ally had more than enough work by delaying many matters for him. He told Sherman in private letters that there was plenty of legal work in the comptroller's office because national bank assets of $40 million were in the hands of his receivers. Dawes was delighted to participate in Sherman's business plans by sending first-class legal work to the Macomb, Illinois, law firm.[3]

Dawes used depositors' money to subsidize his political aspirations. He made sure that Sherman, then Speaker of the Illinois House of Representatives, was fully paid for his legal bills on an expedited basis. A few weeks after Dawes resigned as comptroller of the currency, he returned to Illinois to begin his campaign for the United States Senate. To enhance his chances for election, Dawes and Speaker Sherman combined their respective political organizations. Nevertheless, Dawes lost the 1902 Senate race after his opponent charged that he had squandered depositors' money as comptroller of the currency by hiring political attorneys, including Speaker Sherman, to represent insolvent national banks.[4]

After his defeat, Dawes, who was always planning for the future by mixing politics with his business, immediately hired Sherman as his private attorney. He then sold Sherman stock in the Seattle Lighting Company, one of the companies controlled by Dawes and his brothers. Because the powerful legislator was his attorney and business partner, Dawes was ready to organize the Central Trust Company of Illinois, a state-chartered bank. After it was chartered, the advertising slogan of the Dawes bank was "a banking institution built around friendly contacts." It was an appropriate slogan because Dawes used his political contacts to benefit the bank, and he used the bank to advance his political career.[5]

Sherman's opportunity to run for the United States Senate appeared in 1912, and Dawes was the chief fund-raiser for his successful campaign. Dawes continued the financial support of

With the active support of Comptroller of the Currency Joseph W. McIntosh
(left), Senator Lawrence Y. Sherman *(right)* turned the banking crash into
a legal bonanza.
(Courtesy, Office of the Comptroller of the Currency and Illinois
State Historical Library)

Sherman throughout his career. During his eight years in the Senate, Sherman repaid his political debts many times when Dawes lobbied him regarding issues and appointments. Dawes frequently contacted his obedient friend regarding banking matters. Dawes appreciated their friendship, but he once wrote Sherman that his responsiveness was sometimes an embarrassment. Nevertheless, in that same letter he asked Sherman for a favor. Dawes's brothers, Henry and Rufus, also were not timid about using their influence with Sherman when the Senate was considering legislation that affected the family's business interests.[6]

Sherman resigned from the Senate in 1921 for financial reasons. He recognized that the success of his fledgling law practice depended on Charles Dawes, who was becoming a titan in the Republican party. Shortly after Sherman's resignation, Dawes, then director of the Bureau of the Budget, appointed him to the executive budget committee, which prepared the nation's budget. President Harding later thanked the former senator for his work on the budget committee and assured him that the White House was always open. The president wished Sherman success in his new law practice: "I want to make an expression at this time of my gratitude for the very great help you have given to the administration. . . . I hope an abundance of compensation will come to you."[7]

During June 1924, the same month Sherman, as a delegate to the Republican National Convention, seconded the nomination of Charles Dawes for vice-president, Comptroller of the Currency Henry Dawes granted Sherman a charter for the First National Bank of Daytona Beach. Sherman had vigorously lobbied the convention on behalf of Charles Dawes and had been instrumental in his nomination. After the convention, Dawes wrote his loyal friend expressing appreciation for his significant influence during the nomination process. In a congratulatory letter, Sherman, who was sixty-six years old, reminded the vice-presidential nominee that he was going "to spend the rest of [his] years repairing [his] broken fortune."[8]

Sherman planned to retire to Daytona Beach after the presidential campaign and form a law firm using the new bank as its anchor client. The bank would be an ideal client for the proposed law firm, which would perform no trial work and be limited to office consultations. Sherman's partner in the venture would be

Noah C. Bainum, a sixty-year-old former judge in Illinois who had been his law partner in Springfield. Sherman and Bainum would conveniently have an office in the bank building, and both would serve on the bank's board of directors. Dawes approved Sherman's plans and told him they made good sense.[9]

Sherman maintained a close working relationship with the Dawes brothers after he moved to Florida. Although Sherman had no previous bank management experience, he was approved as president of the First National Bank of Daytona Beach. When his bank opened, Sherman became the correspondent banker for the Dawes brothers in Florida. Comptroller Henry Dawes granted two bank charters in Florida during his tenure in Washington, and Sherman was connected to both: the First National Bank of Daytona Beach and the Palm Beach National Bank.[10]

Sherman guaranteed the approval of his application for a bank charter by promising that the new bank would establish a correspondent banking relationship with the Central Trust Company of Illinois, which was controlled by the Dawes brothers. Less than two weeks before Henry Dawes granted the lucrative bank charter, Charles Dawes, then chairman of the board of the Central Trust Company, thanked Sherman for his assurance that the First National Bank of Daytona Beach would become a correspondent of the Dawes bank.[11]

THE GUARDIAN ANGEL

The election of Calvin Coolidge and Charles Dawes assured Sherman "an abundance of compensation." After the resignation of Henry Dawes, President Coolidge named his deputy comptroller, Joseph McIntosh of Illinois, as the comptroller of the currency. McIntosh in turn appointed Sherman's Daytona Beach law firm as the liquidation attorneys for the Palm Beach National Bank, the First National Bank of Lake Worth, and the National Bank of West Palm Beach. Sherman was in a hurry to repair his "broken fortune" so he blatantly used the power at his disposal.[12]

Friction between him and the comptroller's professional staff began after he submitted his first invoice for the Palm Beach National Bank. Sherman sent a bill for expenses directly to McIntosh in Washington. J. E. Fouts, assistant supervising receiver, advised

Sherman that "in accordance with the custom of the office" his bills for fees and expenses had to be submitted to the local receiver in Florida, not to McIntosh. Fouts then told Cunningham to review Sherman's bills and, if they were reasonable, to send them to Washington. A recommendation from Cunningham was required before payment could be authorized.[13]

Disregarding Fouts's letter, Sherman wrote a private letter to his friend McIntosh asking for advice regarding the amount of the fee. In a handwritten postscript, he said he did not know how much to charge because this was the first time he had represented the comptroller's office. To advance his negotiating ploy, Sherman conveniently forgot that he had represented the office when Charles Dawes was the comptroller.[14]

When Sherman submitted his bill for services, the comptroller's staff was alarmed about its lack of detail. Cunningham was instructed to demand "detailed information" from Sherman. Cunningham assured his supervisors that "in the future all bills rendered by L. Y. Sherman, will carry complete detailed information in support of any and all charges." Cunningham promised that he would prevent Sherman from submitting any more bills directly to McIntosh.[15]

While the professional staff was trying to force the former senator to follow normal office procedures, McIntosh informed Sherman that he planned to visit Florida soon and hoped to meet with him to discuss his fees. McIntosh and Vice-President Dawes would be vacationing in Florida together. In March 1927, McIntosh took the time to resolve the fee dispute on the way to his vacation with the vice-president. Without an itemized bill and outside normal channels, McIntosh personally agreed to a flat fee of $5,000 for Sherman's law firm at the Palm Beach National Bank. He met privately with Sherman in Palm Beach and authorized the payment. McIntosh later told Sherman that he had delivered Sherman's message to Vice-President Dawes.[16]

When McIntosh returned to Washington, he found that more business for Sherman was waiting on his desk. The First National Bank of Lake Worth had failed, and a receivership needed to be established. After appointing Cunningham as the receiver, McIntosh named Sherman as the attorney for the defunct bank. But this time Sherman was required to sign a contract mandating that his fees would be "reasonable, subject to the approval of the Comptroller of the Currency, whose decision as to such fees shall be final."[17]

His law practice was booming because of Vice-President Dawes and Comptroller McIntosh, and Sherman enthusiastically proved that he was a devoted team member in a letter to Charles N. Wheeler, author of *Dawes at Home and Abroad*. Sherman wrote: "Charles G. Dawes is great in peace or war, in office or out of office, in public or private, in business or politics, in all he is touched by the inscrutable hand of destiny to stand out in his generation the gifted man of thought and action that stamps him as a leader in every great emergency that has arisen since he came upon the stage of human affairs." In September, the vice-president showed his appreciation by inviting Sherman and his daughter to stay with the Dawes family at their home in Evanston, Illinois.[18]

Sherman then used his political capital to increase his legal fees. In January 1928, he traveled to Washington to meet privately with McIntosh. Circumventing the comptroller's official policy, Sherman wanted to get his flat fee increased by 50 percent. He requested that McIntosh change their previous agreement and pay his firm an additional $2,500 for the Palm Beach National Bank, which would bring the total fees to $7,500. Although McIntosh was generous with depositors' money, the professional staff asked for an accounting.[19]

Reluctantly, Sherman provided the comptroller's office with a sketchy statement for past services rendered. The statement did not describe the individual cases and the services provided in each action. He admitted it was incomplete because his firm had neglected to maintain accurate timekeeping records. He promised McIntosh, however, that the additional fee would cover all past services rendered by his firm and all services to be rendered in the future. In a follow-up letter stamped "special" by the comptroller's office, Sherman told McIntosh that his firm had given a 50 percent discount because government work was so much larger in volume than legal work in the private sector. Following normal departmental policy, the professional staff rejected the additional payment and requested "a detailed bill" for past services rendered by Sherman's firm.[20]

An irritated Sherman sent the comptroller's staff a seven-page letter, which failed to provide the documentation requested but revealed that he had reached an agreement with McIntosh. The agreement was that Sherman's flat fee would be increased to $7,500. He had already received $5,000, and an additional $2,500 was to be paid when Sherman made a report generally describing his services. He said it was extremely difficult to calculate the amount of time he spent on each collection case so he could not give the comptroller's staff a precise breakdown of his time.[21]

While haggling with the comptroller's office, Sherman wrote Vice-President Dawes to encourage him to run for the presidency in 1928. Twelve years earlier Dawes had promoted Sherman as a presidential candidate, and now their roles were reversed. Dawes, whose bank in Chicago would fail because of insider abuse before the end of the next presidential term, was torn between his business interests and his political aspirations. He thanked his confidant for the support and asked him to entertain an associate who was going to spend his vacation in Daytona Beach.[22]

Sherman, annoyed by the refusal of the comptroller's staff to pay his latest demands, appealed to McIntosh in a personal letter. He asked his protégé to intervene and resolve the controversy. Upset that the comptroller's staff was questioning their arrangement and his latest bill, Sherman said that the difference between the $2,500 charged and the amount of services rendered as shown on his bill was irrelevant. He reminded McIntosh that they had reached an agreement at their private meeting in January. Sherman said he knew his friend of long standing was a man of his word.[23]

Immediately upon receipt of Sherman's letter, McIntosh sent a terse memorandum to Robert D. Garrett, chief supervising receiver, asking him to ensure that the matter was "fixed up." McIntosh firmly told his staff that he thought Sherman was "quite modest in his charges." Two days later, Garrett informed Cunningham that Sherman was "disturbed" and had sent another "personal communication to Colonel McIntosh." Sherman was "anxious" now that the staff had discovered the mistake in his bill. So Cunningham was told to "disregard" the previous instructions by the staff and to pay the former senator.[24]

Before receiving the additional payment, Sherman opined that the borrowers were liable for the bank's legal fees. Sherman advised Cunningham that the promissory notes and security agreements of the Palm Beach National Bank provided for payment of attorney's fees if the borrower defaulted. He failed to mention the difficulty in recovering legal fees from insolvent borrowers. Cunningham sent Sherman's legal opinion to Washington with a cover letter stamped "special," saying that borrowers in default could help offset Sherman's fees.[25]

Based on the flat fee agreement and Sherman's legal opinion, when Cunningham paid Sherman and Bainum he deducted from the payment $547 of fees that they had collected in 1927 from two borrowers. After receiving the $1,953 payment, Bainum, acting for the firm, issued a revised legal opinion that contradicted Sherman's previous opinion and complicated the matter further. Bainum said the deduction was improper and the receiver lacked the authority to reduce their fees. Besides, the two borrowers were liable for fees on a proportional basis.[26]

Cunningham requested assistance from his supervisor in Washington to resolve the new problem with Sherman and Bainum. Now skeptical about the soundness of the legal advice he was receiving, he asked for "special attention" from the senior staff. Based on Bainum's opinion, Cunningham inquired whether the entire $7,500 fee of Sherman and Bainum should be refunded to an escrow account. Then borrowers could pay fees to the law firm on a case-by-case basis.[27]

Because of the fee dispute, Sherman and Bainum refused to pay any expenses in advance. Cunningham complained to Washington that he was in an "embarrassing position," which was creating a "serious handicap" for the receivership. Delays in filing lawsuits would cause depositors to lose money because of the "unrest" in Palm Beach County. Garrett, the chief supervising receiver who had "fixed up" the earlier dispute for Sherman, responded to Cunningham's concerns by departing from the standard procedure of the comptroller's office. He instructed his subordinate to pay Sherman and Bainum's expenses in advance, including their travel cost. Garrett conceded that "ordinarily . . . all of our attorneys pay their expenses in these matters and submit their itemized bill to the Receiver for payment." He also cautioned Cunningham "to keep down any friction" with Sherman.[28]

At a time when a dress shirt cost $1.95 and a good tie cost $1.00 in Palm Beach, Sherman was determined to collect the additional $547. He would soon be a delegate to the Republican National Convention in Kansas City, so he took advantage of the timing to collect the additional fee. On his way to Kansas City, Sherman stopped in Washington to meet with McIntosh and his legal counsel, George P. Barse. Sherman misrepresented his agreement with McIntosh by saying it covered only future services, not past services. According to Sherman's calculations, his fee for representing the Palm Beach National Bank should be $8,047, not $7,500. He said the additional payment would not be a precedent for the two other defunct banks represented by him. Barse advised McIntosh that the payment could be made if the agreement was not a flat fee arrangement covering all legal services performed for the Palm Beach National Bank. For the second time, McIntosh agreed to change the fee agreement with Sherman and to pay him the disputed amount. Three days before the Republican National Convention began, Cunningham paid Sherman $547 in "full settlement of all legal services" for the Palm Beach National Bank.[29]

Sherman must have thought that the first day of the Republican National Convention was a propitious time to pressure the comptroller's office for yet another fee increase. On June 12, from Kansas City, he proposed to McIntosh a flat fee of $15,000 for the First National Bank of Lake Worth or in the alternative a $10,000 retainer plus any fees collected from the borrowers. Sherman, who claimed to be retired in Florida, was seeking a 100 percent fee increase. His proposal seemed to be designed so that depositors would pay for his retirement, and even McIntosh thought it was exorbitant. But McIntosh privately met with him and reached a verbal understanding of $10,000 for the Lake Worth receivership, which was 33 percent more than the fee agreed upon for the Palm Beach National Bank.[30]

Senator Sherman and Judge Bainum were active in the 1928 presidential campaign. Sherman went to Topeka, Kansas, in August as a member of the committee that formally notified Senator Charles Curtis of his selection as the Republican vice-presidential candidate. Bainum served on the committee that traveled to California to advise Herbert Hoover of his nomination. Sherman campaigned for the Republican ticket in the South, declaring: "Herbert Hoover is the best candidate the Republicans could have nominated for the purpose of making the party felt in the south. . . . Senator Curtis, too, will help the ticket in the so-called border states. He is an able man. I served with him in the United States Senate." He predicted that the Republicans would win by a landslide in November and that Hoover could carry the South.

Sherman told the *Illinois State Journal* that he had retired from the "active practice of law," but he felt "fit . . . for a round of politics."[31]

A turning point in Sherman's relationship with the comptroller's office occurred when McIntosh resigned in December 1928. He was succeeded by John W. Pole, the chief of national bank examiners, who was the first career employee to be appointed comptroller of the currency. In a dozen years, the former bank examiner had worked his way through the ranks to the head of the department. Unlike the Dawes brothers and McIntosh, Pole was a professional bank regulator. When he resigned in 1932, Edward Platt, a former member of the Federal Reserve Board, said: "He is the first comptroller of the currency in many years who was not and is not a politician. President Coolidge appointed him in recognition of pure ability, long experience and training in both the theory and practice of banking." Because of the nation's banking crisis, Platt warned Hoover not to appoint "a politician or a political banker" as Pole's successor.[32]

Two weeks after Pole was sworn in, Sherman renewed efforts to increase his fees at the First National Bank of Lake Worth. Sherman asked Pole to change the $10,000 agreement because the legal work was greater than he had anticipated. As additional compensation, he suggested that his firm keep the fees it collected from borrowers. Pole was unreceptive to Sherman's pleas. After his staff complained of receiving "another *long* letter from Mr. Sherman concerning attorneys fees," Pole "closed" the matter.[33]

Several months later, Sherman's firm was criticized by Cunningham for "indifference" and for lacking "the spirit of 'go after it.'" He attributed the firm's "feeling of independence" to a lack of incentive resulting from the substantial fees paid in advance. Privately, the receiver was critical of the firm's "attitude" and work product, but he still treated it with deference. He told Pole that the "utmost friendly relations" existed between him and his attorneys. By parading influential Republicans in front of Cunningham, Sherman reminded him of political realities. Cunningham reported that a friend of Sherman's, John Harris of Harris-Winthrop and Company of New York, appeared "to be a very warm and close friend of Dr. Hubert Work, Mr. Mellon, Mr. West, President Hoover and other high officials of the Government in Washington." Cunningham covered himself by making sure his superiors knew that Sherman held him "in the very highest regard, socially and otherwise."[34]

COURTESY AMONG COLLEAGUES

After the appointment of Pole, Sherman's firm was held account-able for its large fees. An irreconcilable difference developed when the firm refused to make minimal efforts to collect loans from out-of-state borrowers without being paid additional fees. Sherman was reminded that he had agreed to handle all of the legal work at the Palm Beach National Bank and the First National Bank of Lake Worth for a total of $17,500. If his firm had to hire other law firms, it had to pay for their fees.[35]

The issue erupted when Sherman's firm improperly handled the collection of the stale debt of former United States senator Joe Bailey of Texas. Refusing to antagonize a colleague, Sherman treated Bailey with senatorial courtesy even though he had "curtly" refused to pay the outstanding $1,000 on his interest-free note at the Palm Beach National Bank. Bailey was belligerent toward the loan, which involved the Mizner Development Corporation, because his investment had gone sour. To settle the matter quietly and acting without approval from the comptroller's office, Sherman's firm retained the influential Dallas law firm of Davis, Synnott and Hatchell to approach Bailey. Because of Bailey's influence and rep-utation, lawyers in Dallas were reluctant to become entangled in the embarrassing situation.[36]

Davis, Synnott and Hatchell collected the principal and interest of $1,247.70, though the note carried no interest. But the Dallas firm retained 50 percent of the collection, $623.85, for its fee. Senior partner John Davis justified the fee because of the abnormal circumstances involving the loan and the standing of Senator Bailey. Davis stressed the extraordinary difficulty in collecting the loan because Sherman's firm was unwilling to offend Bailey.[37]

Cunningham was appalled. He could not "conceive of a firm of attorneys having the audacity to ask the collection fee of 50%, especially where it was not necessary to file suit." Cunningham understood the difficulty in collecting from Bailey, who had tried to settle the matter with a bad check. But he and his supervisors considered the fee "exorbitant" since the Dallas firm only "wrote two or three letters and possibly called Bailey's office on the telephone." Bainum agreed that the fee was outrageous but advised that the only remedy was to file suit against Davis, Synnott and Hatchell.[38]

Because of their "neglect of duty," Sherman and Bainum were held responsible for the Davis firm's excessive fee. Sherman's firm had failed to require the standard fee contract that gave the comptroller the right to establish a reasonable fee, which in no event would exceed 25 percent of the collection. The comptroller's office took the middle ground by requiring Sherman and Bainum to refund the excess fee of the Davis firm, not their entire fee.[39]

Bainum reacted with a combative letter to Cunningham. Sherman and Bainum refused to accept any responsibility for the Davis firm. Bainum also defended the performance of Davis in such a sensitive situation. He told Cunningham to consider the results: $623.85 recovered from an outstanding balance of $1,000 on an interest-free note. Though Bailey had no legal defense, Bainum emphasized the political fallout of suing a former member of the United States Senate. He admitted, however, that the fee was exorbitant. Yet his firm would litigate against the comptroller's office if necessary.[40]

Comptroller Pole, who had been in office for only a month, answered Bainum's protest by instructing Cunningham to deduct the excess fee of $311.93 from the amount owed to Sherman and Bainum because they were "responsible for the exorbitant charge." Bainum then sent an angry letter to Pole threatening to sue the receiver if their fees were reduced. Sherman's firm also threatened to resign from the three receiverships just when several of the significant cases were ready for trial. One of those cases, *National Bank of West Palm Beach* v. *Atlantic National Bank of Jacksonville,* was on standby for a hearing before the federal judge in Jacksonville. While making the threat to resign, Bainum said that the receiver would lose the cases because no other attorney would have time to prepare properly.[41]

Sherman and Bainum's threats went beyond malpractice. Using extortionate tactics to collect $311.93, the firm exposed the depositors of the three defunct banks to huge losses. Sherman and his law partner also had a conflict of interest which precluded them from zealously prosecuting the case against the Atlantic National Bank of Jacksonville. Their First National Bank of Daytona Beach had a correspondent banking relationship with the Atlantic National Bank of Jacksonville. In 1930, the First National Bank of Daytona Beach formally affiliated with the Atlantic National Bank of Jacksonville and Sherman became a stockholder of both institutions. The threats and conflict of interest could have been the basis of a malpractice lawsuit. But with his connections to the Hoover administration, the comptroller's office, even with Pole as the head of the agency, had to treat Sherman diplomatically.[42]

Instead of refunding the unearned part of its advance fees, Sherman's firm pressured Pole to settle the controversy with an additional payment. Though the withdrawal of the firm prejudiced the receiverships, Bainum demanded an additional $3,000 from the dwindling assets of the First National Bank of Lake Worth. In lieu of time sheets to justify the fee, he reminded Pole that the firm was well-connected in Palm Beach and Washington.[43]

Several major cases were on the trial docket in Miami, so the comptroller's office had to respond quickly to the demand. But Sherman's influence was the deciding factor in the one-sided negotiation. The purging of Sherman from the comptroller's office became an expensive proposition when his firm received the exact amount it demanded. Cunningham reported to Pole that he had reached a "friendly settlement with Messrs. Sherman and Bainum that they felt . . . was just." The wary receiver said, "In severing relations . . . the best of feeling prevails and it would appear no feeling of antagonism exists on their part."[44]

Privately, the comptroller's staff criticized the "attitude" of Sherman and Bainum in refusing to provide any assistance to Cunningham after they resigned. Nevertheless, the lawyers, in search of a quick profit and blind to their conflict of interest, tried unsuccessfully to bid on the remaining assets of the Palm Beach National Bank. The receiver's problems with excessive legal fees ended with the termination of Sherman's firm. Cunningham, who was normally tightfisted with depositors' money, retained the West Palm Beach law firm of Wideman and Wideman, who agreed to charge reasonable fees and to follow the comptroller's standard procedures. Cunningham carefully reviewed each item on the firm's legal bills and challenged a $14 charge for an automobile round trip between Lake Worth and Miami. He refused to pay the bill because the round-trip bus and train fares were $4.50 and $5.84, respectively. He also rejected the legal fee of $75 for a collection case, which he said was "really exorbitant." Revealing the double standard at the comptroller's office, the receiver said that $25 or $30 was an "ample charge." Sanctimoniously, he declared that he had been "too long connected with the service of the United States Government not to know that it does not approve expenditures of funds under its control, directly or indirectly, other than in a most economical manner."[45]

Sherman was handling other matters before Congress and the Hoover administration so he took steps to limit the repercussions from his rupture with the comptroller's office. He wrote former comptroller of the currency McIntosh, thanking him for the legal work but misrepresenting the reasons for his resignation. He told McIntosh that the receiverships were "so nearly administered as to need little or no legal services for the remaining business."[46]

In trying to repair the damage, he even renounced Bainum, who had been his friend for more than thirty-five years. When Bainum had applied for a federal judgeship in 1928, Sherman recommended him to Attorney General John G. Sargent as a man of "character and integrity" who possessed an "eminent professional ability." A couple of years later, Sherman met with Deputy Comptroller F. G. Awalt in Washington "to explain that he had had so much trouble with Mr. Bainum as a law partner that it had become necessary for him to dissolve the partnership." He requested that the records of the comptroller's office reflect that the "difficulty" with his firm was because of his law partner. Sherman said "he felt that Mr. Bainum had been very unreasonable and had not handled matters as he should."[47]

11

THE DEFEAT OF
ERNEST AMOS

I n the aftermath of the crash, many weak banks survived until
depositors learned, by rumors or lawsuits, that they had been
fleeced by insiders. Depositors then panicked, runs followed,
and the banks failed. This phenomenon continued throughout the 1920s. Two of these failures, those of the Seminole County
Bank of Sanford and the Bank of Bay Biscayne, provoked indictments against Ernest Amos for "the crime of malpractice in office." A third failure, that of the Citizens Bank of Tampa, resulted
in impeachment charges against Amos for "willful, wrongful, corrupt or unlawful" acts as comptroller. After six years of controversy, he was finally defeated in 1932.[1]

The Seminole County Bank, ravaged by insider loans, collapsed
in 1927. The local grand jury indicted the bank's president, Forrest
Lake, who was a former president of the Florida Bankers Association and state representative, for bank fraud. After reviewing the
comptroller's confidential regulatory records, jurors also indicted
Amos for "knowingly, unlawfully, wilfully and corruptly" allowing Lake to loot the bank. Amos had known for at least fifteen
months that Lake was engaged in illegal insider lending, but he
had refused to remove him or seize the bank. Proof of his knowl-

edge was a letter he wrote to the bank's directors in May 1926: "Four of your directors are heavily indebted in the institution and the line of credit to the president, Mr. Forrest Lake, is in excess of the entire capital and surplus of the bank."[2]

Amos declared that the indictment was "just another manifestation of the persecution" against him. He said the Seminole County indictment had no more substance than the 1926 Palm Beach County charges. The *Palm Beach Independent* disagreed: "The people being persecuted are the depositors in state banks who have incompetent and dishonest officials. They have lost a lot of money, very few have recovered any, prosecution of bank officers has always failed, and as for Mr. Amos he hasn't missed a meal nor seen the inside of a jail. . . . If the people reelect him . . . we will be sorry for Florida."[3]

Despite the banking crash and indictments for malpractice, Amos won reelection in 1928 by an unprecedented landslide. The Seminole County indictment lured two formidable opponents into the race, but after the Florida Supreme Court dismissed the charges, their campaigns fizzled. State senator James B. Stewart of Fernandina and Emory S. Martin, a respected lawyer and banker, challenged the powerful incumbent. Senator Stewart ran a low-key campaign that relied primarily on his name recognition. Martin, the vice-president and cashier of the Citizens Bank of Williston, who was regarded as "one of the outstandingly clean men in political life," ran an issue-oriented campaign. Both Stewart and Martin failed to realize that in a race against an incumbent his record in office is the issue. They did not criticize Amos or blame him for the record number of bank failures. Martin wasted his limited resources on bland newspaper advertisements supporting "safe and sane" banking and promising to hire "competent and discreet examiners." Martin also stumped for the dismantling of the office he was seeking. He renewed the call for legislation to create a separate banking department headed by a professional regulator. A bill had passed the state House during the previous session but died in the Senate.[4]

The *Tallahassee Daily Democrat,* "a newspaper endorsing and supporting the principles of the Democratic Party," came to the defense of the three-term Democratic cabinet member. Two weeks after the comptroller's indictment and a month before the supreme court blocked his criminal trial, the influential newspaper portrayed Amos as "one of the state's safest and most conservative officials." During the campaign, the *Democrat* endorsed him and said that he deserved reelection because of his "splendid reputation." The paper also supported Amos on its news pages. When he gave his annual speech to the Florida Bankers Association, the *Democrat* printed it on the front page in its entirety with a photograph of the comptroller captioned "Hon. Ernest Amos." Addressing the group that was financing his campaign, Amos praised the bankers for their "courage, grit, resourcefulness, and determination to fight to the last ditch." He predicted that the history of Florida banking would "rout the rantings of demagogues and critics."[5]

Using the powers of his incumbency, Amos routed Senator Stewart and Martin. He led the Democratic ticket and received the most votes of any political candidate in the history of Florida. The comptroller received 154,871 Democratic votes to Stewart's 97,961 votes and Martin's 30,323 votes. The unprecedented landslide for Amos, after his two indictments for gross malpractice, illustrated the folly of challenging an incumbent cabinet member.[6]

His legal problems resurfaced when he was arrested in 1930 following the collapse of the Bank of Bay Biscayne. Amos was charged with official malfeasance by a Miami justice of the peace for "wilfully employing officers, directors, agents and employees of the Bank of Bay Biscayne" to conduct its liquidation audit. He quickly walked across Adams Street and filed for another writ of habeas corpus from the supreme court of Florida. Appearing before the court without counsel, he said: "Your honors, in view of what has been said here today, I feel that there is no need for defense or denials." But he did file a brief asserting many of the arguments that his private lawyer, Fred Davis, had used in 1926.[7]

Davis, who was now the state attorney general, came to the aid of his colleague in the cabinet by filing a motion of disqualification which read like a brief for the accused. Davis informed the court that he had a conflict of interest so he was not qualified to prosecute Amos. Then he argued against the prosecution: "I urged as a proposition of law that the comptroller of the state of Florida could not be charged with nor convicted of the criminal offense of malfeasance for acts done within the scope of his official duties as comptroller in any other county of the state than Leon County, or at all, which opinion I still hold and entertain to be correct in law and by reason thereof I could not conscientiously and honestly argue to the contrary." He also told the court that as attorney general he had defended in his "official capacity the conduct of the said Ernest Amos in regard to the said Bank of Bay Biscayne." Davis appointed a Miami lawyer to discharge his duties as attorney general by representing the state before the supreme court. But he handicapped the prosecution of Amos by refusing to compensate the lawyer for his services or expenses connected with the case.[8]

Following the precedent established in 1926, the supreme court dismissed the charges on procedural grounds. Amos had avoided a trial for the third time because of the high court in Tallahassee. But his practice of appointing officers and directors of failed banks as their liquidators sparked a controversy in Tampa that would lead to his ouster.[9]

TAMPA BANKING PANIC OF 1929

During the banking crash of 1926, depositors in Tampa felt confident, after reading the *Tampa Morning Tribune,* that their banks were in "good shape." Most readers did not realize that the president of Tampa Tribune, Inc., Dr. Louis Bize, was also president of the Citizens Bank and Trust Company of Tampa. Dr. Bize had once piously declared that his goal for the bank was to add to the "world's happiness." But his image in the community changed after he sold his interest in the *Tribune.* When Bize's insolvent bank declared a dividend for the stockholders in July 1929, depositors panicked. While panic swept through Tampa and southwest Florida, the Citizens Bank and Trust Company and nine affiliated banks collapsed.[10]

The closing of the Citizens Bank, a member of the Federal Reserve System, startled Tampa. While the Federal Reserve Bank of Atlanta rushed $5 million to Tampa by airplane and police-escorted armored truck, reporters groped to explain the reason for the closing of the city's largest bank. Directors of the bank, who had converted the landmark into a private casino, made the empty promise that depositors would receive "100 percent on the dollar."[11]

The bankers and their regulators blamed the crisis on "unwise gossip" and the Mediterranean fruit fly. The *New York Times* ran a photograph of the deadly fly, whose "havoc" had supposedly caused the closing of Bize's chain of banks, and reported the official explanation: "Ten banks in Florida failed because of a tiny insect. The banks closed down because the citrus crop failed and the citrus crop was destroyed by the fruit fly. Against the destroyer the federal and state governments are waging a war." The "fearless" eradication of the "invader from abroad" would soon restore Florida's citrus industry and economy.[12]

Governor Doyle E. Carlton, whose campaign supporters included many of the state's bankers and the Anthony family, perpetuated the delusion by saying: "The truth is the Mediterranean Fly scare and not the condition of the banks brought about these disasters." The governor said he expected a "flyless Florida" by October 15. Carlton, a former state senator from Tampa, could not afford to discuss the real reason for the disaster because he and his entities owed $218,578 in forty-three loans to the Citizens Bank and Trust Company at the time of its collapse.[13]

According to the *Tampa Morning Tribune,* depositors should "keep a level head, a guarded tongue, a feeling of faith in the things that merit faith, and you'll help Tampa to stay all right." In a front-page editorial the *Tribune* admonished the public: "The statement of the Federal Reserve Bank that it will furnish money sufficient to pay all the depositors of the banks of Tampa . . . should be sufficient assurance to the people of Tampa that further excitement and further withdrawals are unwarranted." E. D. Lambright, the editor of the *Tribune* when it was controlled by Bize, was still the editor in 1929. Lambright, who gave a speech to the 1927 Florida Bankers Association convention entitled "Florida's Undivided Profits of Opportunity," had a $3,531 loan at the Citizens Bank which was secured by *Tribune* bonds.[14]

The story of the liquidation of the oldest bank in Tampa unfolded on the news pages of the *Tampa Morning Tribune,* not on its editorial page. Though bank secrecy prevented reporters from knowing the extent of the insider abuse, depositors learned enough to know that Amos had deceived them. He had criticized depositors for circulating "too much propaganda" and engaging in "too much agitation." "The people have Samson-like brought down the temple on themselves and as soon as they realize this they will change their attitude." He also accused the fruit fly of causing the liquidity crisis: "Confiscation of fruit made it impossible for growers to meet their obligations to the banks."[15]

When the Citizens Bank and Trust Company of Tampa *(right)* failed, Governor Doyle E. Carlton *(below,* front: second from left) was a major borrower. Treasurer William V. Knott, Comptroller Ernest Amos, and Commissioner of Agriculture Nathan Mayo also used their Cabinet posts to procure bank loans. *Below, front:* R. A. Gray, Carlton, W. S. Cawthon. *Below, back:* Cary D. Landis, Knott, Amos, Mayo. (Courtesy, Florida State Archives)

Tampa's bankers and business establishment agreed with Amos. Depositors who had withdrawn their money before the teller windows closed were belittled and described as "wild eyed" and "timid" people who had lost "possession of their senses." Tampa was divided between depositors with devalued savings and business leaders who had borrowed their money. Peter O. Knight, a business leader and banker, was speaking as vice-president and director of the Exchange National Bank of Tampa when he urged the depositors of remaining banks to exercise restraint and not make "fools of themselves." Knight advised the community: "There was no excuse for the flurry. A night's sleep will convince them they are wrong, that the only danger is through losing their heads and their confidence."[16]

Amos fueled the controversy by hiring Charles Lafayette Knight as the receiver of the Citizens Bank and Trust Company. It was well-known that Knight had been a stockholder and director of the bank. Because Amos and Knight refused to release the liquidation reports, depositors did not know that Knight was one of the Citizens Bank's largest debtors. He and his family's interests, including C. L. Knight and Sons, a real estate company, and Eugene Knight, the oldest son, had borrowed $90,299 from the bank in twenty-four separate loans. Eugene Knight, a stockholder of the Citizens Bank and a vice-president of the affiliated Lafayette Bank, was appointed by his father to manage the bank's trust and securities departments during the liquidation.[17]

After depositors criticized C. L. Knight's appointment, Tampa businessmen, who had substantial loans at the Citizens Bank, scrambled to defend the friendly liquidator. D. Hoyt Woodberry, the secretary and treasurer of the HavaTampa Cigar Company and the Eli Witt Cigar Company, pleaded with Governor Carlton to support Amos in the Knight controversy. Woodberry said that Knight's opponents, the depositors, should be ignored because they were motivated by "personal gain." A review of the final examiner's report of the Citizens Bank negated Woodberry's apparent concern for "the interest of the public" because his companies had borrowed $250,000 from the bank. The HavaTampa Cigar Company had unsecured loans of $138,000, and the Eli Witt Cigar Company had loans of $112,000 at Citizens Bank, which were secured by a "letter of guarantee" from the HavaTampa Cigar Company. Governor Carlton told Woodberry not to worry about Knight's appointment and reassured him that he was working with Amos.[18]

E. W. Coates, who owned the Coates Plumbing Supply Company, wired the governor that the appointment of Knight was supported by the "people" of Tampa. The viability of Coates's company, however, depended on his relationship with the liquidator. Coates and his company owed $119,253 to the Citizens Bank and Trust Company. The battle lines were now drawn with the borrowers of the bank on one side and the depositors on the other.[19]

With the support of Governor Carlton, Amos continued to favor the bankers of Tampa to the detriment of the depositors of the Citizens Bank. Appearing to raise money to pay the depositors a dividend, the receiver agreed to sell the bank's downtown office building to the Alfred I. du Pont interests of Jacksonville, who planned to open the Florida National Bank of Tampa. Fearing competition from Edward Ball, the brother-in-law of Alfred I. du Pont, Peter O. Knight, the vice-president of the Exchange National Bank, mounted a lobbying campaign to kill the bank project. Knight, once described as " 'the best known political manipulator' in Tampa," was a confidant of United States senator Duncan Fletcher of Florida. He had the clout in Tallahassee and Washington to block any state or national bank charter application. Knight gave his friend Governor Carlton a good reason to intervene with Amos: "I think Mr. Ball is quite ambitious to control the situation politically in this state, especially to obtain control, if possible, of the next legislature. And I think the establishment of a bank here by him and his interests is more for political purposes than anything else." Though the du Pont group was willing to capitalize a new bank with $625,000, it was unable to overcome the vigorous opposition from Knight and the Exchange National Bank of Tampa. The depositors of the Citizens Bank suffered significant losses when the du Pont interests were forced to cancel their contract to purchase the high-rise building. Two months later, the Exchange National Bank announced a new stock issue of $375,000 "to provide greater facilities for taking care of increased business in the Tampa territory." Peter O. Knight increased his position in the bank by buying a major block of the stock issue.[20]

Led by J. Tom Watson, a quick-tempered attorney who sometimes settled debates with his fists, depositors formed the Bank Depositors Protective Association of Tampa. After accepting the case without any assurances of being paid, Watson filed suit to remove C. L. Knight as the receiver. The complaint charged that Knight was barred from serving as receiver because of his conflicting interests as a stockholder and director of the bank. As a stockholder, Knight was liable for assessments, and as a director he was "liable for misfeasance or malfeasance of directors in the performance of their duties." Knight, a tough pioneer who had once been a cowboy and steamboat captain, responded by suing Watson to collect a $3,900 loan that he owed to the bank.[21]

Knight's refusal to pay any dividends to the depositors and Amos's refusal to remove him created a furor. Six months after the bank's failure, nearly two thousand depositors attended a rally to demand action against the receiver and Amos. The size and hostility of the crowd prompted Major F. L. D. Carr, chairman of the depositors' association, to caution: "This is not a Bolshevist meeting. . . . We are here for serious work, and we must look at this job in a calm, dignified manner." Then depositors "roared" their approval when Major Carr declared: "It is time we took the head of our banking department out of politics. . . . In charity, I must say that our state comptroller is either insincere and incompetent, or he was a party to conditions that led to the collapse of these Tampa banks."[22]

The Bank Depositors Protective Association adopted a resolution demanding the resignation or impeachment of Amos. The resolution condemned him for his "peculiar subservience" to the officers and directors of the Citizens Bank and its affiliated banks. Because Amos had "betrayed the confidence of the people," the association planned to form a statewide organization of "outraged" depositors to remove the "unfit" comptroller from office. The depositors also urged Governor Carlton to appoint a special prosecutor to investigate the bank failures.[23]

Watson sent a seven-page letter to Amos, demanding his resignation because he had been "continuously guilty of official exploitations." Watson criticized Amos for failing to investigate the insider abuse at the bank. Because he had the power to take sworn depositions and complete access to the records of the bank, Amos should have protected depositors by removing the officers and directors for making illegal loans to themselves. Instead, he allowed the insolvent bank to continue operating for years with impaired capital, in violation of the Florida banking code.[24]

While Watson kept pressure on Amos, Receiver Knight blamed the legal actions of the depositors and their attorney for the freezing of deposits. But the beleaguered receiver lost credibility when he disclosed that the stockholders had paid only a small percentage of their assessments. His refusal to disclose the names of stockholders and if they had repaid their loans raised questions of impropriety and provoked a deluge of headlines. By March 1930, Knight was ready to quit. He said his resignation would remove the "personality" issue from the liquidation process. He expressed to Amos his "deepest appreciation of the steadfast confidence which you have shown in me."[25]

The resignation of Knight did not end the controversy, which won Watson a constituency and propelled him into the Florida House of Representatives. Relying on free newspaper coverage, he ran a low-budget campaign for the House on the promise to impeach Amos. In a hotly contested election, Watson lost by 237 votes on the first count, but he alleged fraud and demanded a recount. After the recount and an investigation, Watson won by 29 votes. Four election officials were later indicted for vote fraud.[26]

Because the legislature's next regular session was not scheduled until the spring of 1931, more than a hundred depositors sent telegrams and letters to Governor Carlton requesting him to call a special legislative session for the impeachment of Amos. Carlton ignored the pleas of the desperate depositors. He told reporters that he had "no public statement to make" regarding the action of the depositors and refused to discuss the matter further.[27]

One of the letters sent to Carlton let him know that his "secret" relationship with Dr. Bize was known in the community. The depositor told the governor: "You do not need to think it is a secret that you accepted bribes to protect such bankers. When you accepted that $250,000 on your personal note from L. A. Bize, also undoubtedly from other bankers. You are an accessory to the crime of theft, knowing before the act." The depositor challenged Carlton to repay his delinquent loans: "Why not be man enough to pay it back? You will never derive benefit from it. And say while you and your family are trying to enjoy a Merry Christmas, think all the time of the many thousands of poor people who were robbed by the many banks closing who have no Christmas on that account. And you not doing a thing to bring the criminal robbers to justice, which shows conclusively that you are implicated. You may get by in this world but there is another place in which you will have to spend eternity. Remember that."[28]

In another letter, Carlton was asked to intervene in the banking crisis because the depositors had "absolutely no faith" in Amos: "Do you not know that the management of the state banking laws by Mr. Amos has brought distrust in the state banks of Florida by every tourist that comes to Fla.? Do you not know that his absolute failure to make any real investigation of the closed state banks is keeping millions of dollars out of Fla.? Do you not know that Mr. Amos allowed these closed banks to continue years after he knew they were insolvent taking hundreds of thousands of dollars from the poor people? Do you not know that after the banks closed Mr. Amos saw to it that men were selected as liquidators who were recommended by its officers and directors, disregarding every interest of the depositors? Do you not know that the people know the state laws, weak as they are, were violated in numerous ways of which Mr. Amos was well aware? Do you not know that the comptrollers of other states put crooked bank officials in the penitentiary? Do you not know that so long as the state allows banks to take in hundreds of thousands of dollars in deposits and then go into bankruptcy and in this way steal the depositors money without any investigation on the part of the state, it creates a situation that demands your most serious and immediate attention?"[29]

The quick-tempered and determined Watson kept the controversy alive with lawsuits until the biennial legislature reconvened. Attorney General Fred Davis personally fought Watson in court on behalf of Amos, generating intense newspaper coverage. Then Watson shifted the battleground to Tallahassee by filing an impeachment resolution against Amos. His arrival in Tallahassee signaled the end of the Amos era.[30]

IMPEACHMENT PROCEEDINGS

In a move that would have defused the impeachment effort, Carlton planned to open the 1931 legislative session by proposing "a non-political banking department." But before the address could be delivered, Watson upstaged the governor and alienated the Democratic establishment. His first official act in Tallahassee, a town that revered cabinet members and expected legislators— especially freshmen House members—to work within the system, made quite an impression.[31]

On the first day of the session, banner front-page headlines announced that Watson was filing impeachment charges against Amos for committing "willful, wrongful, corrupt or unlawful" acts as the regulator and liquidator of the Citizens Bank and Trust Company. Watson called for an end to the politics of banking and introduced a bill to establish a separate banking department headed by a banking commission appointed by the governor. Because Amos had closed the state's banking records, Watson had no way of knowing that Governor Carlton was heavily indebted to the Citizens Bank. Watson's impeachment resolution contained fourteen articles of misfeasance and malfeasance charging that Amos allowed the directors of the Citizens Bank to declare an illegal dividend on the eve of its collapse; that he failed to remove the directors or seize the insolvent bank; that he allowed the bank to own illegal subsidiaries and permitted the unlawful transfer of assets before the bank closed; that he allowed the closing of solvent affiliated banks; and that he misused his power by compromising the debts of borrowers and the liability of stockholders.[32]

Amos began his public relations campaign by denouncing Watson for trying to "Get Even." He claimed he had denied Watson's "insistent" applications to be receiver of the Citizens Bank. Amos brushed aside Watson's lawsuits, which had forced Knight to resign, and declared that he had "kept faith with the people and lived up strictly with his oath of office." In closing his statement, Amos laid the foundation for his next attack on Watson. He said, "If those who owe the banks had paid their obligations we would have had few if any failures."[33]

Without investigating the charges, the *Tallahassee Daily Democrat* rushed to the defense of the cabinet member with an editorial titled "Amos Will Come from Probe with Reputation as Clear as Conscience." The editors had "always believed that Ernest Amos should have an 'a' after the 'E' in his first name." The paper dismissed Watson as a freshman legislator and his charges as "good gravy for the home folks to read that he's making a noble effort to provide them with protection from alleged irregular banking methods." The *Democrat* blamed the debacle on the legislature's refusal to give Amos adequate staff to regulate the banks properly. Ten days later and before an impeachment committee was appointed, the editors declared that it was "TIME FOR ACTION!" After reading the resolution, they wanted it dismissed because "the things complained of are mere matters of judgment and discretion which do not call for impeachment even if the judgment used was not sound."[34]

As the impeachment investigation began, Watson introduced a resolution to compel the comptroller to provide the names of state banks closed since 1926 and the amount of money spent on liquidators and preferred creditors. He was not requesting information on fees paid to legislators by the comptroller because that would "cast aspersions on [his] colleagues." Blunting criticism of his loan default at the Citizens Bank, Watson declared that he was an "honest bankrupt." After a volatile debate, his disclosure resolution passed the House.[35]

The *Democrat* kept the spotlight on Watson, making the future attorney general of Florida appear unstable. The newspaper's front-page headlines read: "Watson Has Tantrum in House," "I'm Honest Bankrupt, He Tells Colleagues," "Tampan Shouts Claim against State Officials," and "Declares That Legislature 'Dilly-Dallies,' While Laws Are Broken." Despite the efforts of the *Democrat* and Amos, hard-charging Watson was gaining credibility. His next allegation was that Amos had allowed state agencies to spend $98,000 on the illegal purchase of automobiles. In a surprise move, Speaker E. Clay Lewis, Jr., appointed the freshman as the chairman of a select committee to investigate the purchases. In lieu of announcing the investigation, the *Democrat* ran as its top headline: "Tom Watson Off on Wild Goose Chase."[36]

With the situation getting out of hand, Amos displayed the power of his office. The conservative leadership in the House then closed ranks around the four-term cabinet member and closed the process to public scrutiny. Representative S. P. Robineau of Miami, chairman of the select Impeachment Committee, ordered that all impeachment hearings be held in executive session and all testimony be confidential. The committee, on a seven-to-one count, even voted to exclude Watson from attending the hearings.[37]

Watson exploded in an "impassioned" speech on the floor of the House. He demanded to be a witness at the hearings and to act as a prosecutor, with the right to cross-examine witnesses. During the lengthy debate that followed, Robineau denounced the political eccentric whose "rancor" toward Amos was turning the House "into an impeachment body exclusively." If Watson participated in the impeachment investigation, Robineau argued, he would "go on a fishing expedition to the embarrassment of the state's political structure." After shedding his coat and loosening his tie, Watson declared that the banking "dictator must be dethroned." In his finest hour, Watson said he was not "Don Quixote" or a "fool," acting with a vindictive motive. After three years of fighting a corrupt system, he had introduced a "constructive" measure to eliminate the elected regulator who had caused the calamity. His argument carried the debate and surprised the packed gallery. In a vote of forty-seven to thirty, the House reversed the Impeachment Committee and allowed Watson to serve as both the accuser and the prosecutor. Amos's defeat was softened, however, by the House's refusal to open the hearings to the public.[38]

Meanwhile, the idea of a professional banking department was gaining momentum. Representative Dan Chappell of Miami introduced another bill to strip banking from the comptroller's office. His proposal followed the Georgia model of a superintendent of banking appointed by the governor. With the two banking bills pending in the House, Franklin O. King, a maverick senator from Orlando, who was planning to run against the "czar" of agriculture, Commissioner Nathan Mayo in 1932, filed legislation in the Senate similar to Chappell's bill. But before the Senate considered King's proposal, the House Banking Committee, chaired by S. E. Teague of Franklin County, who was president of the Apalachicola State Bank and a director of the Capital City Bank of Tallahassee, killed Watson's bill. Teague declared that his committee was opposed to any legislation that removed banking from Amos's office.[39]

Undaunted by the defeat of his banking bill, Watson moved several times on the House floor to introduce a resolution authorizing the hiring of an independent auditor to analyze the confidential records of the Citizens Bank. Chairman Robineau of the Impeachment Committee, who was supposed to be investigating Amos, opposed the hiring of an auditor. House Rules chairman Millard F. Caldwell, a powerful Amos ally who was also from Santa Rosa County, continuously objected to Watson's resolution on the grounds that it was out of order. After Caldwell blocked the motion, Watson shouted: "I am being denied the privilege of making a motion. I am not surprised at the gentleman from Santa Rosa. It almost appears through this session that he was sent here for the sole purpose of keeping me from the floor."[40]

Less than a week later, Watson raised the auditor issue before the full House again. His motion sparked a "heated debate," so the leadership banned the public from the House gallery. In an unusual secret session, House members debated for one hour and fifty minutes. While Robineau was vigorously defending the comptroller, Amos walked onto the House floor to confer with Caldwell. Supported by the House leadership, Robineau defeated Watson's motion. Deciding the investigation was a sham, Watson moved to withdraw his impeachment resolution and Robineau objected: "The petulant action of Mr. Watson indicates that if he cannot run the show he wants to stop it." Robineau and his Impeachment Committee requested and received authority from the House to complete the "investigation." Caldwell then proposed and passed a resolution to preclude House action on any banking bills for the balance of the session. Representative J. M. Lee of Avon Park opposed the heavy-handed tactics and developed a lively interest in the comptroller's office.[41]

After falling victim to the cracker politicians, Watson and John E. Mathews of Jacksonville led an urban coalition in a fight against rural counties over the distribution of the state's gasoline tax receipts. As Peter Tomasello, Jr., of Okeechobee and Mathews debated the issue, Watson leaped over a railing in the House chamber, declaring: "I am going to get out of here. . . . They're like a pair of billy goats." Watson backed up his words with his fists. As a filibuster on the tax issue continued, Watson and R. C. Horne of rural Madison County got in a brawl on the floor of the House chamber.[42]

As the tumultuous session came to an end, the House defeated the abandoned impeachment resolution by a vote of eighty-one to two. But Watson won the public debate. Robineau admitted that the impeachment inquiry was "probably the most arduous and in most instances embarrassing task ever presented to any committee." Teague, the banker, and twenty other members sponsored a resolution "to remove all doubt as to the utmost integrity and efficiency of the banking industry in this state and the comptroller of the state of Florida." The resolution, printed in its entirety on the front page of the *Tallahassee Daily Democrat,* stated that the banking crisis was "due to economic and industrial causes and not due to carelessness on the part of the state officials or laxity in the enforcement of state laws." The House pronounced its "utmost confidence in the ability, integrity, and good intentions of the Honorable Ernest Amos, Comptroller, and . . . perfect faith in the ability and integrity of banks and bankers generally throughout the State of Florida."[43]

Disgusted with the legislative cover-up, Watson simply said the government had lost the public's confidence. He recognized, however, the damage he had inflicted on Amos and his banking clique. He had introduced the impeachment resolution during the first week of the 1931 session, but it was not rejected by the House until the final week. Timing was bad for Amos because he had to stand for a statewide election in 1932. In the interim, state banks continued to fail.[44]

LEE DEFEATS AMOS

Watson decided not to run for comptroller in 1932. Instead, he ran for governor and made banking a key issue in that contest. If elected, he planned to push for a banking commission or a superintendent appointed by the governor. During the legislative fight, his campaign to oust Amos gained an important ally, J. M. Lee, an unknown House member from rural south-central Florida. Lee had fought the House leadership when it blocked a floor vote on the appointed banking commissioner bill. He knew from firsthand experience that Amos had become an embarrassment to the general membership of the House. He also watched as a freshman legislator suddenly developed a statewide name by confronting a powerful cabinet member. Lee's most valuable asset was his courage to challenge the incumbent. His decision to run for comptroller meant that Amos would have at least two opponents to debate in the campaign.[45]

But Amos had history on his side. Only one cabinet member had been defeated in the twentieth century. That was Superintendent of Public Instruction William N. Sheats, who lost his office in 1904 but regained it in 1912. Amos had the solid support of the banking industry and the leaders of the Democratic party. He could rely on his cabinet colleagues, especially Secretary of State

R. A. Gray and Treasurer William V. Knott. Gray had been Amos's assistant comptroller, and Knott, a former comptroller, was now responsible for selecting the banks that received most of the state's deposits. Knott, who lived in an antebellum mansion on Park Avenue in Tallahassee, and Gray had been Democratic insiders for years.[46]

Knott enjoyed a cozy relationship with the banking industry throughout his public career. For example, the Lewis State Bank of Tallahassee dealt with him on both a public and private basis. On July 12, 1916, during the middle of his tough campaign for governor, Comptroller Knott approved conversion of the First National Bank of Tallahassee to the Lewis State Bank. After Knott returned to the cabinet as treasurer, he received substantial personal loans from the bank while he was depositing state funds in the bank. Governor Martin's appointment of Knott as treasurer was effective on September 28, 1928. Five days later, Knott borrowed $1,000 from the Lewis State Bank. By the end of the year, he had borrowed and repaid a total of $4,900. The bank was also accommodating to his brother Charles, the clerk of court for Hillsborough County, who was also a borrower at the Citizens Bank and Trust Company of Tampa. The Knott brothers were partners in numerous speculative land deals around Florida while they both held public office.[47]

By December 1932, Treasurer Knott was maintaining thirteen state bank accounts at the Lewis State Bank totaling $177,275. At the same time, he personally owed the bank $10,700 in four separate loans. When he defaulted on a $7,550 loan, the bank foreclosed on his property in south Florida. The policy loan was secured by a mortgage on real estate located hundreds of miles outside the bank's lending territory. Despite the foreclosure, the bank continued to make loans to him. State Bank Examiner John E. Perkins classified the Knott loans because they represented "large lines of credit."[48]

Knott was not the only cabinet member with bad investments who used his public position to his advantage at the Lewis State Bank. Commissioner of Agriculture Nathan Mayo had endorsed a $7,500 loan for the Lanark Hotel Company at the bank, which was in default by more than seven months. Examiner Perkins classified its repayment as "doubtful." He also classified a personal loan of Mayo's, which had been in default for more than five months. Mayo maintained a number of state accounts at the bank, which held public deposits totaling $712,195 at the end of 1932. The bank's public deposits included city, county, state, and federal funds that amounted to 26.8 percent of its total deposits. State deposits of $291,664 represented the largest category.[49]

Besides the support from his colleagues and the banking industry, Amos was the favorite of Florida's major newspapers. Friendly editors defended the incumbent, though they had no way of evaluating his regulatory performance. As the race ignited, the *Tallahassee Daily Democrat* published "The Consistency of the Gold Dust Twins," saying that Amos had two opponents, Lee and Tom Watson, the gubernatorial candidate. The editors criticized them for blaming the debacle on Amos. "Derelict" men like Lee and Watson were the real culprits because they failed to repay their debts on time.[50]

The editorial noted that a Punta Gorda bank had sued Lee to collect a $544 loan. The defunct bank received a judgment, but he still refused to pay his debt. The *Democrat* reported that during the bank's liquidation, it had deducted Lee's worthless note from its assets. Because the liquidation records were confidential, Amos was using selective disclosure for his political advantage. He also leaked information about Watson's bad loan at the Citizens Bank and Trust Company. The editors concluded that it was time for Lee and Watson to "PAY UP."[51]

Lee sent a clever letter to the *Democrat* declaring that he would contribute $500 to the Florida Children's Home if Amos could prove that he had benefited from the bank loan. Sounding like Senator Joe Bailey, Lee said the bank had purchased "a fraudulent note, secured from [him] by fraud." He berated Amos for failing to prosecute the confidence man. Lee did not explain his refusal to pay the promissory note even after a judgment was entered.[52]

The *Democrat* responded with more editorials, which accused Lee of being a demagogue who was regarded "all over the state as the friend of the poor bank depositor." The editors hammered at his delinquent loan: "Physician, heal thyself." He was called "militant" and condemned for acting above the law. It was "ridiculous" for Lee to blame Amos for his bad deal. After a campaign appearance in Tallahassee, Lee left town with "his robe a bit soiled and with the halo with which he had crowned himself not quite straight upon his head."[53]

Meanwhile, the harsh words of Tom Watson framed the debate in the governor's race. He was facing a crowded field of nine candidates, including former governors Cary Hardee and John Martin. But in the throes of the Great Depression, Hardee, the banker-governor, and Martin, who had presided over the bust, represented big business. Running on a shoestring budget, the irrepressible Watson hoped to attract enough media coverage to convince angry voters to end the "graft and corruption" in Tallahassee. David Sholtz, a Daytona Beach banking lawyer, adopted Watson's message and with a well-financed campaign became the "people's candidate." Sholtz, who had been a stockholder, director, borrower, and the attorney for the Atlantic State Bank and Trust Company of Daytona Beach which failed in 1929, called for "banking laws with teeth."[54]

In the comptroller's race, Amos controlled the flow of information focusing media attention on Lee's bad loan. Amos's own delinquent loans remained strictly confidential because he had sealed the liquidation records. Nevertheless, Lee's personal financial problems and obscure public record compared favorably to Amos's record of indictments and bank failures. Lee had represented Highlands County in the state House of Representatives since 1927, but his major weaknesses were that he came from a small county and had never run for statewide office. His alliance with Watson, however, and their vigorous campaigns gave him the opportunity to become the first person in Florida's history to defeat an incumbent banking commissioner.[55]

Another decisive factor was that Van C. Swearingen, a former mayor of Jacksonville and a former attorney general, was in the race. Swearingen's candidacy assured a run-off election. As Swearingen criticized the Tallahassee establishment, Lee blamed the state's epidemic of bank failures and its depression on Amos. He accused Amos of wasting depositors' life savings by spending $509,000 on the liquidation of 148 state banks between 1926 and 1932. He declared that "thousands of aged, infirm, bent-over men and women [were] walking the highways of Florida" because of Amos's malpractice. Lee said he was the "repair man" who could fix the state's banking system.[56]

While Lee spoke at rallies and picnics, Amos spent his time with the bankers who had been his allies during the past sixteen years. Amos was their defender throughout the troubled times, and now he needed their active support. At the height of the banking crisis, he had praised the Florida Bankers Association as a "body of splendid business men." During the campaign of 1932, the bankers rallied around their besieged leader, who was also the keeper of their secrets.[57]

The Florida Bankers Association assured favorable press coverage for Amos by asking him to open their annual convention in Jacksonville on the Friday before election day. The bankers enthusiastically applauded his speech even though he finally embraced the concept of deposit insurance. He thanked his friends for their "many expressions of confidence" and predicted that they were "face to face with a new era in banking." The reversal of Amos's public position on the controversial deposit insurance issue was a recognition that Lee was gaining ground. Coming at the end of a tough campaign, his new stance had no effect on the members of the Florida Bankers Association. Concerned more about corporate profits than public confidence, the bankers condemned any form of government-sponsored deposit insurance as being contrary to the free enterprise system. But they supported a taxpayer bailout of Florida's bankrupt cities. The FBA urged the legislature to guarantee the payment of municipal bonds in which the banks had heavily invested.[58]

Jacksonville's *Florida Times-Union* supported Amos on both its news and editorial pages. In the editorial "Efficiency Should Be Rewarded," which was reprinted in the *Tallahassee Daily Democrat,* the *Times-Union* endorsed Amos's reelection bid. The editors asked voters to follow the historical precedent "of retaining good men in office for long terms." Trying to prove the point but making another one, the editorial reviewed the history of Florida's elected comptrollers. Only six men had served as comptroller from 1881 to 1932, a fifty-one-year period, and none of them had been defeated in an election. Georgians also recognized longtime incumbents as "invaluable" resources of their state. The comptroller of Georgia, who was not the banking commissioner, held on to his post for more than fifty years and died in office.[59]

Though he had the full support of the power structure, Amos finished the first primary with only a slim lead in the three-man race. He received 95,181 votes to Lee's 91,582 and Swearingen's 62,370. As Amos and Lee entered the second primary, Lee's attacks intensified. The challenger made the incumbent the central issue.

Facing a serious challenge for the first time, Amos became defensive and spent his resources responding to Lee's charges.[60]

Former governor Hardee's dreams of reinstating a "banker government" in Tallahassee were thwarted when he was repudiated by the voters. Then he unsuccessfully lobbied President Franklin D. Roosevelt for an appointment to the Federal Reserve Board and the Reconstruction Finance Corporation. After Florida's Democratic leaders leaned on the White House, Roosevelt's comptroller of the currency, J. F. T. O'Connor, appointed Hardee as the receiver of the Federal American National Bank and Trust Company of Washington, D.C.[61]

Sholtz, a former legislator who ran as an outsider, finished a strong second behind former governor Martin. Tom Watson, whose lack of funds doomed his campaign, ran dead last, but he had laid the groundwork for his election as state attorney general in 1940 and 1944. In the 1940 campaign, Watson defeated four other candidates, including E. B. Donnell of West Palm Beach, who later became chairman of the Democratic Executive Committee. As attorney general, he often sparred with governors Spessard L. Holland and Millard F. Caldwell, and then he ran another unsuccessful race for governor in 1948. After losing a congressional race in 1950, he switched parties and made a bid to become Florida's first Republican governor since Reconstruction. But ten days before the 1954 election, he died of a sudden heart attack.[62]

In the runoff race for comptroller, Amos complained that Lee was conducting a "wholly destructive" negative campaign. The incumbent won the endorsement of the defeated Van Swearingen, a former cabinet colleague, but not the confidence of the voters. Unrelenting, Lee continued the assault. In an advertisement entitled "No Wonder Amos Tried to Hide," Lee accused Amos of mismanaging school funds. He said that taxpayers and schoolteachers were losing money because of the incompetence of Amos.[63]

Instead of ignoring or attacking his opponent, Amos ran advertisements with the slogan: "VOTE FOR ERNEST AMOS—WHO IS HONEST." He admitted a delay in depositing school funds but blamed it on his small staff. He said Lee was making "a 'last minute' misstatement of facts" because no schools had closed and no money was lost. During the final days, Lee crisscrossed the state speaking to crowds that grew with each campaign stop. He promised to reduce taxes by using the comptroller's fiscal function to eliminate wasteful government spending. And he hammered at his theme: it was time to overthrow the banking "dictator."[64]

Finally, Amos halted his retreat and charged that Lee was "a racketeer professional politician" who had promised jobs in the comptroller's office in exchange for political support. He blasted Lee for refusing to pay the loan at the Punta Gorda State Bank, and he attempted to limit his regulatory power by campaign edict. Amos said he was not responsible for bank failures because he had no "veto power over loans made by state banks." Refusing to criticize the bankers for their worthless loans, he blamed irresponsible borrowers such as Lee for the banking crisis. Trying to salvage his seat in the cabinet, Amos renewed the call for an appointed banking commissioner. He also tried belatedly to develop the campaign theme that "words are no substitute for old-fashioned honesty." His advertisements portrayed him as "a simple business man" and "quiet gentleman" who had provided steady leadership during tough economic times.[65]

In the acrimonious governor's race, Sholtz denounced the "rackets" and pork-barrel programs of the "professional politicians" in Tallahassee. He attributed the economic malaise to the backroom deals of former governor Martin's cronies. In response, Martin promised lower taxes and dismissed Sholtz, the Yale graduate and lawyer, as "unknown, untried, untested, and unsafe." He touted himself as "the Florida cracker boy" and warned the voters that they could not "trust a corporation hireling when he comes promising the moon with a ribbon around it."[66]

Sholtz won an overwhelming victory, capturing 63 percent of the vote. He had received the strong support of the business community, including Frank Jennings, who was president of J. R. Anthony's Peninsular Life Insurance Company of Jacksonville. During the campaign, Jennings told the press that Sholtz would stop the "political trading and governmental extravagances" in Tallahassee.[67]

Amos, the polished cabinet member, was no match for his aggressive challenger. Lee defeated Amos by a landslide with more than 57 percent of the vote. Lee received 150,661 votes to Amos's 111,512. Amos became the first comptroller in the history of Florida to be defeated at the polls. On January 3, 1933, six and a half years after the banking crash, Florida had a new banking commissioner. Comptroller Lee was reelected three more times and died in office in 1946. Governor Millard Caldwell then appointed Clarence Gay, the former associate of Manley and Anthony, as Florida's twenty-third comptroller.[68]

EPILOGUE

Six decades after the panic of 1926, fraud and insider abuse were again thriving in Florida's banking system. After the failure of forty-nine state-chartered banks and thrifts, including the spectacular collapse of Cen-Trust Savings Bank of Miami, state representative Art Simon, the Democratic chairman of the House Commerce Committee, initiated an investigation into the regulatory performance of the Florida Department of Banking and Finance. The committee also focused on the fund-raising practices of the state's elected banking commissioner, Comptroller Gerald Lewis, a Democratic cabinet member who began his reign in 1975.[1]

In February 1992, the House Commerce Committee issued a scathing report declaring: "Governmental regulation of financial institutions, especially state-chartered thrifts, is a national disgrace. During the last decade, a record number of financial institutions have been declared insolvent in Florida and nationwide. As a result, billions of dollars in losses will have to be borne by taxpayers, depositors, and innocent stockholders. This crisis was preventable."[2]

The committee also found that the state's regulatory system was compromised by Lewis's "acceptance of large campaign contributions from persons directly responsible for the failure of certain state-chartered financial institutions in Florida, at a time when it was known to the Department that these institutions were suffering from serious financial irregularities and insider abuse." The committee determined that a "cloak of confidentiality" shrouded the Department of Banking and Finance, preventing "meaningful legislative oversight" of the comptroller's regulatory performance.[3]

The House report reached similar conclusions as *A Review of the Regulation of Banking and Securities in Florida,* which was issued by the state Senate in 1986. Responding to a federal grand jury investigation of Lewis and his department, the president of the Florida Senate directed the Governmental Operations Committee "to review the structure of the regulation of banking and securities to determine whether this responsibility is best placed with an elected official or an appointed commissioner. After conducting a nationwide survey, the committee confirmed that "Florida is unique in that it is the only state that has an elected official charged with the responsibility of regulating banking institutions . . . in every other state and federal government structure, the regulation of financial institutions is charged to an appointed official or an appointed public body." The report concluded that "in view of the discretionary aspect" of banking regulation and "the nature of a statewide campaign, the structure does not provide the comptroller, as an elected member of the cabinet, sufficient independence from the regulated industries. The regulator is permitted to accept campaign contributions from the industries he regulates." Therefore, "the regulation of banking and securities would best be statutorily placed with an appointed official or officials."[4]

The Senate report stressed that the comptroller's "excessive authority" and lack of accountability provided "the potential for abuse or exploitation." The "concentrated power" resulted from the "highly improbable" removal procedures established by the state constitution and the exemption of bank regulatory records from the public records law. Lewis, as a cabinet member, could run for unlimited terms and could be removed only by defeat or impeachment. In the history of Florida only two comptrollers have been defeated in the low-profile races, and none has been impeached. The report failed to mention the influence that full-time cabinet members exert over part-time legislators. That power was displayed when the report was buried at the beginning of the 1986 legislative session.[5]

Between 1986 and 1992 regulatory inaction cost taxpayers billions of dollars, yet the comptroller's office escaped another reform effort during the 1992 sunset review of state banking laws. Frustrated by "stonewalling" from Lewis, Representative Jeff Huenink, a Republican member of the House Commerce Committee, repeated history by filing an impeachment resolution against the comptroller. Huenink accused Lewis of running the Department of Banking and Finance with such "favoritism and cronyism" as to constitute "gross misconduct." Capturing daily headlines, Huenink charged that the elected regulator operated a "pay-to-play" system in which he took contributions from bankers and turned his head when they looted their banks. Huenink condemned the "deplorable pattern of fund-raising, campaign contributions, gifts, favors. . . . The regulatory inaction alone is a scandal."[6]

Maneuvering for meaningful reform, Huenink sought to replace the tainted elected regulator with an appointed professional. His efforts were derailed by Democratic House Speaker T. K. Wetherell, whose refusal to appoint an impeachment committee obstructed the process. Admitting his conflict of interest, Wetherell said: "My wife works for Lewis and I got a mortgage company I own that's regulated by him." Lewis survived the impeachment move, and the state regulatory system, with its elected banking commissioner, remained intact. Nevertheless, the conservative Senate was forced to accept an important disclosure provision. It provided that insider loans of officers and directors would become public one year after the failure of a state financial institution. But by resisting the opening of the failed bank records through bizarre legal interpretations, Lewis and his lawyers prevented Florida from becoming the leading disclosure state.[7]

GREED AND SECRECY

The panic of 1926, like today's savings and loan debacle, was caused by greed and secrecy. Gamblers disguised as bankers converted financial institutions into casinos. They played with the public's money until depositors finally realized that it was their chips being thrown away on Florida's roulette table. Addison Mizner, J. R. Anthony, and W. D. Manley set the mood for Florida's boom just as Charles Keating, David Paul, Marvin Warner, and Ivan Boesky did in the 1980s. The activities of these high-powered confidence men were consistent with Boesky's words of advice to the University of California's graduating class of 1986: "Greed is all right. . . . I think greed is healthy. You can be greedy and still feel good about yourself."[8]

During Florida's boom, the state's chief bank regulator, Ernest Amos, joined with Georgia Superintendent of Banks T. R. Bennett and Comptroller of the Currency Joseph McIntosh to help their political friends profit from the frenzy. State and federal regulators allowed Manley's insolvent banking system to operate for years. It collapsed after lawsuits disclosed the fraud and insider deals. Violent bank runs paralyzed two states because official secrecy had prevented depositors from purging Manley's system in an orderly manner.

If depositors had known what regulators knew, the panic could have been averted. Indeed, if depositors had known that Manley had engaged in massive insider abuse from the beginning, his empire would not have grown to two hundred banks, which was large enough to cause a panic when it collapsed. Regulators allowed Manley and his affiliated bankers to defraud depositors by issuing false financial statements, counting worthless loans as valuable assets. Even after lawsuits exposed the corruption, state and federal regulators intentionally deceived the public. Official secrecy concealed the regulatory complicity for fifty years. In the interim most state regulators destroyed the evidence.

Depositors who withdrew their money were denounced and ridiculed by government officials. Those who listened to the regulators lost most of their savings after suffering through more than a decade of liquidators and lawyers. The regulatory records that survived make it clear that depositors who withdrew their money acted prudently.

Disclosure of the examination reports of Manley's banks would have stopped the growth of his rogue banking system. It would have warned depositors to bank elsewhere. But official deceit prevented the public from making an adjustment, and the panic of 1926 became a prelude to the stock market crash of 1929. Both upheavals signaled that the public had lost confidence in its institutions. Congress failed to restore confidence, and the Great Depression followed.

After the Bank Holiday of 1933, Congress finally took action, and President Roosevelt reluctantly signed the Glass-Steagall Act, providing federal insurance for depositors. Roosevelt feared deposit insurance would perpetuate the problem, not solve it. He warned: "We do not wish to make the United States government liable for the mistakes and errors of individual banks, and put a premium on unsound banking in the future." Deposit insurance restored public confidence, but Congress ensured the savings and loan disaster by endorsing a policy of official secrecy.[9]

ABOLISH BANK SECRECY

Depositors with federally insured deposits remained calm throughout the savings and loan crisis while the names of insolvent and troubled institutions were publicized. After requiring taxpayers to pay more than $500 billion for the bailout, how can Congress justify the exclusion of the public from the secrets of banking?[10]

Adam Smith's *Wealth of Nations* and Thomas Jefferson's Declaration of Independence, both published in 1776, promoted competition in a free market and "the consent of the governed." After the collapse of the Soviet Union, capitalism and democracy have become interchangeable. But America's secret banking system, combined with its federal deposit insurance, conflicts with Smith's vision of a free enterprise system and Jefferson's concept of informed consent. Capitalism and democracy cannot function without a well-informed market and electorate. By successfully lobbying to keep the public uninformed, bankers have remained the governors of the banking system. As James Madison said, "Knowledge will forever govern ignorance."[11]

A banking-in-the-sunshine law, mandating full disclosure for financial institutions, their officers and directors, and regulatory agencies, is the only way for the public to regulate its banking system. Disclosure of insider deals, bad loans, and political involvement would empower the public and restrain the rampant insider abuse. Taxpayers have a right to know if a banker has personal loans at federally insured institutions or has made policy loans to regulators and politicians. Release of bank examination reports, which are now sealed by criminal penalties, would also expose delinquent borrowers and prevent bankers from protecting their directors, business partners, and political friends. Bankers, who enjoy the privilege of a public subsidy and who use the public's money for private profit, are public officials. And like other public officials they should be held accountable by disclosing their personal finances. Full disclosure would allow competition to function in the banking industry because informed depositors could select financial institutions free of insider abuse.[12]

Yet the sunshine law would go far beyond reforming the banking industry. Relying on the banking secrets of two generations ago, this book revealed how bankers, regulators, and politicians joined together to violate their public trust. The banking scandals of the 1920s reached from the statehouses of Florida and Georgia to the chambers of the vice-president of the United States. Releasing today's banking secrets would purge the bankers, regulators, and politicians who were responsible for the savings and loan fiasco. Dismantling the system of favoritism, without delay, could also prevent the next banking crisis.

Throughout the American experience, landmark financial reform has been enacted only after a calamity has shocked the nation. The national banking system was formed during the Civil War, the Federal Reserve System was created after the Panic of 1907, and Congress passed the deposit insurance and securities disclosure acts during the 1930s. For the first time since the Great Depression, Americans have the opportunity to abolish bank secrecy. Instead of merely paying for the scandal, they should demand that Congress open the secret vault.

NOTES

ABBREVIATIONS

BB/IHS   Bureau of Banking, Department of Finance, Idaho Historical Society, Boise, Idaho.

BEP/NMA   Bank Examiner Papers, State Records Center and Archives, Santa Fe, New Mexico.

BRHS   Boca Raton Historical Society, Boca Raton, Florida.

CC/DCCC   Civil Cases, Duval County Circuit Court, Jacksonville, Florida.

CC/FCSC   Civil Cases, Fulton County Superior Court, Atlanta, Georgia.

CD/FCSC   Criminal Division, Fulton County Superior Court, Atlanta, Georgia.

CGDP/NUL   Charles G. Dawes Papers, Special Collections, Northwestern University Library, Evanston, Illinois.

CMG/FSA   Clarence M. Gay, Comptroller Campaign Literature, 1947–48, RG 350, Series 426, Florida State Archives, Department of State, Tallahassee, Florida.

DCM/OTAB   Dawson City Museum, Old Territorial Administration Building, Dawson City, Yukon Territory.

DEC/FSA	Governors: 1929–71 (RG 102). Doyle Elam Carlton Administrative Correspondence, 1929–32, Series 204. Department of State, Florida State Archives, Tallahassee, Florida.
DBF/GSA	Department of Banking and Finance Records, RG 20, Georgia State Archives, Atlanta, Georgia.
FSA	Department of State, Florida State Archives, Tallahassee, Florida.
FSCHS	Florida Supreme Court Historical Society, Supreme Court Building, Tallahassee, Florida.
GEM/HASF	George Edgar Merrick Papers, Historical Association of Southern Florida, Miami, Florida.
GO/GSA	Governor's Office Records, Georgia State Archives, Atlanta, Georgia.
HASF	Historical Association of Southern Florida, Miami, Florida.
HSPBC	Historical Society of Palm Beach County, West Palm Beach, Florida.
JBHP/PKYL	James B. Hodges Papers, P. K. Yonge Library of Florida History, University of Florida, Gainesville, Florida.
JMFP/HASF	John M. Frohock Papers, Historical Association of Southern Florida, Miami, Florida.
KFP/FSA	Knott Family Papers, Manuscript Collections, Department of State, Florida State Archives, Tallahassee, Florida.
LSB/FSA	Lewis State Bank Records, Manuscript Collections, Department of State, Florida State Archives, Tallahassee, Florida.
LYSP/ISHL	Lawrence Y. Sherman Papers, Illinois State Historical Library, Springfield, Illinois.
LC/WDC	Library of Congress, Washington, D.C.
PD/DCCC	Probate Division, Duval County Circuit Court, Jacksonville, Florida.
PKYL	P. K. Yonge Library of Florida History, University of Florida, Gainesville, Florida.
RAGP/FSA	Robert Andrew Gray Papers, Manuscript Collections, Department of State, Florida State Archives, Tallahassee, Florida.
SC/FSA	State Comptroller Records, RG 350, Series 64, Closed Bank Records, 1898–1942, Department of State, Florida State Archives, Tallahassee, Florida.

SCD/UM	Special Collections Department, Otto G. Richter Library, University of Miami, Coral Gables, Florida.
SCF/FSA	Supreme Court of Florida Records, RG 970, Series 49, Case Files of Civil and Criminal Appeals, Department of State, Florida State Archives, Tallahassee, Florida.
SS/GSA	Secretary of State Records, Georgia State Archives, Atlanta, Georgia.
USDC/NDF	U.S. District Court Records, Northern District of Florida, Federal Courthouse, Jacksonville, Florida.
USDC/NDG	U.S. District Court Records, RG 21, Northern District of Georgia, 1847–1942, National Archives, Atlanta, Georgia.
USDC/SDF	U.S. District Court Records, RG 21, Southern District of Florida, 1828–1943, National Archives, Atlanta, Georgia.
USOCC/NA	U.S. Office of the Comptroller of the Currency, RG 101, Records of the Division of Insolvent National Banks, 1865–1950, National Archives, Suitland, Maryland.
USOCC/WNRC	U.S. Office of the Comptroller of the Currency, RG 101, Records of the Examining Division, 1863–1935, Washington National Records Center, Suitland, Maryland.

PREFACE

1. *Guide to the National Archives of the United States* (Washington, D.C.: National Archives and Records Administration, 1987), 161.

2. *Miami Herald,* April 4, 1974; *St. Petersburg Times,* April 4, 1974; *Wall Street Journal,* November 3, 1986; *General Acts and Resolutions Adopted by the Legislature of Florida,* Tallahassee, 1974, Ch. 74-84, Sec. 658.10(1)(b).

3. *Florida Times-Union,* September 9, 1974; *General Acts of Florida,* 1980, Ch. 80-273, Sec. 658.057(1)(b),(3),(8); *Florida Statutes 1991,* Sec. 655.057(1)(b),(3),(8).

4. Edward F. Keuchel to Jim Berberich, February 29, 1988, FSA; Henri C. Cawthon to Keuchel, March 10, 1988; Cawthon to S. Craig Kiser, March 23, 1988; William A. Friedlander to Catherine Green, April 13, 1988; Green to Berberich, April 26, 1988, FSA; Friedlander to Benjamin E. Poitevent, February 1, 1989, FSA; Affidavit of Henry W. Cook, Clerk

of the Circuit Court of Duval County, January 31, 1989, FSA; Poitevent to Beverly Burnsed, February 21, 1989, FSA; Green to Burnsed, March 6, 1989, FSA; Green to Ken Rouse, March 13, 1989, FSA; Rouse to Friedlander, March 15, 1989; Friedlander to Rouse, April 4, 1989, FSA; Florida Historical Society Resolution, May 13, 1989.

5. Gerald Lewis to Jim Smith, June 7, 1989, FSA; Rouse to Berberich, June 13, 1989, FSA; Berberich to Keuchel, June 15, 1989; Friedlander to Keuchel, June 23, 1989; *Wall Street Journal,* February 15, May 23, 1989; *St. Petersburg Times,* May 29, June 15, 1989; *Tallahassee Democrat,* June 15, 27, 1989; *Florida Times-Union,* June 15, 1989; *Ft. Lauderdale Sun-Sentinel,* June 15, 1989; *Tampa Tribune,* June 15, 1989; *Orlando Sentinel,* June 15, 1989; *Palm Beach Post,* June 15, 1989; "Opening the Secret Vault," *St. Petersburg Times,* June 25, 1989.

6. *General Acts of Florida,* 1992, Ch. 92-303, Sec. 655.057(2)(g).

7. R. D. Jones, Assistant Supervisor of Banking of Washington, to author, July 9, 1991; Tom Ruller, Alabama Department of Archives and History, to Sidney F. McAlpin, Washington State Archivist, April 30, 1987; Zack Thompson, Alabama Superintendent of Banks, to author, July 10, 1991.

8. Ruller to McAlpin, April 30, 1987.

9. Ibid.; Patrick C. Carroll, California Banking Department, to author, July 8, 1991; Andrew J. Klein, Illinois Department of Banks and Trust Companies, to author, July 16, 1991; Allison M. Haupt, Ohio Superintendent of Banks, to author, September 16, 1991; Russell S. Kropschot, Michigan Commissioner of Financial Institutions, to author, July 17, 1991; James G. Miller, Deputy Commissioner of Commerce of Minnesota, to author, July 22, 1991; James M. Cooper, Indiana Department of Financial Institutions, to author, July 23, 1991; Neil T. Tobin, Massachusetts Office of the Commissioner of Banks, to author, November 13, 1991; Nirja Savill, Connecticut Department of Banking, to author, July 29, 1991; A. Roland Roberge, Bank Commissioner of New Hampshire, to author, October 29, 1991; Henry L. Bryson, Deputy Bank Commissioner of Maryland, to author, November 4, 1991; Thomas W. Stout, Kentucky Department of Financial Institutions, to author, August 2, 1991; Elizabeth Ann Clark, Tennessee Department of Financial Institutions, to author, August 5, 1991; Louie A. Jacobs, South Carolina Commissioner of Banking, to author, August 5, 1991; Sonja A. Hencely, Georgia Department of Banking and Finance, to author, July 16, 1991; *Acts and Resolutions of the General Assembly of the State of Georgia,* Atlanta, 1919, Part I, Title 6, Sec. 19; Thomas L. Wright, Mississippi Commissioner of Banking, to author, July 8, 1991; Mary F. Amedee, Louisiana Office of Financial Institutions, November 18, 1991; James A.

Hansen, Nebraska Director of Banking and Finance, to author, July 10, 1991; Mary Fehring, Iowa Division of Banking, to author, October 30, 1991; Earl L. Manning, Missouri Commissioner of Finance, to author, October 29, 1991; Grant L. C. Brooks, Kansas Banking Department, to author, July 29, 1991; L. Scott Walshaw, Nevada Commissioner of Financial Institutions, to author, July 9, 1991; Christopher G. Driggs, Nevada State Library and Archives, to author, July 16, 1991; Gary D. Preszler, North Dakota Commissioner of Banking and Financial Institutions, to author, November 1, 1991; Beverly Zigler, South Dakota Division of Banking, to author, July 30, 1991; Everett X. Hammacher, Pennsylvania Department of Banking, to author, August 6, 1991; Donald W. Hutchinson, Montana Commissioner of Financial Institutions, to author, July 15, 1991; Clare E. Sykes, New York Banking Department, to author, July 29, 1991.

10. William T. Graham, North Carolina Commissioner of Banks, to author, July 9, 1991; Susan L. Winters, Deputy Bank Commissioner of Delaware, to author, July 11, 1991; Marsha Kramarck, Deputy Attorney General of Delaware, to author, August 1, 1991.

11. Harold L. Miller, State Historical Society of Wisconsin, to author, August 8, 1991, and "Agreement for Use of Restricted Materials"; Leon M. Swerin, Wisconsin Office of Commissioner of Banking, to author, August 14, 1991; Colette L. Mooney, Deputy Superintendent of Banking of Maine, to author, July 23, 1991; Wendell G. Bassett, Vermont Financial Institutions Regulation and Consumer Services Administrator, to author, August 12, 1991; Edward D. Pare, Jr., Associate Superintendent of Banking of Rhode Island, to author, July 31, 1991; Candace A. Franks, Arkansas Bank Department, to author, July 9, 1991; Barbara M. A. Walker, Colorado Bank Commissioner, to author, July 15, 1991; Judith A. Seymour, Arizona Director of Deposit Institutions, to author, August 16, 1991; Sue E. Mecca, Wyoming Banking Commissioner, to author, July 22, 1991; Bill L. Walker, Deputy Commissioner of Financial Institutions of Utah, to author, November 18, 1991.

12. Willis F. Kirkpatrick, Alaska Director of Banking, Securities, and Corporations, to author, July 16, 1991; Fred C. Goodenough, Deputy Attorney General of Idaho, to author, July 17, 1991; James Clark, Oregon State Archives, to author, August 5, 1991.

INTRODUCTION

1. Ravi Batra blamed the economic problems of the 1920s, in part, on deregulation. This was not the case in the banking industry. See Batra, *The Great Depression of 1990* (New York: Simon & Schuster, 1987),

96–104, 134, 193–96, 214; *National Bank Act,* 1927; *Bank Failure: An Evaluation of the Factors Contributing to the Failure of National Banks* (Washington, D.C.: Office of the Comptroller of the Currency, 1988).

2. *U.S.N.B. of LaGrande* v. *Pole,* 2 F.Supp. 153, 157. In 1927, the U.S. Fourth Circuit Court of Appeals ruled that the comptroller of the currency had "almost imperialistic powers" (*Liberty National Bank of South Carolina at Columbia* v. *McIntosh,* 16 F.2d 906); James J. White, *Teaching Materials on Banking Law* (St. Paul, Minn.: West, 1976), 65–67, 868–73; *Ex Parte: Ernest Amos,* 112 Southern Reporter 289, *Cases Adjudicated in the Supreme Court of Florida,* Vol. 93, January Term, 1927; *Acts of Georgia,* 1919, Part I, Title 6, Article V, Sec. 3; *National Bank Act,* 1920, Chapter IV, 434, Sec. 5209; *Palm Beach Independent,* September 24, 1926.

3. Arthur M. Schlesinger, Jr., *The Imperial Presidency* (Boston: Houghton Mifflin, 1973), 332–33.

4. Raymond B. Vickers, "Sleazy Banking in the '20s and Today," *Wall Street Journal,* May 23, 1989.

5. Louis D. Brandeis, *Other People's Money and How the Bankers Use It* (New York: Frederick A. Stokes, 1932), 92–108.

6. Ibid.; Thomas K. McCraw, *The Prophets of Regulation* (Cambridge, Mass.: Harvard University Press, 1984), 1–25; Vincent P. Carosso, *The Morgans: Private International Bankers, 1854–1913* (Cambridge, Mass.: Harvard University Press, 1987), 639–40; Charles H. Hession and Hyman Sardy, *Ascent to Affluence: A History of American Economic Development* (Boston: Allyn and Bacon, 1969), 716–17; James Ring Adams, *The Big Fix: Inside the S&L Scandal* (New York: John Wiley & Sons, 1990), 6, 135.

7. *Wall Street Journal,* September 15, 22, October 6, November 4, 18, 1988, December 22, 1992; *New York Times,* September 18, 1991, July 30, 1992, March 16, 1993; *Washington Post,* June 11, October 29, 1991; Stephen Pizzo, Mary Fricker, and Paul Muolo, *Inside Job: The Looting of America's Savings and Loans* (New York: Harper Perennial, 1991), 486; Martin Mayer, *The Greatest-Ever Bank Robbery: The Collapse of the Savings and Loan Industry* (New York: Charles Scribner's Sons, 1990), 2; Adams, *The Big Fix,* 1991, 281–84; L. William Seidman, *Full Faith and Credit: The Great S&L Debacle and Other Washington Sagas* (New York: Times Books, 1993), 196–97.

8. *Annual Report of the Comptroller of the State of Florida, Banking Department* (Tallahassee, June 30, 1926, and June 30, 1930); *Annual Report of the Comptroller of the Currency,* U.S. Treasury Department (Washington, D.C.: U.S. Government Printing Office, December 2, 1929), 2–5.

9. *Atlanta Constitution,* July 15, November 18, 1926; *New York Times,* July 15, 17, 22, September 1, December 26, 1926; J. E. Dovell, *History of Banking in Florida, 1828–1954* (Orlando: Florida Bankers Association,

1955), 114–16; *Annual Report of the Comptroller of Florida,* June 30, 1930; Charles Bartlett Pinney, "The Effects of the Real Estate Boom on Florida State Banks" (M.A. thesis, University of Florida, Gainesville, 1934), 23; Gaines Thomson Cartinhous, *Branch, Group and Chain Banking* (New York: Macmillan, 1931), 20; *Palm Beach Post,* November 9, 1926; Jan Pogue, *To Wield a Mighty Influence: The Story of Banking in Georgia* (Atlanta: Corporate Stories, 1992), 64–66.

10. John Kenneth Galbraith, *The Great Crash, 1929* (Boston: Houghton Mifflin, 1972), 8–12; Dovell, *History of Banking,* 114–16; *Annual Report of the Comptroller of Florida,* June 30, 1930; Gene Burnett, "Cool Leadership during Florida's Banking Crisis," *Florida Trend* 23 (June 1980): 103–5.

11. Dovell, *History of Banking,* 109–11, 114–20; Galbraith, *Great Crash,* 8–12; Charlton W. Tebeau, *A History of Florida* (Coral Gables: University of Miami Press, 1971), 393–94; Frederick Lewis Allen, *Only Yesterday: An Informal History of the Nineteen-Twenties* (New York: Harper and Brothers, 1931), 280–85; Pinney, "Effects of the Real Estate Boom," 21–23; Frank Bowman Sessa, "Real Estate Expansion and Boom in Miami and Its Environs during the 1920's" (Ph.D. dissertation, University of Pittsburgh, 1950), 319–55; Kenneth Ballinger, *Miami Millions: The Dance of the Dollars in the Great Florida Land Boom of 1925* (Miami: Franklin Press, 1936), 159; Burnett, "Florida's Banking Crisis," 103–5; *Annual Report of the Comptroller of Florida,* June 30, 1926, xiii, xiv, and June 30, 1930, 5; *Commercial and Financial Chronicle,* July 24, 1926, p. 412; *Atlanta Constitution,* October 3, 1926; Tom L. Popejoy, "Analysis of the Causes of Bank Failures in New Mexico, 1920 to 1925," *University of New Mexico Bulletin,* October 1, 1931, p. 7.

12. See the bank examination reports, correspondence, and other regulatory records of failed Florida and Georgia banks in USOCC/ WNRC, USOCC/NA, and SC/FSA; see also *State of Georgia v. W. D. Manley,* Case Nos. 26668, 26729, 26730, 26731, 26732, 26733, 26734, 26735, 26736, 26737, 26738, 26739, 26740, 26741, 26742, 26743, 26744, 26745, 26746, 26747, CD/FCSC; and *United States v. Wesley D. Manley, Joseph A. Sasser, Paul J. Baker, Lorne R. Adams, and John D. Russell,* indictments for fraudulent use of mails, and sentences to the United States penitentiary, Criminal Docket No. 13423, USDC/NDG.

13. Frederick D. Wolf, *Failed Financial Institutions: Reasons, Costs, Remedies and Unresolved Issues,* U.S. General Accounting Office Testimony, January 13, 1989, pp. 9, 10, 11, 13, 21, 22, 40.

14. Teresa Simons, "Banking on Secrecy," *Washington Monthly* 22 (December 1990): 31.

15. Jonathan Daniels, *Ordeal of Ambition: Jefferson, Hamilton, Burr* (Garden City, N.Y.: Doubleday, 1970), 174, 195–97, 269, 272–73; John

Steele Gordon, "Understanding the S&L Mess," *American Heritage* 42 (February–March 1991): 56.

16. Robert V. Remini, *Andrew Jackson* (New York: Harper & Row, 1969), 145; Arthur M. Schlesinger, Jr., *The Age of Jackson* (Boston: Little, Brown, 1950), 84–87.

17. Remini, *Jackson*, 150.

18. Popejoy, "Analysis of the Causes of Bank Failures in New Mexico," 10; Merrill D. Beal and Merle W. Wells, *History of Idaho*, Vol. 2 (New York: Lewis Historical Publishing Company, 1959), 245.

19. Popejoy, "Analysis of the Causes of Bank Failures in New Mexico," 10; Ralph L. Edgel, *A Brief History of Banking in New Mexico, 1870–1959* (Albuquerque: Bureau of Business Research, University of New Mexico, 1962), 10–13; Larry Schweikart, "Early Banking in New Mexico from the Civil War to the Roaring Twenties," *New Mexico Historical Review* 63 (January 1988): 21–23; Lynne Pierson Doti and Larry Schweikart, *Banking in the American West: From the Gold Rush to Deregulation* (Norman: University of Oklahoma Press, 1991), 104–6.

20. Receivers' Reports of McKinley County Bank of Gallup, Farmers State Bank of Maxwell, Farmers and Stockmens Bank of Estancia, First State Bank of Alamogordo, Columbus State Bank, First State Bank of Capitan, Bank of Magdalena, Dexter State Bank, Bank of Roy, Silver City Savings Bank, Socorro State Bank, State Trust and Savings Bank of Albuquerque, and "Bank Suspensions since January 1, 1921," Federal Reserve Committee on Branch, Group and Chain Banking, BEP/NMA; Popejoy, "Analysis of the Causes of Bank Failures in New Mexico," 10.

21. Receiver's Report of Farmers State Bank of Maxwell, New Mexico, BEP/NMA.

22. *Annual Report of the State Bank Examiner of New Mexico*, Santa Fe, 1920, 6, 7.

23. Clara Elizabeth Aldrich, "The History of Banking in Idaho" (M.A. thesis, University of Washington, 1940), 53–54, 59, 65; Beal and Wells, *History of Idaho*, 243; Glen Barrett, *Idaho Banking, 1863–1976* (Boise: Boise State University Press, 1976), 54, 64; *Annual Report of the Bureau of Banking, Department of Finance of the State of Idaho*, Boise (1922), 6.

24. Inventory Reports of Bank of Stites, February 2, 1921; State Bank of Idaho Falls, November 23, 1921; Citizens State Bank of Buhl, December 1, 1921; Fidelity State Bank of Orofino, April 8, 1921; Farmers and Merchants Bank of Rupert, October 20, 1922; Paul State Bank, January 17, 1923; First State Bank of Rockland, February 7, 1923; Bank of Washington County, April 9, 1923; D. W. Standrod & Co. Bankers of Blackfoot, November 28, 1923; Weiser Loan and Trust Company, July 31, 1924; Farmers and Merchants Bank of Rexburg, January 14, 1925;

Citizens State Bank of Gooding, April 18, 1925; State Bank of Middleton, April 22, 1927, BB/IHS.

25. Report of State Bank of Idaho Falls, November 23, 1921, BB/IHS; and see comments of State Bank Examiner Charles S. Loveland, *Proceedings of Idaho Bankers Association, First Annual Session,* May 10, 1905, BB/IHS.

26. Report of State Bank of Idaho Falls, November 23, 1921, BB/IHS.

27. Ibid.; *Annual Report of the Bureau of Banking of Idaho,* 1921.

28. Adams, *Big Fix,* 1990, 135, 156, 184, 187, 190; James Ring Adams, "Tallahassee Vice?" *Forbes* 137 (May 5, 1986): 54, 56, 58; Phillip Longman, "Where Was Gerald?" *Florida Trend* 33 (August 1990): 28, 30–37; Impeachment Resolution against Gerald Lewis, filed by Representative Jeff Huenink in the Florida House of Representatives, March 12, 1992.

CHAPTER 1. PROMOTERS IN PARADISE

1. Pierre Berton, *Klondike: The Last Great Gold Rush, 1896–1899* (Toronto: Penguin Books, 1990), 524; William R. Hunt, *North of 53: The Wild Days of the Alaska-Yukon Mining Frontier, 1870–1914* (New York: Macmillan, 1974), 44, 58, 63, 72–79; Paul S. George, "Brokers, Binders, and Builders: Greater Miami's Boom of the Mid-1920s," *Florida Historical Quarterly* 65 (July 1986): 27–51; George B. Tindall, "Bubble in the Sun," *American Heritage* 16 (August 1965): 76–83, 109–11; Theyre Hamilton Weigall, *Boom in Paradise* (New York: A. H. King, 1932), 30; Alva Johnston, *The Legendary Mizners* (New York: Farrar, Straus, and Young, 1953), 287.

2. William E. Leuchtenburg, *The Perils of Prosperity, 1914–32* (Chicago: University of Chicago Press, 1958), 126–27, 216; George H. Soule, *Prosperity Decade: From War to Depression, 1917–1929* (New York: Harper & Row, 1947), 169; Allen, *Only Yesterday,* 148–50.

3. Galbraith, *Great Crash,* 6–12; Allen, *Only Yesterday,* 132–54; Leuchtenburg, *Perils of Prosperity,* 178–203; John O'Sullivan and Edward F. Keuchel, *American Economic History: From Abundance to Constraint* (New York: Markus Wiener, 1989), 163–65.

4. Galbraith, *Great Crash,* 6.

5. Arthur M. Schlesinger, Jr., *The Age of Roosevelt: The Crisis of the Old Order, 1919–1933* (Boston: Houghton Mifflin, 1957), 57, 73; James J. Flink, *The Car Culture* (Cambridge, Mass.: MIT Press, 1975), 67–68.

6. Galbraith, *Great Crash,* 8–12; Sinclair Lewis, *Babbitt* (New York: New American Library, 1961), 23; Allen, *Only Yesterday,* 225–40; Mark Sullivan, *Our Times,* Vol. 6: *The Twenties* (New York: Charles Scribner's Sons, 1935), 647–48.

7. Ida M. Tarbell, Introduction to *Florida Architecture of Addison Mizner* (New York: William Helburn, 1928), 1–2; George, "Brokers," 31; Tebeau, *History of Florida,* 268–69.

8. *New York Times,* March 22, August 10, 11, 16, 1925; *Wall Street Journal,* January 20, 1925; George Brown Tindall, *The Emergence of the New South, 1913–1945* (Baton Rouge: Louisiana State University Press, 1967), 106; Tindall, "Bubble," 77–78, 109; Lawrence W. Levine, *Defender of the Faith, William Jennings Bryan: The Last Decade, 1915–1925* (New York: Oxford University Press, 1965), 238.

9. Sessa, "Expansion and Boom in Miami," 179–80; Paolo E. Coletta, *William Jennings Bryan,* Vol. 3: *Political Puritan, 1915–1925* (Lincoln: University of Nebraska Press, 1969), 151; George, "Brokers," 38–42; *New York Times,* August 9, 11, 1925, March 13, 1926; Kathryne B. Ashley, *George E. Merrick and Coral Gables, Florida* (Coral Gables: Crystal Bay Publishers, 1985), 40–42.

10. Tindall, "Bubble," 77–80, 109, 111; Ashley, *Merrick,* 1–4; James M. Cox, "Florida," *Enterprise, Education and Economics in Florida* (1926); *Miami and the Story of Its Remarkable Growth* (1925); *The Riviera Section and the University of Miami* (1925); *Miami Riviera of Coral Gables,* September 10, November 15, 1926, January 21, April 8, 1927, SCD/UM; *Miami Herald,* March 4, 15, April 4, 1925.

11. Final Report of Palm Beach Bank and Trust Company, July 28, 1926; Final Report of Commercial Bank and Trust Company, June 26, 1926; Final Report of Bank of Dania, July 28, 1926; Final Report of Bank of Coral Gables, June 10, 1930, SC/FSA; Report of Receivers, *In the Matter of W. D. Manley, Bankrupt,* Docket No. 12055, USDC/NDG; Ashley, *Merrick,* 32.

12. First State Bank of Clermont, Florida, to Oscar E. Dooly, February 2, 1927; Robert H. Jones, Jr., to Dooly, January 28, 1927; Petition of Oscar E. Dooly for Distribution of Coral Gables Corporation Collection, April 5, 1927; Dooly to Harry Dodd, June 2, December 1, 1927; Report of Bankers Trust Company, December 1, 1927; Affidavit of Cliff C. Kimsey, *In the Matter of Bankers Trust Company, Bankrupt,* Docket No. 12046, USDC/NDG.

13. As a comparison, the state of Ohio announced, in June 1925, the construction of the "first 'skyscraper' capitol building" at a cost of $1 million. See *Daytona Beach Journal,* June 4, 1925; *Boca Raton: Florida's Wholly New Entirely Beautiful World Resort,* BRHS; Tindall, "Bubble," 80; Donald W. Curl, *Mizner's Florida: American Resort Architecture* (Cambridge, Mass.: MIT Press, 1985), 145–47; Theodore Pratt, *The Story of Boca Raton* (St. Petersburg: Great Outdoors, 1963), 25.

14. *Boca Raton: Florida's Wholly New Entirely Beautiful World Resort,* BRHS; Curl, *Mizner's Florida,* 125.

15. *Palm Beach Post,* April 15, 1925; *Boca Raton: Florida's Wholly New Entirely Beautiful World Resort,* BRHS.

16. *Palm Beach Post,* April 15, September 1, 1925, February 26, July 14, 1926; *Boca Raton: Florida's Wholly New Entirely Beautiful World Resort,* BRHS; Pratt, *Story of Boca Raton,* 14, 20–25; Curl, *Mizner's Florida,* 138–45.

17. *Boca Raton: Florida's Wholly New Entirely Beautiful World Resort,* BRHS; Tarbell, Introduction, 1–2; Theodore Pratt, *That Was Palm Beach* (St. Petersburg: Great Outdoors, 1968), 44.

18. David Leon Chandler, *Henry Flagler: The Astonishing Life and Times of the Visionary Robber Baron Who Founded Florida* (New York: Macmillan, 1986), 136, 138–40, 240–41, 243, 253; Edward N. Akin, *Flagler: Rockefeller Partner and Florida Baron* (Kent, Ohio: Kent State University Press, 1988), 145–46, 155, 157, 203, 234; Tebeau, *History of Florida,* 284; Pratt, *That Was Palm Beach,* 19–38; Stuart B. McIver, *Yesterday's Palm Beach* (Miami: E. A. Seemann, 1976), 35–50.

19. Tindall, "Bubble," 79; Johnston, *Legendary Mizners,* 212; Pratt, *That Was Palm Beach,* 19, 24; George McEvoy, "Wilson Mizner: Now We See Him," *Orlando Sentinel Florida Magazine,* January 14, 1973.

20. *Palm Beach Post,* April 15, 1925, February 6, 19, December 5, 1926; *Palm Beach Independent,* December 4, 1925; Curl, *Mizner's Florida,* 1, 38–39, 41–44, 46–50, 52–54, 60, 83, 145–47; Joseph Frazier Wall, *Alfred I. du Pont: The Man and His Family* (New York: Oxford University Press, 1990), 346, 348; Marquis James, *Alfred I. du Pont: The Family Rebel* (New York: Bobbs-Merrill, 1941), 288–92; Joseph J. Thorndike, Jr., "Addison Mizner—What He Did for Palm Beach," *Smithsonian* 16 (September 1985): 113–16, 118, 121, 122; Johnston, *Legendary Mizners,* 278–99; "Mizner Came to Florida to Die," *Florida Trend* 16 (September 1973): 94–96, 98, 99; Paris Singer, Foreword to *Florida Architecture of Addison Mizner* (New York: William Helburn, 1928); Donald H. Dyal, *Addison Mizner: The Palm Beach Architect* (Monticello, Ill.: Vance Bibliographies, 1985); Christina Orr, *Addison Mizner: Architect of Dreams and Realities (1872–1933),* 1977, HSPBC; Soule, *Prosperity Decade,* 311; John Burke, *Rogue's Progress: The Fabulous Adventures of Wilson Mizner* (New York: G. P. Putnam's Sons, 1975), 111, 177, 219, 222, 265–67.

21. Curl, *Mizner's Florida,* 145; Examiner's Reports of Palm Beach National Bank, June 17, 1925, and June 15, 1926, USOCC/WNRC.

22. *Palm Beach Post,* April 15, May 15, 1925; *New York Times,* September 23, 1926; Final Report of Palm Beach Bank and Trust Company, July 28, 1926, and Final Report of Commercial Bank and Trust Company, June 26, 1926, SC/FSA.

23. *Palm Beach Post,* April 15, November 30, 1925, February 19, July 14, August 23, 1926; Jack "Doc" Kearns with Oscar Fraley, *The Million*

Dollar Gate (New York: Macmillan, 1966), 27; Burke, *Rogue's Progress,* 52–67; Hunt, *North of 53,* 82, 102, 198–201; Pratt, *Story of Boca Raton;* Johnston, *Legendary Mizners,* 205, 253–54, 264–65, 286; Jean Matheson, "Wilson Mizner: 'The first hundred years are the hardest,'" *Palm Beach Today,* June 14, 1991.

24. Addison Mizner, *The Many Mizners* (New York: Sears, 1932), 228–29; J. Camille Showalter, ed., *The Many Mizners: California Clan Extraordinary,* an exhibition of the Oakland Museum, November 7, 1978–February 5, 1979, pp. 16–18; Tindall, "Bubble," 80; Pratt, *Story of Boca Raton,* 14; Curl, *Mizner's Florida,* 4–9.

25. Curl, *Mizner's Florida,* 11–15; Johnston, *Legendary Mizners,* 28, 78–103; Berton, *Klondike,* 78–79, 335, 491; Burke, *Rogue's Progress,* 23–25; Showalter, *Many Mizners,* 20–21; Neville A. D. Armstrong, *Yukon Yesterdays: Thirty Years of Adventure in the Klondike* (London: John Long, 1936), 57–58; May McNeer, *The Alaska Gold Rush* (New York: Random House, 1960), 21–22; William Bronson with Richard Reinhardt, *The Last Grand Adventure* (New York: McGraw-Hill, 1977); *Palm Beach Daily News,* December 18, 1989.

26. Edward Dean Sullivan, *The Fabulous Wilson Mizner* (New York: Henkle, 1935), 78–79, 93–95, 98, 139; Berton, *Klondike,* 85–86, 105, 331–32, 400, 434–63, 471, 478–79, 483; Johnston, *Legendary Mizners,* 73–77, 82–88, 213; Burke, *Rogue's Progress,* 9–10, 36–46, 54–57; McEvoy, "Wilson Mizner"; Ella Lung Martinsen, *Trail to North Star Gold* (Portland: Metropolitan Press, 1969), 22; Ellis Lucia, *Klondike Kate: The Life and Legend of Kitty Rockwell, The Queen of the Yukon* (New York: Hastings House, 1962), 74; Kearns, *Million Dollar Gate,* ix–xi, 27–29; Hunt, *North of 53,* 193–201; *Klondike Nugget,* January 7, June 28, 1899; Glenn Driscoll, "Dance Halls, Saloons, Gambling Dens and Their Personalities, or How I Lost My Shirt in the Klondike Stampede," DCM/OTAB; *Palm Beach Times,* January 9, 1932; *Palm Beach Daily News,* March 12, 1990.

27. Hunt, *North of 53,* 198–201; Mizner, *Many Mizners,* 178–82; Sullivan, *Wilson Mizner,* 129–40; Burke, *Rogue's Progress,* 48, 51–52, 54, 63; Rex E. Beach, *The Miracle of Coral Gables* (New York: Currier & Harford, 1926); Curl, *Mizner's Florida,* 12–15; Stuart McIver, "The Way We Were," *Sunshine,* March 4, 1984, HSPBC.

28. Curl, *Mizner's Florida,* 12–15.

29. Sullivan, *Wilson Mizner,* 140–42, 174–93; Burke, *Rogue's Progress,* 73–105, 107; Hunt, *North of 53,* 100; Curl, *Mizner's Florida,* 16–37; *Palm Beach Daily News,* December 18, 1989; *New York News,* May 7, 1972; McEvoy, "Wilson Mizner."

30. Burke, *Rogue's Progress,* 119, 130; Sullivan, *Wilson Mizner,* 201; Johnston, *Legendary Mizners,* 141–55; *Palm Beach Daily News,* December 18, 1989; *Palm Beach Post,* September 30, 1991.

31. Burke, *Rogue's Progress,* 10, 149–51, 172–84, 203, 205–6, 209; Johnston, *Legendary Mizners,* 156–59, 205–6, 253; Sullivan, *Wilson Mizner,* 305; McEvoy, "Wilson Mizner"; Jonathan Kwitny, *The Fountain Pen Conspiracy* (New York: Knopf, 1973), 286; Deane Tatum to Governor Doyle E. Carlton, n.d.; and "A Depositor" to Carlton, August 18, 1930, DEC/FSA.

32. Johnston, *Legendary Mizners,* 25; Tindall, "Bubble," 80–81.

33. Curl, *Mizner's Florida,* 235–38; Johnston, *Legendary Mizners,* 212; Pratt, *Story of Boca Raton,* 20; *Palm Beach Post,* August 23, 1925.

34. Statement of All Property of Bankrupt, October 25, 1932, *In the Matter of Donald H. Conkling, Bankrupt,* Docket No. 1284, USDC/SDF; *Palm Beach Post,* April 15, 1925; Final Report of Commercial Bank and Trust Company, June 26, 1926; Inventory and Liquidator's Receipt, October 24, 1929, SC/FSA; Receiver's Quarterly Report of Palm Beach National Bank, June 28, 1926, USOCC/NA; Examiner's Report of Palm Beach National Bank, June 17, 1925, USOCC/WNRC; *Polk's Bankers Encyclopedia* (New York: Bankers Encyclopedia Co.), September 1925, p. 291, March 1926, p. 311; Curl, *Mizner's Florida,* 139–40.

35. Final Report of Commercial Bank and Trust Company, June 26, 1926; Inventory and Liquidator's Receipt of Commercial Bank and Trust Company, October 24, 1929; Final Report of First American Bank and Trust Company, October 12, 1929, SC/FSA; Receiver's Quarterly Reports of Palm Beach National Bank, June 28, September 30, 1926, USOCC/NA.

36. Final Report of First American Bank and Trust Company, October 12, 1929, SC/FSA; *Palm Beach Times,* May 24, 1927; *Palm Beach Independent,* July 2, 1926, May 27, June 3, 1927; *Palm Beach Post,* May 24, 26, 1927.

37. Final Report of Commercial Bank and Trust Company, June 26, 1926; and Inventory and Liquidator's Receipt, October 24, 1929, SC/FSA; Receiver's Quarterly Report of Palm Beach National Bank, June 28, 1926, USOCC/NA; Examiner's Report of Palm Beach National Bank, June 17, 1925, USOCC/WNRC; *Polk's Bankers,* September 1925, p. 291, March 1926, p. 311.

38. *Palm Beach Post,* April 15, August 23, 1925.

39. *Palm Beach Post,* June 30, 1925.

40. *Palm Beach Post,* April 15, 1925.

41. *Palm Beach Post,* September 5, 1925.

42. Curl, *Mizner's Florida,* 140, 147, 153; *Palm Beach Post,* October 10, 1925; *Tampa Morning Tribune,* September 22, 1925.

43. Curl, *Mizner's Florida,* 153–54; *New York Times,* October 10, 1925; Victoria Harden McDonnell, "The Businessman's Politician: A Study of the Administration of John Welborn Martin, 1925– 1929" (M.A. thesis, University of Florida, 1968), 68–69.

44. *New York Times,* October 14, 1925.

45. *New York Times,* November 25, 1925; *Palm Beach Post,* November 6, 1926; *Palm Beach Independent,* December 4, 1925; Burke, *Rogue's Progress,* 242–43; Curl, *Mizner's Florida,* 153–54; Johnston, *Legendary Mizners,* 278–87.

46. Curl, *Mizner's Florida,* 140–41, 147, 149–50, 164; Pratt, *Story of Boca Raton,* 21–22, 27–28; *Palm Beach Post,* September 1, 1925, June 22, 1926; Anona Christina Orr-Cahall, "An Identification and Discussion of the Architecture and Decorative Arts of Addison Mizner (1872–1933)" (Ph.D. dissertation, Yale University, 1979), 62, 64–65; Joan Bream, *Addison Cairns Mizner 1872–1933,* BRHS.

47. Oath to Schedule B, *In the Matter of Mizner Development Corporation, Bankrupt,* Docket No. 252, USDC/SDF; Addison Mizner to Investors at Boca Raton, January 14, 1926, BRHS; *New York Times,* November 29, 1925, September 23, 1926; *Palm Beach Post,* May 15, 1925; Final Report of Palm Beach Bank and Trust Company, July 28, 1926; Final Report of Commercial Bank and Trust Company, June 26, 1926, SC/FSA; Examiner's Reports of Palm Beach National Bank, February 10, June 15, 1926, USOCC/WNRC.

48. Schedule of Creditors Holding Securities, August 4, 1927; Petition of Trustees in Bankruptcy, September 23, 1927; Reply to Order to Show Cause of Central Equities Corporation; Transcript of Hearing before Referee L. Earl Curry, October 10, 1927; Order Dismissing Petition, October 10, 1927, *In the Matter of Mizner Development Corporation, Bankrupt,* Docket No. 252, USDC/SDF.

CHAPTER 2. CAPTURING THE REGULATORS

1. *Annual Report of the Comptroller of Florida,* June 30, 1930; J. B. Cunningham to J. W. Pole, September 3, 1926, and Cunningham to J. W. McIntosh, September 25, 1926, Palm Beach National Bank Records, USOCC/NA; *Daytona Morning Journal,* September 13, 1924; *Palm Beach Post,* December 21, 1926.

2. Dovell, *History of Banking,* 227; Allen Morris, *The Florida Handbook: 1981–1982* (Tallahassee: Peninsular Publishing Company, 1981), 211.

3. Dovell, *History of Banking,* 37, 227; George, "Brokers," 29–30; Sessa, "Real Estate Expansion," 109; Cary A. Hardee, "The Banker and the Government," *Southern Banker,* May 1922, pp. 12–13; Allen Morris, *The Florida Handbook: 1987–1988* (Tallahassee: Peninsular Publishing Company, 1987), 128.

4. *Miami and the Story of Its Remarkable Growth* (1925), SCD/UM; *New York Times,* March 15, 1925.

5. *Miami Herald,* July 28, 1929, February 8, 1942, January 16, 1952, October 22, 24, 1964; *Miami News,* October 22, 1964; Statement of the

Condition of Southern Bank and Trust Company, December 31, 1924, HASE

6. Final Reports of Bank of Bay Biscayne, July 24, 1930, and Southern Bank and Trust Company of Miami, September 5, 1931, and Inventory Report of Dade County Security Company, May 20, 1933, SC/FSA; Mary T. Moore, *Coral Gables History,* March 1950, SCD/UM.

7. Pinney, "Effects of the Real Estate Boom," 23; Examiner's Reports of Palm Beach National Bank, February 10, June 15, 1926, USOCC/WNRC; Receiver's Report of Palm Beach National Bank, June 28, 1926, USOCC/NA; Final Report of Palm Beach Bank and Trust Company, July 28, 1926; Final Report of Commercial Bank and Trust Company, June 26, 1926; and Final Report of Peoples Bank of Jacksonville, July 25, 1929, SC/FSA.

8. *New York Times,* September 23, 1926; *Palm Beach Post,* April 15, 1925; Final Report of Commercial Bank and Trust Company, June 26, 1926; and Final Report of Palm Beach Bank and Trust Company, July 28, 1926, SC/FSA.

9. Examiner's Reports of Palm Beach National Bank, February 10, June 15, 1926, USOCC/WNRC; Receiver's Report of Palm Beach National Bank, June 28, 1926, USOCC/NA; Final Report of Commercial Bank and Trust Company, June 26, 1926; and Final Report of Palm Beach Bank and Trust Company, July 28, 1926, SC/FSA; J. B. Hodges to J. L. Earman, July 28, 1926; Earman to Hodges, August 30, 1926; and T. C. Hawkins to Hodges, February 10, 1934, JBHP/PKYL; *New York Times,* September 23, 1926; *Palm Beach Post,* May 15, 1925.

10. Joe L. Earman, "J. R. Anthony," *Palm Beach Independent,* November 26, 1926; A. P. Anthony, "Report of Chairman, State Bank Section," *Southern Banker,* April 1925, p. 51; *Groveland Graphic,* May 1, 1924; A. P. Anthony to R. A. Gray, June 1, 1921, RAGP/FSA; Final Report of Peoples Bank of Jacksonville, July 25, 1929; Final Report of Palm Beach Bank and Trust Company, July 28, 1926; and Final Report of Commercial Bank and Trust Company, June 26, 1926, SC/FSA; Receiver's Report of Palm Beach National Bank, June 28, 1926, USOCC/NA; *New York Times,* September 23, 1926.

11. Final Report of Peoples Bank of Jacksonville, July 25, 1929, SC/FSA.

12. *Tallahassee Daily Democrat,* February 29, 1928; *Acts and Resolutions Adopted by the Legislature of Florida,* Tallahassee, 1897, 1901, and 1903.

13. When Amos's father died in 1931, at age eighty-eight, the state capitol was closed for his funeral. See *Tallahassee Daily Democrat,* January 22, 1931; Wayne Flynt, *Cracker Messiah: Governor Sidney J. Catts of Florida* (Baton Rouge: Louisiana State University Press, 1977), 116.

14. Selden F. Waldo to Clarence Gay, January 9, 1948, CMG/FSA.

15. *Palm Beach Post,* September 29, 1926; *Palm Beach Independent,* Oc-

tober 1, 1926; Joe L. Earman to J. B. Hodges, September 25, 1926, JBHP/PKYL.

16. Allen Morris, *The Florida Handbook: 1977–1978* (Tallahassee: Peninsular Publishing Company, 1977), 43–50, 75, 87, 90, 93; Flynt, *Cracker Messiah*, 40–43, 63–67; *General Acts of Florida*, 1931, 1933.

17. Receiver's Report of Palm Beach National Bank, June 28, 1926, USOCC/NA; Final Report of Peoples Bank of Jacksonville, July 25, 1929, SC/FSA; *Tallahassee Daily Democrat*, June 5, 1932.

18. Joe L. Earman, "J. R. Anthony," *Palm Beach Independent*, November 26, 1926; Earman, "James Rembert Anthony," *Present Truth Messenger* 29 (November 27, 1924), pp. 25–26.

19. James Rembert Anthony, "Anthony Brothers on the East Coast: 1890–1936" (1936), 1–3, 5–7, PKYL; Total of Inventories, March 29, 1932, *In the Matter of Anthony's, Inc., Bankrupt*, Docket No. 1195, USDC/NDG; James R. Knott, "The Anthony Saga, 1895–1980," *Palm Beach Post*, December 7, 1980; *Palm Beach Post*, June 30, 1940.

20. Anthony, "Anthony Brothers on the East Coast," 10–11, PKYL; and *The First Thirty Years of Miami and the Bank of Bay Biscayne: 1896–1926*, 3–6, 8, PKYL.

21. The Romfhs, a pioneer family from Arkansas, had their name changed from Rumph to Romfh by special act of the Florida legislature. Anthony, "Anthony Brothers on the East Coast," 10–11, PKYL; *Miami Herald*, February 8, 1942, January 16, 1952; *Miami Daily News*, August 13, 1933, July 24, 1902; George Lewis, *Florida Banks* (1942), 2–3, 14–16, PKYL.

22. *The First Thirty Years of Miami and the Bank of Bay Biscayne*, 3–6, 8, PKYL; Chandler, *Henry Flagler*, 179–81, 191–92, 213–14; Akin, *Flagler*, 206–7, 119–20, 170–71; *Palm Beach Post*, June 30, 1940; *Attention Democrats* and *To the Negroes*, JMFP/HASF; William T. Cash, *History of the Democratic Party in Florida* (Tallahassee: Florida Democratic Historical Foundation, 1936), 94, 103.

23. Anthony, "Anthony Brothers on the East Coast," 1, 10–11, PKYL; *Palm Beach Post*, June 30, 1940; *Miami Daily News*, July 24, 1902; "The Bank Account," December 1977, p. 2, HASF.

24. Akin, *Flagler*, 170–71; Chandler, *Henry Flagler*, 149.

25. Anthony, "Anthony Brothers on the East Coast," 1, 10–11, PKYL; E. C. Romfh to John Frohock, March 19, July 15, 23, 1942, JMFP/HASF.

26. Sidney W. Martin, "Flagler's Associates in East Florida Developments," *Florida Historical Quarterly* 26 (January 1948): 259–61; *The First Thirty Years of Miami and the Bank of Bay Biscayne*, 6, PKYL; Akin, *Flagler*, 139, 141, 170–71, 208; E. V. Blackman, *Miami and Dade County, Florida: Its Settlement, Progress and Achievement* (Washington, D.C.: Victor Rain-

bolt, 1921), 47, 109–12; Lewis, *Florida Banks,* 16, PKYL; Donald W. Curl, *Palm Beach County: An Illustrated History* (Northridge, Calif.: Windsor Publications, 1986), 29, 31, 48, 114; *Miami News,* December 6, 1964.

27. Anthony, "Anthony Brothers on the East Coast," 11, PKYL; Lewis, *Florida Banks,* 16, PKYL; *Miami Daily News,* July 24, 1902.

28. *Palm Beach Post,* June 30, 1940; James R. Knott, "The Anthony Saga, 1895–1980," *Palm Beach Post,* December 7, 1980.

29. *Miami Daily News,* July 24, 1902; Curl, *Palm Beach County,* 23.

30. Anthony, "Anthony Brothers on the East Coast," 10, PKYL; *Miami Daily Metropolis,* July 24, 1902.

31. Anthony, "Anthony Brothers on the East Coast," 11, PKYL; *Miami Daily Metropolis,* July 24, 1902; Blackman, *Miami,* 47; *Miami Herald,* February 8, 1942.

32. Anthony, "Anthony Brothers on the East Coast," 25–26, PKYL; *Miami Daily News,* August 13, 1933; *Miami Herald,* February 8, 1942, January 16, 1952; Dovell, *History of Banking,* 102.

33. Lewis, *Florida Banks,* 16–19, PKYL; *The First Thirty Years of Miami and the Bank of Bay Biscayne,* 10–11, PKYL; Anthony, "Anthony Brothers on the East Coast," 23, PKYL; Wayne Flynt, *Duncan Upshaw Fletcher: Dixie's Reluctant Progressive* (Tallahassee: Florida State University Press, 1971), 43.

34. *New York Herald Tribune,* March 14, 1927; Garet Garrett, "Why Some Banks Fail and Others Don't," *Saturday Evening Post* 205 (May 20, 1933): 3–5, 67–70, 72; J. W. McIntosh to L. Y. Sherman, February 25, March 28, 1928; and Sherman to McIntosh, April 6, 1927, LYSP/ISHL; J. B. Cunningham to Comptroller of the Currency, March 11, 1927, Palm Beach National Bank Records; J. W. McIntosh to E. C. Romfh, May 29, 1928 (telegram), American National Bank of Sarasota Records, USOCC/NA; *Tampa Morning Tribune,* July 2, 4, August 18, 20, 1930; Blackman, *Miami,* 111–12; *Miami Herald,* February 8, 1942, January 16, 1952, May 26, 1964; Lewis, *Florida Banks,* 14–21, PKYL; *Who Was Who In America, 1897–1960* (Chicago: Marquis Who's Who, 1960), 3:581; *Miami News,* May 28, 1957.

35. *Commercial and Financial Chronicle,* July 3, 1926, pp. 36–37, December 6, 1926, p. 1.

36. Dovell, *History of Banking,* 192; E. C. Romfh to John Frohock, March 19, July 15, 23, 1942, JMFP/HASF; "The First National Bank of Miami," JMFP/HASF; "The First National Bank, Miami, Florida: Cash and Marketable Securities to Total Deposits," HASF; Statement of Condition of the First National Bank of Miami, June 30, 1930, HASF; *Miami Herald,* January 16, 1952, April 3, 1964; *Miami Daily News,* August 13, 1933, December 6, 1964.

37. Anthony, "Anthony Brothers on the East Coast," 23–24, PKYL; Dovell, *History of Banking,* 82–83, 226, 233; *Annual Report of the Comptroller of Florida,* 1894; Lewis, *Florida Banks,* 5, PKYL; *Palm Beach Post,* June 30, 1940.

38. *Bank of Palm Beach,* HSPBC; *Palm Beach Post,* January 15, 1916, May 18, 1917, July 10, 1918, April 19, July 10, August 5, 24, September 4, 8, 21, 22, December 24, 1919, January 26, May 9, June 27, October 13, 1920, January 25, May 24, June 16, October 23, November 29, 1925, January 1, 1926, December 16, 1927, November 17, 18, December 13, 14, 1928, May 4, 5, 6, 7, 8, 9, 10, 11, 13, 14, 1931; *Palm Beach Independent,* January 4, 1929; *Palm Beach Times,* November 26, December 7, 11, 12, 17, 18, 29, 1928, May 26, 1930; *Tampa Morning Tribune,* November 22, 1929; Final Report of Palm Beach Bank and Trust Company, July 28, 1926, SC/FSA; Biographical Data of David Forrest Dunkle and "Belles of Yesterday," n.d., HSPBC.

39. The Seward Building was named for the family of J. R. Anthony's wife, Rosa Seward Anthony. *Palm Beach Post,* August 14, October 18, 1919, January 28, August 28, 1920; Bank transaction receipt of Bank of Palm Beach, August 1914, HSPBC; Anthony, "Anthony Brothers on the East Coast," 21, 24, PKYL.

40. Final Report of Palm Beach Bank and Trust Company, July 28, 1926, and Final Report of Peoples Bank of Jacksonville, July 25, 1929, SC/FSA; *Palm Beach Independent,* September 24, 1926; *New York Times,* September 23, 1926.

41. Anthony, "Anthony Brothers on the East Coast," 20–21, 26, 29, PKYL; Earman, "James Rembert Anthony," 25–26; James R. Knott, "The Anthony Saga, 1895–1980," *Palm Beach Post,* December 7, 1980.

42. *Annual Report of the Department of Banking of the State of Georgia,* Atlanta, 1920, p. 44, and 1921, p. 71; *Commercial and Financial Chronicle,* September 25, 1926, p. 1583; Minutes of Board of Directors Meetings of Bankers Financing Company of Atlanta, October 21, 23, 1905, *United States v. Wesley D. Manley, et al.,* Criminal Docket No. 13423, USDC/NDG; Pogue, *To Wield a Mighty Influence,* 64; Franklin M. Garrett, *Atlanta and Environs,* Vol. 2 (Athens: University of Georgia Press, 1988), 124–26, 697–99, 727; George, "Brokers," 37.

43. Testimony of W. D. Manley, August 27, 1926, *In the Matter of W. D. Manley, Bankrupt,* Docket No. 12055, USDC/NDG.

44. Ibid.; Testimony of Joseph A. Sasser; Minutes of Board of Directors Meetings of Bankers Financing Company of Atlanta, October 21, 23, 1905; Minutes of Stockholders Meeting of Bankers Trust Company, September 13, 1919, *United States v. Wesley D. Manley, et al.,* Criminal Docket No. 13423, USDC/NDG.

45. Minutes of Board of Directors Meetings of Bankers Financing

Company of Atlanta, October 21, 23, 1905; Testimony of H. E. Rank, *United States* v. *Wesley D. Manley, et al.*, Criminal Docket No. 13423; Testimony of W. D. Manley, August 27, 1926; Report of Receivers, *In the Matter of W. D. Manley, Bankrupt*, Docket No. 12055, USDC/NDG; Garrett, *Atlanta and Environs*, 124–26, 697–99; *Annual Report of the Department of Banking of the State of Georgia*, 1926, p. vi.

46. *Commercial and Financial Chronicle*, August 21, 1926, pp. 936–38; *Atlanta Constitution*, September 4, 1926; *Annual Report of the Department of Banking of the State of Georgia*, 1920, p. 44; 1921, p. 71; 1922, p. 114; 1923, p. 39; and 1924, p. 38.

47. Georgia State Bank Charters, Certificates of Incorporation, Bank and Trust Companies, 1920–39, Certificate Book 2, 11, and Georgia State Bank Charter Amendments, Bank Charters and Amendments, 1920–30, Book K, 1921–24, pp. 141–43, SS/GSA; *Acts of Georgia*, 1919, Part I, Title 6, Article VIII, Section 1(3); *Southern Banker*, June 1924; *New York Times*, July 15, 16, 17, 1926; *Commercial and Financial Chronicle*, July 17, 1926, pp. 285–86, July 31, 1926, pp. 499–501; *Atlanta Constitution*, July 15, 1926; *Annual Report of the Department of Banking of the State of Georgia*, 1924, p. 39.

48. *Atlanta Constitution Journal Magazine*, June 17, 1923; *Palm Beach Post*, November 9, 1926; Pogue, *To Wield a Mighty Influence*, 64, 66.

49. *Atlanta Constitution*, August 15, 20, 24, September 5, November 12, 1926; *New York Times*, August 15, 1926; *Commercial and Financial Chronicle*, August 21, 1926, pp. 936–38; Testimony of Lena Long, August 28, 1926; and Testimony of Mrs. W. D. Manley, August 30, 1926, *In the Matter of W. D. Manley, Bankrupt*, Docket No. 12055; J. A. Sasser to W. D. Manley, August 11, 1917; Testimony of O. B. Tomlinson, *United States* v. *Wesley D. Manley, et al.*, Criminal Docket No. 13423, USDC/NDG; *Rono Memborn* v. *Mrs. W. D. Manley*, Case No. 69345, CC/FCSC.

50. *Chamberlin-Johnson-DuBose Company* v. *Mrs. W. D. Manley*, Case No. 73582, CC/FCSC; Garrett, *Atlanta and Environs*, 731–32.

51. *Lake Butler Bank* v. *Mrs. V. R. Manley*, Case No. 41663, CC/FCSC; *Atlanta Constitution*, August 24, 1926.

52. *Annual Report of the Department of Banking of the State of Georgia*, 1926; *Annual Report of the Comptroller of Florida*, June 30, 1926; George, "Brokers," 37; James R. Knott, "The Anthony Saga, 1895–1980," *Palm Beach Post*, December 7, 1980.

53. Flynt, *Cracker Messiah*, 40–61; Cash, *History of the Democratic Party in Florida*, 124–30; Tebeau, *History of Florida*, 361–64; W. V. Knott to F. O. Spain, October 16, 1922, KFP/FSA.

54. Bankers Financing Company to W. V. Knott, October 4, 1921; W. V. Knott to C. M. Knott, June 17, 1922; see two letters with the same date, W. V. Knott to F. O. Spain, October 16, 1922; W. V. Knott to C. M. Knott, October 17, 1922; J. R. Anthony to W. V. Knott, October 18, 1922;

Spain to W. V. Knott, May 25, 1923; O. C. Sheffield to W. V. Knott, June 4, 1923, KFP/FSA.

55. W. V. Knott to F. O. Spain, October 16, 1922, KFP/FSA.

56. W. V. Knott to F. O. Spain, October 16, 1922; J. R. Anthony to Knott, October 18, 1922; Spain to Knott, May 25, 1923; O. C. Sheffield to Knott, June 4, 1923, KFP/FSA.

57. Final Report of Peoples Bank of Jacksonville, July 5, 1929, SC/FSA; Examiner's Reports of Palm Beach National Bank, February 10, June 15, 1926, USOCC/WNRC; Receiver's Report of Palm Beach National Bank, June 28, 1926, USOCC/NA; Anthony, "Report of Chairman," p. 51.

58. Final Report of Palm Beach Bank and Trust Company, July 28, 1926; Final Report of Commercial Bank and Trust Company, June 26, 1926, SC/FSA; A. P. Anthony to R. A. Gray, June 1, 1921, RAGP/FSA.

59. *Tropical Sun,* January 16, 1925; Final Report of Peoples Bank of Jacksonville, July 5, 1929, SC/FSA; Dovell, *History of Banking,* 215–17.

60. J. B. Hodges to Joe L. Earman, July 23, 26, 28, 31, August 4, 17, 24, 27, 28, September 1, 29, 30, October 16, 1926; Earman to Hodges, July 26, August 30, 1926; Louis McH. Howe to Hodges, May 10, 1933, JBHP/PKYL; Testimony of Earl Haltiwanger, *United States* v. *Wesley D. Manley, et al.,* Criminal Docket No. 13423, USDC/NDG; *Palm Beach Independent,* March 25, 1927; Cash, *History of the Democratic Party in Florida,* 210; William T. Cash, *The Story of Florida,* Vol. 3 (New York: American Historical Society, 1938), 127–28.

61. Final Report of Brevard County Bank and Trust Company, October 15, 1929; Final Report of Bank of Little River, July 2, 1926, SC/FSA; Morris, *Florida Handbook: 1987–1988,* 126; *General Acts of Florida,* 1925, 1927, 1929; Cash, *History of the Democratic Party in Florida,* 227; Cash, *Story of Florida,* 322–23.

62. Testimony of Lorne R. Adams, *United States* v. *Wesley D. Manley, et al.,* Criminal Docket No. 13423, USDC/NDG.

63. *The Depositors Guarantee Fund of the Witham System,* Government Exhibit No. 513, ibid.

64. Dovell, *History of Banking,* 215–16, 228, 233; *Tampa Morning Tribune,* November 9, 1929, July 30, November 5, December 3, 1930; Final Report of Seminole County Bank, August 6, 1927; and Final Report of Citizens Bank and Trust Company of Tampa, August 16, 1929, SC/FSA; *General Acts of Florida,* 1923.

65. Cary A. Hardee, "The Banker and the Government," p. 12.

66. Dovell, *History of Banking,* 33–37.

67. J. R. Anthony, "Annual Address of the President," *Southern Banker,* April 1925, p. 4.

68. Ibid.

69. George, "Brokers," 31; Sessa, "Real Estate Expansion," 146; *Miami Daily News,* April 10, 1925.

70. *Southern Banker,* April 1925, pp. 21, 24.

71. Schlesinger, *Age of Roosevelt,* 62–63; Anthony, "Annual Address of the President," p. 6.

72. Anthony, "Annual Address of the President," p. 6; *Annual Report of the Department of Banking of the State of Georgia,* 1926, p. vi; *Annual Report of the Comptroller of Florida,* June 30, 1926; Adams, *Big Fix,* 1990, 276–78.

73. Testimony and Suggestions of John D. Russell; Minutes of Joint Meeting of the Directors of Georgia State Bank and Bankers Trust Company, May 6, 1925, *United States* v. *Wesley D. Manley, et al.,* Criminal Docket No. 13423, USDC/NDG.

CHAPTER 3. THE MIZNER BANK

1. Examiner's Reports of Palm Beach National Bank, February 10, June 15, 1926, USOCC/WNRC; Charles W. Collins to Attorney General, July 22, September 1, 1926; O. R. Luhring to Comptroller of the Currency, July 27, August 3, 1926; V. H. Northcutt to J. W. Pole, August 3, 1926; E. W. Stearns to Attorney General, July 13, 1926; J. B. Cunningham to Comptroller of the Currency, September 17, 1926, February 6, 1928; Assistant Supervising Receiver to Cunningham, February 18, 1928; Receiver's Reports of Palm Beach National Bank, June 28, September 30, 1926, USOCC/NA; Final Report of Palm Beach Bank and Trust Company, July 28, 1926; Final Report of Commercial Bank and Trust Company, June 26, 1926; Final Report of Farmers Bank and Trust Company, June 15, 1927; Final Report of First American Bank and Trust Company, October 12, 1929, SC/FSA; Schedule A of Creditors, August 4, 1927; First Dividend .001%, March 18, 1930, and other bankruptcy records, *In the Matter of Mizner Development Corporation, Bankrupt,* Docket No. 252, USDC/SDF; Balance Sheet of Mizner Development Corporation, March 31, 1926, and Addison Mizner to the Stockholders of Mizner Development Corporation, April 30, 1926, HSPBC; *New York Times,* September 23, 1926; Curl, *Mizner's Florida,* 153–57, 163–64; Johnston, *Legendary Mizners,* 287, 296; Pratt, *Story of Boca Raton,* 24; McEvoy, "Wilson Mizner."

2. Palm Beach National Bank Records, USOCC/WNRC and USOCC/NA; *Annual Report of the Comptroller of the Currency,* December 10, 1926, p. 193.

3. Lewis, *Florida Banks,* 20, PKYL; *Annual Report of the Comptroller of the Currency,* December 1, 1930, p. 311; *Palm Beach Post,* January 1, 3, 1925.

4. Report of Organization of National Bank, Palm Beach National Bank, November 25, 1924; Comptroller of the Currency to V. H. Northcutt, December 8, 1924; Northcutt to Comptroller of the Currency, December 12, 1924; Northcutt to Cashier, Palm Beach National Bank,

December 12, 1924, USOCC/NA; Final Report of Palm Beach Bank and Trust Company, July 28, 1926, SC/FSA; Examiner's Reports of Palm Beach National Bank, February 10, June 15, 1926, USOCC/WNRC; *Tropical Sun,* January 16, 1925.

5. *Palm Beach Post,* January 1, 3, 1925; *Polk's Bankers,* March 1926; Blackwell and Donnell to Comptroller of the Currency, July 7, 1926 (telegram), Palm Beach National Bank Records, USOCC/NA; *Palm Beach Independent,* November 26, 1926, February 11, 25, 1927.

6. Examiner's Reports of Palm Beach National Bank, February 10, June 15, 1926, USOCC/WNRC; Final Report of Palm Beach Bank and Trust Company, July 28, 1926, SC/FSA; *Palm Beach Post,* September 23, 1926; Receiver's Reports of Palm Beach National Bank, June 28, September 30, 1926, USOCC/NA; Flink, *Car Culture,* 67.

7. Examiner's Report of Palm Beach National Bank, February 10, 1926, USOCC/WNRC; *General Acts of Florida,* 1927, Ch. 11808, p. 10; Affidavit of E. M. Porter, August 9, 1926, Palm Beach Bank and Trust Company Records, SC/FSA.

8. Examiner's Report of Palm Beach National Bank, June 15, 1926, USOCC/WNRC.

9. Joe L. Earman to J. B. Hodges, August 30, 1926, JBHP/PKYL; Ernest Amos to Palm Beach Bank and Trust Company, January 23, 1926, *Palm Beach Independent,* September 24, 1926; *Annual Report of the Comptroller of Florida,* June 30, 1926, June 30, 1927, and June 30, 1928.

10. Final Report of Commercial Bank and Trust Company, June 26, 1926, SC/FSA; T. C. Hawkins to J. B. Hodges, February 10, 1934, JBHP/PKYL.

11. John B. Cunningham to Comptroller of Currency, September 17, 1926, and the lease between the Palm Beach National Bank and the Palm Way Finance Company, October 3, 1924, Palm Beach National Bank Records, USOCC/NA; Curl, *Mizner's Florida,* 145.

12. Examiner's Reports of Palm Beach National Bank, June 17, September 25, 1925, February 10, June 15, 1926, USOCC/WNRC; *Palm Beach Post,* April 15, 1925.

13. *Tampa Tribune,* July 13, 1978, March 3, 1990; Résumé of Victor Huborn Northcutt, *Tampa Tribune* files; Dovell, *History of Banking,* 231.

14. *Tampa Tribune,* July 13, 1978; Examiner's Report of Palm Beach National Bank, June 17, 1925, USOCC/WNRC.

15. Examiner's Report of Palm Beach National Bank, June 17, 1925, USOCC/WNRC.

16. Ibid.

17. Examiner's Report of Palm Beach National Bank, September 25, 1925, USOCC/WNRC.

18. Ibid.

19. Examiner's Report of Palm Beach National Bank, February 10,

1926, and "Florida Banks in Healthy Condition," n.d., clipping in Palm Beach National Bank Records, USOCC/WNRC.

20. Examiner's Reports of Palm Beach National Bank, September 25, 1925, February 10, 1926, USOCC/WNRC.

21. Examiner's Report of Palm Beach National Bank, February 10, 1926, ibid.

22. Ibid.

23. Examiner's Report of Palm Beach National Bank, February 10, June 15, 1926, ibid.; Addison Mizner to the Stockholders of the Mizner Development Corporation, n.d., HSPBC.

24. Examiner's Reports of Palm Beach National Bank, June 17, 1925, June 15, 1926, USOCC/WNRC; Receiver's Report of Palm Beach National Bank, June 28, 1926, USOCC/NA; Statement of All Property of Bankrupt, October 25, 1932, *In the Matter of Donald H. Conkling, Bankrupt,* Docket No. 1284, USDC/NDG; Addison Mizner to Stockholders of Mizner Development Corporation, n.d., HSPBC; Curl, *Mizner's Florida,* 71–76, 118, 145; "Mr. Christopher Dunphy," newspaper clipping, December 14, 1948, HSPBC; *Palm Beach Post,* April 15, 1925.

25. Examiner's Report of Palm Beach National Bank, June 15, 1926, USOCC/WNRC; J. B. Cunningham to Comptroller of the Currency, February 6, 1928; Assistant Supervising Receiver to Cunningham, February 18, 1928, USOCC/NA.

26. Final Report of Palm Beach Bank and Trust Company, July 28, 1926; Final Report of Commercial Bank and Trust Company, June 26, 1926; Final Report of Farmers Bank and Trust Company, June 15, 1927; Final Report of First American Bank and Trust Company, October 12, 1929, SC/FSA; Schedule A of Creditors, August 4, 1927; and First Dividend .001%, March 18, 1930, *In the Matter of Mizner Development Corporation, Bankrupt,* Docket No. 252, USDC/SDF.

27. Examiner's Report of Palm Beach National Bank, June 15, 1926, USOCC/WNRC; Final Report of Palm Beach Bank and Trust Company, July 28, 1926; Final Report of Commercial Bank and Trust Company, June 26, 1926; Final Report of First American Bank and Trust Company, October 12, 1929, SC/FSA; Curl, *Mizner's Florida,* 53, 118, 140–41, 145.

28. Examiner's Report of Palm Beach National Bank, February 10, 1926, USOCC/WNRC; John B. Cunningham to Comptroller of the Currency, January 31, 1927; J. E. Fouts to Cunningham, February 16, 1927; N. C. Bainum to Cunningham, December 21, 1928, Palm Beach National Bank Records, USOCC/NA; *New York Times,* April 15, 1929; Curl, *Mizner's Florida,* 140, 145.

29. J. B. Cunningham to Comptroller of the Currency, January 31, 1927, USOCC/NA.

30. J. B. Cunningham to Comptroller of the Currency, July 15, 1926;

Charles W. Collins to Attorney General, July 22, 1926; O. R. Luhring to Comptroller of the Currency, July 27, August 3, 1926; V. H. Northcutt to J. W. Pole, August 3, 1926, USOCC/NA.

31. J. B. Cunningham to Comptroller of the Currency, July 7, 1926; E. W. Stearns to Attorney General, July 13, 1926, USOCC/NA.

32. Charles W. Collins to Attorney General, September 1, 1926; J. B. Cunningham to J. W. Pole, September 3, 1926; Cunningham to Comptroller of Currency, August 27, September 17, 25, 1926, February 6, 1928; Assistant Supervising Receiver to Cunningham, February 18, 1928; V. H. Northcutt to J. W. Pole, August 3, 1926; Pole to Cunningham, September 9, 1926; J. W. McIntosh to Cunningham, October 11, 1926, USOCC/NA.

33. Examiner's Report of Palm Beach National Bank, June 15, 1926, USOCC/WNRC; *New York Times,* September 23, 1926; Curl, *Mizner's Florida,* 163.

34. *New York Times,* November 25, 1925; William A. White to George S. Graham, January 27, 1926, and Graham to J. W. McIntosh, February 10, 1926, Palm Beach National Bank Records, USOCC/WNRC.

35. Graham was a director of the Columbia American Trust Company; Philadelphia Electric Light and Power Company; Pennsylvania Heat, Light, and Power Company; International Smokeless Powder Chemical Company of New Jersey; and the American Milling Company of New Jersey. See *Biographical Directory of the American Congress, 1774–1961* (Washington, D.C.: U.S. Government Printing Office, 1961), 964; *New York Times,* July 4, 5, 7, 22, 1931; *Martindale's American Law Directory* (New York: Martindale's American Law Directory, 1930), 1546, 1621; Wall, *du Pont,* 346; James, *du Pont,* 289, 291; *Tampa Morning Tribune,* March 5, 1930.

36. William A. White to George S. Graham, January 27, 1926, and Graham to J. W. McIntosh, February 10, 1926, McIntosh to Graham, February 12, 1926, Palm Beach National Bank Records, USOCC/WNRC; *New York Times,* December 3, 19, 21, 1924; *History of the Pure Oil Company,* Vol. 2 (Chicago, 1953), LC/WDC, 26, 28–37.

37. E. F. Quinn to W. W. McBryde, February 13, 1926; W. J. Fowler to W. A. White, February 13, March 11, 1926; McBryde, Memorandum, and Approval of the Application of Palm Beach National Bank, March 11, 1926; Application to Increase Capital of Palm Beach National Bank, March 18, 1926, received on April 1, 1926; White to Fowler, March 29, 1926; Fowler to president of Palm Beach National Bank, April 2, May 13, 1926, Palm Beach National Bank Records, Examiner's Report of Palm Beach National Bank, February 10, 1926, USOCC/WNRC.

38. Examiner's Report of Palm Beach National Bank, June 15, 1926, USOCC/WNRC.

39. Claude G. Bowers, *Beveridge and the Progressive Era* (New York: Literary Guild, 1932), 184–87; *New York Times,* March 4, 12, 1899, July 1, 1902, April 14, 15, 1929; *Biographical Directory of the American Congress,* 503.

40. *Martindale's American Law Directory, 1930,* 932; *The Martindale-Hubbell Law Directory* (New York: Martindale's American Law Directory, 1932), 872, 1096; *New York Times,* February 19, 1920, April 14, 1929; J. B. Cunningham to Comptroller of the Currency, January 31, 1927, Palm Beach National Bank Records, USOCC/NA.

41. Sam Hanna Acheson, *Joe Bailey: The Last Democrat* (New York: Macmillan, 1932), 139–51, 175, 180, 212, 214, 224–27, 231–40; Bob Charles Holcomb, "Senator Joe Bailey: Two Decades of Controversy" (Ph.D. dissertation, Texas Technological College, 1968), 216–22, 237–48, 531–33; *New York Times,* January 3, April 26, 1913.

42. Examiner's Reports of Palm Beach National Bank, February 10, June 15, 1926; W. J. Fowler to Cashier of Palm Beach National Bank, March 11, 1926; George T. Dyer to Comptroller of the Currency, March 17, 1926, USOCC/WNRC; J. B. Cunningham to Comptroller of the Currency, January 31, 1927; J. E. Fouts to Cunningham, February 16, 1927; N. C. Bainum to Cunningham, December 21, 1928, Palm Beach National Bank Records, USOCC/NA.

43. Curl, *Mizner's Florida,* 153–57; Petition of Franklin L. Jones, August 24, 1927, *In the Matter of Mizner Development Corporation, Bankrupt,* Docket No. 252, USDC/SDF; *Palm Beach Independent,* March 19, 1926.

44. Examiner's Report of Palm Beach National Bank, June 15, 1926, USOCC/WNRC; Ellis D. Robb to Comptroller of the Currency, June 12, 1926, Palm Beach National Bank Records, USOCC/NA; *Annual Report of the Comptroller of Florida,* June 30, 1930.

45. Examiner's Reports of Palm Beach National Bank, February 10, June 15, 1926, and Supplemental Report of Palm Beach National Bank, June 15, 1926, USOCC/WNRC.

46. *Palm Beach Independent,* March 12, 1926.

47. Examiner's Report of Palm Beach National Bank, June 15, 1926, USOCC/WNRC; *New York Times,* June 22, 29, 30, 1926; *Palm Beach Post,* June 22, 23, 1926; *Palm Beach Independent,* July 2, 1926; Curl, *Mizner's Florida,* 163.

48. *Palm Beach Independent,* July 2, 1926; "Asks Receiver for Mizner Corporation," clipping, n.d., and "Mizner Corporation to Oppose Receiver," clipping, n.d.; Chief Examiner Robb to U.S. Comptroller, June 29, 1926 (coded telegram); Robb to U.S. Comptroller (translated telegram); and E. W. Stearns to Examining Division, June 29, 1926, Palm Beach National Bank Records, USOCC/NA; Examiner's Report of Palm Beach National Bank, June 15, 1926, USOCC/WNRC; Curl,

Mizner's Florida, 163; Orr-Cahall, "Identification and Discussion," 69; Final Report of Commercial Bank and Trust Company, June 26, 1926; and Final Report of Palm Beach Bank and Trust Company, July 28, 1926, SC/FSA.

49. *Atlanta Constitution,* July 13, 15, 1926; *New York Times,* June 22, 29, 30, July 3, 4, 13, 14, 15, 1926; *Commercial and Financial Chronicle,* July 17, 1926, p. 286; *Annual Report of the Comptroller of the Currency,* December 1, 1930, p. 311; *Palm Beach Post,* June 22, 23, 1926; Haynes McFadden, "Chain Bank Crash in Georgia," *American Bankers Association Journal* 19 (September 1926): 137; Pogue, *To Wield a Mighty Influence,* 64–66.

CHAPTER 4. OFFICIAL DECEIT

1. *Atlanta Constitution,* July 13, 14, 15, 16, 18, 19, 22, November 18, 1926; *New York Times,* June 29, July 3, 4, 13, 14, 15, 16, 17, 18, 20, 21, 22, 1926; *Commercial and Financial Chronicle,* July 17, 1926, p. 286; *Annual Report of the Comptroller of Florida,* June 30, 1926, and 1930; *Tallahassee Daily Democrat,* July 17, 1926; *Chicago Tribune,* July 22, 1926; Pogue, *To Wield a Mighty Influence,* 64, 66.

2. *Atlanta Constitution,* July 17, 1926.

3. Ibid.; *New York Times,* July 17, 1926; Garrett, *Atlanta and Environs,* 252, 499–500, 519, 556, 585, 698, 775, 797, 927; "Atlanta Business Men Who Began on the Farm," *Atlanta Constitution Journal Magazine,* February 1, 1925.

4. *Commercial and Financial Chronicle,* July 17, 1926, p. 286; *Annual Report of the Department of Banking of the State of Georgia,* 1920, 1921, 1922, 1923, 1924; *Atlanta Constitution,* August 27, September 28, 1926; Garrett, *Atlanta and Environs,* 797.

5. *Atlanta Constitution,* July 17, 1926.

6. Final Report of Bank of Dania, July 28, 1926; Final Report of Commercial Bank and Trust Company, June 26, 1926; Final Report of Bank of Little River, July 2, 1926; Final Report of Palm Beach Bank and Trust Company, July 28, 1926; Final Report of Bank of Coconut Grove, July 3, 1926; and Final Report of Bank of Coral Gables, July 2, 1930, SC/FSA.

7. *Tallahassee Daily Democrat,* July 17, 1926; *Atlanta Constitution,* July 15, 16, 1926; *Commercial and Financial Chronicle,* July 24, 1926, p. 412.

8. Remini, *Jackson,* 141–68; White, *Banking Law,* 1–19; Gordon, "Understanding the S&L Mess," 49–51, 54, 56, 58–60, 62–63, 65–66, 68.

9. *Atlanta Constitution,* July 17, 1926; *Annual Report of the Comptroller of Florida,* June 30, 1926.

10. M. B. Wellborn to Mr. Blank, June 22, 1922, in the *Annual Report*

of the Comptroller of Florida, June 30, 1926; Southern Banker, May 1922, p. 9; Atlanta Constitution, August 27, 1926; Federal Reserve Bulletin, July 1926; Annual Report of the Department of Banking of the State of Georgia, 1926, p. vi.

11. Federal Reserve Bulletin, July 1926, p. iii; Examiner's Reports of Palm Beach National Bank, February 10, June 15, 1926, USOCC/ WNRC; Ellis D. Robb to Comptroller of the Currency, June 12, 1926, Palm Beach National Bank Records, USOCC/NA.

12. New York Times, July 17, 1926; Palm Beach Independent, December 17, 1926.

13. Herbert Hoover, The Memoirs of Herbert Hoover: The Great Depression, 1929–1941 (New York: Macmillan, 1952), 9; Galbraith, Great Crash, 32–33; Federal Reserve Bulletin, July 1926; New York Times, July 15, 16, 1926; Commercial and Financial Chronicle, July 17, 1926, p. 286; Atlanta Constitution, July 15, 1926; Annual Report of the Comptroller of Florida, June 30, 1926.

14. J. W. McIntosh to V. H. Northcutt, July 2, 1926; J. B. Cunningham to Comptroller of the Currency, July 7, 15, August 27, 1926; Cunningham to J. W. Pole, September 3, 1926; Cunningham to J. W. McIntosh, September 25, 1926; McIntosh to Cunningham, October 11, 1926, Palm Beach National Bank Records, USOCC/NA; Annual Report of the Comptroller of the Currency, December 10, 1926, p. 193; December 12, 1927, p. 244; December 13, 1928, p. 277.

15. Palm Beach Independent, October 1, 22, November 12, 1926.

16. John D. Russell to W. D. Manley, June 23, 1924; Russell to Manley and Joseph A. Sasser, October 13, 1923, United States v. Wesley D. Manley, et al., Criminal Docket No. 13423, USDC/NDG.

17. John D. Russell to W. D. Manley, June 23, 1924, United States v. Wesley D. Manley, et al., Criminal Docket No. 13423, USDC/NDG; New York Times, November 21, 1928, September 1, 8, 10, 22, 1932.

18. Examiner's Reports of National Bank of West Palm Beach, November 16, 1926, April 15, 1927; "Voluntary Comparative Statement of Condition of the National Bank of West Palm Beach," n.d., newspaper clipping, National Bank of West Palm Beach Records, USOCC/WNRC; Palm Beach Independent, August 6, September 10, 1926, May 20, 1927.

19. A. D. Cutts to E. W. Stearns, July 16, 1926; Stearns to Cutts, July 19, 1926; "National Bank of West Palm Beach," August 5, 1926, newspaper clipping, National Bank of West Palm Beach Records, USOCC/WNRC; Palm Beach Independent, August 6, 1926.

20. Annual Report of the Comptroller of the Currency, 1930, p. 314; Examiner's Reports of First National Bank of Lake Worth, June 18, 1925, July 22, 1926, January 14, 1927, USOCC/WNRC.

21. Palm Beach Post, January 10, 1923; Lake Worth Herald, January 10,

1923; handwritten note on clipping of *Lake Worth Leader,* January 12, 1923; V. H. Northcutt to Comptroller of the Currency, January 12, 1923; and Examiner's Report of First National Bank of Lake Worth, June 18, 1925, USOCC/WNRC.

22. Supplemental Report of Examination of First National Bank of Lake Worth, June 18, 1925; and Examiner's Report of First National Bank of Lake Worth, January 14, 1927, USOCC/WNRC.

23. Examiner's Report of First National Bank of Lake Worth, June 18, 1925, ibid.

24. *New York Times,* March 9, 11, 1927; Receiver's Quarterly Report of First National Bank of Lake Worth, March 12, 1927; Memorandum for Comptroller, October 13, 1933; and John B. Cunningham to Comptroller of the Currency, November 8, 1927, USOCC/NA; *Lake Worth Leader,* November 8, 1927; *Palm Beach Post,* November 8, 1927.

25. J. B. Cunningham to J. W. McIntosh, April 30, May 5, 1927; Cunningham to Comptroller of the Currency, June 22, July 3, 1928, First National Bank of Lake Worth Records, USOCC/NA.

26. J. B. Cunningham to J. W. McIntosh, April 30, 1927, ibid.

27. "Memorandum of V. H. Northcutt, National Bank Examiner, Relative to the Failure of the First National Bank of Lake Worth, Florida," April 18, 1927; and J. B. Cunningham to J. W. McIntosh, April 30, May 5, 1927, ibid.; *Annual Report of the Comptroller of the Currency,* December 12, 1927.

28. Examiner's Reports of National Bank of West Palm Beach, November 16, 1926, April 15, 1927, USOCC/WNRC.

29. Examiner's Report of National Bank of West Palm Beach, November 16, 1926; W. J. Fowles to E. D. Robb, June 29, 1925, ibid.; J. B. Cunningham to E. W. Stearns, July 26, 1927, First National Bank of Lake Worth Records, USOCC/NA; Final Report of Northwood Bank and Trust Company, West Palm Beach, October 26, 1929, SC/FSA.

30. J. W. McIntosh to Board of Directors, National Bank of West Palm Beach, April 30, 1927; and Memorandum of W. W. McBryde, May 5, 1927, USOCC/WNRC.

31. J. B. Cunningham to E. W. Stearns, July 26, 1927, First National Bank of Lake Worth Records, USOCC/NA.

32. Ibid.

33. Ibid.; Examiner's Report of National Bank of West Palm Beach, October 4, 1927, USOCC/WNRC.

34. J. W. McIntosh to Board of Directors, National Bank of West Palm Beach, April 30, 1927; Examiner's Report of National Bank of West Palm Beach, October 5, 1927; and J. B. Cunningham to McIntosh, March 29, 1927, ibid.; *Annual Report of the Comptroller of the Currency,* December 12, 1927; *Palm Beach Independent,* November 25, 1927.

35. *Palm Beach Post,* May 4, 5, 6, 7, 8, 9, 10, 11, 13, 14, 1931.

36. *Atlanta Constitution,* July 16, 1926; *Commercial and Financial Chronicle,* July 24, 1926, p. 286.

37. *Annual Report of the Department of Banking of the State of Georgia,* 1926, p. v; Testimony of E. R. Parker, *United States* v. *Wesley D. Manley, et al.,* Criminal Docket No. 13423, USDC/NDG; Garrett, *Atlanta and Environs,* 706–7.

38. Minutes of Stockholders Meeting of the Amortization Corporation, July 1921; Testimony of E. R. Parker, W. F Floyd, and H. E. Rank; Testimony of H. M. Jernigan and government exhibits 219–42; Testimony of J. D. Hinton and government exhibits 243–46, *United States* v. *Wesley D. Manley, et al.,* Criminal Docket No. 13423, USDC/NDG.

39. T. R. Bennett to Governor Clifford Walker, September 3, 1926, in the *Atlanta Constitution,* September 4, 1926; *Annual Report of the Department of Banking of the State of Georgia,* 1926, p. v; *Acts of Georgia,* 1919, Part I, Title 6, Article VI, Sec. 2 and 3.

40. *Annual Report of the Department of Banking of the State of Georgia,* 1926, pp. v, vi, ix; *Atlanta Constitution,* September 4, 1926; Testimony of Lorne R. Adams, *United States* v. *Wesley D. Manley, et al.,* Criminal Docket No. 13423, USDC/NDG.

41. *Acts of Georgia,* 1919, Part I, Title 6, Article II, Sec. 4; *Annual Report of the Department of Banking of the State of Georgia,* 1926, pp. viii, x.

42. *Annual Report of the Department of Banking of the State of Georgia,* 1926, p. x.

43. Ibid.

44. Testimony of Lena Long, August 28, 1926, *In the Matter of W. D. Manley, Bankrupt,* Docket No. 12055, USDC/NDG.

45. *Tallahassee Daily Democrat,* July 17, 1926.

46. *Tampa Morning Tribune,* April 23, 1915; Final Report of Citizens Bank and Trust Company of Tampa, August 16, 1929, SC/FSA; *Polk's Bankers,* March 1926, p. 314b.

47. *Tampa Morning Tribune,* June 30, July 4, 6, 7, 15, 18, 1926, March 15, 1927.

48. Final Report of Citizens Bank and Trust Company of Tampa, August 16, 1929; Final Audit Report of Citizens Bank and Trust Company of Tampa, July 12, 1939; and Petition to Comptroller for Final Discharge of Liquidator and Release of Bond, July 12, 1939, SC/FSA.

49. *Palm Beach Independent,* July 23, 1926; *Polk's Bankers,* March 1926, p. 314c.

50. Ibid.

51. *New York Times,* July 21, 1926; *Commercial and Financial Chronicle,* July 24, 1926, p. 411.

52. *New York Times,* July 17, 1926; Dovell, *History of Banking,* 228;

"Miami and the Bank of Bay Biscayne," 15–16, 22–23, PKYL; Final Report of Bank of Bay Biscayne, July 24, 1930, SC/FSA; Bernard Gould to Governor Doyle E. Carlton, June 23, 1930; Carlton to Gould, July 2, 1930; "A Depositor" to Carlton, August 18, 1930; Deane Tatum to Carlton, n.d.; L. C. Mount to Carlton, April 25, 1932; Fred Featherstone to Carlton, May 3, 1932; Carlton to Featherstone, May 3, 10, 1932; and B. Shayne to Carlton, n.d., DEC/FSA; *Florida Times-Union,* August 19, 20, 1930; *Ex Parte: Ernest Amos,* 129 Southern Reporter 855, *Cases Adjudicated in the Supreme Court of Florida,* Vol. 100, June Term, 1930.

53. *Annual Report of the Comptroller of Florida,* June 30, 1926.

54. *Coconut Grove Bank and Trust Company as Receiver of the Bank of Coconut Grove v. Farmers and Traders Bank; Bank of Allapattah v. Farmers and Traders Bank; Church Street Bank of Orlando v. Farmers and Traders Bank; First State Bank of Hialeah v. Farmers and Traders Bank; City National Bank and Trust Company of Miami v. Farmers and Traders Bank; Buena Vista Bank and Trust Company v. Farmers and Traders Bank; Little River Bank and Trust Company v. Farmers and Traders Bank,* CC/FCSC.

55. Testimony of Lorne R. Adams; L. R. Adams and John D. Russell to W. D. Manley, May 17, 1926, *United States v. Wesley D. Manley, et al.,* Criminal Docket No. 13423, USDC/NDG; McFadden, "Chain Bank Crash in Georgia," 137.

56. Testimony of Lorne R. Adams and Joseph A. Sasser; Testimony and Suggestions of John D. Russell; Minutes of Joint Meeting of the Directors of Georgia State Bank and Bankers Trust Company, May 6, 1925, *United States v. Wesley D. Manley, et al.,* Criminal Docket No. 13423, USDC/NDG.

57. Testimony of Lorne R. Adams and Joseph A. Sasser, *United States v. Wesley D. Manley, et al.,* ibid.; W. D. Manley to Herbert J. Haas, July 8, 1926, see also the testimony of Herbert J. Haas, August 30, 1926; Testimony of Mrs. W. D. Manley, August 30, 1926, *In the Matter of W. D. Manley, Bankrupt,* Docket No. 12055, USDC/NDG.

58. Receiver's Report of Palm Beach National Bank, June 28, 1926, USOCC/NA; Examiner's Reports of Palm Beach National Bank, February 10, June 15, 1926, USOCC/WNRC; Final Report of Peoples Bank of Jacksonville, July 25, 1929; Affidavit of E. M. Porter, August 9, 1926, Palm Beach Bank and Trust Company Records, SC/FSA.

59. Ernest Amos to T. M. Cook, June 1, 1926, in the *Palm Beach Independent,* September 24, 1926.

60. Ibid.; Final Report of Commercial Bank and Trust Company, June 26, 1926, SC/FSA.

61. "Encouraging Indications," *Palm Beach Independent,* May 21, 1926; "Florida Banks in Healthy Condition," n.d., newspaper clipping, Palm Beach National Bank Records; Examiner's Report of Palm Beach National Bank, February 10, June 15, 1926, USOCC/WNRC.

62. *Palm Beach Independent,* September 24, 1926.

63. Ibid.; Receiver's Report of Palm Beach National Bank, September 30, 1926, USOCC/NA; Joe L. Earman to J. B. Hodges, August 30, 1926; Hodges to Earman, September 1, 1926, JBHP/PKYL.

64. *Palm Beach Independent,* May 7, 21, 1926, February 11, 1927; Liquidation Records of the Palm Beach Bank and Trust Company, SC/FSA; *Tropical Sun,* March 5, 1937.

65. Cartinhous, *Branch, Group, and Chain Banking,* 86–87; *New York Times,* June 29, July 22, 1926; *Atlanta Constitution,* July 22, 1926; *Chicago Tribune,* July 22, 1926; *Commercial and Financial Chronicle,* July 24, 1926, p. 411; *Annual Report of the Comptroller of Florida,* June 30, 1926.

CHAPTER 5. THE INDICTMENT OF FLORIDA'S COMPTROLLER

1. *Palm Beach Post,* September 16, 1926; *Palm Beach Independent,* September 24, October 22, 1926; Joe L. Earman to J. B. Hodges, September 25, 1926, JBHP/PKYL.

2. *Palm Beach Post,* December 10, 16, 1926; *Palm Beach Independent,* September 24, 1926.

3. Ernest Amos to Joe L. Earman, August 18, September 15, 1926, in the *Palm Beach Independent,* August 27, September 24, 1926; *Palm Beach Independent,* October 1, 22, November 26, 1926; *Palm Beach Post,* September 16, 1926.

4. *Palm Beach Post,* September 16, December 10, 16, 1926; *Palm Beach Independent,* September 17, 24, October 22, 1926, May 20, 1927.

5. *New York Times,* September 23, 1926; *Palm Beach Post,* September 23, 24, 1926; *Palm Beach Independent,* September 17, 24, October 22, 1926; Final Report of Palm Beach Bank and Trust Company, July 28, 1926, SC/FSA.

6. Indictment of Ernest Amos, September 22, 1926, SCF/FSA; *New York Times,* September 23, 1926; *Palm Beach Post,* September 23, 1926; *Palm Beach Independent,* September 24, 1926.

7. *Capias in the State of Florida* v. *Ernest Amos,* SCF/FSA; *Palm Beach Post,* September 23, 24, October 13, 14, 1926.

8. *Palm Beach Post,* September 29, 1926; *Palm Beach Independent,* October 1, 1926; Joe L. Earman to J. B. Hodges, September 25, 1926, JBHP/PKYL.

9. J. B. Cunningham to J. W. Pole, September 3, 1926; Blackwell and Donnell to Comptroller of the Currency, July 7, 1926 (telegram), Palm Beach National Bank Records, USOCC/NA; *Palm Beach Independent,* September 24, October 22, 1926, March 11, 1927; Final Report of Palm Beach Bank and Trust Company, July 28, 1926, SC/FSA.

10. First Dividend of .001%, March 18, 1930; Petition for Attorneys Fees of Blackwell, Donnell and Moore, December 16, 1927, *In the Matter of Mizner Development Corporation, Bankrupt,* Docket No. 252, USDC/SDF; Flynt, *Cracker Messiah,* 106, 276–77, 289–90, 293–95; *Palm Beach Post,* June 19, 20, September 15, 1917, August 3, 1918, March 23, June 16, December 24, 1919, March 11, 20, June 16, 1920, March 3, April 8, 1921, August 12, 1927, April 23, 26, 1931, April 7, 17, 1932; *Palm Beach Times,* January 8, 1928, April 4, 7, 18, 21, May 4, 1932; *Palm Beach Times,* n.d., 1923, and newspaper clipping, March 23, 1919, E. B. Donnell File, HSPBC; Allen Morris, *The Florida Handbook,* 3d ed. (Tallahassee: Peninsular Publishing Company, 1952), 191.

11. J. B. Cunningham to J. W. Pole, September 3, 1926, Palm Beach National Bank Records, USOCC/WNRC.

12. Final Report of Palm Beach Bank and Trust Company, July 28, 1926; Resignation of Receiver, September 7, 1929; and Claims Compromised in Liquidation, SC/FSA.

13. *Palm Beach Independent,* July 16, September 24, 1926; Joe S. Earman and Betty Earman, *Big Joe Earman* (Vero Beach: Earman Family, 1977), 9–12, 46–47.

14. Final Report of Palm Beach Bank and Trust Company, July 28, 1926; Final Report of Commercial Bank and Trust Company, June 26, 1926, SC/FSA; *Palm Beach Independent,* September 24, 1926.

15. *Palm Beach Independent,* September 24, 1926.

16. Ibid.

17. Ernest Amos to J. L. Earman, September 15, 1926, in the *Palm Beach Independent,* September 24, 1926.

18. *Palm Beach Independent,* September 17, 24, October 22, 1926, March 25, 1927.

19. Ibid.; Final Report of Palm Beach Bank and Trust Company, July 28, 1926; Final Report of Commercial Bank and Trust Company, June 26, 1926; Inventory and Liquidator's Receipt, October 24, 1929, SC/FSA; *Polk's Bankers,* September 1925, p. 291, and March 1926, p. 311.

20. *Palm Beach Independent,* September 24, 1926.

21. Ibid.; *Palm Beach Post,* July 18, September 16, 1926.

22. Joe Earman to J. B. Hodges, February 11, 1925; Rivers Buford to Hodges, February 9, 11, 16, 1925; Hodges to Earman, February 16, 1925; Hodges to Buford, February 10, 14, 1925, JBHP/PKYL; Flynt, *Fletcher,* 128, 132; Flynt, *Cracker Messiah,* 76, 94, 105–7, 203, 276–79, 289; Earman and Earman, *Big Joe Earman,* 9–12, 47.

23. Flynt, *Cracker Messiah,* 130, 150–51, 176, 341.

24. *Palm Beach Independent,* September 24, 1926.

25. *Palm Beach Independent,* October 22, 1926, September 16, 1927.

26. *Palm Beach Independent,* October 29, 1926; *Palm Beach Post,* December 5, 1926, April 20, 1929.

27. *Palm Beach Post,* December 5, 1926; *General Acts of Florida,* 1925, Ch. 10037, Sec. 4161, and 1913, Ch. 6427, Sec. 1.

28. Ernest Amos to Joe L. Earman, January 14, 1927, in the *Palm Beach Independent,* April 22, 1927; Earman, "J. R. Anthony," *Palm Beach Independent,* November 26, 1926; *Palm Beach Post,* November 19, 1926.

29. *Palm Beach Independent,* November 12, 1926, May 20, 1927; Schlesinger, *Imperial Presidency,* 332–33; *Florida Times-Union,* June 24, 1932; *Tampa Morning Tribune,* March 11, 1930.

30. *Palm Beach Post,* September 23, 1926; *Palm Beach Independent,* September 24, 1926; *Annual Report of the Comptroller of Florida,* June 30, 1926.

31. "Better Laws for Banking," editorial in the *Madison Enterprise Record,* reprinted in the *Palm Beach Independent,* February 4, 1927.

32. *Tallahassee Daily Democrat,* February 29, 1928, January 22, 1931.

33. *Palm Beach Independent,* September 24, 1926, May 20, 27, 1927; *Palm Beach Post,* September 23, 1926; *Tallahassee Daily Democrat,* April 6, May 19, 1927; *Annual Report of the Comptroller of Florida,* June 30, 1926.

34. A. P. Anthony, "Report of Chairman"; *Palm Beach Independent,* October 15, 1926, July 23, May 20, 1927.

35. Garrett, "Why Some Banks Fail."

36. *Palm Beach Independent,* August 20, 1927; *Palm Beach Post,* September 23, December 8, 1926; Curl, *Palm Beach County,* 94; Final Report of Palm Beach Bank and Trust Company, July 28, 1926; Final Report of Commercial Bank and Trust Company, June 26, 1926, SC/FSA.

37. *Palm Beach Post,* July 18, October 3, 1926, June 24, 25, 1927; *Palm Beach Independent,* February 11, 18, 25, May 6, 20, June 17, 24, July 1, 1927; Final Report of Commercial Bank and Trust Company, June 26, 1926; Final Report of Palm Beach Bank and Trust Company, July 28, 1926, SC/FSA.

38. Final Report of Commercial Bank and Trust Company, June 26, 1926; Final Report of Palm Beach Bank and Trust Company, July 28, 1926, SC/FSA; *Palm Beach Independent,* July 16, September 17, 1926.

39. *Palm Beach Post,* May 26, 1927, July 26, 1928; Final Reports of First American Bank and Trust Company, October 12, 1929, and June 30, 1930, SC/FSA; Vincent Oaksmith, "History of Palm Beach County Public Official," HSPBC.

40. Anthony Brothers, Inc., also defaulted on a $11,283 loan, and Anthony's, Inc., defaulted on a $3,623 loan at the First American Bank and Trust Company. Final Reports of First American Bank and Trust Company, October 12, 1929, and June 30, 1930, SC/FSA; *Palm Beach Times,* May 28, 1951.

41. *Palm Beach Post,* September 25, 1926; *Florida Times-Union,* September 25, 1926; *Atlanta Constitution,* September 25, 1926; *Palm Beach Independent,* October 1, 8, 1926.

42. *Palm Beach Post,* September 26, 1926; *Florida Times-Union,* September 26, 1926; *Atlanta Constitution,* September 26, 1926.

43. *Polk's Bankers,* September 1925, pp. 282, 291–92, 295, March 1926, pp. 311, 314a; Receiver's Report of Palm Beach National Bank, June 28, 1926, USOCC/NA; Final Report of Peoples Bank of Jacksonville, July 25, 1929, SC/FSA.

44. John W. Martin to Ernest Amos, September 27, 1926, in the *Palm Beach Post,* September 28, 1926; *Florida Times-Union,* September 28, 1926.

45. *Annual Report of the Comptroller of Florida,* June 30, 1926; *Palm Beach Post,* September 25, 1926.

46. *Palm Beach Independent,* April 29, 1927.

47. Governor John Martin appointed Fred Davis as the state's attorney general in 1927. Davis was elected to the cabinet position in 1928, and Governor Doyle E. Carlton appointed him to the supreme court of Florida in 1931. See *Palm Beach Independent,* May 20, 1927; Cash, *Story of Florida,* 4–5; "Fred Henry Davis," n.d., FSCHS; *Tallahassee Daily Democrat,* January 10, 1923, January 17, March 3, 1931, May 9, 1932.

48. Brief for the Petitioner on Application for Writ of Habeas Corpus, n.d.; Supplemental Brief for Petitioner, September 25, 1926; Writ of Habeas Corpus, September 28, 1926, SCF/FSA; *Palm Beach Post,* September 29, October 4, 1926.

49. *Palm Beach Post,* September 29, October 4, 1926; Brief for the Petitioner on Application for Writ of Habeas Corpus, n.d.; Supplemental Brief for Petitioner, September 25, 1926; Brief on Behalf of Petitioner on Motion to Discharge Prisoner from Custody, October 14, 1926; Reply Brief of Counsel for Petitioner on Motion to Discharge Prisoner, November 18, 1926, SCF/FSA.

50. Brief in Opposition to the Petitioner's Motion for Discharge from Custody, November 8, 1926, SCF/FSA; *Palm Beach Post,* November 9, 1926.

51. *Ex Parte: Ernest Amos,* 112 Southern Reporter 289; Interview of B. K. Roberts, April 21, 1980, FSCHS.

52. Cash, *Story of Florida,* 42–43, 319–20; Julia Whitfield Neeley and Randolph Whitfield, "Our Father, James Bryan Whitfield," *Florida Supreme Court Historical Society Review* 3 (1987–88): 1–3, 10–12; *Tallahassee Daily Democrat,* January 11, 12, 1927; *Ex Parte: Ernest Amos,* 112 Southern Reporter 289.

53. *Ex Parte: Ernest Amos,* 112 Southern Reporter 289.

54. Ibid.

55. Ibid.

56. Ibid.; Morris, *Florida Handbook* (1952), 93.

57. Interview of B. K. Roberts, April 21, 1980, FSCHS; Joe Earman

to J. B. Hodges, February 11, 1925; Rivers Buford to Hodges, February 9, 11, 16, 1925; Hodges to Earman, February 16, 1925; Hodges to Buford, February 10, 14, 1925, JBHP/PKYL.

58. Receiver's Report of Palm Beach National Bank, June 28, 1926, USOCC/NA; Examiner's Reports of Palm Beach National Bank, February 10, June 15, 1926, USOCC/WNRC; Final Report of Peoples Bank of Jacksonville, July 25, 1929; Final Report of Palm Beach Bank and Trust Company, July 28, 1926, SC/FSA; *Palm Beach Post,* September 23, 1926; *Ex Parte: Ernest Amos,* 112 Southern Reporter 289.

59. *Ex Parte: Ernest Amos,* 112 Southern Reporter 289; *Palm Beach Post,* September 26, 1926; *Florida Times-Union,* September 26, 1926; Receiver's Report of Palm Beach National Bank, June 28, 1926, USOCC/NA; Final Report of Peoples Bank of Jacksonville, July 25, 1929, SC/FSA.

60. *State of Florida* v. *Jonathan F. Wershow et al.,* Fla., 343 So. 2d 605, *Cases Adjudicated in the Supreme Court and District Courts of Appeal of Florida, Southern Reporter,* 2d (St. Paul: West Publishing, 1977).

CHAPTER 6. THE RESIGNATION OF GEORGIA'S SUPERINTENDENT OF BANKS

1. *New York Times,* July 22, 1926; *Commercial and Financial Chronicle,* July 24, 1926, p. 411; *Chicago Tribune,* July 22, 1926; *Atlanta Constitution,* July 22, 1926; Garrett, *Atlanta and Environs,* 674, 758, 811, 837, 867–68.

2. *New York Times,* July 17, 22, 1926; *Atlanta Constitution,* July 22, September 4, 1926; *Commercial and Financial Chronicle,* July 24, 1926, p. 411; *Chicago Tribune,* July 22, 1926.

3. *Atlanta Constitution,* September 4, 1926.

4. Ibid.; McFadden, "Chain Bank Crash in Georgia," 137–38; *Acts of Georgia,* 1919, Part I, Title 6, Article XIX, Sec. 5, 6, 7, 8.

5. *Atlanta Constitution,* September 4, 1926.

6. *Atlanta Constitution,* September 4, 5, 1926; *Commercial and Financial Chronicle,* September 11, 1926, pp. 1332–35.

7. Robert M. Moler, *Georgia Department of Banking and Finance: Historical Review with Perspective on the Future, 1920–1982* (December 31, 1981), 37; *New York Times,* July 22, 1926; *Acts of Georgia,* 1919, Part I, Title 6, Article VII, Sec. 10; *Annual Report of the Department of Banking of the State of Georgia,* 1926, vii and viii; Report of Custodian, *In the Matter of Bankers Trust Company, Bankrupt,* Docket No. 12046, USDC/NDG.

8. *Acts of Georgia,* 1919, Part I, Title 6, Article II, Sec. 7; *Atlanta Constitution,* September 4, 5, 1926; *Commercial and Financial Chronicle,* September 11, 1926, pp. 1332–35.

9. *Atlanta Constitution,* September 4, 5, 1926; *Commercial and Financial*

Chronicle, September 11, 1926, pp. 1332–35; *Annual Report of the Department of Banking of the State of Georgia,* 1926, p. vi.

10. *Annual Report of the Department of Banking of the State of Georgia,* 1926, pp. iv, v, vi; *Acts of Georgia,* 1919, Part I, Title 6, Article II, Sec. 18; Article III, Sec. 1, 9; Article V, Sec. 3; and Article XV, Sec. 1, 2.

11. *Annual Report of the Department of Banking of the State of Georgia,* 1926, pp. v, vi, vii, viii.

12. *Atlanta Constitution,* September 4, 1926.

13. *Annual Report of the Department of Banking of the State of Georgia,* 1926, pp. v, vi, vii; Pogue, *To Wield a Mighty Influence,* 66.

14. *Annual Report of the Department of Banking of the State of Georgia,* 1926, pp. v, vi, vii; Testimony of Lorne R. Adams, *United States* v. *Wesley D. Manley, et al.,* Criminal Docket No. 13423, USDC/NDG; *Southern Banker,* June 1924.

15. Testimony of Lorne R. Adams, *United States* v. *Wesley D. Manley, et al.,* Criminal Docket No. 13423, USDC/NDG; *Atlanta Constitution,* September 4, 1926; *Annual Report of the Department of Banking of the State of Georgia,* 1926, pp. iv–v.

16. *Annual Report of the Department of Banking of the State of Georgia,* 1926, p. vii; *Atlanta Constitution,* September 4, 1926.

17. Minutes of Joint Meeting of the Directors of Georgia State Bank and Bankers Trust Company, May 6, 1925; Testimony and Suggestions of John D. Russell; T. R. Bennett to W. D. Manley, January 18, 1926, and L. R. Adams to Manley, n.d., *United States* v. *Wesley D. Manley, et al.,* Criminal Docket No. 13423, USDC/NDG.

18. W. D. Manley to T. R. Bennett, January 19, 1926; Bennett to Manley, February 23, 1926, and L. R. Adams to Manley, n.d., ibid.

19. Testimony and Suggestions of John D. Russell; Meeting of Trustees of Bankers Trust Company, March 9, 1926; Policy Memorandum of L. R. Adams and John D. Russell, March 16, 1926, ibid.

20. L. R. Adams to W. D. Manley, n.d., ibid.

21. John D. Russell to W. D. Manley and J. A. Sasser, January 14, 1923; L. R. Adams to Manley, n.d., ibid.

22. Moler, *Georgia Department of Banking and Finance,* 1–4.

23. Ibid.; "Introduction," DBF/GSA.

24. *Report of Budget and Investigating Commission and Governor's Transmittal,* 1919, pp. 12–13, Summary Commission Reports, GO/GSA; James F. Cook, *Governors of Georgia* (Huntsville, Ala.: Strode, 1980), 233, 235.

25. *Annual Report of the Department of Banking of the State of Georgia,* 1920; Cook, *Governors of Georgia,* 229; *New York Times,* July 15, 1926; *Atlanta Constitution,* September 4, 1926; Garrett, *Atlanta and Environs,* 571, 673–74, 775.

26. Moler, *Georgia Department of Banking and Finance,* 1–4; *Annual Report of the Department of Banking of the State of Georgia,* 1926, p. viii.

27. *Acts of Georgia,* 1888–89, 2:564–67; Moler, *Georgia Department of Banking and Finance,* 5.

28. *Annual Report of the Department of Banking of the State of Georgia,* 1926, pp. vi, vii; *New York Times,* July 15, 1926; *Acts of Georgia,* 1919, Part I, Title 6, Article VIII, and Article I, Sec. 3; Georgia State Bank Charter, State Bank of Cochran Charter, Richland State Bank Charter, Georgia State Bank Charters, Certificates of Incorporation, Bank and Trust Companies, 1920–39, SS/GSA.

29. Georgia Bank Charters and Amendments, 1925–32, Book L, SS/GSA; *New York Times,* July 15, 1926; *Acts of Georgia,* 1919, Part I, Title 6, Article IX, Sec. 5.

30. *Acts of Georgia,* 1919, Part I, Title 6, Article VIII, Sec. 3, 4(5), 8.

31. Ibid., Article I, Sec. 3.

32. *Annual Report of the Department of Banking of the State of Georgia,* 1926, pp. vi–vii; *Acts of Georgia,* 1919, Part I, Title 6, Article III, Sec. 1, 9.

33. *Acts of Georgia,* 1919, Part I, Title 6, Article III, Sec. 2.

34. Ibid., Sec. 3.

35. Ibid., Article V, Sec. 3.

36. Ibid., Article XV, Article VII, Sec. 1; *Annual Report of the Department of Banking of the State of Georgia,* 1926, pp. iv, vii.

37. *Annual Report of the Department of Banking of the State of Georgia,* 1926, p. v.

38. *Atlanta Constitution,* September 4, 1926.

39. *Acts of Georgia,* 1919, Part I, Title 6, Article VII, Sec. 19.

40. *Atlanta Constitution,* July 15, September 2, 5, 1926; *Annual Report of the Department of Banking of the State of Georgia,* 1926, p. viii.

41. *Atlanta Constitution,* September 2, 1926.

42. Garrett, *Atlanta and Environs,* 818; *Atlanta Constitution,* September 10, 11, October 2, 1926.

43. *Atlanta Constitution,* October 7, 1926.

44. *Atlanta Constitution,* October 3, 6, 1926.

45. *Atlanta Constitution,* September 26, October 1, 1926.

46. *Atlanta Constitution,* September 24, 25, 1926.

47. *Atlanta Constitution,* September 6, 9, 27, October 1, 2, 3, 6, 1926.

48. *Atlanta Constitution,* October 1, 2, 1926; Cook, *Governors of Georgia,* 238.

49. *Atlanta Constitution,* October 7, 10, 13, 1926.

50. *Atlanta Constitution,* October 9, 17, 1926.

51. *Annual Report of the Department of Banking of the State of Georgia,* 1926, p. ix.

52. T. R. Bennett to Governor Clifford Walker, October 16, 1926, in

the *Atlanta Constitution,* October 17, 1926; *Annual Report of the Department of Banking of the State of Georgia,* 1926, p. iv.

CHAPTER 7. THE MAD BANKER

1. *Atlanta Constitution,* July 22, August 15, 20, 24, September 5, November 12, 1926; *New York Times,* July 22, August 15, 1926; *Commercial and Financial Chronicle,* July 24, 1926, p. 411, August 21, 1926, pp. 936–38; *Chicago Tribune,* July 22, 1926; *Palm Beach Post,* November 9, 1926; *Atlanta Constitution Journal Magazine,* June 17, 1923; McFadden, "Chain Bank Crash in Georgia," 137–38; *State of Georgia* v. *W. D. Manley,* Case Nos. 26668, 26729, 26730, 26731, 26732, 26733, 26734, 26735, 26736, 26737, 26738, 26739, 26740, 26741, 26742, 26743, 26744, 26745, 26746, 26747, CD/FCSC; *Rono Memborn* v. *Mrs. W. D. Manley,* Case No. 69345, CC/FCSC.

2. Testimony of Ralph Payne and John D. Russell; John D. Russell to W. D. Manley and J. A. Sasser, January 14, October 13, 1923; Russell to Manley, June 23, 1924, *United States* v. *W. D. Manley, et al.,* Criminal Docket No. 13423, USDC/NDG.

3. John D. Russell to W. D. Manley and J. A. Sasser, October 13, 1923; Testimony of Lorne R. Adams, ibid.

4. *Annual Report of the Department of Banking of the State of Georgia,* 1926, p. viii; *Atlanta Constitution,* October 15, November 21, 1926; *Palm Beach Post,* September 1, 1926; McFadden, "Chain Bank Crash in Georgia," 137; James W. Austin to Oscar E. Dooley, February 22, 1927, *In the Matter of Bankers Trust Company, Bankrupt,* Docket No. 12046, USDC/NDG.

5. Report of H. Thomas Amason, C.P.A., to Hugh M. Dorsey, John K. Ottley, and Oscar E. Dooly, Receivers, August 16, 1926, *In the Matter of Bankers Trust Company, Bankrupt,* Docket No. 12046, USDC/NDG; McFadden, "Chain Bank Crash in Georgia," 137; Morris, *Florida Handbook: 1977–1978,* 87, 502.

6. *New York Times,* July 15, 1926; *Atlanta Constitution,* July 15, September 1, 1926; Testimony of W. D. Manley, August 27, 1926, *In the Matter of W. D. Manley, Bankrupt,* Docket No. 12055, USDC/NDG.

7. Testimony of Lena Long, August 28, 1926, and Mrs. W. D. Manley, August 30, 1926; see copy of check from W. D. Manley to Citizens and Southern Bank, June 7, 1926, *In the Matter of W. D. Manley, Bankrupt,* Docket No. 12055, USDC/NDG.

8. Special Investigation of W. D. Manley and Company, Inc.; Testimony of W. D. Manley, August 27, 1926, Isaac M. Wengrow, August 28, 1926, Lena Long, August 28, 1926, Mrs. W. D. Manley, August 30, 1926, and Herbert J. Haas, August 30, 1926, ibid.; Garrett, *Atlanta and Environs,* 459.

9. Testimony of Herbert J. Haas, August 30, 1926, ibid.

10. Testimony of W. D. Manley, August 27, 1926, Isaac M. Wengrow, August 28, 1926, Lena Long, August 28, 1926, Mrs. W. D. Manley, August 30, 1926, and Herbert J. Haas, August 30, 1926, *In the Matter of W. D. Manley, Bankrupt,* Docket No. 12055, USDC/NDG.

11. Report of Receivers, September 27, 1926; In Account with Livingston & Company; Testimony of Mrs. W. D. Manley, August 30, 1926, ibid.

12. *Bank of Dania, Florida* v. *W. D. Manley, W. D. Manley and Company, Inc. and Arthur Acklin,* CC/FCSC; Final Report of Bank of Dania, Florida, July 28, 1926, SC/FSA; Order of District Court Judge Samuel H. Sibley, September 2, 1926, *In the Matter of W. D. Manley, Bankrupt,* Docket No. 12055, USDC/NDG; *Atlanta Constitution,* September 1, 3, 1926.

13. *Commercial and Financial Chronicle,* September 25, 1926, p. 1583; *Coconut Grove Bank and Trust Company as Receiver of the Bank of Coconut Grove* v. *Farmers and Traders Bank of Atlanta,* CC/FCSC; Final Report of Bank of Coconut Grove, September 9, 1926, SC/FSA.

14. *Coconut Grove Bank and Trust Company as Receiver of the Bank of Coconut Grove* v. *Farmers and Traders Bank of Atlanta,* CC/FCSC.

15. Ibid.; *Acts of Georgia,* 1919, Part I, Title 6, Article VII, Sec. 19.

16. Final Report of Trustee, June 27, 1929; Controversies Existing Between the Estate of W. D. Manley and Mrs. Valeria R. Manley, Wife of W. D. Manley, *In the Matter of W. D. Manley, Bankrupt,* Docket No. 12055, USDC/NDG.

17. Petition of Mrs. W. D. Manley, September 1, 1926, ibid.

18. *Atlanta Constitution,* August 15, 1926; *New York Times,* August 15, 1926; *Palm Beach Post,* November 9, 1926; Frederick Lewis, "The Banker Who Went Mad," *Liberty* 17 (March 30, 1940): 37–39.

19. *Atlanta Constitution,* August 20, 1926.

20. *Atlanta Constitution,* August 24, 1926; *New York Times,* August 24, 1926.

21. *Atlanta Constitution,* August 24, 1926; Testimony of Lena Long, August 28, 1926, *In the Matter of W. D. Manley, Bankrupt,* Docket No. 12055, USDC/NDG.

22. Georgia State Bank Charters, Certificates of Incorporation, Bank and Trust Companies, 1920–39, Certificate Book 2, SS/GSA; *Atlanta Constitution,* August 27, 1926; *Annual Report of the Department of Banking of the State of Georgia,* 1920–24.

23. *Atlanta Constitution,* August 27, 1926; *New York Times,* August 27, 1926; C. N. Davie to Harry Dodd, January 27, 1930, *In the Matter of Bankers Trust Company, Bankrupt,* Docket No. 12046, USDC/NDG.

24. Case Nos. 27179, 27180, 27181, 27182, 27183, 27184, 27185, CD/FCSC; *Atlanta Constitution,* September 1, 3, 4, 1926; *New York Times,* September 1, 1926; *Palm Beach Post,* September 1, December 1, 1926.

25. Statement of All Debts of Bankrupt, September 30, 1926, *In the Matter of W. D. Manley, Bankrupt,* Docket No. 12055, USDC/NDG; *Atlanta Constitution,* November 21, 1926.

26. *Atlanta Constitution,* November 9, 10, 11, 1926; *Palm Beach Post,* November 9, 1926; Special Plea of Insanity, and Order of Judge G. H. Howard, *State of Georgia* v. *W. D. Manley,* Case No. 26735, CD/FCSC.

27. Disqualification of Judge G. H. Howard, November 9, 1926, *State of Georgia* v. *W. D. Manley,* Case No. 26735, CD/FCSC; *A. B. Mobley* v. *J. A. Sasser, et al.,* Case No. 72003, CC/FCSC; *Atlanta Constitution,* July 16, November 9, 10, 1926; *New York Times,* July 16, 1926.

28. *Atlanta Constitution,* November 9, 10, 1926.

29. *Atlanta Constitution,* November 11, 1926; *Palm Beach Post,* November 9, 1926.

30. *Atlanta Constitution,* November 11, 12, 13, 1926; *Palm Beach Post,* November 12, 1926.

31. *Atlanta Constitution,* November 12, 1926; *Palm Beach Post,* November 12, 1926.

32. *Atlanta Constitution,* November 8, 9, 10, 11, 12, 13, 16, 17, 1926; *New York Times,* November 16, 1926; *Palm Beach Post,* November 9, 11, 12, 16, 21, 1926; *State of Georgia* v. *W. D. Manley,* Case No. 26735, CD/FCSC.

33. *Atlanta Constitution,* November 17, 1926.

34. *Atlanta Constitution,* November 18, 19, 1926; *Palm Beach Post,* November 19, 1926.

35. *Atlanta Constitution,* November 18, 19, 1926.

36. Ibid.

37. *Atlanta Constitution,* November 19, 1926.

38. Ibid.; *Palm Beach Post,* November 19, 1926; McFadden, "Chain Bank Crash in Georgia," 137.

39. *Atlanta Constitution,* November 20, 1926.

40. Ibid.

41. Ibid.

42. Motion for New Trial; Sentence of W. D. Manley, *State of Georgia* v. *W. D. Manley,* Case No. 26735, CD/FCSC; *Palm Beach Post,* November 21, 22, 1926; *Atlanta Constitution,* November 20, 21, 1926; *New York Times,* November 21, 1926.

43. Order of Judge N. B. Moore, *State of Georgia* v. *W. D. Manley,* Case No. 26735; Motion for Continuance, Case No. 26668, CD/FCSC.

44. The federal grand jury in Atlanta issued subpoenas to the following Georgia bankers: J. F Hamilton, Bank of Abbeville; O. B. Bishop, Bank of Adairsville; R. D. Manning, Milton County Bank, Alpharetta; A. Q. Lifsey, Bank of Arnoldsville; J. S. Thompson, Peachtree Road Commercial Bank, Atlanta; G. C. Adams, Ball Ground Bank; J. R.

Murphy, Bartow Bank; J. G. Smith, Georgia State Bank, Bowdon; L. T. Roundtree, Georgia State Bank, Bronwood; N. A. Thomasson, Bank of Cherokee, Canton; F. D. Smith, Carlton Bank; J. F. Kimsey, Bank of Cassville; A. N. Tumlin, Bank of Cave Spring; W. F. Travis, Georgia State Bank, Chatsworth; W. L. Prickett, Commercial Bank of Crawford; J. L. Burt, Commerce Bank and Trust Company; A. E. Rozar, Farmers and Merchants Bank of Chipley; F. M. Reeves, Habersham Bank of Clarkesville; T. A. Duckett, Bank of Clayton; F. G. Mauney, White County Bank, Cleveland; L. S. Leach, State Bank of Cochran; J. L. Williams, Madison County Bank, Colbert; W. E. Henslee, Comer Bank; J. H. Childs, Georgia State Bank, Cordele; C. C. Kimsey, Cornelia Bank; John D. Black, Georgia State Bank, Cumming; W. A. Gayler, Bank of Cusseta; W. L. DeJarnette, Farmers State Bank of Cuthbert; D. E. Pinkston, Commercial Bank of Dallas; C. R. Faulk, Bank of Danville; J. S. Lunsford, Cornelia Bank, Demorest; J. G. Hickerson, Georgia State Bank, Douglasville; T. F. Guffin, Bank of East Point; R. D. Payne, Fair Mount Bank; C. O. Maddox, Georgia State Bank, Greensboro, and Georgia State Bank, Winder; R. H. Calhoun, Bank of Hamilton; T. H. Weatherly, Bank of Hazelhurst; W. O. Sparks, Bank of Hiawassee; W. C. Leake, Bank of Hiram; B. R. Jones, Twiggs County Bank, Jeffersonville; W. F. Dunham, Bartow County Bank, Kingston; W. T. Anderson, Bank of Leslie; W. D. Loyd, Bank of Lexington; J. H. Tate, Bank of Louisville; E. F. Whitworth, Bank of Lula; Joseph R. Barrett, Bank of Lyerly; W. C. Banks, Farmers and Merchants Bank of Lakeland; A. F. Gill, Commercial Bank of Manchester; M. A. Thompson, Georgia State Bank, Maysville; H. McGukin, Bank of Menlo; R. H. Fletcher, Bank of Molena; W. A. Boles, Macon County Bank, Oglethorpe; R. T. Sims, Bank of Palmetto; F. L. Williams, Bank of Plainville; C. G. Brown, Bank of Powder Springs; O. N. Merritt, Bank of Ringgold; H. P. Fambro, Rockmart Bank; H. C. Nelson, Bank of Roopville; C. C. Fain, Farmers Bank of Royston; C. I. Holcombe, Bank of Smyrna; W. S. McKibben, Social Circle Bank; L. B. Sewell, Bank of Stockbridge; J. H. Edge, Farmers and Merchants Bank of Summerville; M. A. Perry, Bank of Taylorville; L. F. West, Farmers State Bank of Temple; T. W. Anderson, Farmers and Merchants Bank of Toccoa; H. I. Talbot, Bank of Warm Springs; P. W. Vaughn, Bank of Williamson; Y. A. Olive, Citizens Commercial Bank of Woodbury, *United States* v. *W. D. Manley, et al.*, Criminal Docket Nos. 13420–13423, USDC/NDG.

45. The federal grand jury in Atlanta also issued subpoenas to the following Florida bankers: W. T. Adams, Bank of Allapattah, Miami; W. N. Girardeau, State Bank of Orlando; J. J. Murphy, First State Bank of Hialeah; D. O. McDougald, Commercial Bank and Trust Company of West Palm Beach; H. H. Ham, Port Orange State Bank; T. W. Byrd,

Bank of Lake Helen; C. W. Roe, First State Bank of Clermont; J. E. Donald, Lake Butler Bank; W. R. Gary, Bank of Okeechobee; O. E. Dooly, Jr., Ta-Miami Banking Company; C. M. Warren, First Bank and Trust Company of Lake Worth; E. Huddleston, Flagler Bank and Trust Company of Miami; D. G. Spain, Bank of Maitland; J. L. Bush, Farmers Bank and Trust Company of Vero Beach; E. Z. Crowley, Bank of Homestead; G. E. Spires, State Bank of Eau Gallie; A. G. Evans, Delray Bank and Trust Company; G. A. Peed, Bank of St. Cloud; W. O. Ham, Citizens Bank of Eustis; W. J. Siddall, Indian River State Bank, Titusville, ibid.

46. *Atlanta Constitution,* September 2, 1926; *New York Times,* September 2, 1926; McFadden, "Chain Bank Crash in Georgia," 137–38.

47. *Atlanta Constitution,* September 3, 1926; *New York Times,* September 3, 1926; *Florida Times-Union,* September 3, 1926; Grand Jury Indictment, *United States* v. *Wesley D. Manley, et al.,* Criminal Docket No. 13423, USDC/NDG; Articles of Agreement of the Depositors Guarantee Fund, and Final Report of Bank of Coconut Grove, September 9, 1926, SC/FSA.

48. Grand Jury Indictment and Motion for Continuance, *United States* v. *Wesley D. Manley, et al.,* Criminal Docket No. 13423, USDC/NDG.

49. Testimony of H. E. Rank, ibid.

50. John D. Russell to W. D. Manley and Joseph A. Sasser, October 13, 1923, ibid.

51. Testimony of George O. King, ibid.

52. Testimony of Paul J. Baker and H. E. Rank, ibid.

53. Testimony of E. M. Webster, A. G. Evans, C. C. Kimsey, R. L. Anderson, John L. Grice, W. F. Floyd, N. L. Greene, R. D. Manning, and Earl Haltiwanger, ibid.

54. Final Report of Fidelity Bank of New Smyrna, January 23, 1931, SC/FSA.

55. Testimony of H. E. Rank, *United States* v. *Wesley D. Manley, et al.,* Criminal Docket No. 13423, USDC/NDG.

56. Testimony of Joseph A. Sasser and John D. Russell, ibid.

57. L. R. Adams and John D. Russell to W. D. Manley, May 17, 1926; Testimony of John D. Russell, Lorne R. Adams, and Joseph A. Sasser, ibid.

58. L. R. Adams and John D. Russell to W. D. Manley, May 17, 1926, ibid.

59. Testimony of Lorne R. Adams, ibid.; *Atlanta Constitution,* September 3, 1926; General Indexes of Plaintiffs and Defendants, Docket Nos. 2687, 3101, 3213, 3214, USDC/NDF.

60. *Atlanta Constitution,* October 25, 1929, October 16, 1934, March 14, 1935.

61. President of the United States of America to Judges of the Supreme Court of Georgia, February 18, 1929; Order of the Supreme Court of Georgia, April 8, 1929, *State of Georgia* v. *W. D. Manley,* Case No. 26735, CD/FCSC.

62. *Atlanta Constitution,* October 16, 18, 1929; Lewis, "Banker Who Went Mad," 37–41.

63. *Atlanta Constitution,* October 16, 17, 1929.

64. *Atlanta Constitution,* October 18, 20, 1929.

65. *Atlanta Constitution,* October 18, 21, 22, 23, 1929; Testimony of Joseph A. Sasser; Government Exhibit No. 424, *United States* v. *Wesley D. Manley, et al.,* Criminal Docket No. 13423, USDC/NDG.

66. *Atlanta Constitution,* October 24, 1929; W. D. Manley to J. A. Sasser, August 15, 1917; Sasser to Manley, August 11, 14, 1917; Testimony of Joseph A. Sasser and H. E. Rank; Government Exhibit No. 508, *United States* v. *Wesley D. Manley, et al.,* Criminal Docket No. 13423, USDC/NDG.

67. *The Depositors Guarantee Fund of the Witham System,* Government Exhibit No. 513, *United States* v. *Wesley D. Manley, et al.,* Criminal Docket No. 13423, USDC/NDG.

68. *Atlanta Constitution,* October 25, 1929; Lewis, "Banker Who Went Mad," 41; Galbraith, *Great Crash,* 103–7; Allen, *Only Yesterday,* 271–75.

69. *Atlanta Constitution,* October 25, 1929, October 16, 1934, March 14, 1935.

70. Ibid.; Lewis, "Banker Who Went Mad," 41.

CHAPTER 8. A SYSTEM OF PROTECTION

1. Joe L. Earman, "J. R. Anthony," *Palm Beach Independent,* November 26, 1926; Earman, "James Rembert Anthony," 25–26; Final Report of Palm Beach Bank and Trust Company, July 28, 1926; Final Report of Commercial Bank and Trust Company, June 26, 1926, SC/FSA; Testimony of Joseph A. Sasser; Government Exhibit No. 424, *United States* v. *Wesley D. Manley, et al.,* Criminal Docket No. 13423, USDC/NDG; McFadden, "Chain Bank Crash in Georgia," 137.

2. Anthony, "Annual Address of the President," p. 6.

3. Final Report of Palm Beach Bank and Trust Company, July 28, 1926, SC/FSA; *Palm Beach Post,* December 4, 1918, June 30, 1940; *Tropical Sun,* January 16, 1925; W. D. Manley to Herbert J. Haas, July 8, 1926, and the testimony of Herbert J. Haas, August 30, 1926, *In the Matter of W. D. Manley, Bankrupt,* Docket No. 12055, USDC/NDG; Testimony of Joseph A. Sasser, Lorne R. Adams, and John D. Russell; L. R. Adams and John D. Russell to W. D. Manley, May 17, 1926, *United States* v. *Wesley D. Manley, et al.,* Criminal Docket No. 13423, USDC/NDG.

4. L. R. Adams and John D. Russell to W. D. Manley, May 17, 1926, *United States* v. *Wesley D. Manley, et al.,* Criminal Docket No. 13423, USDC/NDG; *New York Times,* September 23, 1926; *Palm Beach Post,* September 23, 1926.

5. Final Report of Peoples Bank of Jacksonville, July 25, 1929, SC/FSA.

6. Testimony of Joseph A. Sasser, Lorne R. Adams, John D. Russell, Fred C. Allen, and H. E. Rank; L. R. Adams and John D. Russell to W. D. Manley, May 17, 1926; Government Exhibit No. 508, *United States* v. *Wesley D. Manley, et al.,* Criminal Docket No. 13423, USDC/NDG.

7. *New York Times,* September 23, 1926; *Palm Beach Post,* September 23, 1926; Indictment of Ernest Amos, September 22, 1926, SCF/FSA; Examiner's Report of Palm Beach National Bank, June 15, 1926, USOCC/WNRC; Final Report of Commercial Bank and Trust Company, June 26, 1926, SC/FSA.

8. Report of Organization of Palm Beach National Bank, November 25, 1924; Examiner's Reports of Palm Beach National Bank, June 17, 1925, February 10, 1926, USOCC/WNRC; Final Report of Palm Beach Bank and Trust Company, July 28, 1926; Final Report of Commercial Bank and Trust Company, June 26, 1926, SC/FSA; *New York Times,* September 23, 1926; *Palm Beach Post,* January 25, April 15, 1925, September 23, 1926; *Palm Beach Independent,* July 23, September 24, 1926.

9. Final Report of Peoples Bank of Jacksonville, July 25, 1929; Final Report of Commercial Bank and Trust Company, June 26, 1926, SC/FSA; Examiner's Reports of Palm Beach National Bank, February 10, June 15, 1926, USOCC/WNRC; Joe L. Earman to J. B. Hodges, August 30, 1926; T. C. Hawkins to Hodges, February 10, 1934, JBHP/PKYL.

10. *Palm Beach Independent,* February 11, 25, 1927.

11. *Palm Beach Independent,* February 18, 25, 1927; Final Report of Palm Beach Bank and Trust Company, July 28, 1926, SC/FSA.

12. *Palm Beach Times,* December 6, 1926; *Palm Beach Independent,* February 11, March 1, April 22, 1927; Joe L. Earman to J. B. Hodges, August 30, 1926; Hodges to Earman, September 1, 1926, JBHP/PKYL.

13. Dovell, *History of Banking,* 149–50, 218; Morris, *Florida Handbook: 1977–1978,* 87, 502; *Palm Beach Independent,* May 6, 1927; Eve Bacon, *Orlando: A Centennial History,* Vol. 2 (Chuluota, Fla.: Mickler House, 1977), 48, 53, 57.

14. "O'Kea O'Shea," Station WRHP Tallahassee, April 18, 1948; "Friends and Fellow Citizens," CMG/FSA.

15. *Return C. M. Gay as Comptroller,* 1948, CMG/FSA.

16. Selden F. Waldo to Clarence Gay, January 9, 1948; Waldo to R. J. Bishop, February 18, 1948; Joe Burnett to William H. Chandler, February 12, 1948, CMG/FSA.

17. Records of Palm Beach Bank and Trust Company, SC/FSA; *Palm Beach Independent,* February 11, 1927; *Tropical Sun,* March 5, 1937.

18. Sec. 4146, *General Acts of Florida,* 1925; Ernest Amos to Officers, Directors and Stockholders of Palm Beach Bank and Trust Company, October 7, 1926, and Petition to Comptroller for Final Discharge of Liquidator and Release of Bond, August 1, 1938, Records of Palm Beach Bank and Trust Company, SC/FSA.

19. Final Report of Palm Beach Bank and Trust Company, July 28, 1926; Final Report of Commercial Bank and Trust Company, June 26, 1926, SC/FSA; Examiner's Reports of Palm Beach National Bank, February 10, June 15, 1926, USOCC/WNRC; Testimony of Ralph Payne, *United States v. Wesley D. Manley, et al.,* Criminal Docket No. 13423, USDC/NDG.

20. Final Report of Commercial Bank and Trust Company, June 26, 1926, and Inventory and Liquidator's Receipt of Commercial Bank and Trust Company, October 24, 1929, SC/FSA; *Palm Beach Independent,* September 24, November 26, 1926; *Palm Beach Post,* November 19, 1926.

21. Final Report of Commercial Bank and Trust Company, June 26, 1926; Final Report of Palm Beach Bank and Trust Company, June 28, 1926, SC/FSA; Examiner's Report of Palm Beach National Bank, June 15, 1926, USOCC/WNRC; Ellis Robb to Comptroller of the Currency, June 29, 1926, (telegram), Palm Beach National Bank Records, USOCC/NA; *Palm Beach Independent,* July 2, 1926.

22. Hearings of August 27, 28, 30, 1926; Petition of Dorsey, Howell, and Heyman, May 25, 1927; W. D. Manley to Herbert J. Haas, July 8, 1926, and the testimony of Herbert H. Haas, August 30, 1926; Petition of J. D. Robinson, April 19, 1928; Order of Referee Harry Dodd, April 28, 1928, *In the Matter of W. D. Manley, Bankrupt,* Docket No. 12055; Testimony of Paul J. Baker, Lorne R. Adams, and Joseph A. Sasser, *United States v. Wesley D. Manley, et al.,* Criminal Docket No. 13423, USDC/NDG.

23. Order of Referee Harry Dodd, July 23, 1927, *In the Matter of W. D. Manley, Bankrupt,* Docket No. 12055; Oscar E. Dooly to Harry Dodd; Report of Bankers Trust Company, December 1, 1927, *In the Matter of Bankers Trust Company, Bankrupt,* Docket No. 12046, USDC/NDG; Final Report of Peoples Bank of Jacksonville, July 25, 1929, SC/FSA.

24. Petition of Trustee J. D. Robinson, April 30, 1928; Order of Referee Harry Dodd, May 4, 1928; Report of Appraisers, July 11, 1927, *In the Matter of W. D. Manley, Bankrupt,* Docket No. 12055, USDC/NDG.

25. See bankruptcy records, *In the Matter of Thomas M. Cook, Bankrupt,* Docket No. 1305; and *In the Matter of Donald H. Conkling, Bankrupt,* Docket No. 1284, USDC/SDF.

26. Statement of All Debts of Bankrupt, Statement of All Assets of

Bankrupt, and Summary of Debts and Assets, December 23, 1932, *In the Matter of Thomas M. Cook, Bankrupt,* Docket No. 1305, USDC/SDF; Final Audit Report of Commercial Bank and Trust Company, December 31, 1937, to July 28, 1938, SC/FSA.

27. Lewis, *Florida Banks,* 8; Final Report of Commercial Bank and Trust Company, June 26, 1926, SC/FSA.

28. Statement of All Debts of Bankrupt, Statement of All Assets of Bankrupt, and Summary of Debts and Assets, December 23, 1932, *In the Matter of Thomas M. Cook, Bankrupt,* Docket No. 1305, USDC/SDF.

29. Statement of All Assets of Bankrupt, December 23, 1932, ibid.

30. Statement of All Debts of Bankrupt, December 23, 1932, ibid.

31. Ibid.

32. Ibid.

33. Statement of All Assets of Bankrupt, ibid.; Biographical Data of Thomas McBride Cook for the *Tropical Sun* and "Thomas McBride Cook" article, HSPBC; *Palm Beach Post,* November 13, 1960.

34. Statement of All Property of Bankrupt, October 25, 1932, *In the Matter of Donald H. Conkling, Bankrupt,* Docket No. 1284, USDC/SDF; First Dividend of .001%, March 18, 1930; Proof of Claim and Power of Attorney of Post Publishing Company, June 30, 1927, *In the Matter of Mizner Development Corporation,* March 18, 1930, Docket No. 252, USDC/SDF; Final Report of Commercial Bank and Trust Company, June 26, 1926; Final Report of First American Bank and Trust Company, October 12, 1929, SC/FSA; Receiver's Quarterly Reports of Palm Beach National Bank, June 28, September 30, 1926, USOCC/NA; *Polk's Bankers,* September 1925, p. 291; *Palm Beach Times,* December 3, 1930; Flynt, *Cracker Messiah,* 106.

35. Final Report of First American Bank and Trust Company, October 12, 1929, SC/FSA; *Palm Beach Independent,* July 2, 1926; *Palm Beach Times,* May 24, 1927; *Palm Beach Post,* May 24, 26, 1927.

36. Final Report of First American Bank and Trust Company, October 12, 1929, SC/FSA; Statement of All Debts of Bankrupt, October 25, 1932, *In the Matter of Donald H. Conkling, Bankrupt,* Docket No. 1284, USDC/SDF.

37. Statement of All Debts of Bankrupt, October 25, 1932, *In the Matter of Donald H. Conkling, Bankrupt,* Docket No. 1284, USDC/SDF; James R. Knott, *Palm Beach Revisited* (1987), 75–87; Curl, *Palm Beach County,* 43–45, 112; McIver, *Yesterday's Palm Beach,* 21, 73–74, 105–6, 126.

38. *New York Herald,* March 4, 1915; *New York Sun,* March 9, 1915.

39. Statement of All Debts of Bankrupt, October 25, 1932, *In the Matter of Donald H. Conkling, Bankrupt,* Docket No. 1284, USDC/SDF; Final Report of Farmers Bank and Trust Company of West Palm Beach, June 15, 1927, SC/FSA; Curl, *Palm Beach County,* 112.

40. General Indexes of Plaintiffs and Defendants, Docket Nos. 3101, 3213, 3214, 4185, USDC/NDF.

41. Anthony, "Anthony Brothers on the East Coast," 30, PKYL; Last Will and Testament of Rosa Seward Anthony, July 27, 1948; Appraisal of Estate, May 6, 1958; Annual Returns, March 31, 1958, March 19, 1959; Inventory of Estate and Claim of Rosa Seward Anthony, September 19, 1957, *In re: Estate of Rosa Seward Anthony,* No. 23567-D, PD/DCCC; Final Report of Palm Beach Bank and Trust Company, July 28, 1926; Final Report of Peoples Bank of Jacksonville, July 25, 1929, SC/FSA; *Polk's Bankers,* March 1928, p. 336; Testimony of E. D. Anthony, April 30, 1932, *In the Matter of Anthony's, Inc., Bankrupt,* Docket No. 1195, USDC/SDF; Testimony of D. S. Goodrich, *United States* v. *Wesley D. Manley, et al.,* Criminal Docket No. 13423, USDC/NDG.

42. Testimony of E. D. Anthony, April 30, August 17, 1932, *In the Matter of Anthony's, Inc., Bankrupt,* Docket No. 1195, USDC/SDF; Anthony, "Anthony Brothers on the East Coast," 20–21, 29–30, PKYL; James R. Knott, "The Anthony Saga, 1895–1980," *Palm Beach Post,* December 7, 1980; Final Report of Palm Beach Bank and Trust Company, July 28, 1926; Final Report of First American Bank and Trust Company, SC/FSA.

43. Petition of Consolidated Florida Co., Palm Beach Daily News, and B. D. Cole, Inc., March 25, 1932, *In the Matter of Anthony's, Inc., Bankrupt,* Docket No. 1195, USDC/SDF.

44. Testimony of E. D. Anthony, August 17, 1932; Petition of Anthony Investment Company, October 27, 1932; Receiver's Petition for Application of Rents Accrued Prior to Bankruptcy, October 31, 1932; Trust Agreement between Anthony Investment Company and Anthony Brothers, Incorporated, May 15, 1923; Unpaid Taxes and Interest Accrued, 1929–32; Order of Involuntary Bankruptcy, March 26, 1932; Creditors' Meetings, May 18, August 17, 1932; Petitions of Anthony Investment Company, September 20, October 27, 1932, ibid.; Anthony, "Anthony Brothers on the East Coast," 20–21, PKYL.

45. Order Appointing Receiver, September 30, 1932, *Joseph S. White* v. *Anthony Investment Company;* Receiver's Petition for Application of Rents Accrued Prior to Bankruptcy, and Order of Referee, October 31, 1932; Petitions of Joseph S. White, as Successor-Trustee, August 4, 16, 1932; Order of Referee L. Earl Curry, August 5, 1932; Hearing of December 7, 1932, *In the Matter of Anthony's, Inc., Bankrupt,* Docket No. 1195, USDC/SDF.

46. Testimony of E. D. Anthony and Luella E. McGuire, April 30, 1932; Indenture between Anthony Investment Company and Anthony Brothers, Incorporated and Palm Beach Bank and Trust Company, May 15, 1923; Balance Sheet of Anthony's, Inc., February 1932; Statement of

Assets and Liabilities of Anthony Holding Company, March 26, 1932, ibid.

47. Testimony of Luella E. McGuire, April 30, 1932, ibid.

48. Petition of Anthony Investment Company, October 27, 1932; Statement of Assets and Liabilities of Anthony Holding Company, March 26, 1932, ibid.

49. Petition for Reclamation of Jacob Elishewitz and Sons Company, May 4, 1932; Trustee's Answer to the Petition for Reclamation, December 7, 1932; Order of Referee L. Earl Curry, December 20, 1932; Petition for Review of Order, December 28, 1932; Certificate of Referee on Review, January 16, 1933, ibid.

50. Testimony of E. D. Anthony, August 17, December 7, 1932; Proof of Debt of Florida Bank and Trust Company, West Palm Beach, May 18, 1932, and the Promissory Note of Anthony's, Inc., March 14, 1932, ibid.; Final Report of Palm Beach Bank and Trust Company, July 28, 1926; Final Report of First American Bank and Trust Company, October 12, 1929, SC/FSA.

51. Offer of Composition, June 24, 1932; Meeting to Offer Composition, August 17, 1932; Receiver's Reports, April 30, May 18, 1932; Hearing to Vote on Composition, September 14, 1932; First and Final Dividend of 25%, October 31, 1932, *In the Matter of Anthony's, Inc., Bankrupt,* Docket No. 1195, USDC/SDF; *Palm Beach Independent,* November 26, 1926; Final Report of Palm Beach Bank and Trust Company, July 28, 1926, SC/FSA.

52. Petition of Consolidated Florida Co., March 25, 1932; Special Meeting of Board of Directors of Anthony's, Inc., March 28, 1932; Order of Referee L. Earl Curry, March 29, 1932; Petition to Confirm Sale of Assets, October 5, 1932; Order Confirming Sale, October 5, 1932; Testimony of E. D. Anthony, April 30, December 7, 1932, *In the Matter of Anthony's, Inc., Bankrupt,* Docket No. 1195, USDC/SDF

53. Testimony of E. D. Anthony, December 7, 1932; First and Final Dividend of 25%, October 31, 1932, ibid.; *Palm Beach Times,* May 6, 9, 13, 31, 1930, April 8, 1932.

54. Petition of Consolidated Florida Co., Palm Beach Daily News, and B. D. Cole, Inc., March 25, 1932; First and Final Dividend of 25%, October 31, 1932, *In the Matter of Anthony's, Inc., Bankrupt,* Docket No. 1195, USDC/SDF; Final Report of First American Bank and Trust Company, June 18, 1928, and Statement of Condition of First American Bank and Trust Company, June 30, 1930, SC/FSA; *Palm Beach Post,* September 13, 1925.

55. Anthony, "Anthony Brothers on the East Coast," 30, PKYL; Order of Referee Harry Dodd, July 23, 1927; Petition of Trustee J. D. Robinson, April 30, 1928; Order of Referee Harry Dodd, May 4, 1928, *In*

the Matter of W. D. Manley, Bankrupt, Docket No. 12055, USDC/NDG; General Indexes of Plaintiffs and Defendants, Docket Nos. 3101, 3213, 3214, 4185, USDC/NDF; Petition of Anthony Investment Company, October 27, 1932; *Joseph S. White* v. *Anthony Investment Company, In the Matter of Anthony's, Inc., Bankrupt,* Docket No. 1195, USDC/SDF; *The Blue Book: A Social Register of Jacksonville, Florida* (St. Augustine: Record Company, 1929–31, 1933–35), *Polk's Jacksonville City Directory* (Jacksonville: R. L. Polk, 1918, 1921, 1922, 1926, 1930–31, 1935–40).

56. William Knott had held the position of state treasurer from 1903 to 1912. See Bankers Financing Company to W. V. Knott, October 4, 1921; W. V. Knott to C. M. Knott, June 17, 1922; see two letters with the same date, W. V. Knott to F. O. Spain, October 16, 1922; W. V. Knott to C. M. Knott, October 17, 1922; J. R. Anthony to W. V. Knott, October 18, 1922; Spain to W. V. Knott, May 25, 1923; O. C. Sheffield to W. V. Knott, June 4, 1923, KFP/FSA; T. Frederick Davis, *History of Jacksonville, Florida, and Vicinity, 1513 to 1924* (St. Augustine: Florida Historical Society, 1925), 304.

57. Anthony, "Anthony Brothers on the East Coast," 30, PKYL; *Palm Beach Post,* June 30, 1940; Appraisal of Estate of Rosa Seward Anthony, May 6, 1958, *In re: Estate of Rosa Seward Anthony,* No. 23567-D, PD/DCCC; *Polk's Jacksonville City Directory,* 1938–42.

CHAPTER 9. FRIENDS OF VICE-PRESIDENT DAWES

1. J. W. McIntosh to L. Y. Sherman, July 2, 1926; McIntosh to First National Bank of Daytona Beach, July 8, 1926 (telegram); Noah C. Bainum to McIntosh, July 8, 1926 (telegram); Bainum to McIntosh, July 8, 1926, Palm Beach National Bank Records, USOCC/NA.

2. J. W. McIntosh to L. Y. Sherman, July 2, 1926, ibid.; C. G. Dawes to Sherman, August 11, 1904, LYSP/ISHL; *Daytona Morning Journal,* March 4, 1926; Bascom N. Timmons, *Portrait of an American: Charles G. Dawes* (New York: Henry Holt, 1953), 68–69, 107–10, 122, 149–51, 161–62, 208; Charles G. Dawes, *A Journal of the McKinley Years* (Chicago: Lakeside Press, R. R. Donnelley & Sons, 1950), 260, 287, 293, 302–4, 309, 332–34, 337, 345–46, 354, 372, 390, 440–42.

3. *History of the Pure Oil Company,* 26, 28–37, LC/WDC; *Annual Report of the Comptroller of the Currency,* 1968, p. 189; Charles G. Dawes, *Notes as Vice President, 1928–1929* (Boston: Little, Brown, 1935), 154; *Who Was Who,* 214–15, 581; *Poor's Register of Directors of the United States: 1929* (New York: Poor's Publishing Company, 1929), 421; *New York Times,* February 2, April 8, August 18, 1923, December 3, 4, 19, 1924, May 16, 1927, November 21, 1928; *Daytona Morning Journal,* October 1, 1924.

4. J. B. Cunningham to Comptroller of the Currency, October 18,

1926, and Agreement between Mizner Development Corporation and Central Equities Corporation, July 19, 1926; J. E. Fouts to J. B. Cunningham, October 21, 1926; Cunningham to J. W. Pole, October 22, 1926, Palm Beach National Bank Records, USOCC/NA; *Palm Beach Post,* July 2, 20, October 19, 1926; *Palm Beach Independent,* July 23, 1926; *Palm Beach Times,* July 9, 19, 20, 1926; *New York Times,* July 21, 1926; Curl, *Mizner's Florida,* 163–64; Pratt, *Story of Boca Raton,* 24–25, 30, 33–36; Marjie Gates Giffin, *Water Runs Downhill: A History of the Indianapolis Water Company and Other Centenarians* (New York: Newcomen Society, 1981), 27.

5. Blackwell and Donnell to Comptroller of the Currency, July 7, 1926 (telegram); E. W. Stearns to J. B. Cunningham, July 8, 1926 (telegram), Palm Beach National Bank Records, USOCC/NA.

6. L. Y. Sherman to J. W. McIntosh, July 10, 13, 1926 (telegrams); Sherman to McIntosh, July 20, 1926; J. E. Fouts to J. B. Cunningham, September 22, 1926, Palm Beach National Bank Records, USOCC/NA.

7. J. B. Cunningham to Comptroller of the Currency, September 1, 1926 (telegram), and J. E. Fouts to Cunningham, September 1, 1926 (telegram), Palm Beach National Bank Records, USOCC/NA; Curl, *Mizner's Florida,* 142.

8. J. B. Cunningham to Comptroller of the Currency, February 6, 1928; Assistant Supervising Receiver to Cunningham, February 18, 1928, Palm Beach National Bank Records, USOCC/NA.

9. J. B. Cunningham to Comptroller of the Currency, September 1, 1926 (telegram); J. E. Fouts to Cunningham, September 1, 1926 (telegram), and September 2, 1926; Suspense Account and J. B. Cunningham to Comptroller of the Currency, February 6, 1928, ibid.

10. Wilson Mizner had pledged 408 shares of the Mizner Development Corporation to the Palm Beach National Bank as collateral for his personal loans. J. B. Cunningham to Comptroller of the Currency, October 18, 1926; Agreement between Mizner Development Corporation and Central Equities Corporation, July 19, 1926; J. E. Fouts to Cunningham, October 21, 1926, Palm Beach National Bank Records, USOCC/NA; *Palm Beach Post,* July 20, 1926.

11. Agreement between Mizner Development Corporation and Central Equities Corporation, July 19, 1926, USOCC/NA; Balance Sheet of Mizner Development Corporation, March 31, 1926, HSPBC.

12. *Poor's Register: 1929,* 422–23; *New York Times,* March 30, April 8, 1923, December 10, 11, 1926; William L. Shirer, *The Rise and Fall of the Third Reich: A History of Nazi Germany* (New York: Simon and Schuster, 1960), 112, 136, 943.

13. Agreement between Mizner Development Corporation and Central Equities Corporation, July 19, 1926, Palm Beach National Bank

Records, USOCC/NA; *Palm Beach Post,* July 2, 20, October 19, 1926; *New York Times,* July 21, 1926.

14. *Palm Beach Post,* October 19, 1926.

15. Petition of Jack Lindy, H. F. Underwood, and Sidney Adler, March 7, 1927, *In the Matter of Mizner Development Corporation, Bankrupt,* Docket No. 252, USDC/SDF; *Palm Beach Post,* April 23, 1927; *New York Times,* March 10, 1927; J. B. Cunningham to J. W. Pole, October 22, 1927, and *Palm Beach Post,* n.d., newspaper clipping, Palm Beach National Bank Records, USOCC/NA.

16. Schedule of Creditors Holding Securities, August 4, 1927; Petition of Trustees in Bankruptcy, September 23, 1927, *In the Matter of Mizner Development Corporation, Bankrupt,* Docket No. 252, USDC/SDF.

17. Petition of Riddle Engineering Company, Ahrens & Sons, Inc., and the Palm Beach Mercantile Company, June 23, 1927; Adjudication in Bankruptcy of the Mizner Development Corporation, July 26, 1927, ibid.

18. Petition of Trustees in Bankruptcy, September 23, 1927; Reply to Order to Show Cause of Central Equities Corporation; Hearing of October 10, 1927; Order Dismissing Petition, October 10, 1927, ibid.

19. First Dividend of .001%, March 18, 1930, ibid.

20. First Dividend of .001%, March 18, 1930; Petition for Attorneys Fees of Blackwell, Donnell and Moore, December 16, 1927, ibid.

21. Proof of Unsecured Debt of Florida Power and Light Company, September 1927; Proof of Claim of Warren and Wetmore, October 20, 1927; First Dividend of .001%, March 18, 1930, ibid.

22. Hearing of October 27, 1927; Stipulation and Agreement of Max Specktor, C. H. Geist, and J. D. Gedney, November 8, 1927, ibid.; *Palm Beach Post,* April 15, 1925, April 23, October 28, November 6, 9, 1927; *Palm Beach Independent,* October 21, November 25, 1927; *Palm Beach Times,* October 19, 28, November 1, 2, 20, 1927; *New York Times,* October 20, 1926, March 10, November 7, 1927, June 13, 1938; J. B. Cunningham to J. W. Pole, October 22, 1927, and *Palm Beach Post,* n.d., newspaper clipping, Palm Beach National Bank Records, USOCC/NA; Donald W. Curl and John P. Johnson, *Boca Raton: A Pictorial History* (Virginia Beach, Va.: Donning Company, 1990), 79; Giffin, *Water Runs Downhill,* 23–27; "Report of Syndicate Manager, April 1, 1928," in the *Spanish River Papers* 16 (1987–88).

23. Schedule of Creditors Holding Securities, August 4, 1927, *In the Matter of Mizner Development Corporation, Bankrupt,* Docket No. 252, USDC/SDF; In Account with Addison Mizner, Incorporated; Creditors Whose Claims Are Unsecured, July 24, 1933; First Meeting of Creditors, August 23, 1933, *In the Matter of Mizner Industries, Inc., Bankrupt,* Docket No. 1325, USDC/SDF.

24. Final Report of Referee L. Earl Curry, November 9, 1938; Statement of all creditors who are to be paid in full, or to whom priority is secured by law, July 24, 1933; Income Tax Claim of Collector of Internal Revenue, August 16, 1933; Petition of United States of America, December 22, 1933; Order of Fifth Circuit Court of Appeals, February 7, 1935; Petition of Paty, Warwick and Mooney, August 27, 1935; Hearing of July 8, 1936, ibid.; Curl, *Mizner's Florida*, 53–59.

25. Petition of West Palm Beach Atlantic National Bank, August 23, 1933; Promissory Note of Mizner Industries, Inc., December 15, 1932; Creditors Whose Claims Are Unsecured, July 24, 1933; Petition of Lainhart and Potter, Inc., Frank E. Martin, and Sinclair Refining Company, April 29, 1933; Balance Sheet of Mizner Industries, Incorporated, July 30, 1932; Oath of Appraisers, October 23, 1933, *In the Matter of Mizner Industries, Inc., Bankrupt*, Docket No. 1325, USDC/SDF.

26. Debtor's Petition in Proceedings Under Section 77-B of the Bankruptcy Act, May 11, 1935; Order of Halsted L. Ritter, May 13, 1935; Petition of Intervention of Atlantic National Bank of Jacksonville, June 11, 1935; Affidavit of E. Harris Drew, March 7, 1936; Decree Confirming Plan of Reorganization, March 9, 1936, *In the Matter of Addison Mizner, Inc., Debtor*, Docket No. 1495, USDC/SDF.

27. Debtor's Petition in Proceedings Under Section 77-B of the Bankruptcy Act, May 11, 1935, ibid.; Curl, *Mizner's Florida*, 113–15, 201; Orr-Cahall, "Identification and Discussion," 56–57.

CHAPTER 10. SENATORIAL PRIVILEGE

1. J. B. Cunningham to J. W. McIntosh, April 11, 1927, and McIntosh to Cunningham, April 11, 1927, Palm Beach National Bank Records, USOCC/NA.

2. *The National Cyclopaedia of American Biography Being the History of the United States*, Vol. 3 (New York: James T. White & Company, 1893), 527–28, and Vol. 15 (1916), 101; *Biographical Directory of the American Congress*, 788–89, 1689; Dawes, *McKinley Years*, 260.

3. C. G. Dawes to L. Y. Sherman, February 13, 18, 19, 23, March 23, April 20, May 4, June 11, 1901; Dawes to D. G. Tunnicliff, February 13, 1901; Tunnicliff to Sherman, July 13, 1901, LYSP/ISHL.

4. D. G. Tunnicliff to C. G. Dawes, March 22, 1901; Dawes to L. Y. Sherman, June 30, August 2, 31, 1901, August 11, 1904, LYSP/ISHL; Dawes, *McKinley Years*, 287, 295–96, 308–9.

5. Dawes, *McKinley Years*, 293; C. G. Dawes to L. Y. Sherman, August 11, 1904, LYSP/ISHL; Charles G. Dawes, *Essays and Speeches* (Boston: Houghton Mifflin, 1915), 330–31; *Polk's Bankers* 1 (March 1926): 445; *Chicago Tribune*, October 19, 1926.

6. C. G. Dawes to L. Y. Sherman, July 2, 15, 1913, January 8, 1915, February 1, 26, May 22, August 1, 1916, February 21, 1917; Sherman to C. G. Dawes, February 19, 1912, June 3, 1914, February 4, 27, May 27, 1916; H. M. Dawes to Sherman, December 3, 1916; R. C. Dawes to Sherman, February 1, October 24, 1918; Sherman to R. C. Dawes, November 6, 1918, LYSP/ISHL; *New York Times,* February 2, March 27, 1913.

7. Charles G. Dawes, *The First Year of the Budget of the United States* (New York: Harper & Brothers, 1923), 84; W. G. Harding to L. Y. Sherman, October 11, 1921, LYSP/ISHL.

8. L. Y. Sherman to C. G. Dawes, June 14, 1924; Sherman to N. K. Defreitas, June 18, 1924; Dawes to Sherman, June 19, 1924, LYSP/ISHL; *Annual Report of the Comptroller of the Currency,* 1966, p. 189; *Daytona Morning Journal,* September 19, 1924; *Biographical Directory of the American Congress,* 1593.

9. C. G. Dawes to L. Y. Sherman, May 21, 1924, and "Sherman Seen as Candidate for Governor," n.d., newspaper clipping, LYSP/ISHL; *Daytona Morning Journal,* September 19, 1924.

10. The original name of Sherman's bank was the First National Bank of Seabreeze, but the bank changed its name to the First National Bank of Daytona Beach in 1926. Lewis, *Florida Banks,* 20.

11. L. Y. Sherman to N. K. Defreitas, June 18, 1924; C. G. Dawes to Sherman, May 21, 1924, LYSP/ISHL; *Daytona Morning Journal,* September 19, 1924; *Polk's Bankers,* September 1925, p. 285; Lewis, *Florida Banks,* 20.

12. L. Y. Sherman to J. W. McIntosh, January 4, 1927, Palm Beach National Bank Records, USOCC/NA.

13. Ibid.; Expense Bill to McIntosh from Sherman; J. E. Fouts to Sherman, January 10, 1927; Fouts to J. B. Cunningham, January 10, 1927, ibid.

14. L. Y. Sherman to J. W. McIntosh, January 22, 1927, and Bill for Services Rendered, Palm Beach National Bank Records, USOCC/NA; C. G. Dawes to Sherman, August 31, 1901, LYSP/ISHL.

15. J. B. Cunningham to Comptroller of the Currency, February 11, 1927, Palm Beach National Bank Records, USOCC/NA.

16. L. Y. Sherman to J. W. McIntosh, January 22, 1927; J. B. Cunningham to Comptroller of the Currency, March 11, 16, 26, 1927; Voucher No. 115, Receiver J. B. Cunningham in favor of Sherman and Bainum for $2,500, March 9, 1927; J. E. Fouts to Cunningham, March 24, 1927; Expense Statement of Sherman and Bainum to J. B. Cunningham, April 2, 1927, Palm Beach National Bank Records, USOCC/NA; J. W. McIntosh to L. Y. Sherman, February 25, March 28, 1927; Sherman to McIntosh, April 6, 1927, LYSP/ISHL; *New York Herald Tribune,* March 14, 1927.

17. *Annual Report of the Comptroller of the Currency,* 1930, p. 314; J. B. Cunningham to J. W. McIntosh, April 11, 1927 (telegram); J. W. McIntosh to Cunningham, April 11, 1927, First National Bank of Lake Worth Records, USOCC/NA.

18. L. Y. Sherman to C. N. Wheeler, June 10, 1927; C. G. Dawes to Sherman, September 8, 1927, LYSP/ISHL.

19. L. Y. Sherman to J. W. McIntosh, December 30, 31, 1927, LYSP/ISHL.

20. Statement of Expenses of Sherman and Bainum, January 2, 1928; L. Y. Sherman to J. W. McIntosh, January 3, 11, 1928; A. B. Merritt to J. B. Cunningham, January 17, 1928; Cunningham to Comptroller of the Currency, January 20, 26, 1928, Palm Beach National Bank Records, USOCC/NA.

21. L. Y. Sherman to J. B. Cunningham, January 31, 1928; Cunningham to Comptroller of the Currency, February 1, 6, 28, 1928; J. E. Fouts to Cunningham, February 17, 1928, Palm Beach National Bank Records, USOCC/NA.

22. C. G. Dawes to L. Y. Sherman, February 11, 1928, LYSP/ISHL; Timmons, *Portrait of an American,* 161–63; Richard Garrett Sherman, "Charles G. Davis: An Entrepreneurial Biography, 1865–1951" (Ph.D. dissertation, University of Iowa, 1960), 106–39.

23. L. Y. Sherman to J. W. McIntosh, March 2, 1928, and N. C. Bainum to J. B. Cunningham, March 10, 1928, Palm Beach National Bank Records, USOCC/NA.

24. J. W. McIntosh to R. D. Garrett, March 5, 1928; Garrett to J. B. Cunningham, March 7, 1928; Cunningham to Comptroller of the Currency, March 23, 1928; Cunningham to Sherman and Bainum, March 29, 1928, and Voucher No. 179, Palm Beach National Bank Records, USOCC/NA.

25. N. C. Bainum to J. B. Cunningham, March 10, 1928; Cunningham to Comptroller of the Currency, March 23, 1928; J. E. Fouts to Cunningham, March 31, 1928, ibid.

26. J. B. Cunningham to Sherman and Bainum, March 29, 1928, and attached Voucher No. 179; J. E. Fouts to Cunningham, April 1, 1928; N. C. Bainum to Cunningham, April 4, 1928; L. Y. Sherman to Cunningham, March 10, 1928; Cunningham to Comptroller of the Currency, April 4, 1928, ibid.

27. J. B. Cunningham to R. D. Garrett, April 5, 1928, ibid.

28. J. B. Cunningham to R. D. Garrett, April 14, 1928; A. B. Merritt to Cunningham, April 16, 1928; Cunningham to Comptroller of the Currency, April 21, 1928; Garrett to Cunningham, May 11, 1928, ibid.

29. *Biographical Directory of the American Congress,* 1593; Paul F. Boller, Jr., *Presidential Campaigns* (New York: Oxford University Press, 1985),

223; *Palm Beach Independent,* January 22, 1926; G. P. Barse to J. W. McIntosh, May 25, 1928; A. B. Merritt to J. B. Cunningham, June 6, 1928; Cunningham to Sherman and Bainum, June 9, 1928, and Voucher No. 197; Cunningham to Comptroller of the Currency, June 12, 1928, Palm Beach National Bank Records, USOCC/NA.

30. Sherman's personal letter to McIntosh could not be found by the comptroller's staff after "a thorough search" of their files. L. Y. Sherman to J. W. McIntosh, October 22, 1928; F. G. Awalt to J. B. Cunningham, August 16, 1928; Cunningham to Comptroller of the Currency, August 30, 1928; R. D. Garrett to Cunningham, November 5, 1928, First National Bank of Lake Worth Records, USOCC/NA; R. E. Niven to L. Y. Sherman, October 1, 1928, LYSP/ISHL; Boller, *Presidential Campaigns,* 223; *Illinois State Journal,* August 15, 1928.

31. *Illinois State Journal,* August 15, 1928.

32. *New York Times,* November 21, 1928, September 1, 8, 10, 22, 1932; Ross M. Robertson, *The Comptroller and Bank Supervision: A Historical Appraisal* (Washington, D.C.: Office of the Comptroller of the Currency, 1968), 106.

33. L. Y. Sherman to J. W. Pole, December 6, 1928, First National Bank of Lake Worth Records, USOCC/NA.

34. J. B. Cunningham to Comptroller of the Currency, February 1, 6, 1929; Cunningham to R. D. Garrett, March 13, 1929, ibid.

35. F. G. Awalt to J. B. Cunningham, August 16, 1928; Cunningham to Comptroller of the Currency, February 6, 1929; Sherman and Bainum to Cunningham, February 4, 1929, ibid.

36. J. B. Cunningham to Comptroller of the Currency, January 31, 1927; John Davis to Comptroller of the Currency, August 13, 1928; J. W. McIntosh to Cunningham, September 19, 1928; N. C. Bainum to Cunningham, December 21, 1928; N. C. Bainum to J. W. Pole, March 13, 1929, Palm Beach National Bank Records, USOCC/NA; Examiner's Reports of Palm Beach National Bank, February 10, 1926, June 15, 1926, USOCC/WNRC.

37. John Davis to Sherman and Bainum, April 30, 1928; Davis to Comptroller of the Currency, August 13, 1928, Palm Beach National Bank Records, USOCC/NA.

38. J. B. Cunningham to Comptroller of the Currency, May 5, June 30, 1928; J. E. Fouts to Cunningham, May 12, July 17, 1928; N. C. Bainum to Cunningham, June 28, 1928, ibid.

39. John Davis to Comptroller of the Currency, August 13, 1928; J. W. McIntosh to J. B. Cunningham, September 19, 1928; N. C. Bainum to J. W. Pole, March 13, 1929, ibid.

40. J. B. Cunningham to Comptroller of the Currency, December 4,

1928; J. E. Fouts to Cunningham, December 15, 1928; N. C. Bainum to Cunningham, December 21, 1928, ibid.

41. J. W. Pole to J. B. Cunningham, January 9, 1929; N. C. Bainum to Pole, March 13, 1929, ibid.; J. B. Cunningham to R. D. Garrett, March 13, 1929, First National Bank of Lake Worth Records, USOCC/NA.

42. N. C. Bainum to J. W. Pole, March 13, 1929; Receiver's Report, June 28, 1926, Palm Beach National Bank Records; J. B. Cunningham to R. D. Garrett, March 13, 1929, First National Bank of Lake Worth Records, USOCC/NA; R. E. Niven to L. Y. Sherman, August 25, October 1, 7, 13, 1930, September 28, 1933, September 24, 25, 1935; Sherman to Niven, October 10, 16, 1930; Sherman to Atlantic National Bank of Jacksonville, December 29, 1933; Assistant Vice-President of Atlantic National Bank of Jacksonville to Sherman, December 30, 1933; To the Shareholders of the Atlantic National Bank of Jacksonville, April 1, July 1, October 1, 1930, July 2, 1931, July 1, 1933; Account statement of the Atlantic National Company of Jacksonville, March 5, 1930; Cashier of Atlantic National Bank of Jacksonville to L. Y. Sherman, July 13, 1934; Receipt of sale for Lawrence Y. Sherman's stock in the First Atlantic National Bank of Daytona Beach and Atlantic National Bank of Jacksonville, September 17, 1935, LYSP/ISHL; *Illinois State Journal,* August 15, 1928; Lewis, *Florida Banks,* 20; Dovell, *History of Banking,* 126; *Polk's Bankers,* March 1927, p. 278.

43. N. C. Bainum to J. W. Pole, March 15, 1929, First National Bank of Lake Worth Records, USOCC/NA.

44. N. C. Bainum to J. W. Pole, March 15, 1929; Pole to Sherman and Bainum, March 30, 1929; Receipt and Release, April 1, 1929; J. B. Cunningham to Comptroller of the Currency, April 2, 1929, ibid.

45. N. C. Bainum to J. B. Cunningham, April 16, 1929; Cunningham to Comptroller of the Currency, April 17, 29, October 22, 30, November 16, 1929, February 7, 20, March 8, May 8, 26, June 12, July 9, 1930; F. G. Awalt to Cunningham, April 23, 1929; Wideman and Wideman to Cunningham, April 28, September 6, 16, 1929, February 14, April 23, 1930; Voucher No. 253 in favor of Wideman and Wideman, November 25, 1929; Cunningham to Wideman and Wideman, November 6, 25, 1929, February 5, March 8, May 24, June 10, 1930, Palm Beach National Bank Records, USOCC/NA.

46. L. Y. Sherman to J. W. McIntosh, May 1, 1929, LYSP/ISHL.

47. H. C. Hengstler to L. Y. Sherman, April 11, 1928; C. E. Mason to Sherman, April 12, 1928; Sherman to J. G. Sargent, January 23, February 23, 1928; John Marshall to Sherman, January 27, 30, February 28, 1928; Sherman to Marshall, January 27, 1928, LYSP/ISHL; F. G. Awalt to J. E. Fouts, June 24, 1930, Palm Beach National Bank Records, USOCC/NA.

CHAPTER 11. THE DEFEAT OF ERNEST AMOS

1. *Tallahassee Daily Democrat,* October 15, 1927, April 9, 1931; *Florida Times-Union,* August 19, 20, 1930, June 29, 1932; *Palm Beach Independent,* October 28, 1927.

2. *Palm Beach Independent,* September 23, October 28, 1927; Final Report of Seminole County Bank, August 6, 1927, SC/FSA; *Ex Parte: Ernest Amos,* 114 Southern Reporter 760; *Tallahassee Daily Democrat,* October 15, 1927; Dovell, *History of Banking,* 228; *General Acts of Florida,* 1923.

3. *Tallahassee Daily Democrat,* October 15, 1927; *Palm Beach Independent,* September 23, October 21, 1927.

4. *Ex Parte: Ernest Amos,* 114 Southern Reporter 760; Petition for Writ of Habeas Corpus, October 17, 1927; Writ of Habeas Corpus, October 19, 1927; Answer of Petitioner, October 26, 1927; Brief in Behalf of Petitioner, October 26, 1927; Brief of J. M. Jones, Acting Attorney General, November 1, 1927, SCF/FSA; *Tallahassee Daily Democrat,* May 25, 1928.

5. *Tallahassee Daily Democrat,* November 3, December 6, 1927, February 29, April 14, 1928.

6. *Tallahassee Daily Democrat,* June 23, 1928.

7. Petition of Ernest Amos for Writ of Habeas Corpus, August 11, 1930; Brief of Petitioner in Support of Motion to Discharge, August 18, 1930, SCF/FSA; *Florida Times-Union,* August 19, 20, 1930.

8. Certificate of Disqualification of Attorney General, August 14, 1930, SCF/FSA.

9. *Florida Times-Union,* August 19, 20, 1930.

10. *Tampa Morning Tribune,* April 23, 1915, July 18, 1926, July 18, September 5, 1929.

11. *Tampa Morning Tribune,* July 18, 1929.

12. Ibid.; *New York Times,* July 28, 1929.

13. F. L. Middleton to D. E. Carlton, July 22, 1929; Carlton to Middleton, July 31, 1929, DEC/FSA; Final Report of Citizens Bank and Trust Company of Tampa, August 16, 1929, SC/FSA; *Who's Who and What to See in Florida* (St. Petersburg: Current Historical Company of Florida, 1935), 63; *Palm Beach Independent,* September 2, 1927.

14. *Tampa Morning Tribune,* July 18, 1926, July 18, 1929; *New York Times,* July 28, 1929; Tebeau, *History of Florida,* 395; Program of the Florida Bankers Association Convention, 1927, PKYL; Final Report of Citizens Bank and Trust Company of Tampa, August 16, 1929, SC/FSA.

15. *Tampa Morning Tribune,* July 18, 1929.

16. Ibid.; Flynt, *Cracker Messiah,* 218, 222, 226–28.

17. After his ordeal in West Palm Beach, Amos maintained that liquidation reports were "quasi-confidential." *Tampa Morning Tribune,* November 1, 1929, August 20, 21, 30, September 4, 1929, March 11, 1930; Final Report of Citizens Bank and Trust Company of Tampa, August 16, 1929, SC/FSA; Leland Hawes, " 'Knight's Run' Commemorates Rugged Tampa Pioneer," *Tampa Tribune,* July 15, 1990.

18. D. H. Woodberry to D. E. Carlton, August 20, 1929 (telegram); Carlton to Woodberry, August 21, 1929, DEC/FSA; Final Report of Citizens Bank and Trust Company of Tampa, August 16, 1929, SC/FSA.

19. E. W. Coates to D. E. Carlton, August 1, 1929 (telegram), DEC/FSA; Final Report of Citizens Bank and Trust Company of Tampa, August 16, 1929, SC/FSA.

20. P. O. Knight to Ernest Amos, April 23, 1930; Knight to D. E. Carlton, April 23, 1930; Carlton to Knight, April 26, 1930; J. T. Watson to Amos, December 6, 1930; Carlton to Watson, December 9, 1930, DEC/FSA; *Tampa Morning Tribune,* January 8, June 7, August 15, 1930; Flynt, *Fletcher,* 44, 107, 167.

21. *Tampa Morning Tribune,* September 5, 20, 1929, January 22, February 6, 1930; Final Report of Citizens Bank and Trust Company of Tampa, August 16, 1929, SC/FSA; Leland Hawes, " 'Knight's Run' Commemorates Rugged Tampa Pioneer," *Tampa Tribune,* July 15, 1990.

22. *Tampa Morning Tribune,* January 22, 28, 1930.

23. *Tampa Morning Tribune,* January 28, 1930; Final Report of Citizens Bank and Trust Company of Tampa, August 16, 1929, SC/FSA; Resolution of the Depositors Protective Association of Tampa, August 20, 1930; H. K. Wells to D. E. Carlton, August 23, 1930; Carlton to Wells, September 2, 1930, DEC/FSA.

24. J. T. Watson to Ernest Amos, February 10, 1930 (copy), DEC/FSA.

25. *Tampa Morning Tribune,* October 5, November 14, 1929, January 21, March 29, April 1, 4, August 21, 1930; C. L. Knight to Ernest Amos, March 28, 1930 (telegram), Records of Citizens Bank and Trust Company of Tampa, SC/FSA.

26. *Tampa Morning Tribune,* August 8, November 14, 1929, March 20, May 26, June 5, 30, July 1, 19, 24, August 2, December 12, 1930.

27. *Tampa Morning Tribune,* February 15, 1930.

28. Anonymous to D. E. Carlton, n.d., DEC/FSA.

29. A Friend to D. E. Carlton, November 29, 1930, ibid.

30. Leland Hawes, "Tampa Lawyer Helped to Defeat Comptroller," *Tampa Tribune,* December 16, 1990; *Tampa Morning Tribune,* August 27, September 26, 27, 1930.

31. *Tampa Tribune,* December 16, 1990; *Tampa Morning Tribune,* August 27, September 26, 27, 1930.

32. *Tallahassee Daily Democrat,* April 7, 8, 1931; *Tampa Morning Tribune,* April 8, 9, 1931.

33. *Tallahassee Daily Democrat,* April 9, 1931; *General Acts of Florida,* 1931.

34. *Tallahassee Daily Democrat,* April 9, 19, 1931.

35. *Tallahassee Daily Democrat,* April 14, 1931.

36. *Tallahassee Daily Democrat,* April 14, 15, 17, 1931; *Biennial Report of the Attorney General, State of Florida,* J. Tom Watson, Attorney General, Tallahassee, Florida, 1942; *General Acts of Florida,* 1931.

37. *Tallahassee Daily Democrat,* April 27, 28, 1931.

38. *Tallahassee Daily Democrat,* April 28, 1931; *General Acts of Florida,* 1931.

39. *Tallahassee Daily Democrat,* April 15, May 4, 7, 1931, June 3, 1932; *General Acts of Florida,* 1931; *Polk's Bankers,* September 1925, p. 260, March 1926, p. 315a, March 1928, p. 335.

40. *Tallahassee Daily Democrat,* May 8, 1931.

41. *Tallahassee Daily Democrat,* May 12, 1931.

42. *Tallahassee Daily Democrat,* May 28, June 1, 1931; *General Acts of Florida,* 1931.

43. *Tallahassee Daily Democrat,* June 4, 1931; *General Acts of Florida,* 1931.

44. *Tallahassee Daily Democrat,* April 9, June 4, 1931.

45. Ibid., May 12, 1931.

46. Morris, *Florida Handbook: 1977–1978,* 47; *Florida Times-Union,* June 9, 1932.

47. Mark F. Boyd, "A Century of Confidence and Conservatism Culminates in the Lewis State Bank of Tallahassee, Florida," Supplement of *Florida Historical Quarterly* 34 (April 1956): 39; "The Lewis Family and Its Sprightly Old-Time Bank," *Burroughs Clearing House* 51 (July 1967): 68; Lewis, *Florida Banks,* 7; Flynt, *Cracker Messiah,* 40–43, 63–67; Morris, *Florida Handbook: 1977–1978,* 90; Promissory notes of W. V. Knott, October 5, 30, November 14, 26, 1928, November 3, 17, 1931; G. E. Lewis to W. V. Knott, December 5, 1928; P. B. McDougall to W. V. Knott, September 24, 1931; Promissory note of C. M. Knott and W. V. Knott, September 30, 1930; G. E. Lewis to C. M. Knott, October 30, 1931; C. M. Knott to W. V. Knott, October 31, 1931; P. B. McDougall to W. V. Knott, January 13, 1931, KFP/FSA; Final Report of Citizens Bank and Trust Company of Tampa, August 16, 1929, SC/FSA.

48. Examiner's Report of Lewis State Bank of Tallahassee, March 14, 1933, LSB/FSA.

49. Ibid.

50. *Tallahassee Daily Democrat,* May 13, 15, June 1, 1932.

51. *Tallahassee Daily Democrat,* May 13, 1932.

52. *Tallahassee Daily Democrat,* May 25, 1932.

53. *Tallahassee Daily Democrat,* May 25, 26, 1932.

54. *Tallahassee Daily Democrat,* May 8, 12, 13, 15, 17, 1932; *Florida Times-Union,* June 7, 19, 20, 1932; Final Report of Atlantic State Bank and Trust Company of Daytona Beach, August 6, 1929, SC/FSA.

55. Cash, *History of the Democratic Party in Florida,* 216.

56. *Florida Times-Union,* June 14, 28, 1932; Flynt, *Cracker Messiah,* 71, 101, 173–76; *Tallahassee Daily Democrat,* May 17, 26, 1932.

57. *Annual Report of the Comptroller of Florida,* June 30, 1926, pp. xiii–xiv.

58. *Tallahassee Daily Democrat,* May 8, June 2, 3, 1932; *Florida Times-Union,* June 2, 3, 4, 5, 1932.

59. *Florida Times-Union* editorial in the *Tallahassee Daily Democrat,* June 5, 1932; *General Acts of Florida,* 1885, 1891, 1895, 1897, 1901, 1911, 1913, 1915, and 1917; Morris, *Florida Handbook: 1977–1978,* 87.

60. *Tallahassee Daily Democrat,* June 12, 1932; *Florida Times-Union,* June 12, 1932; Morris, *Florida Handbook: 1949–1950,* 300; *Florida Times-Union,* June 24, 26, 27, 1932.

61. Rivers Buford to Franklin Roosevelt, April 13, 1933; C. A. Hardee to Buford, April 15, 1933; J. B. Hodges to G. B. Hills, May 2, 1933; Hodges to Roosevelt, May 6, 1933; L. M. Howe to Hodges, May 10, 1933; Hardee to Hodges, May 16, 1933; Hardee to Hodges, August 21, 1934, JBHP/PKYL.

62. *Tampa Morning Tribune,* May 13, 19, 1950, October 25, 1954; *Tampa Tribune,* December 16, 1990; Thomas R. Wagy, *Governor LeRoy Collins of Florida: Spokesman of the New South* (Tuscaloosa: University of Alabama Press, 1985), 41; Morris, *Florida Handbook* (1952), 93, 183–84, 191.

63. *Florida Times-Union,* June 26, 1932.

64. *Florida Times-Union,* June 18, 24, 26, 27, 1932.

65. *Florida Times-Union,* June 18, 24, 26, 27, 28, 1932.

66. *Florida Times-Union,* June 14, 21, 22, 1932.

67. *Florida Times-Union,* June 21, 1932.

68. *Florida Times-Union,* June 29, 1932; *General Acts of Florida,* 1933; Morris, *Florida Handbook: 1949–1950,* 300; Eve Bacon, *Orlando: A Centennial History* (Chuluota, Fla.: Mickler House, 1977), 2:48, 53, 57; Morris, *Florida Handbook* (1952), 94.

EPILOGUE

1. *Explanation of Major Provisions of CS/HB 2471 Financial Institutions Regulatory Reform Act of 1992 and Regulatory Sunset Report,* Florida House of Representatives, Committee on Commerce, Art Simon, Chairman, February 26, 1992.

2. Ibid.

3. Ibid.

4. *A Review of the Regulation of Banking and Securities in Florida,* Florida Senate Committee on Governmental Operations, John Vogt, Chairman, March 1986, 1, 3, 6, 7, 81.

5. Ibid., 82–85, 104.

6. Impeachment Resolution against Gerald Lewis filed by Representative Jeff Huenink in the Florida House of Representatives, March 12, 1992; *Tampa Tribune,* November 15, 1991, February 9, 14, 19, 29, March 2, 3, 4, 6, 7, 11, 13, 17, 20, 25, 1992; *St. Petersburg Times,* November 15, 19, 1991, February 20, 29, March 1, 3, 4, 5, 6, 7, 8, 13, 17, 20, 22, 25, 1992; *Tallahassee Democrat,* February 29, March 1, 4, 5, 13, 1992; *Fort Lauderdale Sun-Sentinel,* March 3, 4, 13, 1992; *Orlando Sentinel,* March 3, 9, 26, 1992; *Florida Times-Union,* March 3, 20, 1992; *Palm Beach Post,* March 3, 4, 13, 23, 1992; *Miami Herald,* February 23, March 3, 4, 7, 13, 1992; *Lakeland Ledger,* February 6, March 6, June 1, 1992; *Gainesville Sun,* February 8, March 4, 1992; *Sarasota Herald Tribune,* March 3, 1992; *Daytona Beach News-Journal,* March 4, 1992.

7. *St. Petersburg Times,* March 12, 1992; *General Acts of Florida,* 1992, Ch. 92-303, Sec. 655.057 (2)(g).

8. James B. Stewart, *Den of Thieves* (New York: Simon and Schuster, 1991), 223.

9. White, *Banking Law,* 715; Carosso, *Investment Banking in America,* 352–81; Gordon, "Understanding the S&L Mess," 65; Adams, *Big Fix,* 1990, 11–12.

10. Pizzo, Fricker, and Muolo, *Inside Job,* 486; Mayer, *Greatest-Ever Bank Robbery,* 2; *Wall Street Journal,* December 22, 1992; *New York Times,* September 18, 1991, July 30, 1992, March 16, 1993; *Washington Post,* October 29, 1991; Seidman, *Full Faith and Credit,* 196–97.

11. Schlesinger, *Imperial Presidency,* 332–33; Paul M. Angle, *By These Words: Great Documents of American Liberty, Selected and Placed in Their Contemporary Settings* (New York: Rand McNally, 1954), 56–61.

12. Gordon, "Understanding the S&L Mess," 65.

BIBLIOGRAPHY

GOVERNMENT DOCUMENTS AND PUBLICATIONS

Acts and Resolutions Adopted by the Legislature of Florida. Tallahassee, 1885–1911.

Acts and Resolutions of the General Assembly of the State of Georgia. Atlanta, 1888–1935.

Annual Report of the Bureau of Banking, Department of Finance of the State of Idaho. Boise, 1905–30.

Annual Report of the Comptroller of the Currency, U.S. Treasury Department. Washington, D.C.: U.S. Government Printing Office, 1888–1935.

Annual Report of the Comptroller of the State of Florida, Banking Department. Tallahassee, 1889–1935.

Annual Report of the Department of Banking of the State of Georgia. Atlanta, 1920–35.

Annual Report of the Federal Reserve Board. Washington, D.C.: U.S. Government Printing Office, 1920–32.

Annual Report of the State Bank Examiner of New Mexico. Santa Fe, 1920–30.

Applications for Appointments as Receivers of National Banks and to Other Positions in the Office of the Comptroller of the Currency, 1880–1900. National Archives, Suitland, Maryland.

Baird, Charles F. "What the Canadians Know." *GAO Journal,* Spring/Summer 1992, pp. 33–37.

Bank Examiner Papers, State Records Center and Archives, Santa Fe, New Mexico.

Bank Failure: An Evaluation of the Factors Contributing to the Failure of National Banks. Washington, D.C.: Office of the Comptroller of the Currency, 1988.

Bank Failures: Independent Audits Needed to Strengthen Internal Control and Bank Management. U.S. General Accounting Office Report, May 1989.

Biennial Report of the Attorney General, State of Florida. J. Tom Watson, Attorney General. Tallahassee, 1941–48.

Biographical Directory of the American Congress, 1774–1961. Washington, D.C.: U.S. Government Printing Office, 1961.

Budget Issues: Information on FDIC and FSLIC Notes Payable. U.S. General Accounting Office Fact Sheet, August 1988.

Bureau of Banking, Department of Finance, Idaho Historical Society, Boise, Idaho.

Card Record of Compensation Paid to Attorneys, 1898–1918. National Archives, Suitland, Maryland.

Cases Adjudicated in the Supreme Court and District Courts of Appeal of Florida, Southern Reporter, 2d. St. Paul: West Publishing, 1958–91.

City of Boca Raton Records, Boca Raton, Florida.

Civil Cases, Duval County Circuit Court, Jacksonville, Florida.

Civil Cases, Fulton County Superior Court, Atlanta, Georgia.

Civil Cases, Palm Beach County Circuit Court, West Palm Beach, Florida.

Commercial Banking: Trends in Performance from December 1976 through June 1987. U.S. General Accounting Office Report, July 1988.

Corrigan, E. Gerald. "Commercial Banking in the United States: A Look Back and a Look Ahead." *GAO Journal,* Spring/Summer 1992, pp. 10–14.

Criminal Division, Fulton County Superior Court, Atlanta, Georgia.

The Currency. U.S. Senate Document No. 161. 63d Cong., 1st sess. 1913.

Department of Banking and Finance Records, RG 20. Georgia State Archives, Atlanta, Georgia.

Dividend Schedules: 1893–1944, Comptroller of the Currency Records. National Archives, Suitland, Maryland.

Ex Parte: Ernest Amos. 112 Southern Reporter 289. *Cases Adjudicated in the Supreme Court of Florida.* Vol. 93, January Term, 1927.

Ex Parte: Ernest Amos. 114 Southern Reporter 760. *Cases Adjudicated in the Supreme Court of Florida.* Vol. 94, June Term, 1927.

Ex Parte: Ernest Amos. 129 Southern Reporter 855. *Cases Adjudicated in the Supreme Court of Florida.* Vol. 100, June Term, 1930.

Examination Reports of Insolvent National Banks, 1918–30. Records of the Comptroller of the Currency, RG 101, Division of Examinations. Washington National Record Center, Suitland, Maryland.

Explanation of Major Provisions of CS/HB 2471 Financial Institutions Regulatory Reform Act of 1992 and Regulatory Sunset Report. Florida House of Representatives, Committee on Commerce, Art Simon, Chairman. February 26, 1992.

Failed Bank: FDIC Documentation of Crossland Savings, FSB, Decision Was Inadequate. U.S. General Accounting Office Report, July 1992.

Failed Banks: FDIC's Asset Liquidation Operations. U.S. General Accounting Office Report, September 1988.

Failed Thrift: Lengthy Government Control of Sunbelt Savings Bank. U.S. General Accounting Office Report, April 1992.

Failed Thrifts: FDIC Oversight of 1988 Deals Needs Improvement. U.S. General Accounting Office Report, July 1990.

Failed Thrifts: No Compelling Evidence of a Need for the Federal Asset Disposition Association. U.S. General Accounting Office Report, December 1988.

Federal Reserve Bulletin. 1920–35.

Financial Analysis: FADA's Preliminary and Final 1987 Financial Statements. U.S. General Accounting Office Fact Sheet, August 1988.

Financial Audit: Bank Insurance Fund's 1991 and 1990 Financial Statements. U.S. General Accounting Office Report, June 1992.

Financial Audit: Federal Asset Disposition Association's 1987 Financial Statements. U.S. General Accounting Office Report, December 1988.

Financial Audit: Federal Home Loan Banks' 1987 Financial Statements. U.S. General Accounting Office Report, December 1988.

Financial Audit: Federal Savings and Loan Insurance Corporation's 1987 and 1986 Financial Statements. U.S. General Accounting Office Report, July 1988.

Financial Audit: Resolution Trust Corporation's 1991 and 1990 Financial Statements. U.S. General Accounting Office Report, June 1992.

Financial Audit: Savings Association Insurance Fund's 1990 and 1989 Financial Statements. U.S. General Accounting Office Report, January 1992.

Financial Audit: Savings Association Insurance Fund's 1991 and 1990 Financial Statements. U.S. General Accounting Office Report, June 1992.

Financial Services Industry Issues. U.S. General Accounting Office Transition Series, November 1988.

Florida Statutes, 1941–93. Tallahassee: State of Florida.

General Acts and Resolutions Adopted by the Legislature of Florida. Tallahassee, 1913–1980.

General Correspondence File of the Comptroller of the Currency, 1865–1944, Records of the Comptroller of the Currency, RG 101, Division of Insolvent National Banks. National Archives, Suitland, Maryland.

Georgia Bank Charters and Amendments, 1925–32, Book L. Secretary of State Records, Georgia State Archives, Atlanta, Georgia.

Georgia State Bank Charter Amendments, Bank Charters, and Amendments, 1920–30. Secretary of State Records, Georgia State Archives, Atlanta, Georgia.

Georgia State Bank Charters, Certificates of Incorporation, Bank and Trust Companies, 1920–39. Secretary of State Records, Georgia State Archives, Atlanta, Georgia.

Governors: 1929–71, RG 102. Doyle Elam Carlton Administrative Correspondence, 1929–32, Series 204, Department of State. Florida State Archives, Tallahassee, Florida.

Governor's Office Records. Georgia State Archives, Atlanta, Georgia.

Guide to the National Archives of the United States. Washington, D.C.: National Archives and Records Administration, 1987.

High Yield Bonds: Nature of the Market and Effect on Federally Insured Institutions. U.S. General Accounting Office Hearing, May 1988.

Impeachment Resolution against Gerald Lewis, Filed by Representative Jeff Huenink in the Florida House of Representatives, March 12, 1992.

Indictment of Ernest Amos, September 22, 1926. Supreme Court of Florida Records, RG 970, Series 49, Case Files of Civil and Criminal Appeals, Department of State, Florida State Archives, Tallahassee, Florida.

Lacovara, Philip A. "Modernize Banking . . . But with Care." *GAO Journal,* Spring/Summer 1992, pp. 15–20.

Letters from the Comptroller of the Currency to Receivers, July 1, 1884–November 30, 1934. National Archives, Suitland, Maryland.

Letters from the Comptroller of the Currency to Receivers, January 7, 1925–November 26, 1934. National Archives, Suitland, Maryland.

Letters from Receivers, 1880–85 and 1902–5, Comptroller of the Currency Records. National Archives, Suitland, Maryland.

List of Attorneys Showing Trusts and Fees, 1899, Comptroller of the Currency Records. National Archives, Suitland, Maryland.

Mayo, Nathan, Florida Commissioner of Agriculture. *Florida: An Advancing State, 1907–1917–1927.* Tallahassee: 1928.

Miscellaneous Administrative Papers, 1884–1930, Comptroller of the Currency Records. National Archives, Suitland, Maryland.

Miscellaneous Correspondence File of the Comptroller of the Currency, 1883–1926. National Archives, Suitland, Maryland.

Miscellaneous Letters of Receivers, Attorneys, and Examiners, 1893–1907. National Archives, Suitland, Maryland.

Moler, Robert M. *Georgia Department of Banking and Finance: Historical Review with Perspective on the Future, 1920–1982.* December 31, 1981. Department of Banking and Finance Records, RG 20, Georgia State Archives, Atlanta, Georgia.

The National Bank Act as Amended and Other Laws Relating to National Banks. Washington, D.C.: U.S. Government Printing Office, 1920–35.

The New Mexico Blue Book. Santa Fe: Office of Secretary of State, 1919–27.

Obligations Limitation: Resolution Trust Corporation's Compliance as of December 31, 1990. U.S. General Accounting Office Report, October 1991.

Obligations Limitation: Resolution Trust Corporation's Compliance as of March 31, 1991. U.S. General Accounting Office Report, March 1992.

Official Letters of the Comptroller of the Currency, October 28, 1898–February 26, 1904. National Archives, Suitland, Maryland.

Price, William. "A Nonbanker's Perspective on Banking Reform." *GAO Journal,* Spring/Summer 1992, pp. 29–32.

Probate Division, Duval County Circuit Court. Jacksonville, Florida.

Receivers' Final Reports, 1913–44, Comptroller of the Currency Records. National Archives, Suitland, Maryland.

Receivers' First Report Books, 1915–44, Comptroller of the Currency Records. National Archives, Suitland, Maryland.

Receivers' Quarterly Reports, 1913–44, Comptroller of the Currency Records. National Archives, Suitland, Maryland.

Receivership Records Sent to the Comptroller of the Currency by Receivers, 1865–1927. National Archives, Suitland, Maryland.

Records of the Division of Insolvent National Banks, Comptroller of the Currency Records, RG 101. National Archives, Suitland, Maryland.

Records of the Examining Division, Comptroller of the Currency Records, RG 101. Washington National Records Center, Suitland, Maryland.

Register of Letters from the Comptroller of the Currency to Receivers, 1900–1901 and 1909–10. National Archives, Suitland, Maryland.

Report of Budget and Investigating Commission and Governor's Transmittal. 1919. Summary Commission Reports, Box 1, Governor's Office Records. Georgia State Archives, Atlanta, Georgia.

Report to the President of the United States by the Director of the Bureau of Budget. Washington, D.C.: U.S. Government Printing Office, 1922.

A Review of the Regulation of Banking and Securities in Florida. Florida Senate Committee on Governmental Operations, Senator John Vogt, Chairman. March 1986.

Robertson, Ross M. *The Comptroller and Bank Supervision: A Historical Appraisal.* Washington, D.C.: Office of the Comptroller of the Currency, 1968.

Secretary of State Records. Georgia State Archives, Atlanta, Georgia.

Semi-Official Letters of the Comptroller of the Currency, December 30, 1897–June 2, 1899. National Archives, Suitland, Maryland.

Shareholders Agents' Fidelity Bonds and Court Orders, 1865–1945. National Archives, Suitland, Maryland.

Simmons, Craig A., and Stephen C. Swaim. "Girding for Competition." *GAO Journal,* Spring/Summer 1992, pp. 3–9.

Special Acts Adopted by the Legislature of Florida. Tallahassee, 1913–35.

State Comptroller Records, RG 350, Series 64, Closed Bank Records, 1898–1942, Department of State. Florida State Archives, Tallahassee, Florida.

State Comptroller Records, RG 350, Series 1007, Closed Bank Ledgers, 1889–1949, Department of State. Florida State Archives, Tallahassee, Florida.

Statement Showing Condition of Insolvent National Banks, Litigation, Cost of Administration and Fees Paid to Receivers, and Attorneys, January 1898. National Archives, Suitland, Maryland.

State Treasurer Records. Georgia State Archives, Atlanta, Georgia.

Summary Tabular Statements of Receiverships, 1921–26, Comptroller of the Currency Records. National Archives, Suitland, Maryland.

Supreme Court of Florida Records, RG 970, Series 49, Case Files of Civil and Criminal Appeals, Department of State. Florida State Archives, Tallahassee, Florida.

Telegrams from the Comptroller of the Currency to Receivers, January 6, 1897–November 30, 1934. National Archives, Suitland, Maryland.

Thrift Industry: Trends in Thrift Industry Performance, December 1977 through June 1987. U.S. General Accounting Office Report, May 1988.

Thrift Resolutions: FSLIC 1988 and 1989 Assistance Agreement Costs Subject to Continuing Uncertainties. U.S. General Accounting Office Report, August 1992.

Todd, Walker F. *Lessons of the Past and Prospects for the Future in Lender of Last Resort Theory.* Working Paper 8805. Federal Reserve Bank of Cleveland, August 1988.

U.S. Bureau of the Census. *Thirteenth Census of the United States, 1910, Population, II.* Washington, D.C.: U.S. Government Printing Office, 1913.

U.S. Bureau of the Census. *Fourteenth Census of the United States, 1920, Population, III.* Washington, D.C.: U.S. Government Printing Office, 1922.

U.S. District Court Records, Northern District of Florida. Federal Courthouse, Jacksonville, Florida.

U.S. District Court Records, RG 21, Southern District of Florida, 1828–1943. National Archives, Atlanta, Georgia.

U.S. District Court Records, RG 21, Northern District of Georgia, 1847–1942. National Archives, Atlanta, Georgia.

U.S. Office of the Comptroller of the Currency, RG 101, Records of the Division of Insolvent National Banks, 1865–1950. National Archives, Suitland, Maryland.

U.S. Office of the Comptroller of the Currency, RG 101, Records of the Examining Division, 1863–1935. Washington National Records Center, Suitland, Maryland.

Wexler, Bernard. "How Did Glass-Steagall Happen?" *GAO Journal,* Spring/Summer 1992, pp. 21–28.

Wolf, Frederick D. *Failed Financial Institutions: Reasons, Costs, Remedies and Unresolved Issues.* U.S. General Accounting Office Testimony, January 13, 1989.

———. *The Federal Savings and Loan Insurance Corporation: Current Financial Condition and Outlook.* U.S. General Accounting Office Testimony, May 19, 1988.

———. *The Federal Savings and Loan Insurance Corporation's Use of Notes and Assistance Guarantees.* U.S. General Accounting Office Testimony, September 8, 1988.

MANUSCRIPT COLLECTIONS AND HISTORICAL SOCIETIES

Boca Raton Historical Society. Town Hall, Boca Raton, Florida.

Bryan, William Jennings. Papers. Library of Congress, Washington, D.C.

Dawes, Charles G. Papers. Special Collection Department, Northwestern University Library, Evanston, Illinois.

Dawson City Museum, Old Territorial Administration Building, Dawson City, Yukon Territory.

Fisher, Carl. Papers. Historical Association of Southern Florida, Miami, Florida.

Florida Collection. Dorothy Dodd Room, State Library of Florida, Tallahassee, Florida.

Florida Supreme Court Historical Society. Supreme Court Building, Tallahassee, Florida.

Frohock, John M. Papers. Historical Association of Southern Florida, Miami, Florida.

Gay, Clarence M. Campaign Literature, 1947–48, RG 350, Series 426, Department of State, Florida State Archives, Tallahassee, Florida.

Gray, Robert Andrew. Papers. Manuscript Collections, Department of State, Florida State Archives, Tallahassee, Florida.

Historical Society of Palm Beach County. West Palm Beach, Florida.

Hodges, James B. Papers. P. K. Yonge Library of Florida History, University of Florida, Gainesville, Florida.

Jacksonville Historical Society. Jacksonville University, Jacksonville, Florida.

Knight, Peter O. Papers. P. K. Yonge Library of Florida History, University of Florida, Gainesville, Florida.

Knott Family Papers. Manuscript Collections, Department of State, Florida State Archives, Tallahassee, Florida.

Lewis Family Papers. Manuscript Collections, Department of State, Florida State Archives, Tallahassee, Florida.

Lewis State Bank Records. Manuscript Collections, Department of State, Florida State Archives, Tallahassee, Florida.

Merrick, George Edgar. Papers. Historical Association of Southern Florida, Miami, Florida.

Robert Manning Strozier Library. Special Collections Department, Florida State University, Tallahassee, Florida.

Sherman, Lawrence Y. Papers. Illinois State Historical Library, Springfield, Illinois.

Special Collections Department, Otto G. Richter Library, University of Miami, Coral Gables, Florida.

NEWSPAPERS

Atlanta Constitution. 1920–30.
Chicago Tribune. 1900–1945.
Daytona Beach News-Journal. 1992.
Daytona Morning Journal. 1920–35.
Douglas Enterprise. 1926.
Florida Times-Union. 1920–32, 1989, 1992.
Fort Lauderdale Sun-Sentinel. 1986, 1989, 1992.
Gainesville Sun, 1992.
Groveland Graphic. 1924, 1933.
Illinois State Journal. 1928.
Jacksonville Journal. 1920–32.
Klondike Nugget. 1898–1900.
Lakeland Ledger. 1992.
Lake Worth Herald. 1923.
Lake Worth Leader. 1923, 1927.
Miami Daily Metropolis. 1900–1910.
Miami Daily News. 1902–32, 1957, 1964.
Miami Herald. 1900–1932, 1942, 1952, 1964, 1974, 1985–87, 1989, 1992.
Miami Riviera of Coral Gables. 1925–27.
New York Herald Tribune. 1890–1932.
New York News. 1972.
New York Sun. 1915.
New York Times. 1890–1952, 1989–93.
Orlando Sentinel. 1920–32, 1973, 1985, 1986, 1989, 1992.
Palm Beach Daily News. 1989, 1990.

Palm Beach Independent. 1925–27.
Palm Beach Post. 1916–32, 1940, 1980, 1989, 1991, 1992.
Palm Beach Times. 1922–51.
St. Augustine Evening Record. 1920–32.
St. Petersburg Evening Independent. 1920–32.
St. Petersburg Times. 1920–32, 1985, 1986, 1989, 1991, 1992.
Sarasota Herald Tribune. 1920–32, 1992.
Tallahassee Daily Democrat. 1889–1945.
Tallahassee Democrat. 1985, 1986, 1989, 1992.
Tampa Morning Tribune. 1915–32, 1950, 1954.
Tampa Tribune. 1978, 1986, 1989, 1990, 1991, 1992.
Tropical Sun. 1925–37.
Wall Street Journal. 1890–1950, 1985–87, 1989–93.
Washington Post. 1890–1950, 1989–93.

PERIODICALS AND ARTICLES

Adams, James Ring. "Tallahassee Vice?" *Forbes* 137 (May 5, 1986): 54, 56, 58.

Anthony, A. P. "Report of Chairman, State Bank Section." *Southern Banker,* April 1925, p. 51.

Anthony, J. R. "Annual Address of the President." *Southern Banker,* April 1925, pp. 4–6.

"Atlanta Business Men Who Began on the Farm." *Atlanta Constitution Journal Magazine,* February 1, 1925.

Babson, Roger W. "Does the Florida 'Boom' Hinge on Business Conditions?" *Forbes* 17 (October 15, 1925): 9–11, 40, 44; 17 (November 1, 1925): 12–14, 46, 48.

Ball, Edward. "Group Banking: A Florida Success Story." *Burroughs Clearing House* 45 (April 1961): 44–46, 100–102.

Boyd, Mark F. "A Century of Confidence and Conservatism Culminates in the Lewis State Bank of Tallahassee, Florida." Supplement of *Florida Historical Quarterly* 34 (April 1956): 1–51.

Burnett, Gene. "Cool Leadership during Florida's Banking Crisis." *Florida Trend* 23 (June 1980): 103–5.

Carosso, Vincent P. "The Wall Street Money Trust from Pujo through Medina." *Business History Review* 47 (Winter 1973): 421–37.

Commercial and Financial Chronicle. Vols. 116–54. New York: William B. Dana, 1923–41.

Curl, Donald W., ed. "Clarence Geist and Boca Raton." *Spanish River Papers* 16 (1987–88).

Doti, Lynne Pierson. "Nationwide Branching: Some Lessons from California." In *Essays in Economic and Business History: Selected Papers from the Economic and Business Historical Society, 1987*, ed. Edwin J. Perkins. Vol. 6, pp. 141–60. Los Angeles: History Department, University of Southern California, 1988.

Earman, Joe L. "James Rembert Anthony." *Present Truth Messenger* 29 (November 27, 1924): 25–26.

———. "J. R. Anthony." *Palm Beach Independent,* November 26, 1926.

Edgel, Ralph L. *A Brief History of Banking in New Mexico, 1870–1959.* Albuquerque: Bureau of Business Research, University of New Mexico, 1962.

Essary, J. Frederick. "Have Faith in Florida!" *New Republic* 44 (October 14, 1925): 194–96.

"Fact and Comment." *Forbes* 17 (February 15, 1926): 24–28.

"The Florida Madness." *New Republic* 45 (January 27, 1926): 258–59.

Flynn, John T. "Inside the R.F.C.: An Adventure in Secrecy." *Harper's Monthly Magazine* 166 (January 1933): 161–69.

Garrett, Garet. "Why Some Banks Fail and Others Don't." *Saturday Evening Post* 205 (May 20, 1933): 3–5, 67–70, 72.

George, Paul S. "Brokers, Binders, and Builders: Greater Miami's Boom of the Mid-1920s." *Florida Historical Quarterly* 65 (July 1986): 27–51.

Gordon, John Steele. "Understanding the S&L Mess." *American Heritage* 42 (February–March 1991): 49–51, 54, 56, 58–60, 62–63, 65–66, 68.

Hardee, Cary A. "The Banker and the Government." *Southern Banker,* May 1922, pp. 12–13.

Hawes, Leland. "Tampa Lawyer Helped to Defeat Comptroller." *Tampa Tribune,* December 16, 1990.

Jordan, John S. "What's Left in Florida: Fevered Speculation Gone, Stable Values Remain." *World's Work* 52 (September 1926): 571–77.

Knott, James R. "The Anthony Saga, 1895–1980." *Palm Beach Post,* December 7, 1980.

"The Lewis Family and Its Sprightly Old-Time Bank." *Burroughs Clearing House* 51 (July 1967): 32–33, 67–68.

Lewis, Frederick. "The Banker Who Went Mad." *Liberty* 17 (March 30, 1940): 37–41.

Longman, Phillip. "Where Was Gerald?" *Florida Trend* 33 (August 1990): 28–37.

McEvoy, George. "Wilson Mizner: Now We See Him." *Orlando Sentinel Florida Magazine,* January 14, 1973.

McFadden, Haynes. "Chain Bank Crash in Georgia." *American Bankers Association Journal* 19 (September 1926): 137–38.

McIver, Stuart. "The Way We Were." *Sunshine,* March 4, 1984. Historical Society of Palm Beach County, West Palm Beach, Florida.

Mackle, Elliott. "Two-Way Stretch: Some Dichotomies in the Advertising of Florida as the Boom Collapsed." *Tequesta* 33 (1973): 17–29.

McMorrow, Thomas. "To Let on Flagler Street." *Saturday Evening Post* 198 (February 6, 1926): 16–17, 94, 96, 98, 101–2.

Martin, Sidney W. "Flagler's Associates in East Florida Developments." *Florida Historical Quarterly* 26 (January 1948): 256–63.

Matheson, Jean. "Wilson Mizner: 'The first hundred years are the hardest.'" *Palm Beach Today*, June 14, 1991.

"Mizner Came to Florida to Die." *Florida Trend* 16 (September 1973): 94–96, 98–99.

Neeley, Julia Whitfield, and Randolph Whitfield. "Our Father, James Bryan Whitfield." *Florida Supreme Court Historical Society Review* 3 (1987–88): 1–3, 10–12.

Popejoy, Tom L. "Analysis of the Causes of Bank Failures in New Mexico, 1920 to 1925." *University of New Mexico Bulletin* 1 (October 1, 1931): 7–46.

"Report of Syndicate Manager, April 1, 1928," in the *Spanish River Papers* 16 (1987–88).

Roberts, Kenneth L. "Florida Diversions." *Saturday Evening Post* 198 (February 20, 1926): 24–25, 141–42, 145.

———. "Florida Fever." *Saturday Evening Post* 198 (December 5, 1925): 6–7, 207, 209–10.

———. "Good Warm Stuff." *Saturday Evening Post* 198 (January 9, 1926): 12–13, 78, 80, 82.

———. "Tropical Parasites." *Saturday Evening Post* 198 (January 2, 1926): 12–13, 78, 80, 83.

Rukeyser, M. S. "Is Florida Coming Back? In Speculation, No: In Substantial Progress, Yes." *World's Work* 55 (March 1928): 471–81.

Schweikart, Larry. "Early Banking in New Mexico from the Civil War to the Roaring Twenties." *New Mexico Historical Review* 63 (January 1988): 1–24.

Sessa, Frank B. "Miami in 1926." *Tequesta* 16 (1956): 15–36.

Shelby, Gertrude Mathews. "Florida Frenzy." *Harper's Monthly Magazine* 152 (January 1926): 177–86.

Simons, Teresa. "Banking on Secrecy." *Washington Monthly* 22 (December 1990): 31–37.

Singer, Paris. Foreword to *Florida Architecture of Addison Mizner.* New York: William Helburn, 1928.

Tarbell, Ida M. "Florida—And Then What? Impressions of the Boom." *McCall's Magazine* 53 (May 1926): 6–7, 57, 89–92.

———. Introduction to *Florida Architecture of Addison Mizner.* New York: William Helburn, 1928.

Thorndike, Joseph J., Jr. "Addison Mizner—What He Did for Palm Beach." *Smithsonian* 16 (September 1985): 112–16, 118, 120–23.

Tindall, George B. "Bubble in the Sun." *American Heritage* 16 (August 1965): 76–83, 109–11.

Townsend, Reginald T. "The Gold Rush to Florida." *World's Work* 50 (June 1925): 179–86.

Vanderblue, Homer B. "The Florida Land Boom." *Journal of Land and Public Utility Economics* 3 (May 1927): 113–31.

Vickers, Raymond B. "Sleazy Banking in the '20s and Today." *Wall Street Journal,* May 23, 1989.

Villard, Henry S. "Florida Aftermath." *Nation* 126 (June 6, 1928): 635–36.

BOOKS AND UNPUBLISHED WORKS

Acheson, Sam Hanna. *Joe Bailey: The Last Democrat*. New York: Macmillan, 1932.

Adams, James Ring. *The Big Fix: Inside the S&L Scandal*. New York: John Wiley & Sons, 1990 and 1991.

Akin, Edward N. *Flagler: Rockefeller Partner and Florida Baron*. Kent, Ohio: Kent State University Press, 1988.

Aldrich, Clara Elizabeth. "The History of Banking in Idaho." M.A. thesis, University of Washington, 1940.

Allen, Frederick Lewis. *The Big Change: America Transforms Itself 1900–1950*. New York: Harper & Brothers, 1952.

———. *Only Yesterday: An Informal History of the Nineteen-Twenties*. New York: Harper & Brothers, 1931.

———. *Since Yesterday*. New York: Harper & Brothers, 1940.

Angle, Paul M. *By These Words: Great Documents of American Liberty, Selected and Placed in Their Contemporary Settings*. New York: Rand McNally, 1954.

Anthony, James Rembert. "Anthony Brothers on the East Coast: 1890–1936." 1936. P. K. Yonge Library of Florida History, University of Florida, Gainesville, Florida.

Armstrong, Nevill A. D. *Yukon Yesterdays: Thirty Years of Adventure in the Klondike*. London: John Long, 1936.

Ashley, Kathryne B. *George E. Merrick and Coral Gables, Florida*. Coral Gables: Crystal Bay Publishers, 1985.

Ashton, Jacqueline. *Boca Raton: From Pioneer Days to the Fabulous Twenties*. Boca Raton: Dedication Press, 1979.

Bacon, Eve. *Orlando: A Centennial History*. Vol. 2. Chuluota, Fla.: Mickler House, 1977.

Ballinger, Kenneth. *Miami Millions: The Dance of the Dollars in the Great Florida Land Boom of 1925*. Miami: Franklin Press, 1936.

Barrett, Glen. *Idaho Banking, 1863–1976*. Boise: Boise State University Press, 1976.

Batra, Ravi. *The Great Depression of 1990*. New York: Simon & Schuster, 1987.

———. *Surviving the Great Depression of 1990*. New York: Dell Publishing, 1988.

Beach, Rex E. *The Miracle of Coral Gables*. New York: Currier & Harford, 1926.

Beal, Merrill D., and Merle W. Wells. *History of Idaho*. Vol. 2. New York: Lewis Historical Publishing Company, 1959.

Berton, Pierre. *Klondike: The Last Great Gold Rush, 1896–1899*. Toronto: Penguin Books, 1990.

Blackford, Mansel G., and K. Austin Kerr. *Business Enterprise in American History*. Boston: Houghton Mifflin, 1986.

Blackman, E. V. *Miami and Dade County, Florida: Its Settlement, Progress and Achievement*. Washington, D.C.: Victor Rainbolt, 1921.

The Blue Book: A Social Register of Jacksonville, Florida. St. Augustine: Record Company, 1923–24, 1929–31, 1933–35.

Boller, Paul F., Jr. *Presidential Campaigns*. New York: Oxford University Press, 1985.

Bowers, Claude G. *Beveridge and the Progressive Era*. New York: Literary Guild, 1932.

Brandeis, Louis D. *Letters of Louis D. Brandeis*. Edited by Melvin I. Urofsky and David W. Levy. Albany: State University of New York Press, 1971.

———. *Other People's Money and How the Bankers Use It*. New York: Frederick A. Stokes, 1932.

Bronson, William, with Richard Reinhardt. *The Last Grand Adventure*. New York: McGraw-Hill, 1977.

Bryan, William Jennings, and Mary Bryan. *Memoirs of William Jennings Bryan*. Philadelphia: John C. Winston, 1925.

Burke, John. *Rogue's Progress: The Fabulous Adventures of Wilson Mizner*. New York: G. P. Putnam's Sons, 1975.

Carosso, Vincent P. *Investment Banking in America: A History*. Cambridge, Mass.: Harvard University Press, 1970.

———. *The Morgans: Private International Bankers, 1854–1913*. Cambridge, Mass.: Harvard University Press, 1987.

Cartinhous, Gaines Thomson. *Branch, Group and Chain Banking*. New York: Macmillan, 1931.

Cash, William T. *History of the Democratic Party in Florida*. Tallahassee: Florida Democratic Historical Foundation, 1936.

———. *The Story of Florida*. Vol. 3. New York: American Historical Society, 1938.

Chandler, David Leon. *Henry Flagler: The Astonishing Life and Times of the Visionary Robber Baron Who Founded Florida*. New York: Macmillan, 1986.

Cole, Terrence. *E. T. Barnette: The Strange Story of the Man Who Founded Fairbanks*. Anchorage: Alaska Northwest Publishing Company, 1981.

Coletta, Paolo E. *William Jennings Bryan*. Vol. 3: *Political Puritan, 1915–1925*. Lincoln: University of Nebraska Press, 1969.

Cook, James F. *Governors of Georgia*. Huntsville, Ala.: Strode, 1980.

Coolidge, Calvin. *Autobiography of Calvin Coolidge*. New York: Cosmopolitan Book Corporation, 1929.

———. *The Price of Freedom: Speeches and Addresses*. New York: Scribner, 1924.

Crooks, James B. *Jacksonville after the Fire, 1901–1919: A New South City*. Jacksonville: University of North Florida Press, 1991.

Curl, Donald W. *Mizner's Florida: American Resort Architecture*. Cambridge, Mass.: MIT Press, 1985.

———. *Palm Beach County: An Illustrated History*. Northridge, Calif.: Windsor Publications, 1986.

Curl, Donald W., and John P. Johnson. *Boca Raton: A Pictorial History*. Virginia Beach, Va.: Donning Company, 1990.

Cushman, Dan. *The Great North Trail: America's Route of the Ages*. New York: McGraw-Hill, 1966.

Daniels, Jonathan. *Ordeal of Ambition: Jefferson, Hamilton, Burr*. Garden City, N.Y.: Doubleday, 1970.

Davis, T. Frederick. *History of Jacksonville, Florida, and Vicinity, 1513 to 1924*. St. Augustine: Florida Historical Society, 1925.

Dawes, Charles G. *The Banking System of the United States and Its Relation to the Money and Business of the Country*. Chicago: Rand McNally, 1894.

———. *Essays and Speeches*. Boston: Houghton Mifflin, 1915.

———. *The First Year of the Budget of the United States*. New York: Harper & Brothers, 1923.

———. *Journal as Ambassador to Great Britain*. New York: Macmillan, 1939.

———. *A Journal of the Great War*. Boston: Houghton Mifflin, 1921.

———. *A Journal of the McKinley Years*. Chicago: Lakeside Press, R. R. Donnelley & Sons, 1950.

———. *Notes as Vice President, 1928–1929*. Boston: Little, Brown, 1935.

Dolbeare, Harwood B., and Merle O. Barnd. *Forewarnings of Bank Failure: A Comparative Study of the Statements of Certain Failed and Successful Florida State Banks, 1922–1928*. Gainesville: University of Florida Press, 1931.

Doti, Lynne Pierson, and Larry Schweikart. *Banking in the American West: From the Gold Rush to Deregulation*. Norman: University of Oklahoma Press, 1991.

Dovell, J. E. *History of Banking in Florida, 1828–1954*. Orlando: Florida Bankers Association, 1955.

Earman, Joe S., and Betty Earman. *Big Joe Earman*. Vero Beach: Earman Family, 1977.

Eichler, Ned. *The Thrift Debacle*. Berkeley: University of California Press, 1989.

Faulkner, Harold U. *From Versailles to the New Deal*. New Haven: Yale University Press, 1950.

Flink, James J. *The Car Culture*. Cambridge, Mass.: MIT Press, 1975.

Flynt, Wayne. *Cracker Messiah: Governor Sidney J. Catts of Florida*. Baton Rouge: Louisiana State University Press, 1977.

———. *Duncan Upshaw Fletcher: Dixie's Reluctant Progressive*. Tallahassee: Florida State University Press, 1971.

Folsom, Merrill. *More Great American Mansions and Their Stories*. New York: Hastings House, 1967.

Freidel, Frank Burt. *Franklin D. Roosevelt*. Boston: Little, Brown, 1952.

Friedman, Milton, and Anna Jacobson Schwartz. *The Great Contraction, 1929–1933*. Princeton: Princeton University Press, 1965.

Galbraith, John Kenneth. *Economics in Perspective: A Critical History*. Boston: Houghton Mifflin, 1987.

———. *The Great Crash, 1929*. Boston: Houghton Mifflin, 1972.

Garrett, Franklin M. *Atlanta and Environs*. Vol. 2. Athens: University of Georgia Press, 1988.

Gates, John D. *The du Pont Family*. New York: Doubleday, 1979.

Goedeken, Edward Adolph. "Charles G. Dawes in War and Peace, 1917–1922." Ph.D. dissertation, University of Kansas, 1984.

Hession, Charles H., and Hyman Sardy. *Ascent to Affluence: A History of American Economic Development*. Boston: Allyn and Bacon, 1969.

Hicks, John D. *Republican Ascendancy, 1921–1933*. New York: Harper & Row, 1960.

Hofstadter, Richard. *The American Political Tradition and the Men Who Made It*. New York: Knopf, 1970.

———. *The Paranoid Style in American Politics*. New York: Knopf, 1966.

Holcomb, Bob Charles. "Senator Joe Bailey: Two Decades of Controversy." Ph.D. dissertation, Texas Technological College, 1968.

Hoover, Herbert. *The Memoirs of Herbert Hoover: The Great Depression, 1929–1941*. New York: Macmillan, 1952.

———. *The State Papers and Other Public Writings of Herbert Hoover*. Edited by William Starr Myers. Garden City, N.Y.: Doubleday, Doran, 1934.

Hoover, Herbert, and Calvin Coolidge. *Campaign Speeches of 1932*. Garden City, N.Y.: Doubleday, Doran, 1933.

Hunt, William R. *North of 53: The Wild Days of the Alaska-Yukon Mining Frontier, 1870–1914*. New York: Macmillan, 1974.

Hutchinson, William Thomas. *Lowden of Illinois: The Life of Frank O. Lowden*. Chicago: University of Chicago Press, 1957.

James, Marquis. *Alfred I. du Pont: The Family Rebel*. New York: Bobbs-Merrill, 1941.

Johnston, Alva. *The Legendary Mizners*. New York: Farrar, Straus and Young, 1953.

Jones, Jesse H., with Edward Angly. *Fifty Billion Dollars: My Thirteen Years with the RFC (1932–1945)*. New York: Macmillan, 1951.

Kearns, Jack "Doc," with Oscar Fraley. *The Million Dollar Gate*. New York: Macmillan, 1966.

Kennedy, Susan Estabrook. *The Banking Crisis of 1933*. Lexington: University Press of Kentucky, 1973.

Kinney, Henry. *Once Upon a Time: The Legend of the Boca Raton Hotel and Club*. Miami: Arvida Corporation, 1974.

Koenig, Louis W. *Bryan: A Political Biography of William Jennings Bryan*. New York: G. P. Putnam's Sons, 1971.

Kormendi, Roger C., Victor L. Bernard, S. Craig Pirrong, and Edward A. Snyder. *Crisis Resolution in the Thrift Industry: A Mid America Institute Report*. Boston: Kluwer Academic Publisher, 1989.

Kwitny, Jonathan. *The Fountain Pen Conspiracy*. New York: Knopf, 1973.

Leach, Paul Roscoe. *That Man Dawes*. Chicago: Reilly & Lee, 1930.

Leuchtenburg, William E. *The Perils of Prosperity, 1914–32*. Chicago: University of Chicago Press, 1958.

Levine, Lawrence W. *Defender of the Faith, William Jennings Bryan: The Last Decade, 1915–1925*. New York: Oxford University Press, 1965.

Lewis, Sinclair. *Babbitt*. New York: New American Library, 1961.

Lowy, Martin. *High Rollers: Inside the Savings and Loan Debacle*. New York: Praeger, 1991.

Lucia, Ellis. *Klondike Kate: The Life and Legend of Kitty Rockwell, The Queen of the Yukon*. New York: Hastings House, 1962.

McCraw, Thomas K. *The Prophets of Regulation*. Cambridge, Mass.: Harvard University Press, 1984.

McDonald, Forrest. *Insull*. Chicago: University of Chicago Press, 1962.

McDonnell, Victoria Harden. "The Businessman's Politician: A Study of the Administration of John Welborn Martin, 1925–1929." M.A. thesis, University of Florida, 1968.

McIver, Stuart B. *Fort Lauderdale and Broward County*. Woodland Hills, Calif.: Windsor Publications, 1983.

———. *Yesterday's Palm Beach*. Miami: E. A. Seemann, 1976.

McNeer, May. *The Alaska Gold Rush*. New York: Random House, 1960.

Maggin, Donald L. *Bankers, Builders, Knaves, and Thieves: The $300 Million Scam at ESM*. Chicago: Contemporary Books, 1989.

Malin, James C. *The United States after the World War*. Boston: Ginn and Company, 1979.

Martindale's American Law Directory. New York: Martindale's American Law Directory, 1930.

The Martindale-Hubbell Law Directory. New York: Martindale's American Law Directory, 1929 and 1932.

Martinsen, Ella Lung. *Trail to North Star Gold.* Portland: Metropolitan Press, 1969.

Mason, Alpheus Thomas. *Brandeis: A Free Man's Life.* New York: Viking Press, 1946.

Mayer, Martin. *The Greatest-Ever Bank Robbery: The Collapse of the Savings and Loan Industry.* New York: Charles Scribner's Sons, 1990.

Mitchell, Broadus. *Depression Decade: From New Era through New Deal, 1929–1941.* New York: Harper & Row, 1969.

Mizner, Addison. *The Many Mizners.* New York: Sears, 1932.

Moos, Malcolm Charles. *The Republicans: A History of Their Party.* New York: Random House, 1956.

Morris, Allen. *The Florida Handbook: 1949–1950.* Tallahassee: Peninsular Publishing Company, 1950.

————. *The Florida Handbook.* 3d ed. Tallahassee: Peninsular Publishing Company, 1952.

————. *The Florida Handbook: 1977–1978.* Tallahassee: Peninsular Publishing Company, 1977.

————. *The Florida Handbook: 1981–1982.* Tallahassee: Peninsular Publishing Company, 1981.

————. *The Florida Handbook: 1987–1988.* Tallahassee: Peninsular Publishing Company, 1987.

Muir, Helen. *Miami U.S.A.* New York: Holt, 1953.

The National Cyclopaedia of American Biography Being the History of the United States. Vols. 3, 5, 15, and 30. New York: James T. White and Company, 1893, 1916, and 1943.

Nolan, David. *Fifty Feet in Paradise: The Booming of Florida.* San Diego: Harcourt Brace Jovanovich, 1984.

O'Connor, Richard. *High Jinks on the Klondike.* Indianapolis: Bobbs-Merrill, 1954.

Orr-Cahall, Anona Christina. "An Identification and Discussion of the Architecture and Decorative Arts of Addison Mizner (1872–1933)." Ph.D. dissertation, Yale University, 1979.

O'Shea, James. *The Daisy Chain: How Borrowed Billions Sank a Texas S&L.* New York: Pocket Books, 1991.

O'Sullivan, John, and Edward F. Keuchel. *American Economic History: From Abundance to Constraint.* New York: Markus Wiener, 1989.

Pancake, John S. *Thomas Jefferson and Alexander Hamilton.* Woodbury, N.Y.: Barron's Educational Series, 1974.

Peters, Thelma. *Miami 1909: With Excerpts from Fannie Clemons' Diary.* Miami: Banyan Books, 1984.

Pilzer, Paul Zane, with Robert Deitz. *Other People's Money: The Inside Story of the S&L Mess.* New York: Simon and Schuster, 1989.

Pinney, Charles Bartlett. "The Effects of the Real Estate Boom on Florida State Banks." M.A. thesis, University of Florida, Gainesville, 1934.

Pizzo, Stephen, Mary Fricker, and Paul Muolo. *Inside Job: The Looting of America's Savings and Loans*. New York: Harper Perennial, 1991.

Pogue, Jan. *To Wield a Mighty Influence: The Story of Banking in Georgia*. Atlanta: Corporate Stories, 1992.

Polk's Bankers Encyclopedia. New York: Bankers Encyclopedia Co., 1920–35.

Polk's Jacksonville City Directory. Jacksonville: R. L. Polk, 1918, 1921, 1922, 1926, 1930–31, 1935–42.

Poor's Register of Directors of the United States: 1929. New York: Poor's Publishing Company, 1929.

Pratt, Theodore. *The Story of Boca Raton*. St. Petersburg: Great Outdoors, 1963.

———. *That Was Palm Beach*. St. Petersburg: Great Outdoors, 1968.

Remini, Robert V. *Andrew Jackson*. New York: Harper & Row, 1969.

Schlesinger, Arthur M., Jr. *The Age of Jackson*. Boston: Little, Brown, 1950.

———. *The Age of Roosevelt: The Crisis of the Old Order, 1919–1933*. Boston: Houghton Mifflin, 1957.

———. *The Imperial Presidency*. Boston: Houghton Mifflin, 1973.

Seidman, L. William. *Full Faith and Credit: The Great S&L Debacle and Other Washington Sagas*. New York: Times Books, 1993.

Sessa, Frank Bowman. "Real Estate Expansion and Boom in Miami and Its Environs during the 1920's." Ph.D. dissertation, University of Pittsburgh, 1950.

Sherman, Richard Garrett. "Charles G. Dawes: An Entrepreneurial Biography, 1865–1951." Ph.D. dissertation, University of Iowa, 1960.

Shirer, William L. *The Rise and Fall of the Third Reich: A History of Nazi Germany*. New York: Simon and Schuster, 1960.

Smith, Rixey, and Norman Beasley. *Carter Glass: A Biography*. New York: Longmans, Green, 1939.

Soule, George H. *Prosperity Decade: From War to Depression, 1917–1929*. New York: Harper & Row, 1947.

Sprague, Irvine H. *Bailout: An Insider's Account of Bank Failures and Rescues*. New York: Basic Books, 1986.

Stewart, James B. *Den of Thieves*. New York: Simon and Schuster, 1991.

Sullivan, Edward Dean. *The Fabulous Wilson Mizner*. New York: Henkle, 1935.

Sullivan, Mark. *Our Times*, Vol. 6: *The Twenties*. New York: Charles Scribner's Sons, 1935.

Tebeau, Charlton W. *A History of Florida*. Coral Gables: University of Miami Press, 1971.

Timmons, Bascom N. *Jesse H. Jones: The Man and the Statesman*. New York: Henry Holt, 1956.

———. *Portrait of an American: Charles G. Dawes*. New York: Henry Holt, 1953.

Tindall, George Brown. *The Emergence of the New South, 1913–1945*. Baton Rouge: Louisiana State University Press, 1967.

Vickers, Raymond B. "The Banking Panic of 1926." Ph.D. dissertation, Florida State University, 1990.

Wagy, Thomas R. *Governor LeRoy Collins of Florida: Spokesman of the New South*. Tuscaloosa: University of Alabama Press, 1985.

Walker, Franklin. *Jack London and the Klondike: The Genesis of an American Writer*. San Marino, Calif.: Huntington Library, 1972.

Wall, Joseph Frazier. *Alfred I. du Pont: The Man and His Family*. New York: Oxford University Press, 1990.

Ward, James Robertson, and Dena Elizabeth Snodgrass. *Old Hickory's Town: An Illustrated History of Jacksonville*. Jacksonville: Old Hickory's Town, 1985.

Weigall, Theyre Hamilton. *Boom in Paradise*. New York: A. H. King, 1932.

White, James J. *Teaching Materials on Banking Law*. St. Paul, Minn.: West, 1976.

White, William Allen. *Calvin Coolidge: The Man Who Is President*. New York: Macmillan, 1925.

———. *A Puritan in Babylon: The Story of Calvin Coolidge*. New York: Macmillan, 1938.

Who's Who and What to See in Florida. St. Petersburg: Current Historical Company of Florida, 1935.

Who Was Who In America, 1897–1960. Vol. 3. Chicago: Marquis Who's Who, 1960.

PAMPHLETS AND PAPERS

Bank of Palm Beach. Historical Society of Palm Beach County, West Palm Beach, Florida.

Boca Raton: Florida's Wholly New Entirely Beautiful World Resort. Boca Raton Historical Society, Boca Raton, Florida.

Bream, Joan. *Addison Cairns Mizner, 1872–1933*. Boca Raton Historical Society.

Cox, James M. "Florida." *Enterprise, Education and Economics in Florida*. 1926. Special Collections Department, Otto G. Richter Library, University of Miami, Coral Gables, Florida.

The Depositors Guarantee Fund of the Witham System. Government Exhibit No. 513. *United States* v. *Wesley D. Manley, Joseph A. Sasser, Paul J.*

Baker, Lorne R. Adams, and John D. Russell. Criminal Docket No. 13423, U.S. District Court Records, RG 21, Northern District of Georgia, 1847–1942, National Archives, Atlanta, Georgia.

Dial, William H. *History of the Banking Laws of Florida*. St. Paul, Minn.: West, 1954.

Driscoll, Glenn. "Dance Halls, Saloons, Gambling Dens and Their Personalities or How I Lost My Shirt in the Klondike Stampede." Dawson City Museum, Old Territorial Administration Building, Dawson City, Yukon Territory.

Dyal, Donald H. *Addison Mizner: The Palm Beach Architect*. Monticello, Ill.: Vance Bibliographies, 1985.

The First Thirty Years of Miami and the Bank of Bay Biscayne: 1896–1926. P. K. Yonge Library of Florida History, University of Florida, Gainesville, Florida.

Giffin, Marjie Gates. *Water Runs Downhill: A History of the Indianapolis Water Company and Other Centenarians*. New York: Newcomen Society, 1981.

History of the Pure Oil Company. Vol. 2. Chicago, 1953. Library of Congress, Washington, D.C.

Knott, James R. *Palm Beach Revisited: Historical Vignettes of Palm Beach County*. West Palm Beach, 1987.

Lewis, George. *Florida Banks*. 1942. P. K. Yonge Library of Florida History, University of Florida, Gainesville, Florida.

Miami and the Story of Its Remarkable Growth. 1925. Special Collections Department, Otto G. Richter Library, University of Miami, Coral Gables, Florida.

Moore, Mary T. *Coral Gables History*. March 1950. Special Collections Department, Otto G. Richter Library, University of Miami, Coral Gables, Florida.

Orr, Christina. *Addison Mizner: Architect of Dreams and Realities (1872–1933)*. West Palm Beach: Norton Gallery and School of Art, 1977.

Powell-Brant, Evanell K. *Debauched Proverbs and Other Miznerisms of Addison Mizner and Wilson Mizner*. Tampa: 1979.

Proceedings of Idaho Bankers Association, First Annual Session. May 10, 1905. Bureau of Banking, Department of Finance, Idaho Historical Society, Boise, Idaho.

Program of the Florida Bankers Association Convention, 1926, 1927, and 1928. P. K. Yonge Library of Florida History, University of Florida, Gainesville, Florida.

Return C. M. Gay as Comptroller. 1948. Clarence M. Gay, Campaign Literature, 1947–48, RG 350, Series 426, Department of State, Florida State Archives, Tallahassee, Florida.

The Riviera Section and the University of Miami. 1925. Special Collections

Department, Otto G. Richter Library, University of Miami, Coral Gables, Florida.

Rufus Cutler Dawes, 1867–1940. Chicago: A Century of Progress, 1940. Library of Congress, Washington, D.C.

Showalter, J. Camille, ed. *The Many Mizners: California Clan Extraordinary.* Oakland, Calif.: The Oakland Museum, 1978.

INDEX

References to illustrations are printed in **boldface**.

Holder, John N., 124–26
Hoover, Herbert, 185–86; quoted, 80
Hoover, J. Edgar, and Manley case, 134, 145–48
Howard, G. H., 136–37, 140
Howard, William S., 78
Huenink, Jeff, 217

impeachment proceedings: against Amos, 199–206; against Lewis, 215–18
indictments. *See* grand jury
insanity pleas, Manley's, 134–38, 141, 145–46
insider abuse, 5–9, 150–52, 215–19; Earman's attempts to reveal, 99–102; and Manley-Anthony banking system, 154–56; and Manley banking system, 78, 115, 118–20; official knowledge of, 61–65, 80–81, 83–85, 90–93, 191–92 (*see also* secrecy, official); revealed during Manley investigation, 130–31, 139–42

Jackson, Andrew, 6–7, 34, 45, 79
Jefferson, Thomas, and Declaration of Independence, vii, 13, 219
Jelliffe, Smith Ely, 137–38
Jennings, William S., 41
Johnson, J. B., 110–11

Kahn, Otto H., 73
Keating, Charles, 218
Kennedy, Joseph P., 159
King, Franklin O., 204
King, George O., 142
"King of the Chain Banks." *See* Anthony, J. R.
Kingsley, Willey Lyon, 66
Knight, Charles Lafayette, 197–200
Knight, Peter O., 197–98
Knight, Telfair, 19, 21
Knott, William V., **52, 196;** and Amos, 38–39, 207; and Anthony, 39, 51–53, 166

Knox, Philander C., 159

Lake, Forrest, 55, 191–92
Lambright, E. D., 195
land boom, Florida's, 5, 10, 17–19; Boca Raton, **15,** 21–24, 31, 35, 59; Coral Gables, 19–21; Palm Beach, 22, 39–42
Landis, Cary D., **196**
Law and Order League of Palm Beach County, 160
Lee, James Martin, 205, 206–13
Leffler, Charles D., 34
legal proceedings, 162–65 (*see also* grand jury; impeachment proceedings); against Adams, 135–36, 141–45; against Amos, 95–97, 109–13, 191–94; against Anthony's partners, 150–52; against Manley, 129–34, 138–41, 145–48 (*see also* insanity pleas, Manley's); against Manley's partners, 141–45; against Mizner, 171–75
Lewis, Gerald, xii–xiii, 13, 215–17
Lindy, Jack, 171
Livermore, Jesse L., 23
Long, Lena V., 131–32, 135
Lummus, James E., 34, 42
Luning, J. C., 38–39

Madison, James, quoted, vii, 2, 220
mail fraud, 141–49
Manley, Valeria Rankin, 50, 131–32; as witness, 134–35, 137
Manley, W. D., 10–12, 19, 36, 218 (*see also* Manley-Anthony banking system; Manley banking system); accused of bank fraud conspiracy, 73, 77–78; attempts by, to protect assets, 131–34; and insanity pleas, 134–38, 141, 145–46; legal proceedings against, 129–31, 138–41, 145–48; partners of, on trial, 141–45; and Witham banking system, 47–50
Manley-Anthony banking system, 10,

ABOUT THE AUTHOR

Raymond B. Vickers is an attorney in Tallahassee, Florida, who has represented more than a hundred financial institutions. From 1975 to 1979, he served as Assistant Comptroller of Florida, the top appointed official in the Department of Banking and Finance. He received a B.S., J.D., M.A., and Ph.D. in economic and business history from Florida State University, where he is now an adjunct assistant professor of history.